French Utopias

French Utopias

An ANTHOLOGY OF IDEAL SOCIETIES

Edited, with an Introduction and Translations by

Frank E. Manuel and Fritzie P. Manuel

THE FREE PRESS, *New York*

COLLIER-MACMILLAN LIMITED, *London*

CONTENTS

Contents

French Utopias

Introduction

While a rich utopian tradition was inherited from antiquity, three works are primarily responsible for establishing the type in modern European literature —Thomas More's *Utopia* (1516), which gave a name to the genre, Tommaso Campanella's *City of the Sun* (1623), and Francis Bacon's *New Atlantis* (1627). Translated soon after their appearance, they quickly took hold in France. Campanella's influence on Cyrano de Bergerac and Vairasse, More's on Morelly, Francis Bacon's on Condorcet are transparent and freely avowed. Utopian literature did not flourish in post-Renaissance Italy, nor was it ever a distinguished form in either Spain or Germany. For four centuries, it has remained predominantly English and French, and though the English utopias may have greater originality of conceit, the French chain binding Rabelais to Anatole France is the more strongly linked. After the type had been acclimated in France in the seventeenth century—the anonymous *Histoire du grand et admirable royaume d'Antangil* (1616) is usually regarded as the first full-fledged French utopia—successive generations had a way of repeating one another's main themes, with variations of course: Cyrano echoes in Restif de la Bretonne, and Restif in Fourier. The hey-day of the French utopia, when it was almost universal in its cultural impact, spans the century from about 1750 to 1850. When Marx adopted "utopian socialism" as a term of opprobrium to dissociate his own "scientific socialism" from current French and English radical writings, he unwittingly bestowed upon the literature a new lease on life. In many parts of the modern world these works are still read and studied primarily as a prologue to Marxist thought, though of late there has been revived interest in the French utopias in their own right as penetrating revelations of grave faults in the structure of society and of the aspirations of men to remold it. By the twentieth century the utopian spirit had departed from France. "Socialist dreams" like the one incorporated into Anatole France's novel *The White Stone* are mechanically syncretistic, pieced together from bits of Saint-Simon, Fourier, and Proudhon. The French Republics, Third through Fifth, have been so thoroughly imbued with a

1

realistic temper that they have banished all dreams of paradisiacal happiness. While there is in present-day France a proliferation of "programs" for the future, these are the work of matter-of-fact social planners who approach their task with the same practical spirit as do planners in any communistic or capitalistic society. If there is a contemporary French utopian in the grand manner, he is Teilhard de Chardin, and we have included him.

The selections in *French Utopias* are drawn from works that in brief compass, though often with excessive and prosy detail, describe an imaginary and ideal society, or present a program for organizing such a society. We have begun with Mandeville's adaptation of a passage from Vincent of Beauvais, in order to establish a filiation with the medieval and classical tradition. Rabelais's delightful description of the Abbey of Theleme in the *Gargantua*, though not a discrete utopia, already reflects the influence of Thomas More in France. While some authors strain to introduce dramatic episodes into their books—Vairasse is an example of the futile attempt to enliven a ponderous recital with anecdotes—most utopias are matter-of-fact and earnest treatises which plod rather laboriously through the major aspects of social organization. The early utopias have a curtain raiser in which the hero-narrator recounts how he happened to visit utopia and an epilogue in which he explains how he got back to European civilization. By the eighteenth century the stage props are sometimes dispensed with; and the great nineteenth-century utopias, which had pretensions to scientific historical prophecy, usually found them superfluous. But on occasion even they resorted to the artificial machinery of the shipwreck, the dream, and the waking vision.

Offhand it seems paradoxical that the utopia should have become stylish in France, cultivated more extensively there than elsewhere on the continent. The land of clear and distinct ideas has not been remarkable for its whimsicality. A forthright French reaction to utopia ought to have been a shrug of incredulity and a flood of ridicule. On further reflection, however, it becomes obvious that the utopian temper is not an affront to Cartesian clarity. Since it is nowhere, utopia, unlike real life, can be simple, consonant with itself, mathematical, "logical" in its arrangements, compartmentalized, defined, sharply limned and demarcated. Utopias are not fuzzy. Their laws are perhaps all too clear and their societies all too smoothly engineered. The fascination of utopian thought for École Polytechnique students in the nineteenth century is understandable.

Utopias have rarely been great works of art; their aesthetic qualities are meagre and they fit more readily into a history of social thought than into a history of literature. Their implicit condemnation of contemporary life is often more telling than their evocation of the future. They are dream-mirrors of existence as much as they are anticipations. Since they predict so many imaginary worlds, it is not surprising that they sometimes prognosticate the shape of things to come with a measure of accuracy. Like all dreams, they are an admixture of dissonant elements and they may reflect universal, perhaps eternal fantasies of mankind, along with particular embodiments of the universal in time and place.

In their social origins, the French visionaries ranged from top to bottom of the hierarchy; and their invention of utopias doubtless appeased a wide gamut of psychic needs. Our selection includes the free intellectual play of the libertine Renaissance humanists Rabelais and Cyrano de Bergerac; the moral preachments of Archbishop Fénelon for the guidance of princes; the rigid plans for reform of the human species by Restif de la Bretonne, an eighteenth-century peasant's profligate son; vast projects of world organization by Henri Saint-Simon, a declassed noble of the Revolutionary epoch; the erotic daydreams of Charles Fourier, a frustrated clerk of the Restoration; the megalomaniac structures of that academic *raté*, Auguste Comte, who was rejected by the university potentates of the July Monarchy; and the rather disenchanted musings of one of the great scholars of the nineteenth century, Ernest Renan.

The individual fortunes of the French utopians were touched with failure and tragedy. Cyrano de Bergerac, estranged from his ducal patron, died in misery of a wound accidentally inflicted by a servant. Diderot was imprisoned in Vincennes, and subversive pieces like the *Supplement to the Voyage of Bougainville* could be published only after his death. Condorcet wrote his vision of the future scientific society while hiding from Robespierre's police in a garret, and he died in a sans-culottes detention cell. Babeuf was guillotined for his attempt to implement the *Manifesto of the Equals*. Restif de la Bretonne lived in abject poverty during his declining years, though he did receive a rather grand official funeral under Napoleon. Saint-Simon stood trial for publishing the *Parable*, charged with inciting the Duke of Berry's assassination, and in his advanced age despair drove him to an attempt at suicide. Though the Saint-Simonian leaders were rehabilitated and "returned to the world" after serving a short term in a not uncomfortable jail for committing acts which outraged public morals, many adepts perished in North Africa seeking the Female Messiah. A hapless lot of Frenchmen set sail to establish Cabet's Icaria in Texas and succumbed to fever in the swamplands. Fourier and Comte died in obscurity—a modern martyrdom.

The French social utopias have always been more than wild personal phantasmagorias. The wish-fantasy of the writer, whatever its genesis, has been tamed, adapted, and generalized. Utopias are to be distinguished from private worlds and mad delusions. Their publication alone is proof that they are not solipsistic but are, at the very least, *folie à deux*—of the writer and the printer. Sometimes they expressed so forcefully a poignant longing of masses of men that their words reverberated throughout society. Volney's *Ruins* enjoyed an international renown; Morelly's austere *Nature's Code* inspired lawmakers of successive French revolutions; and Condorcet's *Sketch* became official liberal doctrine for more than a century. Saint-Simon, the Saint-Simonians, Fourier, and Comte exerted a far-flung influence upon committed groups of disciples, from the lower depths of Czarist Russia through the intellectual elite of Latin America. In response to their summons, social movements were organized and dreams were translated into concrete institutional practices. Attempts to pragmatize the French utopias were more numerous in the experimental communities of the United States than anywhere else in the world.

But even when the utopias did not become the pattern for communities such as those inspired in the nineteenth century by Fourier and his follower Cabet, they indirectly affected political programs. The utopia was in time reduced to encompassable social goals, many of which were eventually fulfilled. The Saint-Simonian cultists of the thirties turned bankers and senators under the Second Empire—but with a residue of utopian imagery in their souls—are a classical instance of this contraction of the boundless ideal to the real in the course of a generation. There is of course no way of gauging whether a utopia is merely a sensitive recording of change that is taking place anyway or is itself the spark plug of social reform—most great utopias have been both reflections and stimuli.

In this collection, the term utopians has not been restricted to those writers who expected to see an ideal society usher in a golden age in their own time or for their immediate posterity. If this were the criterion for admission into the French canon, only Condorcet, Babeuf, Saint-Simon and the Saint-Simonians, Fourier, Cabet, and Auguste Comte would be certain of a place; perhaps Mercier and Morelly, also. Though they described the future only in vague terms, the historical prognoses of Volney and Renan have been included because they presuppose the existence of a new framework of social institutions. Rabelais and Cyrano depict life in an imaginary abbey and on the sun and moon to castigate by implication the France of their day, without commitment to every image of their literary "fancies"; but whatever their principal intent they have been read as utopians and are so considered here.

A seventeenth-century work, the *History of the Sevarambians*, has been selected as a transition type: Vairasse does not believe in the possibility of this imaginary world any more than did Rabelais in the Abbey of Theleme or Cyrano in his lunar society, but the emphasis is shifting; the reformist zeal is becoming more pronounced. Only in the eighteenth century do the utopias grow really serious, and then they are dead serious, though Diderot still remains ambivalent about the introduction of Tahitian ways into the kingdom of France.

The French social utopia of the eighteenth century is sometimes confounded with run-of-the-mill depictions of primitive societies, either in the authentic travel literature which saw contemporary savages through heavily tinted rose glasses or in garret-produced fantasies about the lives of aborigines by men who had never ventured outside of Paris. Great moralists like Diderot and Rousseau were able to raise their "primitivism" to another level. Rousseau's description of both the historical and the contemporary primitive was a contrasting image held up to his society. He steadfastly asserted that he did not remotely advocate a return to the state of nature, and it is probably right to read the *Discourse on Inequality* the way Kant did, as a critical introduction to the ideal future political state of mankind delineated in the *Social Contract*. Diderot's dialogue about life in Tahiti, which lies on the border between the primitivist daydream and a proper utopia, merits inclusion for its rare aesthetic quality, as well as for its mordant satire on sexual morality in eighteenth-century France.

Once a serious social purpose becomes predominant among the utopians, they are impatient for immediate fulfillment. Fénelon described a productive enlightened monarchy that seemed quite practicable to the eighteenth century. There was nothing fantastic about the legislative program of Morelly and the hopes of Volney. Condorcet thought in terms of the next decade for the initiation of his world republic of science. As for Saint-Simon and the Saint-Simonians, Fourier, Comte, and Proudhon, they conceived of themselves as social prophets not in the sense that they were prognosticating for a distant future but for tomorrow at nine. In fact, they persistently upbraided their fellow citizens for delaying the institution of a felicity to which there were no longer any historical, scientific, or technological barriers. The world was stupid, mad, cruel, and impractical to ignore "the system"; they, whom others called utopian, were the supreme realists. Toward the second half of the nineteenth century, the optimist groundswell began to subside. Renan's dream, with its uncertainties and anxieties, stands on the borderline of the negative utopia. The time scale of realization has again become shrouded in a verbal mist.

The general tone of utopias varies, and does not easily define the genre as a form of intellectual expression. Even when a work is primarily satirical, for example a depiction of the contemporary world in an alien costume either to escape censorship or to pique the reader's curiosity, it may still preserve genuine utopian qualities. *Jérôme Paturot in Quest of the Best of Republics* by Louis Reybaud, a witty nineteenth-century antecedent of the negative utopias of George Orwell and Zamiatin, remains half-possessed by the beliefs it is ridiculing. Occasionally a utopia appears to be sheer whimsy, though it is difficult to conceive of man at this sort of game without the intrusion of a serious purpose. Playful and literary elements are most marked in the earlier French works, those of Rabelais and Cyrano, perhaps Vairasse, men who never expected their utopia to be realized, though like Thomas More they may have wished for it. By contrast, the nineteenth-century utopians were conspicuously lacking in humor; they were party leaders, directors of movements for whom the written text of the utopia was a gospel for a new religion.

In eighteenth-century France, the description of imaginary societies which were nowhere, idealized places that were supposedly somewhere in the Americas or the Southern Seas, and accounts of what a good society should or might look like at some future date were not sharply distinguishable one from another. While it is possible to separate out pastoral dreams of bygone days, imaginary worlds with no prospect of realization, fictitious portrayals of distant lands, and works written with the conscious purpose and expectation that the world can and should be transformed into utopia, the simon-pure forms are few. As the newly discovered continents came to be taken for granted, there was perhaps some tendency to move utopias away from contemporary exotic lands and to locate them in the historical future of Europe; distance in time replaced distance in space. But it is difficult to establish a clear-cut progression in the geography of utopias. The extraplanetary utopia, for example, is as ancient as Lucian and as new as the most recent work of science fiction.

Most utopias can be significantly illuminated by a study of the economic and social conditions of the periods in which they were composed, despite their absorption with the world of the future. Scholars have shown that Thomas More's communist utopia reflects the problems of the disinherited during the English enclosure movement of the sixteenth century. Similarly, the historical context of French eighteenth- and nineteenth-century utopias is readily definable. In the eighteenth century, an extraordinary preoccupation with uniform regulations expresses a wish that the chaotic legal and institutional structure of the ancient regime might be simplified, normalized, so that the bewildering feudal and customary laws would cease interfering with the achievement of elementary rational goals of production and consumption. The regulated character of work in the eighteenth-century utopias is largely an extension to the whole of society of certain prevailing corporate practices in the compulsory organization of artisans. Instead, however, of the bewildering variety of rules, distinct for each of hundreds of crafts which had survived from the Middle Ages, the uniform provisions governing labor in utopia reflect the simple uniformities of life perceived in the new physical science.

The eighteenth-century utopias promise agrarian security either through guaranteed individual holdings to farmers or through communistic peasant cooperatives. Small-scale agriculture remains the productive base, whether the future government of society is envisaged as an enlightened monarchy in Fénelon, Restif de la Bretonne, and Mercier, or as a democracy in Volney. Manual labor on the land is the primary source of health and prosperity, and the evils of the city are painted in lurid colors. The doctrines of the physiocrats and of Rousseau fortified each other in French eighteenth-century utopias. The threat of industrial problems to come is faint; it is only on the distant horizon. The relationship of the French Revolution to the ideal legal codes and systems spawned during the century which preceded it is, in retrospect, clear enough. Many writers had a premonition that a revolution was in the offing. For Morelly, despite his disavowals, communist legislation was a practical plan to be adopted forthwith once men had resolved to return to a natural way of life and to sweep aside the debris of the old order. For Restif de la Bretonne, the communist agrarian system had more complex roots: through his carefully regulated social mechanisms he hoped to avoid the bloody horrors of a revolution that would inevitably follow once "the people," whose passions he had diagnosed with such brutal honesty, broke their chains and were let loose upon society.

By the nineteenth century, French utopias respond directly to the upheavals engendered by the industrial-scientific revolution. Whether the Fourierists proposed a system of phalansteries with a high degree of local autonomy or their rivals the Saint-Simonians planned a worldwide industrial-scientific-artistic society, these were alternative remedies, equally sovereign, for the manifold economic and psychological ills of the times. The French utopians were precocious. Using English examples and parallels, or generalizing from the experience of the few factory centers established in France in the early years of the century, they drew a dramatic picture of social and spiritual chaos. Men had to recoil in horror at the prospect before them and flee for refuge to utopia. Under the "new systems," the cyclical economic crises which brought starvation, the brutal factory regulations which denatured man, the pestiferous living conditions of industrial cities which ruined his health, the cheats of false bourgeois love which degraded him, and the deadly wars of competition would all be abolished. The physical sufferings of the proletariat and the psychic pain of the rootless members of the other classes would end. Association would replace the antagonisms of capitalist society. There would be neat little houses or communal dwellings, orderly work arrangements, cleanliness, peace and tranquillity, and love aplenty for everybody.

Within the chronological arrangement which parallels changing social and economic conditions, French utopias since Rabelais can, broadly speaking, be divided along the lines of the major cleavage between the rival ancient prescriptive moral philosophies of the eudaemonist tradition: those which hoped to achieve a state of perfect happiness by arousing, multiplying, increasing, and varying sensations, and those which established a tolerable minimum of pleasure that they tried to maintain as stable as possible, training the inhabitants to find complete satisfaction within the fixed norms. There are thus expansive and restrictive utopias: Rabelais and Fourier would clearly belong to the former type, Fénelon, the Morelly of *Nature's Code*, and Restif to the latter. In general in the eighteenth century, the hard utopias predominate over the visions of the soft and luxurious blessed isles in the manner of Diderot. The stark *Manifesto of the Equals* is the final programmatic statement of the more common Spartan ideal of the age. But as with all categorizing, this dichotomy of the expansive and the restrictive has its inadequacies. One of the least sensate utopias of modern times, Auguste Comte's description of the ultimate stage of Humanity after the subjective synthesis has been achieved, is extolled by its author as emotionally the most free. It is sexless, procreation being accomplished by women without the intervention of male bodies, and alimentation consists solely of liquids and gases. Once men are emancipated from material needs and desires, time is whiled away in the invention of ever new expressions of spiritual love; the *gaie science,* Comte calls it.

Perhaps a more fruitful distinction could be made between the static and the dynamic utopias. Here too the chronological arrangement which we adopted in our presentation lends itself to a logical division. The prenineteenth-century utopias tend to be static. If their authors could witness the establishment of a never-changing society, they would look upon their work as done and pronounce it good. The imitation of the natural order of the Newtonian universe is intentional. Constant sameness is the ideal; the revolutions of planets in accordance with a lawful design in a finite universe was adopted as the most appropriate model for the social world. Not unlike the ancient Greeks whom they admired, the early eighteenth-century utopians believed that continual innovation was evil, that only the unchanging was good. Utopia should therefore approximate a state of immutability, or at least invariance, as nearly as possible. The utopian reformer sought out those elements in human nature and in the organization of society which tended to create disturbances in domestic tranquillity and either curbed them, transformed them, or ruthlessly eradicated them—at least on paper. This was easily accomplished by limiting severely the number of artifacts and social variables a society would have to cope with; hence the predilection for the Spartan, the Roman republican, and the Puritan ideals. When the sensualist Restif de la Bretonne turned to writing his stream of utopias, he drew up authoritarian schemes for the sharp curtailment of pleasures by law. In a personal sense, this was an expression of the reverse side of his nature, the Jansenist one, but it is also symbolic for the age. When a society soaked in the sensationalist philosophy, acutely aware of the "ravages of the passions," drafts laws for itself, it resorts to simple and often inflexible rules. Trouble comes to utopia when differences and distinctions multiply and unregulated innovations disrupt the rational social forms bringing civil strife in their wake. To romantic moderns with their striving for the infinite, this image of a static utopia without confrontations and conflicts is deadly. The idyllic peacefulness would drive some of us to distraction, and so would the unrelieved sameness. But to the prenineteenth-century utopian, this constancy was the essence of the good life. It was the prosy embodiment of the ideal of pastoral poetry. When Aristotle analyzed the nature of the social maladies which generated change and described the circular variations in the government of the polity to which they gave rise, revolutions were all conceived as departures from the enduring good. Ixion's fate is not a happy one. Progression in either an Augustinian sense or in the late eighteenth-century secularized version of Condorcet is a derogation of the utopia itself because perfection cannot be improved upon. When toward the end of the Enlightenment the idea of progress took possession of utopia, it radically altered the nature of the dream.

If poetry and music are not banished from the eighteenth-century utopian republics, history usually is. At best, history is a record of horrible examples of inhuman conduct preserved from barbarous times. Static utopians like Mercier do not know quite how to treat the historical. Shall they expunge its evil images from the memory of man forever and limit the history of the past to the history of the good which led to the perfect, lest the example of past wickedness be contagious even in utopia? Or shall they retain the history of recorded evil in all its odious forms to teach moral lessons? Whatever the solution, the historical is substantially devalued.

The nineteenth-century utopias, unlike their predecessors, are profoundly historical in character. Condorcet (who for our purposes is more intimately related to his successors than to his eighteenth-century antecedents), Saint-Simon, Fourier, and Comte are reformers who may start out with a trenchant critique of the existing order that is often the most cogent part of their writings; but a historical analysis of how the present came to assume its shape is essential for their extrapolation of the curve of social development in utopia. Full-scale philosophies of historical progression invariably accompany the attacks on contemporary society; they demonstrate that the ultimate fulfillment of their social ideal is inevitable. There is usually some leeway in the determinist prediction: it may come about fast or it may be delayed; the process may be peaceful or it may be revolutionary; but a utopia is always the culmination of the historical series. The whole of the past has been building up to a moment of crisis; the present transition stage, painful though it is, will pass; and the future is a dynamic crescendo of ever-increasing joys about to commence. Whereas the ordinary eighteenth-century utopias settled down to reasonable steadiness, those of the nineteenth century, beginning with Condorcet—who bridges the gap even though he died in 1795—were committed to indefinite perfectibility. The process was not envisaged as growth toward a final goal, known and fixed; it was a proclamation of infinite progress, like mathematical infinity; for the new higher goal as well as its achievement could only be revealed in time. Up to the nineteenth century, purposes were set: the "social art" of which the prerevolutionary utopian was master consisted in devising and implementing a plan, like the mythical lawgiver of antiquity, and then maintaining it in the face of natural tendencies toward corruption. After the concept of progress suffused utopia, the ideal order lost its static and finished quality. Heaven itself became changeable. The image of the good society became as dynamic as the vision of the expanding universe was in the new astronomy.

If they are examined as a body of psychological rather than historical documents, many utopias appear to be expressions of the obsessive, somewhat paranoid personality. How else shall one interpret the regulatory minutiae of Restif and Fourier, the repetitive details, the reduction of reality to a symmetrical uniform structure, the autarchy and isolation of most ideal commonwealths, the piling up of restrictions, the artificiality of relationships? They describe a two-dimensional world which lacks emotional depth. There may be some sorrow allowable but nothing tragic, some orderly joy but no ecstasy. Life is flattened out: everything is adequate, nothing magnificent. The extremes of existence have been lopped off. The petty bourgeois, strait-laced Frenchman of the nineteenth century could move into the better utopias without knowing the difference. Poets are not ousted from modern French utopias, as they were from Plato's *Republic*; but they are required to behave themselves.

Marriage, education, work, distribution and consumption, civil punishment, festivals, and religion are the "departments" of life covered seriatim in most utopias and their solutions are often remarkably similar: a monogamous family in which partners have some free choice; a gentle rather than a harsh education with more emphasis on virtue than bookish knowledge; compulsory labor for all, accompanied by a rehabilitation of the worth of the manual arts; more or less equal consumption of an adequate quantity of simple products, avoiding the vices of excess; equal and rather lenient punishments for all miscreants (Beccaria's little treatise has found its way into the consciousness of the utopians and punishment is always made to fit the crime); a religion which is an amalgam of deism and inspirational civic ceremonies. Scientific culture is favored over the literary—in Anatole France's utopia, reading declines and communication becomes phonographic. The arts serve to inspire social virtues. There is widely diffused love and an atmosphere of respect for human dignity. Good health is based on continent and regular habits. Reason is everywhere in control and the passions, though not condemned outrightly, are held in check. With the appearance of the nineteenth-century romantic utopians, there is a movement to dethrone Reason in the name of Love as the guiding principle, but still the love is reasonable, not extravagant or destructive.

The utopian treats of society and each individual who comprises it as a manipulable object, as "it." He stands in sharp contrast to the mythopoeic view of the cosmos and society where man faces all creatures and things as "thou." Almost by definition, the utopian is alienated from the social order in which he actually lives, so alienated that he is driven to construct another world out of synthetic blocks and people it with creatures whom he disposes like dressed dolls in a model for a stageset. All utopias exude this spirit of the inanimate. Those utopians who created an imaginary contemporary character magically transported to a future age constructed a man who, despite his admiration for the ways of the new society, never was emotionally part of it. Attempts to describe utopian feelings, when they do occur, are always dismal failures. Utopias are generally wooden, mechanical, contrived. When we say they are dreamlike, we are probably misleading; they have none of the powerful affective qualities of the dream. Their emotional range is extraordinarily narrow. Rarely do they succeed in conveying what it is like to live in utopia—perhaps because there are no utopian feelings other than the mild contentment and sense of adequacy experienced in an eventemperatured room. Looked at from this viewpoint, the emotionally impoverished utopias may be considered a presage of the well-policed, comfortable civil societies of our advanced technological age. Cabet's Icaria was a fiasco in nineteenth-century Texas and in Nauvoo, Illinois, but with certain organizational changes, it could be looked upon as a social blueprint with recognizable affinities to contemporary suburbia.

Most utopias would be considered harshly authoritarian by the standards of nineteenth-century liberals like John Stuart Mill; they surely did not abide by his principles of tolerance and forbearance. Some of them express a niggardly, closed spirit. They do not allow for spontaneity: the details of supervision are meticulous, often boring, like government regulations anywhere. Only from utopia there is no escape to utopia because you are already in it.

Utopias tend to be plainly utilitarian. You can describe a more perfect organization of the distribution of produce, but how do you depict a new art or literature? Mercier tried without much success. Beginning with the eighteenth century, the idea of "socially conscious" art assumed its place in the utopias, but it did not flower in the center of the utopian gardens until the Saint-Simonians. When religion was preserved it was of the Roman civic type—the theophilanthropic cults of the French Revolution had many antecedents and followers—or it was "generalized science" called religion as in Saint-Simon's project for a High Council of Newton. There is no room for the mystical in any of these matter-of-fact little worlds and the practical excludes even the intuitive. Excellence is usually cultivated by hard work, and though it is recognized that talents vary and natural superiority is esteemed, there is no appreciation of romantic genius.

Love in utopia is, more often than not, respectable. Even in Rabelais's Abbey of Theleme, the magnificently costumed inmates taking their pleasure in exercise, display, and learned conversation, were decently paired off. When Vairasse allowed his public officials a measure of polygamy, he may have been introducing a realistic note, but he overstepped the bounds of most French utopias. By a consensus of utopians, monogamy is the only permissible social practice. The Saint-Simonians provided for some variety in love relationships, but only under the guidance of the great priests of mankind, who had an insight into the amorous character of their adepts. Morelly permitted divorce, a radical proposal in eighteenth-century France, but he enveloped the procedures with so many restrictions that it was no light matter. Only the Marquis de Sade and Fourier would open wide the floodgates of promiscuous sexual encounters to those who desired them. De Sade's companies of pleasure-seekers were rather elitist in character, but in our selection from *La Philosophie dans le boudoir*, he adapted his prescriptions to all ranks of society in the French Republic and there is sound reason for welcoming him among the social utopians. Restif de la Bretonne in his *Andrographe* portrays a rather proper little agrarian society of patriarchal units that is virtually indistinguishable from that of Mercier or Morelly, except that it is more rigid and sexually restrictive. Diderot's commitment to the free love of Tahiti is far from absolute, nothing like Fourier's faith in the amorous series of the phalanstery. But while Diderot did not expect to introduce the amatory customs of the South Seas into France, he used this ideal image of natural behavior in his plea against the terrible punishments which certain prohibited sexual relations entailed in his own society. Since in Comte's future state of Humanity sex has abolished itself, love is a spiritualized and sublimated relationship, rich in its incorporeal expressions. In the Positivist Religion of Humanity, marriage remains indissoluble and widowhood eternal—a more rigorous rule than the Catholic state of France ever imposed.

With the possible exception of Renan's dream, eugenics do not play a crucial role in the French utopias. For the most part, essential human nature remains fixed and biological transformations reflecting the influence of a crude Darwinism are lacking. If Auguste Comte envisioned a change in man's sexual and appetitive nature, it was to come about through the power of religion rather than sexual selection. Such eugenic measures as were proposed in the seventeenth- and eighteenth-century utopias aimed to improve the species, to breed healthier progeny—but not to alter man's nature.

Of all the utopians, only Fourier seriously attacks the family structure as the basic unit of social life. The others direct themselves toward strengthening the relationship, ennobling it, purifying it of dross. Equality for women is forthrightly espoused only by the Saint-Simonians and in late nineteenth-century imitations of their ideas in Anatole France, though most utopias provide for a rise in the social status of women from their position of subjection in the patriarchal family structure of France. This holds true for utopias written both under the ancient regime and the postrevolutionary bourgeois state.

Since the utopians wish to teach a new way of life, they always give prominence to a new system of education. Again Fourier's reflections on the nature of children have greatest originality. On the whole, there is a predilection for practical education, in marked opposition to the emphasis on classical literature in the prevailing system. Children are trained to fit into pre-established social niches in an economy where all persons are productive and there is no leisure class. Utopias written after Rousseau's *Émile* were all subject to his influence and the novel systems deal with education by example, by doing, rather than with learning things by rote or by rational argument. The educational projects of utopias, whether in Vairasse or in the Saint-Simonian lectures, are among their most significant sections, even more prominent than those on courtship and marriage.

While passion for equality is marked among the Frenchmen of the eighteenth century, it is condemned by the "classical utopians" of the nineteenth. The eighteenth-century plans are often mechanically egalitarian—all men eat the same food and perform virtually the same amount of labor with a minimal differentiation of tasks. Men are like interchangeable counters. The nineteenth-century organizations were more complex: the egalitarian ideal took the shape of an opportunity for equal self-actualization, and because desires and capacities varied, the whole fabric of the utopia tended to become more intricate. With the introduction of imagery from the biological sciences, men were regarded as parts of a social organism and they assumed distinctive characters as well as functions in the Saint-Simonian, Fourierist, Comtist, and Proudhonian systems. Differences among men were innate qualities in these organismic analogies. Fourier recognized that human psychological needs were radically varied, hence a complicated social mechanism with many alternative work patterns. The Saint-Simonians, in the spirit of their master emphasizing profound variations in human capacity, built a society out of gigantic professional hierarchies of natural talent. The Marxist dictum of the Gotha Program which combined total actualization of *all* needs and *all* capacities was clearly derivative from these French utopians. From the eighteenth century through the middle of the nineteenth, the utopians are without exception anti-aristocratic, though not necessarily anti-elitist; Renan's vision of a world ruled by scientists who become virtual supermen represents the elitist tendency driven to its logical extreme.

Most utopias are humanitarian asylums where nothing ill befalls anyone who stays within the rules. Punishments are both deterrent and corrective, and there is frequent resort to the vague sanctions of public obloquy in place of physical force, though seventeenth-century utopias like the *History of the Sevarambians* still retain whipping as a punishment for adultery. In the eighteenth-century utopias—Mercier's "Execution of a Criminal," for example—there are grim touches of totalitarian modernity when the criminal is brought to realize the justice of his punishment and to welcome it.

Utopias are unanimous in their elimination of the violent clashes of great armies that western society has known. Cyrano de Bergerac's playful mind substituted a combat of champions or a well-regulated war in which honorable forms, often rather outlandish ones, were strictly observed. The eighteenth- and nineteenth-century utopias were premised on the feasibility of the total abolition of war, either through the complete atrophy of the aggressive instinct or its sublimation. Fourier stands out as an exception in recognizing the persistence of the combative and competitive instincts even in the state of Harmony and, more than any other utopian, he devoted himself to dreaming up sham battles of the sexes with captives of love as the reward to the victorious army. No modern utopians have been able to countenance the massacres which have been the reality of life. In this respect, as in so many others, the French follow the early utopians, More and Campanella. As we move into the nineteenth century, universal peace becomes the overriding passion of utopia; even the minor limited wars of Thomas More's isolated island no longer seem tolerable. From Emeric Crucé and the Abbé de Saint-Pierre through Anatole France, Frenchmen multiplied the schemes for a universal federation of mankind. Utopia had to become international to be real, and peace was indivisible.

Since the French Revolution, "utopian" has often been an abusive epithet. As might be expected, one man's architectural plan for heaven on earth became another man's blueprint for hell. Reflections on social change with which one disagreed were labeled "utopian," though the visionaries of a new social order conceived of themselves as the great realists, and their enemies who rejected the universal happiness which was proffered to mankind, as evil men blind with illusion.

Contemporary attitudes vary. The twentieth-century French sociologist Raymond Ruyer has described utopias as a mental exercise or play on the "lateral possibilities of reality"; while he recognizes their uses his general tone is critical. A school of German sociology has made the distinction between ideology and utopia into a major systematic premise. In England, a theoretician of science has levelled a ferocious attack against "utopia" as contrasted with the realistic engineering of social change. Lewis Mumford's felicitous definition of the twenties still has great merit, though our generation is understandably cool or at best ambivalent toward the utopian vision after so many horrible crimes have been committed in its name.

Utopia has long been another name for the unreal and the impossible. We have set utopia over against the world. As a matter of fact, it is our utopias that make the world tolerable to us; the cities and mansions that people dream of are those in which they finally live. The more men react upon their environment and make it over after a human pattern, the more continuously do they live in utopia; but when there is a breach between the world of affairs and the overworld of utopia, we become conscious of the part that the will-to-utopia has played in our lives, and we see our utopia as a separate reality.

The selections that follow aim to present a balanced sampling of French utopian thought—its fertile inventiveness as well as its stretches of barren wasteland—from among the hundreds of works that have appeared in the last four centuries. While the excerpts may not be long enough to convince the skeptical reader of the intellectual riches which lie hidden beneath the surface of some utopias, they do spare him the aridity and monotony of others.

SIR JOHN MANDEVILLE
(ca. 1300–1372)

The Blessed Isles of
Prester John*

Mandeville is reputed to be an English traveler who was long supposed to have set out on a voyage to the East in 1322, and whose narrative seems to have first appeared in Norman French—early manuscripts give 1356 and 1357 as the date of completion. In a documentary history of French utopias, the justification for the intrusion of this Englishman—if Englishman he was—is twofold. All extant versions of his tales are apparently derived from French originals. Moreover, it is now generally agreed that these travels were not solely an account of Mandeville's peregrinations, but in large measure a compilation of other authors, among them Vincent de Beauvais (d. 1264), from whose encyclopedic *Speculum Mundi* it drew heavily. The *Speculum* itself was a compendium into which flowed many rivulets from the utopian and paradisiacal tradition of Greco-Roman and Oriental antiquity, and it can thus serve as a starting point for the French tradition. Mandeville's famous thirty-second chapter, with its image of the good society of the "Bragmans," had a tenacious hold on European imaginations.

*From Sir John Mandeville, *Mandeville's Travels*, texts and translations by Malcolm Letts from the Douai (1624) edition (London: The Hakluyt Society, 1953), I, pp. 204–10.

Woodcut, illustration for Mandeville's *Travels*, ca. 1500.

Of the Goodness of the Folk of the Isle of Bragman; of King Alexander; and Wherefore the Emperor of India Is Clept Prester John

Beyond this isle is another isle good and great and full of folk; and they are good folk and true and of good faith and good life after the manner of their conversation. And if all it be so that they are not Christian men, not forbye by law of kind they live a commendable life, and are folk of good virtue and flee all vices and sin and malice, and they keep well the Ten Commandments, for they are neither proud, ne covetous, ne lecherous, ne gluttons; and they do nought to another man but as they would were done to themselves. They set nought by riches of this world, ne by having of earthly goods. They make no leasings, ne swear none oaths for nothing, but simply say it is or it is not; for they say he that swears is about to beguile his neighbour. This isle that this folk dwells in is called the Isle of Bragmans; and some men call it the Land of Faith. And through this isle runs a great river, the which is called Thebe. And generally all the men of that isle and of other isles thereby are truer and rightwiser than are in other countries. In this isle are no thieves, ne men murderers, ne common women, ne liars, ne beggars; but they are als clean men of conversation and als good as they were men of religion. And, for als mickle as they are so true folk and so good, there is nevermore in that country neither thunder ne levening [lightning], hail ne snow, ne other tempests of ill weathers; ne hunger, ne pestilence, ne war, ne other tribulations come there none among them, as do among us because of our sin. And therefore it seems that God loves them well and is well paid of their living and of their faith. They trow in God that made all thing, and him they worship at all their might; and all earthly things they set at nought. And they live so temperately and so soberly in meat and drink that they are the longest living folk of the world; and many of them die for pure eld [age] without sickness when the kind fails.

When Alexander the conqueror reigned and conquered all the world, in that time he came by that isle and sent his letters to them that dwelt in that

isle and said that he would come and destroy their land, but if they would be
under his subjection, as other lands were. And they wrote letters again til him
in this manner: 'What thing might suffice to that man, to whom all the world
may not suffice? Thou shall find nothing with us wherefore thou should
werray [make war] upon us; for we have no riches of this world, ne none
covet for to have. All the places of our land and all our goods mobile and
unmobile are common til ilk man. All our riches that we have is our meat and
our drink, wherewith we sustain our bodies; our treasure is peace and accord
and love that is among us. Instead of array of our bodies we use a vile cloth
for to cover with our caitiff carrion. Our wives also are not proudly ne richly
arrayed to pleasing of our eyes, for we hold such enornement great folly to put
to the wretched body more beauty than God has kindly given it; our wives
covet no more beauty than kind has given them. Our land serves us of two
things, that is to say of our lifelade [livelihood], which we live with, and of
sepulture, when we are dead. And aye to this time have we been in peace, of
the which thou will now despoil us and disherit us. A king we have among us,
not for to do right to any man, for among us no man does wrong til other,
but all only to lere [teach] us to be obedient. Judges need us none to have
among us, for none of us does til other but as he would were done til him.
Forbye from us may thou reave nothing but peace, the which has aye unto
this time been among us.' And when king Alexander had seen their letters
and read them, him thought in his heart that it were great harm and great
unmanhood to grieve such folk or trouble them, and he granted them surety
of peace, and bade that they should continue forth their good manners and
use their good customs without dread having of him, for he should not dere
[harm] them.

Near beside that isle is another isle that men call Oxidrace, and another
that is called Gynoscriphe, where for the most part they hold the manners of
the Bragmans, living innocently in lewty [loyalty] and in love and charity
ilk one til other; and they go evermore naked. Into these isles came Alexander
the conqueror; and from the time that he saw their conversation and their
lewty [loyalty] and love ilk one til other, he said he would not grieve them,
but bade them ask of him whatso they would, and he should grant them.
And they answered and said that worldly riches would they none ask ne have,
but all only meat and drink wherewith the feeble body might be sustained.
For the goods and the riches of this world, quoth they, are not lasting but
deceivable. But and he might give them things that were ayelasting and not
deadly, then would they thank him mickle. The king answered them and
said that that might he not do, for he was deadly himself als well as they.

'Whereto, then' quoth they 'gathers thou the riches of this world, that are transitory and may not last; but, whether thou will or not, they shall leave thee, or else thou them, as it has befallen to them that were before thee. And out of this world shall thou bear nothing with thee, but naked as thou came thither shall thou pass hence, and thy flesh shall turn again to earth that thou was made of. And therefore should thou think that nothing may last ever-more, but God that made all the world. And yet, not having regard thereto, thou art so presumptuous and so proud that, right as thou were God, thou would make all the world subject unto thee, and thou knows not the term of thy life, ne the day ne the hour.' When Alexander had heard these words and such other, he had great wonder thereof and was greatly compunct and went from them and did them no dis-ease. And if all it be so that this manner of folk have not the articles of our belief, nevertheless I trow that for their good faith that they have of kind and their good intent, God loves them well and holds him well paid for their living, as he did of Job, the which was a paynim, and not forbye his deeds were acceptable to God as of his loyal servants. And if all there be many divers laws and divers sects in the world, never the latter I trow that God evermore loves well all those that love him in sooth-fastness and serve him meekly and truly and set not by the vainglory of the world, as this folk does and as Job did. And therefore said our Lord by the Prophet Ysai [Hosea], *Ponam eis multiplices leges meas,* that is to say, 'I shall put to them my laws manifold'. And also in the Gospel he says, *Alias oves habeo, que non sunt ex hoc ovili,* that is to say, 'I have other sheep which are not of this fold', as if he said, 'Other servants I have than are under Christian law.' And hereto accords the vision that was showed to Saint Peter in the city of Jaffa, how an angel came from heaven and brought with him all manner of beasts and nedders [snakes] and fowles, and bade him take and eat; and Saint Peter answered and said, 'I eat never of unclean beasts.' And the angel said again to him, *Quod deus mundavit, tu ne immundum dixeris,* that is to say, 'Call thou not unclean that that God has cleansed.' This was done in token that men despise no men for the diversity of their laws. For we wot not whom God loves ne whom he hates; and therefore when I pray for the dead and say my *De Profundis,* I say it for all Christian souls and also for all the souls that are to be prayed for. And of this folk I say thus mickle, that I trow they are full acceptable to God, they are so true and so good. And there are many prophets among them and have been of old time; for in these isles was some time the incarnation of Christ prophesied, how he should be born of a maiden, yea three thousand year and more before the time of his incarnation. And they trow well the incarnation of Christ, but they know not the manner of his passion.

Beyond these isles is another isle that is called Pytan, where the folk neither till ne sow no land, ne neither eat ne drink. And nevertheless they are right fair folk and well coloured and well shapen after the stature that they are of; for they are little like dwarfs, somewhat more than the pigmens. This folk live with the smell of wild apples that grow there; and, if they gang over far from home, they take with them of these apples, for alsone as they forgo the smell of them they die. This folk is not full reasonable, but right simple and as it were beasts.

There near is another isle, where the folk are all full of feathers and rough, out-taken the visage and the palms of the hand. These men go all well upon the water as upon the land; and they eat flesh and fish raw. In this isle is a great river the breadth of two mile; and it is called Wymare. Beyond that river is a great wilderness, as men told me, for I saw it not, ne came not beyond the river. But men that dwell near the river told us that in those deserts are the Trees of the Sun and the Moon, which spake til King Alexander and told him of his death. And men say that folk that keep the trees eat of the fruit of them and of the balm that grows there, and they live four hundred year or five through the virtue of that fruit and of that balm. For there grows great plenty of balm and nowhere else that I could hear of, out-taken in Egypt beside Babylon, as I told you before. My fellows and I would fain have gone thither; but, as men told us, a hundred thousand men of arms should unnethe pass that wilderness because of the great multitude of wild beasts that are in that wilderness, as dragons and divers manners of nedders and other ravissant beasts that slay and devour all that they may get. In this foresaid isle are many elephants all white and some all blue and of other colour without number; there are also many unicorns and lions and many other hideous beasts. Many other isles there are in the lordship of Prester John and many marvels and also mickle riches and noblay of treasure and precious stones and other jewels, the which were over long to tell.

Now will I tell you why this emperor is called Prester John. There was some time an emperor in that land which was a noble prince and a doughty; and he had many knights with him that were Christian, as he has that now is emperor there. And on a time this emperor thought that he would see the manner of the service in Christian kirks. And that time occupied Christian men many countries towards those parts, that is to say, Turkey, Syria, Tartary, Jerusalem, Palestine, Arabia, Aleppo and all Egypt. And so it fell that this emperor and a Christian knight with him came into a kirk in Egypt upon a Saturday in Whitsun week, when the bishop gave Orders. And the emperor beheld the service and the manner of the making of priests, how solemnly and how busily and devoutly they were ordained. And then he asked the knight that was with him what manner of folk those were that were so ordained and what they hight; and he said that they were priests. And then the emperor said he would no more be called king ne emperor but priest, and also he would have the name of the first priest that came out of the kirk. So it fell that the first priest that came first out of the kirk hight John; and therefore that emperor and all other emperors syne have been called Prester John, that is als mickle at say as Priest John. In the land of Prester John are many good Christian men and well living, and men of good faith and of good law, and namely of men of the same country. And they have priests among them that sing them masses; but they make the sacrament of leavened bread, as the Greeks do. And also they say not their masses in all things as our priests do; but they say all only the *Pater Noster* and the words of the consecration with which the sacrament is made, as Saint Thomas the Apostle taught them in old time. But of the ordinances and additions of the court of Rome which our priests use ken they nought.

FRANÇOIS RABELAIS

(ca. 1495–1553)

The Abbey of Theleme*

François Rabelais was born at La Devinière in Touraine. Successively a Franciscan, a Benedictine, a physician in a Lyons hospital, a courtier, this vagabond spirit shifted back and forth between religious and secular employments. Rabelais was an enthusiast for the new, liberal learning and merciless in deriding some aspects of religious life and dogma. His fortunes fluctuated as orthodoxy waxed and waned in France. During his years at Lyons, where he was part of an enlightened and intellectual society, the first of his great satiric tales appeared, and was forthwith condemned by the Sorbonne theologians for obscenity and sacrilege (1533). Despite skirmishes with the religious authorities, Rabelais made several journeys to Italy in the retinue of the humanist Bishop, later Cardinal, Jean du Bellay and of his brother Guillaume, and through their patronage secured livings at Meudon and St. Christophe de Jambet. It is doubtful, however, that the "canon of Meudon" ever presided there, and in the last year of his life he resigned these benefices to take up the honorary court post of *maître des requêtes*. Rabelais's powerfully inventive stories of Gargantua and Pantagruel, published piecemeal over a period of two decades and issued in a complete edition (1567) only after his death, are animated by a robust wit, a sharp sense of ridicule, and a reformer's zeal. His own experience of monastic life gives the chapters on Theleme an especially pungent flavor.

*From François Rabelais, *Gargantua and Pantagruel*, trans. Sir Henry Urquhart and Peter Le Motteux (newly annotated; Oxford: Oxford University Press, 1934), I, pp. 147–9, 154–60.

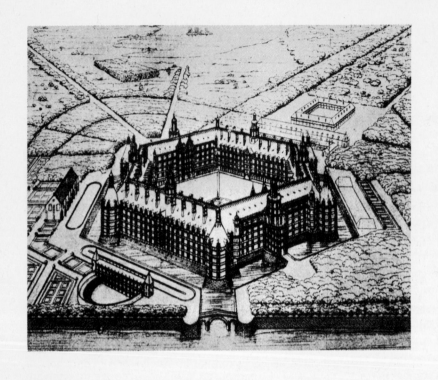

The Abbey of Theleme, as conceived by Charles Lenormant in his *Rabelais et l'architecture de la Renaissance. Restitution de l'Abbaye de Thélème*, Paris, 1840.

How Gargantua Caused To Be Built for the Monk the Abbey of Theleme

There was left onely the Monk to provide for, whom *Gargantua* would have made Abbot of *Seville*, but he refused it; he would have given him the Abbey of *Bourgueil*, or of Sanct *Florent* which was better, or both, if it pleased him; but the Monk gave him a very peremptory answer, that he would never take upon him the charge nor government of Monks; For how shall I be able (said he) to rule over others, that have not full power and command of my self: if you think I have done you, or may hereafter do any acceptable service, give me leave to found an Abby after my owne minde and fancie; the motion pleased *Gargantua* very well, who thereupon offered him all the Countrey of *Thelem* by the river of *Loire,* till within two leagues of the great forrest of *Port-huaut*: the *Monk* then requested *Gargantua* to institute his religious order contrary to all others. First then (said *Gargantua*) you must not build a wall about your convent, for all other Abbies are strongly walled and mured about: See (said the *Monk*) and not without cause (*seeing wall and mure signifie but one and the same thing*;) where there is *Mur* before, and *Mur* behinde, there is store of *Murmur*, envie, and mutual conspiracie. Moreover, seeing there are certaine convents in the world, whereof the custome is, if any woman come in (I mean chaste and honest women) they immediately sweep the ground which they have trod upon; therefore was it ordained that if any man or woman entered into religious orders, should by chance come within this new Abbey, all the roomes should be throughly washed and cleansed through which they had passed; and because in all other Monasteries and Nunneries all is compassed, limited, and regulated by houres, it was decreed that in this new structure there should be neither Clock nor Dial, but that according to the opportunities, and incident occasions, all their hours should be disposed of; for (said *Gargantua*) The greatest losse of time that I know, is to count the hours, what good comes of it? now can there be any greater dotage in the world, then for one to guide and direct his courses by the sound of a Bell, and not by his owne judgement and discretion.

Item, Because at that time they put no women into Nunneries, but such as were either purblinde, blinkards, lame, crooked, ill-favoured, mis-shapen, fooles, senselesse, spoyled or corrupt; nor encloystered any men, but those that were either sickly, subject to defluxions, ill-bred lowts, simple sots, or peevish trouble-houses: but to the purpose; (said the *Monk*) A woman that is neither faire nor good, to what use serves she? To make a Nunne of, said *Gargantua:* Yea (said the *Monk*) and to make shirts and smocks; therefore was it ordained that into this religious order should be admitted no women that were not faire, well featur'd, and of a sweet disposition; nor men that were not comely, personable and well conditioned.

Item, Because in the convents of women men come not but under-hand, privily, and by stealth, it was therefore enacted that in this house there shall be no women in case there be not men, nor men in case there be not women.

Item, Because both men and women that are received into religious orders after the expiring of their noviciat or probation-year, were constrained and forced perpetually to stay there all the days of their life; it was therefore ordered, that all whatever, men or women, admitted within this Abbey, should have full leave to depart with peace and contentment, whensoever it should seem good to them so to do.

Item, for that the religious men and women did ordinarily make three Vows, to wit, those of chastity, poverty & obedience, it was therfore constituted and appointed, that in this Convent they might be honourably married, that they might be rich, and live at liberty. In regard of the legitimat time of the persons to be initiated, and years under and above, which they were not capable of reception, the women were to be admitted from ten till fifteen, and the men from twelve til eighteen.

*　　*　　*

What Manner of Dwelling the Thelemites Had

In the middle of the lower Court there was a stately fountain of faire Alabaster; upon the top thereof stood the three Graces, with their *cornucopias,* or hornes of abundance, and did jert out the water at their breasts, mouth, eares, eyes, and other open passages of the body; the inside of the buildings in this lower Court stood upon great pillars of *Cassydonie* stone, and *Porphyrie* marble, made arch-wayes after a goodly antick fashion. Within those were spacious galleries, long and large, adorned with curious pictures, the hornes of Bucks and

Unicornes: with *Rhinoceroses*, water-horses called *Hippopotames*, the teeth and tusks of Elephants, and other things well worth the beholding. The lodging of the Ladies (*for so we may call those gallant women*) took up all from the tower *Arctick* unto the gate *Mesembrine*: the men possessed the rest. Before the said lodging of the Ladies, that they might have their recreation, between the two first towers, on the out-side, were placed the tilt-yard, the barriers or lists for turnements, the *hippodrome* or riding Court, the *theater* or publike play-house, and *Natatorie* or place to swim in, with most admirable bathes in three stages, situated above one another, well furnished with all necessary accommodation, and store of myrtle-water. By the river-side was the faire garden of pleasure: and in the midst of that the glorious labyrinth. Between the two other towers were the Courts for the tennis and the baloon. Towards the tower *Criere* stood the Orchard full of all fruit-trees, set and ranged in a *quincuncial* order. At the end of that was the great Park, abounding with all sort of Venison. Betwixt the third couple of towers were the buts and marks for shooting with a snap-work gun, an ordinary bowe for common archery, or with a Crosse-bowe. The office-houses were without the tower *Hesperie*, of one story high. The stables were beyond the offices, and before them stood the falconrie, managed by Ostridge-keepers and Falconers, very expert in the Art, and it was yearly supplied and furnished by the *Candians*, *Venetians*, *Sarmates* (now called *Moscoviters*) with all sorts of most excellent hawks, *eagles*, *gerfalcons*, *gosehawkes*, *sacres*, *lanners*, *falcons*, *sparhawks*, *Marlins*, and other kindes of them, so gentle and perfectly well manned, that flying of themselves sometimes from the Castle for their own disport, they would not faile to catch whatever they encountred. The Venerie where the Beagles and Hounds were kept, was a little farther off drawing towards the Park.

All the halls, chambers, and closets or cabinets, were richly hung with tapestrie, and hangings of divers sorts, according to the variety of the seasons of the year. All the pavements and floors were covered with green cloth: the beds were all embroidered: in every back-chamber or withdrawing room there was a looking-glasse of pure crystal set in a frame of fine gold, garnished all about with pearles, and was of such greatnesse, that it would represent to the full the whole lineaments and proportion of the person that stood before it. At the going out of the halls, which belong to the Ladies lodgings, were the perfumers and trimmers, through whose hands the gallants past when they were to visit the Ladies; those sweet Artificers did every morning furnish the Ladies chambers with the spirit of roses, orange-flower-water and *Angelica*; and to each of them gave a little precious casket vapouring forth the most odoriferous exhalations of the choicest aromatical sents.

*   *   *

How the Men and Women of the Religious Order of Theleme Were Apparelled

The Ladies at the foundation of this order, were apparelled after their own pleasure and liking: but since that of their own accord and free will they have reformed themselves, their accoutrement is in manner as followeth. They wore stockins of scarlet crimson, or ingrained purple die, which reached just three inches above the knee, having a list beautified with exquisite embroideries, and rare incisions of the Cutters Art. Their garters were of the colour of their bracelets, and circled the knee a little, both over and under. Their shoes, pumps, and slippers were either of red, violet, or crimson-velvet, pinked and jagged like Lobster wadles.

Next to their smock they put on the pretty kirtle or vasquin of pure silk chamlet; above that went the taffatie or tabie vardingale, of white, red, tawnie, gray, or any other colour: Above this taffatie petticoat they had another of cloth of tissue or brocado, embroidered with fine gold, and interlaced with needlework, or as they thought good, and according to the temperature and disposition of the weather, had their upper coats of sattin, damask or velvet, and those either orange, tawnie, green, ash-coloured, blew, yelow, bright red, crimson or white, and so forth; or had them of cloth of gold, cloth of silver, or some other choise stuffe, inriched with purle, or embroidered according to the dignity of the festival dayes and times wherein they wore them.

Their gownes being still correspondent to the season, were either of cloth of gold frizled with a silver-raised work; of red sattin, covered with gold purle: of tabie, or taffatie, white, blew, black, tawnie, &c., of silk serge, silk chamlot, velvet, cloth of silver, silver tissue, cloth of gold, gold wire, figured velvet, or figured sattin tinselled and overcast with golden threads, in divers variously purfled draughts.

In the summer some dayes in stead of gowns they wore light handsome mantles, made either of the stuffe of the aforesaid attire, or like *Moresco* rugs, of violet velvet frizled, with a raised work of gold upon silver purle: or with a knotted cord-work of gold embroiderie, every where garnished with little *Indian* pearles. They alwayes carried a faire *Pannache*, or plume of feathers, of the colour of their muffe, bravely adorned and tricked out with glistering spangles of gold. In the winter-time they had their taffatie gownes of all colours, as above-named: and those lined with the rich furrings of hinde-wolves, or speckled linxes, black-spotted weesils, martlet-skins of *Calabria*, sables, and other costly furres of an inestimable value. Their beads, rings, bracelets, collars, carcanets and neck-chaines were all of precious stones, such as carbuncles, rubies, baleus, diamonds, saphirs, emeralds, turkoises, garnets, agates, berilles, and excellent margarits. Their head-dressing also varied with the season of the yeare, according to which they decked themselves. In winter it was of the *French* fashion, in the spring of the *Spanish*: in summer of the fashion of *Tuscanie*, except only upon the holy dayes and Sundayes, at which times they were accoutred in the *French* mode, because they accounted it more honourable, and better befitting the garb of a matronal pudicity.

The men were apparelled after their fashion: their stockins were of tamine or of cloth-serge, of white, black, scarlet, or some other ingrained colour: their breeches were of velvet, of the same colour with their stockins, or very near, embroidered and cut according to their fancy; their doublet was of cloth of gold, of cloth of silver, of velvet, sattin, damask, taffaties, &c. of the same colours, cut, embroidered, and suitably trimmed up in perfection: the points were of silk of the same colours; the tags were of gold well enameled: their coats and jerkins were of cloth of gold, cloth of silver, gold, tissue or velvet embroidered; as they thought fit: their gownes were every whit as costly as those of the Ladies: their girdles were of silk, of the colour of their doublets; every one had a gallant sword by his side, the hilt and handle whereof were gilt, and the scabbard of velvet, of the colour of his breeches, with a chape of gold, and pure Goldsmiths work: the dagger was of the same: their caps or bonnets were of black velvet, adorned with jewels and buttons of gold: upon that they wore a white plume, most prettily and minion-like parted by so many rowes of gold spangles, at the end whereof hung dangling in a more sparkling resplendencie faire rubies, emeralds, diamonds, &c. But there was such a sympathy betwixt the gallants & the Ladies, that every day they were apparelled in the same livery: and that they might not misse, there were certain Gentlemen appointed to tell the youths every morning what vestments the Ladies would on that day weare; for all was done according to the pleasure of the Ladies. In these so handsome clothes, and abiliaments so rich, think not that either one or other of either sex did waste any time at all; for the Masters of the wardrobes had all their raiment and apparel so ready for every morning, and the chamber-Ladies so well skilled, that in a trice they would be dressed, and compleatly in their clothes from head to foot. And to have those accoutrements with the more conveniency; there was about the wood of *Teleme* a row of houses of the extent of half a league, very neat and cleanly, wherein dwelt the Goldsmiths, Lapidaries, Jewellers, Embroiderers, Tailors, Gold-drawers, Velvet-weavers, Tapestrie-makers and Upholsters, who wrought there every

one in his own trade, and all for the aforesaid jollie Friars and Nuns of the
new stamp; they were furnished with matter and stuffe from the hands of the
Lord *Nausiclete,* who every year brought them seven ships from the *Perlas &
Cannibal*-islands, laden with ingots of gold, with raw silk, with pearles and
precious stones. And if any *margarites* (called *unions*) began to grow old, and
lose somewhat of their natural whitenesse and lustre, those with their Art
they did renew, by tendering them to eat to some pretty cocks, as they use to
give casting unto hawkes.

*   *   *

How the Thelemites Were Governed and of Their Manner of Living

All their life was spent not in lawes, statutes or rules, but according to their
own free will and pleasure. They rose out of their beds, when they thought
good: they did eat, drink, labour, sleep, when they had a minde to it, and
were disposed for it. None did awake them, none did offer to constrain them
to eat, drink, nor to do any other thing; for so had *Gargantua* established it.
In all their rule, and strictest tie of their order, there was but this one clause
to be observed.

Do what thou wilt.

Because men that are free, well-borne, well-bred, and conversant in honest
companies, have naturally an instinct and spurre that prompteth them unto
vertuous actions, and withdraws them from vice, which is called *honour.*
Those same men, when by base subjection and constraint they are brought
under and kept down, turn aside from that noble disposition, by which they
formerly were inclined to vertue, to shake off and break that bond of servitude,
wherein they are so tyrannously inslaved; for it is agreeable with the nature
of man to long after things forbidden, and to desire what is denied us.

By this liberty they entered into a very laudable emulation, to do all of
them what they saw did please one; if any of the gallants or Ladies should say,
Let us drink, they would all drink: if any one of them said, *Let us play,* they all
played; if one said, *Let us go a walking into the fields,* they went all: if it were to
go a hawking or a hunting, the Ladies mounted upon dainty well-paced nags,

seated in a stately palfrey saddle, carried on their lovely fists, miniardly be-gloved every one of them, either a Sparhawk, or a Laneret, or a Marlin, and the young gallants carried the other kinds of Hawkes: so nobly were they taught, that there was neither he nor she amongst them, but could read, write, sing, play upon several musical instruments, speak five or sixe several languages, and compose in them all very quaintly, both in Verse and Prose: never were seene so valiant Knights, so noble and worthy, so dextrous and skilful both on foot and a horseback, more brisk and lively, more nimble and quick, or better handling all manner of weapons then were there. Never were seene Ladies so proper and handsome, so miniard and dainty, lesse froward, or more ready with their hand, and with their needle, in every honest and free action belonging to that sexe then were there; for this reason when the time came, that any man of the said Abbey, either at the request of his parents, or for some other cause, had a minde to go out of it, he carried along with him one of the Ladies, namely her whom he had before that chosen for his Mistris, and were married together: and if they had formerly in *Theleme* lived in good devotion and amity, they did continue therein and increase it to a greater height in their state of matrimony: and did entertaine that mutual love till the very last day of their life, no no lesse vigour and fervency, then at the very day of their wedding. . . .

ANONYMOUS

The Civil and Religious Constitution of Antangil*

The first "complete" French utopia, describing in circumstantial detail the geography, political institutions, army, educational system, and religion of an imaginary kingdom, appeared anonymously in Saumur in 1616, a whole century after More's *Utopia*. The creator of Antangil dilates at such length upon its military establishment that some have conjectured his profession was soldiering. He was apparently a Protestant, but nothing more about his person can be said with certainty, despite a number of scholarly attempts at identification. The style of his work is rather wooden and its syntax defective. It has none of the wit, charm, elegance, and ambiguity of the earlier utopian fragments of Rabelais, nor the fantasy of Cyrano. The book had no traceable influence, and lay buried in oblivion for three centuries until uncovered by Frédéric Lachèvre in 1922. Its primary and perhaps sole distinction is its priority.

*From *L'Histoire du Royaume d'Antangil*, ed. Frédéric Lachèvre (Paris: La Connaissance, 1933), pp. 38–42, 124–5; translated by the editors.

HISTOIRE
DV GRAND
ET ADMIRA-
BLE ROYAVME
D'ANTANGIL.

Incogneu jusques à present à tous Historiens
& Cosmographes : composé de six vingts
Provinces tref-belles & tref-fertiles. Avec
la description d'icelui, & de sa police nom-
pareille, tant civile que militaire. De l'instruction de la jeunesse. Et de la Religion.

Le tout compris en cinq livres,

Par I. D. M. G. T

A LEIDEN,
Par Iean le Maire.
M. DC. XVI.

Title-page, *Le Royaume d'Antangil*, Saumur, 1616.

The Confusion of All the Provinces of This Empire before They Were Joined Together, and the Means Employed to Unite Them

Some 2,200 years ago this great expanse of territory that we have described was divided among a number of kings, princes, lords, and republics. Because of the disorder of their governments as well as the multiplicity of rulers, they were perpetually involved in wars and disputes; and the land had been made a virtual desert by the battles and continual massacres resulting from the ambition and covetousness of each of them. At long last, the wisest of them, tired of the eternal chaos and clearly seeing that they faced utter ruin, met with the kings, princes, and ambassadors of the republics in a neutral place easy of access. And they mutually swore by all the gods they worshiped that they would maintain and hold inviolate whatever was resolved and determined by that solemn assembly. This done, each one proposed the form of government he judged most appropriate, useful, and fitting for the preservation of the nobility, the city-dwellers, and the ordinary people.

Finally, after everything was weighed, debated, and carefully considered, they ordained the government of this flourishing Monarchy in such a manner—described below—that we must believe God, the enemy of all disorder and confusion, presided over this venerable assembly. For human minds would not have been able to transform such deplorable conditions into such a state of perfection that for the last 2,200 years there has been no need to remodel, change, or alter any of the laws, statutes, and regulations then promulgated. And this has neither been seen nor will be seen in any other kingdom or monarchy, no matter how well governed and administered it may be.

The Division of the Kingdoms, Principalities, and Republics into Provinces. The Establishment of Capital Cities and Their Authority

They first decreed that the whole of this great continent of land, which had once held so many different sovereignties, should be united into a single kingdom to be called Antangil, signifying celestial grace, since they were thoroughly agreed to found a permanent and invincible empire, without any heed to infringements on the authority and sovereign power of any one of them.

After they dealt with dividing the land into 120 provinces, they provided that each one would have a capital city bearing its name, and that under its jurisdiction would be 100 other cities and parishes over which it would have power and authority as a court of last resort.

This done, it was decreed that all houses—those of the capital as well as those of the other cities, towns, and villages dependent upon it—would be grouped by tens, hundreds, thousands, ten thousands, and hundred thouands, if warranted by the size and extent of the cities. Over each ten houses, the most competent and able family man among them was to take command, watching over their conduct, calling them to account and admonishing them, keeping informed at all times of the value of their property, movable goods as well as real estate, up to the last half-farthing. It was his duty furthermore to prevent the quarreling and disputes that arise among neighbors, to make them work and live in an orderly and modest manner as befits gentle folk. If it happened that those under his jurisdiction were refractory, or there was a dispute difficult to decide, he would appeal to his Chief-of-Hundred, and the other nine Chiefs-of-Ten having assembled, they would resolve the problem and summarily impose on the disobedient one any punishment short of death, this last being reserved solely for sovereign judges. And if the matter was of still greater consequence, the Chief-of-Hundred was obliged to notify the Chief-of-Thousand, who summoned his ten Chiefs-of-Hundred to consider the matter and conclude it if possible. If not, he would advise the Chief-of-Ten Thousand, who then assembled his Chiefs-of-Thousand and, if necessary, summoned the Chief-of-Hundred Thousand, and together they would settle the dispute—all this while enjoined from taking any salary or gift, under penalty of death.

This manner of proceeding cuts off a world of disputations and litigations apparently born of nothing, which are thus stifled right from the start without any trouble.

The Council of State and Why It Was Established

After the division into provinces had been made, and the cities, towns, and villages had been grouped by tens, hundreds, thousands, ten thousands, and hundred thousands, it was decreed that from each province three men who were distinguished, prudent, wise, and informed—to wit, a noble, a city dweller, and a man for the towns and villages—would assemble in the number of 360 to constitute the Estates General. This body would represent the entire people and would permanently reside in Sangil to give advice and help to the King and his Council regarding all matters which seemed to them to involve the public weal, to approve or reject as they pleased, to receive the instructions of His Majesty, transmit them to the provinces, and lay before the Council the business with which the provinces had charged them. In sum, they were to act as if the entire people was assembled.

It was further provided that every deputy be clad in the colors of his province and wear on his breast and back the arms and name of his capital city, that he might be identified and that such adornments might render the court more brilliant and impressive.

The deputies' term of office was limited to one year, as much to prevent the corruption that is bred by too long a tenure as to train more people in managing affairs and to recognize their value and merit by making them administrators.

The Council of His Royal Majesty

All these great statesmen saw that it was not enough to have established the Council of Provinces, since if some serious difference arose among them there would be no one to restore harmony and also the yearly rotation would make them novices in affairs of state. And it would not even be as satisfactory as a small number chosen and selected from among the most capable men of all the provinces.

Moved by this consideration, they resolved then to elect a hundred great and wise personages, the first in the Kingdom not in riches, prestige, and power, but in competence and good will. These men would be more concerned with the public good than with their own welfare. They would be at least forty years of age (for youth is fit not for governance, but rather for hasty action, and though there are some modest, wise, and informed young men, they are quite rare and cannot have the training that time and experience give). Inasmuch as the King and this Council were to constitute but one body and without it he could not dispose of important matters of state, it was named the Council of His Royal Majesty and was given sovereign authority, for instance, to choose the King or Viceroy, determine peace or war, regulate finances and subsidies, confirm or invalidate alliances or make new ones, elect judges, removing and punishing anyone derelict in his duty, and act in the same way with the King and Viceroy should they try to disturb existing arrangements or introduce new ones into the state or disregard the instructions of the Council. In short, every sovereign power is vested in them, save when there is a question of provincial interest, in which event the Council of States deliberates, and grants, refuses, or modifies the request.

All these venerable Senators wear long robes of crimson velvet embroidered with gold rosettes and hats of the same color, also covered with embroidery, along with a ribbon of gold and of white silk. Their slippers are of the same material and color, their cassocks of white satin.

For their maintenance, the people give them annually two thousand crowns in wages, plus a magnificent house near the royal palace. Besides, they receive several tributes of honor from princes and neighboring republics as well as from the generosity of the Provinces. The gifts are brought each year to Sangil in recognition of their merit and splendid service to the state and are equally distributed among all. In this way they can live decently and comfortably in accordance with the honor and dignity of their position.

*   *   *

How the Idols Were Removed and True Divine Service Was Established

By Senatorial decree published throughout the provinces, all the idols were removed from the temples and stowed in a designated place; for once the abuse was corrected, it grieved these gentlemen that so many fine statues and pictures, which could adorn public buildings and private houses, should be shattered and totally ruined. Also, all the inscriptions honoring the false gods were effaced, and were replaced by the most meaningful passages from Scripture in veneration of God Almighty and renunciation of error. Then curved benches were installed in the form of an amphitheatre, and others were divided in the middle by aisles to seat the women. There were still others for the clergy, and a lofty seat for the bishop, as will be later described.

When the temples had been cleansed and equipped with everything needed for the divine service, that great personage, Byrachil, asked the Senate to tell him about the civil administration of the state and its appurtenances, so that he might set up the ecclesiastical establishment in accordance with it. They graciously acceded to this request. And when he had absorbed and understood everything, he told them how he truly recognized that God had at all times been a particular concern of their republic, since it was so well administered that they lacked only the last details of perfection, and these the true religion had supplied. Thus he found it expedient to place a bishop in each of the 120 capital cities, who would reside with his clergy near the greatest temple to celebrate the divine service there and to have supervision and authority over all the little cities and parishes comprised in his diocese. As it would be difficult for one man to keep his eye on so many pastors, for every ten parishes there would be a suffragan or archpriest, who would have oversight of their conduct, doctrine, and faith, who would live among them and visit them once a month to report to the bishop on their deportment. Once a year, at the Easter holiday, these pastors would appear before the bishop, along with three elders of each parish who would testify to their lives, conduct, and faith, so that in accordance with their attitude toward their duties they would receive the praise they had earned, or the blame and punishment they deserved. The most severe penalty was deprivation of office. If the clergy committed some crime against the ordinances and civil laws, the bishop would not take cognizance of it, since he had jurisdiction only over purely ecclesiastical matters. But the magistrates would punish them much more severely than laymen, since they had been better instructed and had more knowledge of virtue and piety, and thus their misdeeds were more reprehensible and deserving of punishment.

SAVINIEN CYRANO DE BERGERAC
1619–1655

Warfare on the Moon[*]

Well-born and educated—he is said to have studied at one time with the philosopher Gassendi—Cyrano de Bergerac had a brief though colorful career as an officer in a Gascon regiment. (Two-and-a-half centuries later his prodigious nose and dueling exploits were celebrated in Rostand's famous play.) After sustaining grave wounds in the Siege of Arras, Cyrano abandoned the military profession in 1641 and turned to literature. He wrote novels, dramatic works, and the posthumously published *Comic History of the States of the Moon* (1657) and *Comic History of the States of the Sun* (1662). In these satiric tales, from which Swift drew inspiration for *Gulliver's Travels,* Cyrano mocks the institutions and beliefs of his own society by weaving a fantasy about the lunar and solar worlds, though he treats them lightly and portrays them as having not a few foibles of their own.

*From Savinien Cyrano de Bergerac, *Voyages to the Moon and the Sun,* trans. Richard Aldington (London, New York: George Routledge and Sons, Ltd., E. P. Dutton and Co., 1923), pp. 109–13. Copyright © Madame Catherine Guillaume (nee Aldington).

Engraving from *Government of the World in the Moon*, first English translation, London, 1659.

Conversation with a Lunar Lady

At last when they saw that I kept bawling this and nothing else, save that they were not more learned than Aristotle, and that I had been forbidden to argue with those who denied his Principles, they concluded with one accord that I was not a man but perhaps some sort of ostrich, seeing I carried my head upright like that bird; and so the falconer was ordered to take me back to the cage. I passed my time amusingly enough, for my possessing correctly their language was a cause that the whole Court diverted itself by making me chatter. Among others the Queen's ladies-in-waiting always thrust some scraps of food into my basket, and the prettiest of them all conceived a certain friendship for me. Once when we were alone I discovered to her the mysteries of our religion and I discoursed principally of our bells and our relics; she was so transported with joy that she vowed with tears in her eyes that if ever I were able to fly back to our world she would gladly follow me.

One day I woke up early with a start and saw her tapping against the bars of my cage. "I have good news for you!" said she, "yesterday the council declared for war against the great King; and I hope, with the bustle of preparation and the departure of our Monarch and his subjects, to find an opportunity to set you free."

"War!" I interrupted immediately, "do the Princes of this world quarrel among themselves like those of ours? Tell me, I beseech you, how they fight."

"The Umpires elected by the consent of both parties," she replied, "fix the time allowed for arming, the time of marching, the number of combatants, the day and place of the battle; all with such impartiality that neither army has a single man more than the other. On each side the maimed soldiers are enrolled in one company and on the day of battle the Generals are careful to send them against the maimed soldiers on the other side. The giants are opposed by the colossi, the fencers by the nimble, the valiant by the courageous, the weak by the feeble, the unhealthy by the sick, the robust by the strong; and if someone should strike any but his prescribed enemy he is found guilty of cowardice unless he can clear himself by showing it was a mistake. After the battle they count the wounded, the dead and the prisoners, for none is ever seen to run away. If the losses are equal on each side they draw lots as to who shall be proclaimed the victor. But although a King may have defeated his enemy in open war he has achieved little; there are other less numerous armies of men of wit and learning, upon whose disputes depends wholly the real triumph or servitude of States. A man of learning is opposed to another, men of wit and judgment are set against their like; and the triumph gained by a State in this way is considered equal to three victories of brute force. When a nation is proclaimed victorious, they break up the assembly and the conquering people chooses for its King either their own or that of their enemies."

I could not forbear laughing at this scrupulous manner of making war and as an example of a far stronger policy I alleged the customs of our Europe, where the Monarch takes care to omit no opportunity of conquest; and she answered me in this way:

"Tell me," said she, "do your Princes justify their arms by anything save the right of force?"

"Yes indeed," replied I, "with the justice of their cause."

"Why then," she continued, "do not they choose arbitrators above suspicion to reconcile them? And if there is as much right on the one side as on the other let them stay as they were or let them play a hundred up at piquet for the Town or Province about which they are disputing. And yet, while they are the cause that more than four millions of better men than themselves get broken heads, they are in their cabinets joking over the circumstances of the massacre of these poor boobies. But I am wrong to blame the courage of your brave subjects; they do well to die for their country; 'tis an affair of importance, a matter of being the vassal of a King who wears a ruff or of a King who wears falling bands."

"But," I replied, "why all these circumstances in your manner of fighting? Is it not enough for armies to be equal in numbers?"

"Your judgment is all astray," she replied. "On your faith now, do you think that if you overcome your enemy in the field face to face, that you have beaten him in fair warfare if you wear mail and he does not? If he has only a dagger and you a rapier? Finally, if he is one-armed and you have both your arms? Yet with all the equality you recommend so much to your gladiators, they never fight on equal terms; one will be tall, another short; one skilful, the other will never have handled a sword; one will be strong, the other weak. And even if these proportions are equalised, if they are equally tall, equally nimble and equally strong, they will still not be on an equal footing, for one of the two will perhaps be more courageous than the other. And because a brutal fellow will not consider the peril, will be bilious and will have more blood, will have a heart more set with the qualities which make for courage (as if this were not an arm his enemy does not possess, just like a sword!), he will rush violently upon his adversary, terrify him and deprive of life a poor man who saw the danger, whose vital heat was stifled in phlegm and whose heart is too large to collect the spirits necessary to get rid of that ice we call poltroonery. So you praise a man for having killed his enemy when he had him at an advantage, and by praising his boldness you praise him for a sin against Nature, since boldness tends to its own destruction.

"You must know that a few years ago a Remonstrance was sent up to the council of war, demanding a more circumspect and more conscientious regulation of combats. The philosopher who sent up the notice spoke in these words:

" 'You imagine, gentlemen, that you have equalised two combatants when you have chosen them both hardy, both tall, both active, both courageous, but this still is not enough; the conqueror must win by skill, by force or by chance. If it were by skill, he has doubtless struck his adversary in a place he has not expected, or more quickly than seemed likely; or, feigning to attack him on one side, he paid him home on the other. This is finesse, deceiving, betraying. And such finesse, such deceit, such treason should not contribute to the fair fame of a true gentleman. If he has triumphed by force, will you consider his enemy beaten because he has been overwhelmed? No, doubtless; any more than you would say that a man had lost the victory if he should be overwhelmed by the fall of a mountain, since it was not in his power to gain it. Moreover he has not been overcome, because at that moment he was not disposed to be able to resist the violence of his adversary. And if he has beaten his enemy by chance, you should crown Fortune, not him, for he has contributed nothing; and the loser is no more to be blamed than a dice-player who sees eighteen thrown when he has cast seventeen.' "

It was admitted that he was right, but that it was impossible in all human probability to remedy it and that it was better to yield to one small inconvenience than to give way to a thousand of greater importance.

DENIS VAIRASSE D'ALLAIS

(ca. 1630–ca. 1700)

The Economy and Education of the Sevarambians*

Few facts in the life of Vairasse are known or even surmised. Some biographers have fixed his birthplace as the town of Alais not far from Nîmes, and he was apparently a Protestant, who ended his days as a refugee in Holland. He seems to have had both military and legal training early in his career. It is certain that he passed a part of his youth in England and made the acquaintance of Pepys, of Shaftesbury, and of Locke, whose ideal constitution for the Carolina settlement may have influenced the framework of the Sevarambian state. In the service of the Duke of Buckingham (probably 1665–74), Vairasse returned to France when that nobleman fell into disgrace. In his native land, Vairasse taught English and French, wrote books on French grammar, and published the *Histoire des Sévarambes* (Paris, 1677–79), of which Part I had already appeared in English (London, 1675). The work saw a number of editions in French, as well as translations into Flemish, German, and, as recently as 1956, into Russian. In the Sevarambia of Vairasse's fancy, moderation, orderliness, and equality prevailed under an enlightened despot. The inhabitants, without anxiety or avarice to "destroy their souls," lived in communal dwellings called *osmasies*, and often reached the age of 100 or more. Vairasse invented a host of institutions for his dollhouse society, and even devised for it a new onomatopoeic language, as befitted a philologist. Captain Siden, narrator of the tale, and Sevarias, its lawgiver, are anagrams for the author's name.

*From Denis Vairasse d'Allais, *Histoire des Sévarambes* (Amsterdam: E. Roger, 1702), I, 3, pp. 315–33; translated by the editors.

49

Engraving from the first German translation of the *History of the Sevarambians,*
Sulzbach, 1689.

Laws, Manners, and Customs of the Sevarambians

I believe it is now time to explain how this great state subsists, how its public stores are accumulated, and what disposition is made of them.

We have already said that one of the major policies of the government was to confiscate all private property and vest it in the sovereign. This has been steadily practiced since the rule of Sevarias, in order to support the people and allow everyone to live comfortably. All things necessary and useful are gathered into public warehouses. There is similar stockpiling of commodities that contribute to decent pleasures. From these stores goods are withdrawn for each *osmasie* in accordance with its needs. Every *osmasie* has its own warehouse, which is supplied from time to time from the general warehouse, in order that each person may be allotted whatever he needs for subsistence and for practicing his skill or trade. In the rural *osmasies*, the principal occupation is cultivating the soil, and its inhabitants are nourished on the fruits of the harvest. First, each *osmasie* takes as much corn, wine, oil, and other products as required to further agriculture and feed its people. The surplus is sent to the public warehouse. The same procedure is followed with cattle in places largely devoted to their breeding.

There are prefects of hunting, fishing, and all kinds of manufactured articles, who collect the materials necessary for this work from the areas where they are produced, and have them transported to the points where they are utilized. For instance, there are places where cotton, linen, hemp, and silk are made. Those in charge of the work gather up the raw materials and send them to the towns, where they are made into fabrics; thence they are distributed throughout the country to whatever *osmasies* are in need of them. The same thing happens with wool, leather, and all other goods employed in daily life. As for building materials, the construction supervisor sees to it that there are stockpiles, and from them he draws whatever is needed for new buildings, as well as for repair and maintenance of existing ones.

The same system is in force with respect to public festivals, solemn occasions, and spectacles. For everything there are supervisors, and under them, officers in charge of a certain number of persons assigned to the work. There are various *osmasies* where the children are raised, each sex apart from the other, and every such *osmasie* has its directors and teachers to instruct the youth. There are some where arts and trades are taught. Each *osmasie* has its own stores, officers, and a number of slaves to do the lowliest tasks. These stores furnish whatever is needed for each one's support.

If one reflects on the way of life of other nations, one sees that in fact there are similar storehouses everywhere; that the towns take from the country and vice-versa; that some work with their hands and others with their heads; that some are born to obey and others to command; that there are schools to educate the young and masters to teach them trades; that among the daily tasks, some are needed for subsistence, others provide the comforts of life, still others serve purely pleasurable ends. In short, things are fundamentally the same everywhere, but the manner of distribution is different. Among us, there are people who are stuffed with goods and wealth, while others are in dire want. We have persons who pass their lives in idleness and luxury, while others toil ceaselessly to earn a wretched livelihood. There are those of high rank who are neither worthy nor capable of exercising the privileges of office. And finally, we have deserving persons who, lacking the authority and appurtenances of wealth, stagnate miserably in the mire and are forever condemned to a servile state.

Among the Sevarambians, on the contrary, no one is poor or in want of the things that are necessary and useful for existence. Every one participates in pleasures and public diversions, with no need to torment body and soul by difficult and excessive toil in order to enjoy them. A moderate activity of eight hours daily procures all these advantages for the Sevarambian, for his family, for all his children, however many he has. No one is obliged to pay taxes or duties, or to amass wealth to enrich his children, provide dowries for his daughters, or buy estates. Free of all these cares, Sevarambians are rich from the cradle. And if all of them do not achieve high office, at least they have the satisfaction of seeing that those who do are elevated by their merit and the esteem of their fellow-citizens. All are at the same time nobles and commoners. No one can reproach another for his lowly birth or boast of being high-born himself. No one feels the resentment of seeing others wallow in idleness, while he works to support their pride and vanity. In short, if one thinks about the happiness of this people, one will conclude that it is as perfect as it can be in this world, and that all other nations are most unlucky in comparison.

Similarly, if one compares the lot of kings, princes, and other sovereigns with that of Sevarambia's Viceroy of the Sun, one will find notable differences. The first customarily encounter trouble getting subsidies to run their states, and they are often constrained to use force, even cruelty, to achieve their ends. The Viceroy of the Sun never resorts to any such means. He is already master of all the nation's goods, and no subject can either refuse to obey him or claim any special exemption. He gives and takes away as he pleases. He makes peace and war as he deems proper. Everybody obeys him and no one would dare to thwart his will. He is not exposed to rebellions and popular uprisings. No one challenges his authority and everyone submits to it. He owes it to nobody, and thus nobody would make bold to deprive him of it. For who would be so rash as to revolt against the Sun and his ministers? Who would be so vain as to regard himself more worthy to command than those whom the Resplendent King has chosen for his lieutenants? And even if some madman wished to usurp the government, how could he do it, and where would he find people willing to support his folly and become slaves to make him king? Add to this that religion strongly binds the Sevarambians to obey their superiors. For they not only recognize the Sun as their king, but they worship him as their god, and believe he is the source of all the goods they possess. Thus they have great respect for the laws and for the government, which they think he established among them through the ministry of Sevarias. Moreover, as their system of education is good, they are early trained to strict observance of their laws. It comes naturally to them, and then it is also a matter of free and deliberate choice, as they grow old enough to reflect and find that their laws are just and reasonable.

Education of the Sevarambians

The wise legislator who gave his people such excellent laws could hardly neglect to apply himself to the problem of rearing the young; for he was well aware that their education would determine whether those laws would be preserved intact or undermined, and that moral corruption generally begets gross deception in political affairs. It is difficult indeed for a man who is vicious and has had a poor upbringing ever to become a capable minister or a worthy subject. The violence of his passions betrays him into vice, while his ignorance does not let him distinguish properly between good and evil, true and false. Men have a strong natural penchant for vice, and if good laws, good examples, and good education do not exercise a corrective influence, the seeds of wickedness sprout and grow strong, and usually choke the seeds of virtue that nature has implanted. Then do they abandon themselves to their dissolute appetites, and allowing wild and reckless passions to master their reason, they plunge into every sort of evil. Thus are bred violence and pillage, envy, hatred, pride and the will to dominate, rebellions, wars, massacres, conflagrations, sacrilege, and all the other afflictions with which mankind is beset.

A good education very often controls, and sometimes even smothers the vicious seeds in men, and nourishes whatever seeds of virtue may be in them.

This the great Sevarias well understood, and therefore he made a number of regulations for the education of children. Recognizing at the outset that parents frequently spoil them through fond indulgence or too strict a discipline, he was unwilling to leave these tender plants in the hands of persons so little fit to cultivate them.

To that end he established public schools, where common education was provided under the guidance of specially selected and able persons who, unprejudiced by love or hate, would instruct all the children impartially through precept, reprimand, and example, in order to inculcate in them an aversion to vice and a love of virtue. And, that they might not be thwarted in the discharge of their duties by the parents, after they had given their children the paternal care of the first years and had early displayed their affection to these precious fruits of their love, it was his aim to divest them of paternal authority and bestow it upon the state and the magistrates, the political fathers of the country.

In accordance with the law, on fixed days four times a year, fathers and mothers of children who have reached the age of seven are required to take them to the temple of the sun. There, after they have shed the white clothing they have worn since birth, they are washed, their heads are shaved, they are anointed with oil, they are decked in yellow robes, and they are then consecrated to the deity. The fathers and mothers completely renounce the authority over them which nature has given them, reserving for themselves only love and respect, and from that moment their offspring become children of the state. They are sent without delay to the public schools, where for four whole years they are trained to obey the laws, taught to read and write, and developed physically through dancing and military drills.

When they have thus passed four years at school and their bodies have gained strength, they are moved to the country, where for three years they learn to till the soil, working at it four hours a day, while they spend another four hours practicing the skills they have previously acquired in school. Girls are raised in much the same way as boys, but in different places, for there are *osmasies* for each sex, and those in the country tend to be distant one from another.

When the young people are fourteen, their domiciles are changed and so are their costumes. The yellow habit is given up for a green one, and they are thenceforth called *Edirnai* in the language of the country, signifying that they are in the third septenary of their lives. Those in the first septenary are called *Adirnai*, and those in the second, *Gadirnai*. Or they are named from the color of their garments: *Alistai*, that is, white clothes; *Erimbai*, or yellow clothes; and *Forruai*, or green clothes. In the case of the girls, the suffix *ai* is merely transformed to *ei*, as in *Adirnei*, *Alistei*, and so on. At this time they are taught the principles of grammar and given a choice of vocation. After a period of trial, if they seem suited for the work, they are turned over to masters who are charged with their instruction; but if they show no particular aptitude, they have the alternative of becoming laborers or masons, the two principal occupations in the land.

The girls are trained for tasks appropriate to their sex, less toilsome than those of the boys. They busy themselves with spinning, sewing, clothmaking, and other activities that are not very arduous.

Girls of sixteen and boys of nineteen are allowed to think of love and marriage, which is brought about in the following way.

Having come of age, they may see each other in the presence of their guardians during walks, dances, hunts, parades, and all public ceremonies. On such occasions the boys may address the girls and freely say to them, "I love you," and the girls may hear their declarations unblushingly. Neither birth, wealth, position, nor any other gift of fortune makes any matter among them, for they are all equal in these respects and differ only as to sex and the three years which separate them. Disparities in marriage are countenanced only when a girl is unable to find a husband of her own and must have recourse to a public official to rescue her from virginity. Those whom some natural infirmity or accident exempts from the obligation to marry are despatched to Sporumbia, for the Sevarambians do not look kindly upon them. At gatherings of girls and boys, love plays its role and makes its conquests. Each youth tries to inspire love with his good looks and intellectual endowments. The ones who combine shining qualities of mind and body with integrity and virtue are usually preferred to the rest; for shrewd girls can foresee that these young men will readily succeed to public office, and thus the honors and dignities that fall to them will be shared by their wives. But prudent considerations move some girls in an altogether different direction: out of fear that a man of merit who becomes a functionary may also exercise the privilege of office, which is to have more than one wife if he so desires, they would rather marry someone undistinguished than attach themselves to a man who, as his fortunes rise, might divide a heart which they wish to possess entire. And so everybody adapts his course to his inclination; some love pleasure, others prestige, and everyone follows his own bent.

Since the Sevarambians are naturally intelligent, and are wellbred and refined, when lovers meet the young men do not fail to call to their aid flowers and fruits, laughter, poetry, and pretty speeches to witness their passion to their mistresses. All of this is allowable, and no-one finds anything amiss in it. On the contrary, those who seem untouched by love are objects of contempt; they are regarded as naturally wicked, as citizens unworthy of the nation's interest.

Yet, on all these occasions, it is rare for anyone to ignore the rules of proper deportment, and nothing is done or said which could offend modesty; for that is expressly forbidden, and even the most brazen would not presume to violate decorum, since they speak to the girls only in public and in front of their chaperones.

For eighteen months marriageable girls, called *Enibei*, and boys, *Sparai*, are at leisure to see one another, to become acquainted, and to fall in love without making any commitments; but at the end of that period, it is customary to be engaged and exchange vows; thereafter rejected suitors withdraw and a girl receives only her betrothed. When the time of the *osparénibon*, the nuptial ceremony, arrives, they go to the temple and are wed in the manner described in the first part of this history.

Once married the lads, now twenty-one, are clad in blue; likewise their wives; but to indicate that a girl has not yet reached her fourth *dirnemis*, that is, has not passed twenty-one, she wears green sleeves on her blue habit until she has completed her twenty-first year; then she veils her head and conceals her hair, which has hitherto been uncovered.

On the wedding night bride and groom are feted at a banquet, enlivened by music and dancing, and attended by a great throng of people of every age and sex. It takes place in one of the halls of the *osmasie* where the couple will live and where two rooms on the same floor have been prepared for them, one giving on the street and the other on the courtyard. There they consummate the marriage. They are permitted to sleep together, however, only one night out of three during the first three years of their union, then one night out of two until their twenty-eighth year; after that they are free to sleep together whenever they please. The highest honor for a woman is to love her husband and to raise several children for the fatherland. Among wives of private citizens, those are most esteemed who have the greatest number of children; but among the wives of magistrates, it is the husband who counts. Sterile women are much scorned, and when a man has kept one for five years, he may marry some widow or girl who has not found a husband, or keep a slave as concubine. The only way sterile women may erase their shame is to tend the sick, or, if they are qualified, to occupy themselves with the education of the young. Every mother must nurse her child, unless she is too weak to do so without seriously endangering her health; in that case the child is given another nurse from among those who have lost their children; such women are greatly respected, since, deprived of their own offspring, they nurse that of another and rear a child for the fatherland.

This is the normal upbringing and training the youth of Sevarambia receive. But those children who have extraordinary talent and who are suited for the liberal arts and sciences are not raised in the same way: they are excused from physical work in order to engage in intellectual work. Thus schools have been designed expressly for their education, and it is from their number that people are selected every seven years to travel on our continent and to learn about anything unique that we may have. This has been the custom since Sevaristas re-established commerce with us and decreed that such journeys should be made. The travelers cannot depart the country without leaving behind at least three children to assure their return. I do not know whether that is why they always go home if they possibly can; but I have not heard tell of anyone who, since this custom was initiated, deserted his country to live elsewhere, or, if he survived his voyages, did not try to reach his native land again.

These travels explain how it is that several persons at Sevarind and the cities round about know how to speak the various tongues of Asia and Europe, which are usually taught the voyagers-elect before they embark. It is the reason Sermodas, Carchida, and the rest were able to converse with us straightway; they already knew some of our languages, having lived for years among Asiatics and Europeans without revealing from what country they hailed, for they commonly passed for Persians or Armenians.

GABRIEL DE FOIGNY

(ca. 1630–1692)

On Life and Death among
the Australians*

Like Rabelais a century-and-a-half before him, Foigny was one of those
restless, imaginative clerics who could not be contained within the
bounds of conventional monastic life. While still a young man, he abandoned the Franciscan Order and ran off to Switzerland to embrace Protes-
tantism. After a riotous existence at Geneva and Lausanne, he secured a
post as a minor church official in Morges, but was expelled and subsequently supported himself as a tutor. In Switzerland Foigny married and
fathered four children. Widowed in 1683, he soon returned to France and
withdrew to a convent of his order in Savoy. There he spent the remainder
of his days as a penitent. His *La Terre australe connue: c'est à dire, la description
de ce pays inconnu jusqu'ici* (Geneva, 1676), later translated into English and
other languages, describes a thirty-five year sojourn in the "Southern
World" by the shipwrecked Jacques Sadeur. There he discovers a nation of
rationalist androgynes, living in an ideal society where goods are held in
common and the form of worship, without dogma, ritual, or ministers,
approaches natural religion.

*From Gabriel de Foigny, *A New Discovery of Terra Incognita Australis, or the Southern World*, by
James Sadeur, a French-man (London: J. Dunton, 1693), pp. 84–106.

Je ne pensois alors a autre chose qu'à tenir ferme.

Engraving by Clément-Pierre Marillier for the *Aventures de Jacques Sadeur*, in Garnier's *Voyages imaginaires*, Amsterdam, 1787–89.

Of the Opinion of the Australians Touching This Life

I have only three things to remark upon the Sentiments of the *Australians* concerning the present Life: The first is in respect to the beginning; the second, the continuation thereof; and the third, the end. Their manner of receiving Life, preserving and ending it.

I have already declared, in what manner the *Australians* come into the world; but as it is one of the principal points of this History, so I believe my self obliged yet to say something more of it.

They have so great an aversion for whatsoever regards the first beginning of their Lives, that in a year or thereabouts after my arrival amongst them, two of the Brethren having heard me speak something of it, with-drew from me, with as many signs of horrour, as if I had committed some great Crime. One day when I had discovered my self to my Old Philosopher, after having censured me a little upon this Subject, he entred into a long Discourse, and brought many Proofs to oblige me to believe, that Children grew within them like Fruits upon the Trees; but when he saw all his reasons made no impression on my mind, and that I cou'd not forbear smiling, he left me without accomplishing it, reproaching me that my incredulity proceeded from the corruption of my manners.

It happen'd another time, about six months after my arrival, that the extraordinary Caresses of the Brethren, caused some unruly motions in me, which some of them perceiving, were so very much scandaliz'd at it, that they left me with great indignation: Wherefore I soon became odious to them all, as I have already said; and they had infallibly destroy'd me, had it not been for the particular assistance of this good Old man.

Nevertheless, in about thirty two years that I have lived with them, I cou'd never learn their way of Generation; yet be it as it will, their Children have neither the *Meazles* nor *Small Pox,* nor other the like accidents, which the *Europeans* are subject unto.

As soon as an *Australian* has conceived, he quits his Apartment, and is carried to the *Hab,* where he is received with Testimonys of an extraordinary Bounty, and is nourished without being oblig'd to work. They have a certain high place, upon which they go to bring forth their Child, which is received upon certain *Balsamick Leaves*; after which the Mother (or person that bore it) takes it and rubs it with these Leaves, and gives it suck, without any appearance of having suffer'd any pain.

They make no use of Swadling Cloaths, or Cradles. The Milk it receives from the Mother, gives it so good nourishment, that it suffices it without any other food for two years: And the Excrements it voids, are in so small a quantity, that it may almost be said, it makes none. They generally speak at eight months; they walk at a years end, and at two they wean them. They begin to reason at three; and as soon as the Mother quits them, the first Master of the first Company teaches them to read, and at the same time instructs them in the first Elements of a more advanced knowledge. They usually are three years under the Conduct of the first Master, and after pass under the Discipline of the second, who teaches them to write, with whom they continue four years; and so with the others in proportion, till they are thirty years of Age, at which time they are perfect in all sorts of Sciences, without observing any difference amongst them, either for Capacity, Genius, or Learning. When they have thus accomplish'd the course of all their Studies, they may be chose for Lieutenants, that is, to supply the place of those that wou'd leave this Life.

I have in the fifth Chapter spoken of their humour, which is mixt with a certain sweetness full of Gravity, that forms the temperament of the most reasonable men, and such as are the fittest for Society. They are strong, robust, and vigorous, and their Health is never interrupted by the least sickness. This admirable Constitution comes without doubt from their Birth and excellent Nourishment, which they always take with moderation; for our Sicknesses are always the consequences of the corruption of that Blood whereof we are form'd, and the excess of the ill Food which we are nourished with. In fine, our Parents generally communicate to us all the defects that they have contracted by their irregular Lives; their Intemperance fills us with such an abundance of superfluous Humours, which destroy us how strong soever we may be, if we purge not our selves often. It is the excessive Heats that they kindle in their Blood by their Debauches, which cause in us such Risings in the Flesh, and all those scorbutick Distempers which spread throughout the whole Body. Their Choller gives us a disposition to the same Vice, their Wantonness augments our Concupiscence; in a word, they make us just what we are, because they give us what they have.

The *Australians* are exempted from all these Passions; for their Parents never being subject to them, cannot communicate 'em; and as they have no principle of alteration, so they live in a kind of indifference which they never forsake, except it be to follow the motions that their reason impresses on them.

We may very near make the same consequences touching the nourishment of the *Australians*; for if the *Europeans* have the misfortune only to have such Viands for their subsistence as are unhealthful, it commonly happens, that they eat more than nature requires: and 'tis these excesses that cause in them such weak Stomachs, Feavers, and other the like Infirmities which are wholly unknown to the *Australians*. Their admirable Temperance, and the goodness of their Fruits, upon which they live, maintains them in such a frame of health, as is never interrupted by any Sickness: They are likewise so far from placing any glory in Eating, or making sumptuous Feasts as we do, that they hide themselves, and only eat in secret; they sleep very little, because they are persuaded, that Sleep is too Animal an Action, from which man ought if it was possible, wholly to abstain.

They all agree, that this Life is only a motion full of trouble and agitation; they are persuaded, that what we call Death is their Happiness, and that the greatest good of Mankind is to arrive to this term, which puts an end to all his pains: from whence they are indifferent for life, and passionately wish for Death. The more I seem'd to apprehend Death, the more they were confirm'd in the thought that I cou'd be no man, since according to their Ideas, I sinned against the *first Principles of Reason*. My Old man often times spoke to me of it, and these are very near the same reasons he gave me; *We differ from Beasts,* said he, *in that their Understandings penetrate not into the bottom of things, they judge of them only by Appearance and coulour. 'Tis from thence they fly their destruction, as the greatest evil, and endeavour to preserve themselves as the greatest Good, not considering that since 'tis an absolute necessity that they perish; all the pains they take to prevent it, becomes vain and useless. Even to argue,* continued he, *upon what regards us, it is necessary, that we should consider Life as an Estate of Misery, altho it consist in the union of a spiritual Soul with a material Body, whereof the Inclinations are perfectly opposite the one to the other.*

So that to desire to live, is to desire to be always enduring the violent Shock of these oppositions; and to desire Death, is but to aspire to that Rest, which each of those parts enjoys, when they are both in their Center.

And, as we have nothing *Dearer to us, than our selves,* added he, nor can look upon our selves to be any thing else, but so many Compounds, whose Dissolution is certain and infallible, we more properly *languish than live*; and the case being so with us, would it not be better for us not to be at all, than to be to no other purpose, than to know, that shortly we shall be no more? The care we take to preserve our selves, is to no purpose, since after all, we must die at last. The consideration of our *Rarest Talents*, and most exquisite improvements in Knowledge, gives us a *second torment*, since we can look upon them as no other, than Transitory Enjoyments, whose acquisition has cost us a Thousand pains, and yet, whose loss it is no way in our power to prevent. *In fine*, all that we reflect upon, both *within and without* us, contributes to render our Life so much the more odious and insupportable to us.

I answered to all that, That in my opinion, these Arguments proved too much; and that to give them their full force, it would follow, that I must needs be sorry for knowing any thing that surpasses my Understanding, which yet is false, because *the goodness of Judgment consists in being able to rest content with our condition*, and to put away those troublesome Thoughts that serve only to afflict us, especially when we know not how by any means to remedy them. There is something of Solidity in thy answer, replyed he; but yet it is weak in two particulars: The one is, in supposing we are able to suspend our Judgment; and the other, in thinking it possible we should love our selves without detesting our Dissolution: To be able to do the first, is to be able, with open Eyes, not to see what is continually before us; and to be able to do the second, is, to love to be something, without hating to be nothing. 'Tis a great weakness to imagine, we can possibly live, without being deeply affected with the Sense of our own Destruction; and 'tis still a greater to torment our selves with the fear of what we know will infallibly come upon us: But it is the *utmost degree of folly*, to seek after preservatives, in order to avoid what we know to be absolutely inavoidable. To be able to live without the Sense of Death, is to be able to live without knowing any thing of our selves, since Death is inseparable from our Nature; and that to consider our selves, in all our several parts, is to see we have nothing but what is mortal in us. To be capable of fearing Death, supposes us able to reconcile two Contradictions, since to fear, supposes some doubt in us, whether what we fear will happen or no, and that we certainly know we shall infallibly die, and it is still more absurd to go about to take any Preservatives, to prevent it, when we know that to be impossible. I replied, That we might justly fear, not Death it self, but its Approaches; and that Preservatives were useful, because they might at least stave it off from us for a while. Very good, replied he again, but dost thou not see, that since the necessity of dying is indispensible, and the putting it off for a while, can be of no other service to us, than to keep us the longer under continual pain, grief, and anguish. I answered him, that these Reasons would be of much more weight among our *Europeans*, than among them who know not what it is to suffer; whereas the Life of the *Europeans* was nothing else but a *continued Chain* of Miseries and Sufferings.

How, says he, have you any other Infirmities than those of being *Mortal,* and knowing your selves to be daily advancing towards Death? Yes, I assured him, that our People commonly died *many Deaths,* before they came to die for good and all, and that Death came not upon our *Europeans,* but by the Violence of those Diseases that knockt them down, and made them at last faint away under them. This answer was to him a *Mystery*: And as I was endeavouring to make him comprehend our *Gouts,* our *Headaches,* and our *Colicks*; I found he understood me not, and therefore to make him apprehend my meaning, I was forced particularly to explain to him the Nature of some of those Diseases we suffer; which as soon as he understood, *Is it possible,* cried he, *that any one should be in love with such a Life as that?* I answered, that our People did not only love it, but used all manner of means to prolong it; from whence he took a fresh occasion to condemn us, either for insensibility, or extravagance, not being able, as he said, to conceive how a reasonable Man that was assured of his Death, and that saw himself daily dying, by several sorts of Sufferings, and that could not protract his Life, but in continual Languishment, could possibly forbear desiring Death, as his greatest happiness. Our opinions, in this matter, are vastly different, says he, from yours: For we, assoon as we come to understand our selves, because we think our selves obliged to love our own selves, and look upon our selves, but as so many *Victims of a superiour Cause,* that is able every moment to destroy us, we therefore make very small account of our Life, and esteem it but as a *Happiness, which we can enjoy but as a Passenger,* whilst it is fleeting and passing from us. The time in which we enjoy it, is burthensome to us, because it serves for nothing but to raise in us a grief for the loss of that happiness, which it more lightly takes from us, than at first it gave it us. In fine, We are weary of living, because we durst not fix our *Affection upon our selves with all that tenderness,* we might otherwise have, for fear of enduring too great violences of Reluctance, when we shall be forced to part from a being we have so much doated on. To that I answered him, That Reason teaches us, that it was *always better to be, than not to be, and that 'twas better to live, tho' but for a day, than never to live at all*: To which he replyed, that we were to distinguish two things in our Being; one was our general existence, that perishes not, and the other our particular Existence, or *Individuality* that perishes. The first is indeed better than privation, and that 'tis in that sense, 'tis true; that being is preferable before not being; but that the second, *viz.* the being of our *Individuality,* or particular being is oftentimes worse than not being, especially when 'tis accompanied with a Knowledge that renders us unhappy. I answered again, that if being in general were better than not being, it must needs follow,

That being likewise in particular, was better than its Privation: But he satisfied me, by proposing to me the very State in which I had lately been. Tell me, I prithee, says he, when thou consideredst thy condition in the place of which thou toldst us, *environned on all sides by Death*; could thou possibly esteem thy Life at that time a Happiness, and could thou value it better than nothing? Is it not true, that the Knowledge thou hadst, served then only to *augment thy misery*? It is then to no purpose to maintain that Knowledge that afflicts me, is not only no Happiness to me, but an unhappiness so much the more sensible, as I know it the more perfectly: It is from *that principle that flows our true Misery*, that we know what we are, and what we must be, we know that we are noble, and excellent beings: In a word, worthy of an eternal Duration, and yet we see that for all our Nobleness and Excellence, we depend of a *Thousand other Creatures*, that are inferiour to us, which is the cause we look upon our selves, as beings that were brought up only to be rendered so much the more unhappy, and that it is which makes us chuse rather *not to be at all*, than to be at the same time so excellent, and so miserable.

Our *Ancestors* were so strongly perswaded of this Truth; that they *sought Death with the greatest passion* in the World: But because by that means our Country begun to grow desolate, and dispeopled, reasons were found out to perswade those which remained, to spare themselves for some time: for it was represented to them, that so very *fine and spacious a Country*, ought not to be left useless; that we are an *Ornament of the Universe*, and therefore ought to endure Life, tho' it were but to please that *Soveraign Master* that gave it us. Upon which, some time after, in order to Re-implace those that had sought for Rest in a voluntary Death, all that remained alive, obliged themselves to present no less than *three Children to the Hebs*; by which means, all the Country being well Repeopled, an order was published, that no Person should have permission to go to his *Long Rest*, but such a one who should present another Man to the *Heb*, either his own Son, or another, who was willing to be his Lieutenant, and to supply his place; and it was ordered, at the same time, that none should have the priviledge, neither to demand such a Permission, till he had lived at least 100 Years, or could shew some Wound that extreamly incommoded him. Just as he had *finished* those words, we were joyned by *two Brethren*, for which I was very sorry, because I never found my *Old Man* in so good a humour to discover to me the *Mysteries* of all those things, of which I demanded of him some Explication.

And now to proceed with our *Narration*, there never is held any *Assembly* at the *Heb*, at which there is not twenty or thirty Persons that demand the Liberty to return to their rest, and they never refuse any, be they who they will, that produce just Reasons for it: And when any one has *obtained Permission to go out of this Life,* he presents his Lieutenant, who must be at least 36 years of age. The Company receives him with Joy, and gives him the Name of the *old Man* that has a Mind to die; which done, they represent to him the brave actions of his Predecessors, and tell him they are confident, he will not degenerate from the vertue of him, whose place he is going to supply. When that *Ceremony* is over, the *old Man* goes merrily to the Table, furnished for that effect, with the *Fruit of Rest,* where he eats to the number of eight of them, with a smiling and calm Countenance; when he has eaten *Four* of them, his Heart begins to dilate, and his Spleen to enlarge it self; so that the extraordinary joy he feels within him, makes him commit several extravagancies, as *dancing, leaping,* and *talking* all manner of idle foolish things, which the Brethren take no notice of, as coming from a Man that has lost his reason: then they present him two more, that quite distract his Brain; after which, his Lieutenant, and another Person conduct him to the place, he before-hand chose for a *Sepulchre,* where they give him two more of the aforesaid Fruits, which plunge him into an *Eternal Sleep.* Then they close up his Tomb, and return back, beseeching the *Soveraign Being,* to advance those happy Moments, in which they may have the Priviledge to enjoy the *like Rest* with their departed Brother. In this manner are the *Australians* born, and thus they live and die.

FRANÇOIS DE SALIGNAC DE LA MOTHE-FÉNELON

(1651–1715)

Salentum: Frugal and Noble Simplicity*

At the time he was ordained, Fénelon was a scholarly young man of noble lineage but without fortune. He occupied himself with pedagogy as director of a sisterhood for young converts and author of a treatise on the education of girls. His influence mounted with his appointment as tutor (1689) to the young Duke of Burgundy, the dauphin's son, and in 1695 he was named Archbishop of Cambrai. Four years later, however, his defense of Madame Guyon's quietist doctrines led to his condemnation by the Holy See and his banishment from court. To inculcate moral virtues in his royal pupil he had earlier written the *Adventures of Telemachus*, weaving around Greek figures of the heroic age the story of an austere kingdom where reason, justice, and humanity prevailed. As a grand-seigneur, Fénelon saw in monarchy the ideal state, but he was a staunch foe of despotism and luxury. When the book was published in 1699, without his knowledge, it was interpreted as an implied criticism of Louis XIV's government, and despite the favor of a new pope Fénelon was never recalled from retirement.

*From François de Salignac de la Mothe-Fénelon, *The Adventures of Telemachus*, trans. John Hawkesworth from *Les Aventures de Télémaque*, revised by G. Gregory (New York: T. and J. Swords, 1800), I, pp. 338–57.

Mentor entretient Télémaque des réformes
qu'il a faites à Salente pendant son absence.

Engraving by J. B. Tilliard after Ch. Monnet, from *Les Aventures de Télémaque*,
Paris, 1785.

The Reforms of Mentor

When the army was gone, Idomeneus led Mentor into every quarter of the city. "Let us see," said Mentor, "how many people you have, as well in the city as the country; let us number the whole; and let us also examine how many of them are husbandmen. Let us inquire how much corn, wine, oil, and other necessaries, your lands will produce one year with another: we shall then know whether your country will subsist its inhabitants, and whether it will yield a surplus for foreign trade. Let us also see how many vessels you have, and how many sailors to man them, that we may be able to judge of your strength." He then visited the port, and went on board every vessel: he informed himself of the several ports to which they traded, what merchandize they carried out, and what they brought back in return; what was the expence of the voyage; what were the loans of the merchants to each other, and what trading societies were established among them, that he might know whether their articles were equitable and faithfully observed. He also inquired what was the risk of the several voyages, and to what losses the trade was exposed, that such restrictions might be made as would prevent the ruin of the merchants, who sometimes, from too eager a desire of gain, undertake what they are not in a condition to accomplish.

He ordered that bankruptcy should be punished with great severity, because it is generally the effect of rashness and indiscretion, if not of fraud: he also formed regulations, by which bankruptcies might easily be prevented. He obliged the merchants to give an account of their effects, their profits, their expences, and their undertakings, to magistrates established for that purpose. He ordered that they should never be permitted to risk the property of another, nor more than half their own; that they should undertake by association, what they could not undertake singly; and that the observance of the conditions of such association should be enforced by severe penalties. He ordered, also, that trade should be perfectly open and free; and, instead of loading it with imposts, that every merchant who brought the trade of a new nation to the port of Salentum should be entitled to a reward.

These regulations brought people in crowds from all parts, and the trade of Salentum was like the flux of the sea: riches flowed in upon it, with an impetuous abundance, like wave impelling wave: every thing was freely brought in and carried out of the port: every thing that was brought was useful, and every thing that was carried out left something of greater advantage in its stead. Justice presided over the port, which was the center of innumerable nations, with inflexible severity; and from the lofty towers that were at once its ornament and defence, freedom, integrity, and honour, seemed to call together the merchants of the remotest regions of the earth: and these merchants, whether they came from the shores of the east, where the sun rises from the parting wave to begin the day; or from that boundless ocean, where, wearied with his course, he extinguishes his fires; all lived together in Salentum, as in their native country, with security and peace.

Mentor then visited the magazines, warehouses, and manufactories of the interior part of the city. He prohibited the sale of all foreign commodities that might introduce luxury or effeminacy: he regulated the dress and the provisions of the inhabitants of every rank, and the furniture, the size, and ornaments of their houses. He also prohibited all ornaments of silver and gold. "I know but one thing," said he to Idomeneus, "that can render your people modest in their expences—the example of their prince. It is necessary that there should be a certain dignity in your appearance; but your authority will be sufficiently marked by the guards, and the great officers of your court, that will always attend you. As to your dress, be content with the finest cloth of a purple colour: let the dress of your principal officers be of cloth equally fine: and let your own be distinguished only by the colour, and a slight embroidery of gold round the edge: different colours will serve to distinguish different conditions, without either gold, or silver, or jewels; and let these conditions be regulated by birth.

"Put the most ancient and illustrious nobility in the first rank: those who are distinguished by personal merit, and the authority of office, will be content to stand second to those who have been long in possession of hereditary honour. Men who are not noble by descent will readily yield precedence to those that are, if you take care not to encourage a false opinion of themselves, by raising them too suddenly and too high; and never fail to gratify those with praise who are modest in prosperity. No distinction so little excites envy as that which is derived from ancestors by a long descent.

"To stimulate virtue, and excite an emulation to serve the state, it will be sufficient to reward public merit with honorary distinctions; a crown or a statue, which may be made the foundation of a new nobility, for the children of those to whom they are decreed.

"The habit of persons of the first rank may be white, bordered with a fringe of gold: they may also be distinguished by a gold ring on their finger, and a medal of gold, impressed with your image, hanging from their neck. Those of the second rank may be dressed in blue, with a silver fringe, and be distinguished by the ring without the medal. The third rank may be dressed in green, and wear the medal without either fringe or ring. The colour of the fourth class may be a full yellow; the fifth a pale red; the sixth a mixture of red and white; and the seventh a mixture of white and yellow. Dresses of these different colours will sufficiently distinguish the freemen of your state into seven classes. The habit of slaves should be dark grey: and thus each will be distinguished according to his condition, without expence; and every art which can only gratify pride will be banished from Salentum. All the artificers, which are now employed so much to the disadvantage of their country, will betake themselves to such arts as are useful, which are few, or to commerce or agriculture. No change must ever be suffered to take place, either in the quality of the stuff or the form of the garment. Men are, by nature, formed for serious and important employments; and it is unworthy of them to invent affected novelties in the clothes that cover them, or to suffer the women, whom such employment would less disgrace, to fall into an extravagance so contemptible and pernicious."

Thus Mentor, like a skilful gardener, who lops from his fruit-trees the useless wood, endeavoured to retrench the parade that insensibly corrupts the manners, and to reduce every thing to a frugal and noble simplicity. He regulated even the provisions, not of the slaves only, but those of the highest rank. "What a shame is it," said he, "that men of exalted stations should place their superiority in eating such food as effeminates the mind, and subverts the constitution! They ought to value themselves for the regulation of their own desires, for their power of dispensing good to others, and for the reputation which the exercise of private and public virtue will necessarily procure. To the sober and temperate, the simplest food is always pleasant: and the simplest food only can produce the most vigorous health, and give, at once, capacity and disposition for the purest and highest enjoyments. Your meal should consist of the best food; but it should always be plainly dressed: the art of cookery is the art of poisoning mankind, by rendering appetite still importunate, when the wants of nature are supplied."

Idomeneus easily conceived that he had done wrong in suffering the inhabitants of this new city to corrupt and effeminate their manners, by violating the sumptuary laws of Minos; but Mentor further convinced him, that the revival of those laws would produce little effect, if the king did not give them force by his example: he, therefore, immediately regulated his own table, where he admitted only plain food, such as he had eaten with other Grecian princes at the siege of Troy, with the finest bread, and a small quantity of the wine of the country, which was generous and well flavoured. No man dared to murmur at a regulation which the king imposed upon himself; and the profusion and false delicacy of the table were given up without a struggle.

Mentor suppressed also two kinds of music; the soft and effeminate strains which dissolve the soul into languishment and desire, and the Bacchanalian airs, that transport it with causeless, tumultuous, and opprobrious joy. He allowed only that sacred and solemn harmony which, in the temples of the Gods, kindles devotion, and celebrates heroic virtue. To the temples also he confined the superb ornaments of architecture, columns, pediments, and porticos: he gave models in a simple but elegant style of building, for houses that would contain a numerous family, on a moderate extent of ground; so designed that they should be at once pleasant and convenient; that they should have a healthful aspect, and apartments sufficiently separated from each other; that order and decency might be easily preserved, and that they might be repaired at a small expence. He ordered that every house above the middling class should have a hall, and a small peristyle, with separate chambers for all the free persons of the family; but he prohibited, under severe penalties, the superfluous number and magnificence of apartments, that ostentation and luxury had introduced. Houses erected upon these models, according to the size of the family, served to embellish one part of the city at a small expence, and give it a regular appearance; while the other part, which was already finished according to the caprice and vanity of individuals, was, notwithstanding its magnificence, less pleasing and convenient. This city was built in a very short time; because the neighbouring coast of Greece furnished very skilful architects; and a great number of masons repaired thither from Epirus, and other countries, upon the promise that, after they had finished their work, they should be established in the neighbourhood of Salentum, where land should be granted them to clear, and where they would contribute to people the country.

Painting and sculpture were arts which Mentor thought should by no means be proscribed; but he permitted the practice of them to few. He established a school under masters of an exquisite taste, by whom the performances of the pupils were examined. "There should be no mediocrity," said he, "in the arts which are not necessary to life; and, consequently, no youth should be permitted to practise them, but such as have a genius to excel: others were designed, by nature, for less noble occupations; and may be very usefully employed in supplying the ordinary wants of the community. Sculptors and painters should be employed only to preserve the memory of great men and great actions; and the representations of whatever has been atchieved by heroic virtue, for the service of the public, should be preserved only in public buildings, or on the monuments of the dead." But whatever was the moderation or frugality of Mentor, he indulged the taste of magnificence in the great buildings that were intended for public sports, the races of horses and chariots, combats with the cestus, wrestling, and all other exercises which render the body more agile and vigorous.

He suppressed a great number of traders that sold wrought stuffs of foreign manufacture; embroidery of an excessive price; vases of silver and gold, embossed with various figures in bas-relief; distilled liquors and perfumes: he ordered, also, that the furniture of every house should be plain and substantial, so as not soon to wear out. The people of Salentum, therefore, who had been used to complain of being poor, began to perceive that they abounded in superfluous riches; but that this superfluity was of a deceitful kind; that they were poor in proportion as they possessed it, and that, in proportion as they relinquished it only, they could be rich. "To become truly rich," said they, "is to despise such riches as exhaust the state, and to lessen the number of our wants, by reducing them to the necessities of virtue."

Mentor also took the first opportunity to visit the arsenals and magazines, and examine whether the arms, and other necessaries of war, were in a good condition. "To be always ready for war," said he, "is the surest way to avoid it." He found many things wanting, and immediately employed artificers in brass and iron to supply the defects. Furnaces were immediately built; and smoke and flame ascended in cloudy volumes, like those that issue from the subterranean fires of Mount Aetna. The hammer rang upon the anvil, which groaned under the stroke: the neighbouring shores and mountains re-echoed to the sound; and a spectator of these preparatives for war, made by a provident sagacity during a profound peace, might have thought himself in that island where Vulcan animates the Cyclops, by his example, to forge thunder for the Father of the Gods.

Mentor then went with Idomeneus out of the city, and found a great extent of fertile country wholly uncultivated; besides considerable tracts that were cultivated but in part, through the negligence or poverty of the husbandmen, or the want of spirit, or the want of hands. "This country," said he to the king, "is ready to enrich its inhabitants, but the inhabitants are not sufficient to cultivate the country; let us, then, remove the superfluous artificers from the city, whose professions serve only to corrupt the manners of the people, and let us employ them in fertilizing these plains and hills. It is a misfortune that these men, having been employed in arts which require a sedentary life, are unused to labour: but we will try to remedy this evil: we will divide these uncultivated lands in lots among them, and call in the neighbouring people to their assistance, who will gladly undertake the most laborious part of the work, upon condition that they shall receive a certain proportion of the produce of the lands they clear. They may afterwards be made proprietors of part of it, and be thus incorporated with your people, who are by no means sufficiently numerous. If they prove diligent, and obedient to the laws, they will be good subjects, and increase your power. The artizans, whom you shall transplant from the city to the fields, will bring up their children to the labours of rural life; and the foreigners, whom you have employed to assist in building your city, have engaged to clear part of your lands, and become husbandmen. These men, as soon as they have finished the public buildings, you should incorporate with your people: they will think themselves happy to pass their lives under a government so gentle as that which you have now established; and as they are robust and laborious, their example will animate the transplanted artificers with whom they will be mixed; and, in a short time, your country will abound with a vigorous race, wholly devoted to agriculture.

"When this is done, be in no pain about the multiplication of your people: they will, in a short time, become innumerable, if you facilitate marriage; and the most simple way of facilitating marriage is the most effectual. All men are naturally inclined to marry; and nothing prevents them from indulging this inclination, but the prospect of difficulty and distress: if you do not load them with taxes, their families will never become a burden: the earth is never ungrateful, but always affords sustenance to those who diligently cultivate it: it refuses its bounty only to those who refuse their labour. Husbandmen are always rich, in proportion to the number of their children, if their prince does not make them poor; for their children afford them some assistance, even from their infancy: the youngest can drive the flock to pasture, those that are farther advanced can look after the cattle, and those of the third stage can work with their father in the field. In the mean time the girls assist the mother, who prepares a simple but wholesome repast for those that are abroad, when they return home fatigued with the labour of the day. She milks her cows and her sheep, and the pails overflow with longevity and health; she brings out her little stores, her cheeses and her chesnuts, with fruits that she has preserved from decay; she piles up the social fire, and the family gathers round it; every countenance brightens with the smile of innocence and peace; and some rural ditty diverts them till the night calls them to rest. He that attended the flock returns with his pipe; and, when the family is got together, he sings them some new song, that he has learnt at the neighbouring village. Those that have been at work in the fields come in with their plough, and the weary oxen that hang down their heads, and move with a slow and heavy pace, notwithstanding the goad, which now urges them in vain. All the sufferings of labour end with the day. The poppies which, at the command of the Gods, are scattered over the earth by the hand of sleep, charm away every care: sweet enchantment lulls all nature into peace; and the weary rest without anticipating the troubles of to-morrow. Happy, indeed, are these unambitious, mistrustless, artless people, if the Gods vouchsafe them a king that disturbs not their blameless joy; and of what horrid inhumanity are they guilty, who, to gratify pride and ambition, wrest from them the sweet product of the field, which they owe to the liberality of nature and the sweat of their brow! In the fruitful lap of nature there is inexhaustible plenty for temperance and labour. If none were luxurious and idle, none would be wretched and poor."

"But what shall I do," said Idomeneus, "if the people that I scatter over this fertile country should neglect to cultivate it?" "You must do," said Mentor, "just contrary to what is commonly done. Rapacious and inconsiderate princes think only of taxing those who are most industrious to improve their lands; because, upon these, they suppose a tax will be more easily levied; and they spare those whom idleness has made indigent. Reverse this mistaken and injurious conduct, which oppresses virtue, rewards vice, and encourages a supineness that is equally fatal to the king and to the state. Let your taxes be heavy upon those who neglect the cultivation of their lands; and add, to your taxes, fines and other penalties if it is necessary; punish the negligent and the idle as you would a soldier who should desert his post. On the contrary, distinguish those who, in proportion as their families multiply, cultivate their lands with the greater diligence, by special privileges and immunities: every family will then become numerous; and every one will be animated to labour, not by the desire of gain only, but of honour. The state of husbandry being no longer wretched, will no longer be contemptible: the plough, once more held in honour, will be guided by the victorious hands that have defended the country: and it will not be less glorious to cultivate a paternal inheritance in the security of peace, than to draw the sword in its defence, when it is endangered by war. The whole country will bloom around you: the golden ears of ripe corn will again crown the temples of

Ceres: Bacchus will tread the grapes in rich clusters under his feet; and wine, more delicious than nectar, will flow from the hills like a river: the valleys will resound to the song of the shepherds, who, dispersed along the banks of a transparent stream, shall join their voices with the pipe; while their flocks shall frolic round them, and feast upon the flowery pasture without fear of the wolf.

"O Idomeneus! will it not make you supremely happy to be the source of such prosperity; to stretch your protection, like the shadow of a rock, over so many people, who repose under it in security and peace? Will you not, in the consciousness of this, enjoy a noble elation of mind, a calm sense of superior glory; such as can never touch the bosom of the tyrant, who lives only to desolate the earth, and who diffuses, not less through his own dominions than those which he conquers from others, carnage and tumult, horror and anguish, consternation, famine and despair? Happy, indeed, is the prince, whom his own greatness of soul, and the distinguishing favour of the Gods, shall render thus the delight of his people, and the example of succeeding ages! The world, instead of taking up arms to oppose his power, will be found prostrate at his feet, and suing to be subject to his dominion."

"But," said Idomeneus, "when the people shall be thus blessed with plenty and peace, will not their happiness corrupt their manners; will they not turn against me the very strength I have given them?" "There is no reason to fear that," said Mentor: "the sycophants of prodigal princes have suggested it as a pretence for oppression; but it may easily be prevented. The laws which we have established with respect to agriculture will render life laborious; and the people, notwithstanding their plenty, will abound only in what is necessary, for we have prohibited the arts that furnish superfluities: and the plenty even of necessaries will be restrained within due bounds, by the facility of marriage and the multiplication of families. In proportion as a family becomes numerous, their portion of land being still the same in extent, a more diligent cultivation will become necessary; and this will require incessant labour. Luxury and idleness only render people insolent and rebellious. They will have bread, indeed, and they will have bread enough; but they will have nothing more, except what they can gain from their own ground, by the sweat of their brow.

"That your people may continue in this state of mediocrity, it will be necessary that you should now limit the extent of ground that each family is to possess. We have, you know, divided your people into seven classes, according to their different conditions; and each family, in each class, must be permitted to possess only such an extent of ground as is absolutely necessary to subsist it. This regulation being inviolably observed, the nobles can never get possession of the lands of the poor: every one will have land, but so much only as will make a diligent cultivation necessary. If, in a long course of years, the people should be so much increased that land cannot be found for them at home, they may be sent to form colonies abroad, which will be a new advantage to the mother country.

"I am of opinion that care should be taken, even to prevent wine from being too common in your kingdom. If you find that too many vines are planted, you should cause them to be grubbed up. Some of the most dreadful mischiefs that afflict mankind proceed from wine: it is the cause of disease, quarrels, sedition, idleness, aversion to labour, and every species of domestic disorder. Let wine, then, be considered as a kind of medicine, or as a scarce liquor, to be used only at the sacrifices of the Gods, or in seasons of public festivity. Do not, however, flatter yourself that this regulation can ever take place without the sanction of your own example.

"The laws of Minos, with respect to the education of children, must also be inviolably preserved. Public schools must be established, to teach them the fear of the Gods, the love of their country, a reverence for the laws, and a preference of honour, not only to pleasure, but to life. Magistrates must be appointed to superintend the conduct, not of every family only, but every person: you must keep also your own eye upon them; for you are a king only to be the shepherd of your people, and to watch over your flock night and day. By this unremitted vigilance you will prevent many disorders and many crimes: such as you cannot prevent, you must immediately punish with severity; for, in this case, severity to the individual is clemency to the public: it stops those irregularities at their source, which would deluge the country with misery and guilt: the taking away of one life upon a proper occasion, will be the preservation of many; and will make a prince sufficiently feared, without general or frequent severity. It is a detestable maxim, that the security of the prince depends only upon the oppression of his people. Should no care be taken to improve their knowledge or their morals? Instead of being taught to love him whom they are born to obey, should they be driven, by terror, to despair, and reduced to the dreadful necessity, either of throwing off the yoke of their tyrant, or perishing under its weight? Can this be the way to reign with tranquillity? can this be the path that leads to glory?

"Remember that the sovereign who is most absolute, is always least powerful: he seizes upon all, and his grasp is ruin. He is, indeed, the sole proprietor of whatever his state contains; but, for that reason, his state contains nothing of value: the fields are uncultivated, and almost a desert;

the towns lose some of their few inhabitants every day; and trade every day declines. The king, who must cease to be a king when he ceases to have subjects, and who is great only in virtue of his people, is himself insensibly losing his character and his power, as the number of his people, from whom alone both are derived, insensibly diminishes; and his dominions are at length exhausted of money and of men: the loss of men is the greatest and the most irreparable he can sustain. Absolute power degrades every subject to a slave: the tyrant is flattered, even to an appearance of adoration; and every one trembles at the glance of his eye: but, at the least revolt, this enormous power perishes by its own excess. It derived no strength from the love of the people; it wearied and provoked all that it could reach; and rendered every individual of the state impatient of its continuance. At the first stroke of opposition, the idol is overturned, broken to pieces, and trodden under foot: contempt, hatred, fear, resentment, distrust, and every other passion of the soul, unite against so hateful a despotism. The king who, in his vain prosperity, found no man bold enough to tell him the truth, in his adversity finds no man kind enough to excuse his faults, or to defend him against his enemies."

Idomeneus then hastened to distribute his uncultivated lands, to people them with useless artificers, and to carry all the counsels of Mentor into execution; reserving for the builders such parts as had been allotted them, which they were not to cultivate till they had finished the city.

CHARLES IRÉNÉE CASTEL, ABBÉ DE SAINT-PIERRE
(1658–1743)

A Proposal for Everlasting Peace*

Born near Cherbourg, this scion of an ancient noble family was educated by the Jesuits and subsequently took holy orders. In Paris, he frequented aristocratic salons and in 1695 became almoner of the Duchess of Orleans. In the same year he was elected to the Academy, but was expelled in 1718 for the offence given by a work in which he advocated royal governance with the aid of a council rather than of a single minister. As a critic of political and social institutions he had a marked influence on Rousseau. During a long lifetime the Abbé de Saint-Pierre circulated many projects for the reform of society and the state. His renown rests principally on his peace plans, first drafted in 1711 and submitted to his friends for criticism, then published in a two-volume revision in 1713 as *Projet pour rendre la paix perpétuelle en Europe.* Saint-Pierre was at that time secretary to the French plenipotentiary at Utrecht, where the great powers had convened to draft the treaty that would end the War of the Spanish Succession.

---

*From Charles Irénée Castel, Abbé de Saint-Pierre, *A Project for Settling an Everlasting Peace in Europe, First Proposed by Henry IV of France, and approved of by Queen Elizabeth, and most of the then Princes of Europe, and now discussed at large, and made practicable* (London, 1714), preface.

M.r L'ABBÉ DE S.t PIERRE
Né au Chateau de S.t Pierre près
Valogne en Basse Normandie le 13
Feврier 1658.
Mort à Paris le 29 Avril 1743.
à 86 Ans.

Abbé de Saint-Pierre, engraving.

The Author's Preface Giving a General Idea of the Project

My Design is to propose Means for settling an Everlasting Peace amongst all the Christian States. Let not any Body ask me, what Capacity I have acquired, to handle a Subject of so very high a Nature. 'Tis a Question I can make no Answer to; for tho' for above these three and twenty Years I have done all I could to Instruct my self thoroughly in Matters of political Government; because 'tis my Opinion, that Such chiefly deserve the Attention of a good Citizen; yet, perhaps, I have attain'd none of the Qualities necessary to make a Man serviceable to his Country. But, to judge of the Value of a Work, does the Reader stand in need of any thing besides the Work itself?

About four Years ago, after having finish'd an Essay useful for the interiour Commerce of the Kingdom, being both an Eyewitness of the extreme Misery to which the People were reduc'd by the heavy Taxes, and also inform'd, by divers particular Relations, of the excessive Contributions, the Forragings, the Destructions, the Violences, the Cruelties, and the Murthers which the unhappy Inhabitants of the Frontiers of Christian States daily suffer; in short, being sensibly touch'd with the Evils which War causes to the Princes of *Europe,* and their Subjects, I took a Resolution to penetrate into the first Sources of this Evil, and to find out by my own Reflections, whether It was so inseparable from the Nature of Sovereignties and Sovereigns, as to be absolutely without Remedy; I applied my self to examine this Affair, in order to discover whether it was not possible to find out some practicable Means to terminate their future Differences *without War*; and so to render the Peace perpetual amongst them.

I bestow'd formerly, at different times, some Thoughts upon this Matter, as the most useful that great Genius's could employ themselves upon; but those Thoughts were always without any Success: The Difficulties which arose one from t'other, and even from the Nature of Mankind itself, always discouraged me: 'Tis true, I thought of it only in Places, where, tho' my Mornings were wholly spent in reading, or in meditating upon Subjects of this Nature, yet my Mind was a little too much taken off, either by Duties or Amusements; whereas in the Country, being assisted by the Strength which the Mind receives from the calmness and leisure of Solitude, I thought I might, by an obstinate and continued Meditation, exhaust a Subject, which 'till then had not perhaps ever been examin'd with so much Attention, as in it self it deserved to be.

I thought it necessary to begin, by making some Reflections upon the Happiness it would be, as well to the Sovereigns of *Europe*, as to private Men, to live in Peace, united by some permanent Society; and upon the Necessity they are at present in to have continual Wars with each other, about the Possession or Division of some Advantages; and finally upon the Means which they have hitherto used, either to avoid entering upon those Wars, or not to sink under them, when once they Have entered upon them.

I found that all those Means consisted in making mutual Promises, either in Treaties of Commerce, of Truce, of Peace, wherein Limits of Dominion, and other reciprocal Pretentions are regulated; or else in Treaties of Guarantie, or of League offensive and defensive, to establish, to maintain, or to re-establish the *Equilibrium* of Power between the Principal Houses; a System which hitherto seems to be the highest Degree of Prudence, that the Sovereigns of *Europe*, or their Ministers, ever carried their Policy to.

I soon perceived, that so long as they contented themselves with such Methods, they would never have any *sufficient security* for the Execution of Treaties, nor sufficient Means for terminating equitably, and above all *without War*, their future Differences; and that unless they could find out some better Ways, the Christian Princes must never expect any thing but an almost continual War, which can never be interrupted but by some Treaties of Peace, or rather by Truces, which are the necessary Productions of Equality of Forces, and of the Weariness and Exhaustion of the Combatants, and which in the End must be the total Ruin of the Vanquished. 'Tis these Reflections that are the Subject of the first Discourse. I have reduced them all into two Heads, or two Propositions, which I propose to my self to demonstrate.

1st. *The present Constitution of* Europe *can never produce any thing else but almost continual Wars, because it can never procure any* sufficient Security *for the Execution of Treaties.*

2dly. *The* Equilibrium *of Power between the House of* France, *and the House of* Austria, *cannot procure any* sufficient Security *either against Foreign Wars, or against Civil Wars, and consequently cannot procure any* sufficient Security *either for the Preservation of Territory, or for the Preservation of Commerce.*

The first Step necessary to the obtaining a Cure for a Disease great, or inveterate, and for which alone nothing but ineffectual Medicines have hitherto been used, is to endeavour, on the one Side, to find out the different

Causes of the Disease; and, on the other, the Disproportion of those Medicines with the Disease it self.

I afterwards consider'd, whether Sovereigns might not find some *sufficient Security* for the Execution of mutual Promises, by establishing a perpetual Arbitration; and I find, that if the eighteen Principal Sovereignties of *Europe*, in order to maintain the present Government, to avoid War, and to procure the Advantages of an uninterrupted Commerce between Nation and Nation, would make a Treaty of Union, and a perpetual Congress, much after the Model, either of the seven Sovereignties of *Holland*, the thirteen Sovereignties of the *Swisses*, or the Sovereignties of *Germany*, and form an *European Union*, from what is best in those Unions, and especially in the *Germanic Union*, which consists of above two hundred Sovereignties: I found, I say, that the weakest would have a *sufficient Security*, that the great Power of the strongest could not hurt them; that every one would exactly keep their reciprocal Promises; that Commerce would never be interrupted, and that all future Differences would be terminated *without War*, by means of Umpires, a Blessing which can never be obtain'd any other Way.

These are the eighteen Principal Christian Sovereignties, which should each of them have a Voice in the general Diet of *Europe: 1. France, 2. Spain, 3. England, 4. Holland, 5. Portugal, 6. Switzerland,* and the Associates, *7. Florence,* and the Associates, *8. Genoa,* and Associates, *9.* The Ecclesiastick State, *10. Venice, 11. Savoy, 12. Lorrain, 13. Denmark, 14. Courland* and *Dantzick,* &c. *15.* The Emperor and Empire, *16. Poland, 17. Sweden, 18. Muscovy.* I set down the Empire only as one Sovereignty, because it is but one Body: *Holland* too is mention'd but for one Sovereignty, because that Republick, tho' it consists of seven Sovereign Republicks, is but one Body; the same of *Switzerland*.

In examining the Government of the Sovereigns of *Germany*, I did not find that there would be more Difficulty in forming the *European Body* now, than formerly there was in forming the *Germanick Body*, in executing *in great* that which has been already executed *in little*; on the contrary, I found that there would be fewer Obstacles, and more Facility, in forming the *European Body*; and what greatly perswaded me that this Project was no Chimera, was the Information I received from one of my Friends, soon after I had shewn him the first Sketch of this Work: He told me that *Henry IV*. had form'd a Project, which, in the main, was much the same; and so I found in the Memoirs of the Duke of *Sully*, his Prime Minister; and in Monsieur *de Perefixe's* History of his Reign: Nay more, I found that this Project had been even agreed to by a great many Princes, in the Beginning of the last Century: This gave me

Occasion from thence to draw some Inferences, to prove that the Thing was far from being impracticable: And this is the Subject of the Second Discourse.

1st. *The same Motives and the same Means that formerly sufficed to form a* permanent Society *of all the Sovereignties of* Germany, *are within the reach and Power of the present Sovereigns, and may suffice to form a* permanent Society *of all the Christian Sovereignties of* Europe.

2dly. *The Approbation which most of the Sovereigns of* Europe *gave to the Project for* an European Society, *which* Henry the Great *proposed to them, proves that it may be hoped such a Project will be approved of by their Successors.*

These Models of permanent Societies, the Approbation that was given, an hundred Years ago, to the Project of *Henry* the Great, are sufficient to produce two very great Prepossessions in favour of the Possibility of this: I know the Weight of Prepossessions, and that they make more Impressions upon the Generality of Minds, than true Arguments, fetch'd from the very Bottom of the Subject, and from necessary Consequences of the first Principles; but I plainly foresee they will never be sufficient entirely to determine Spirits of the first Order; that They will be continually finding out Differences and Inequalities between the *European Society*, which I propose, and the Societies I quote as Models; that *Henry IV*, might after all be deceived in thinking That *possible*, which was in reality *impossible*. Thus I find my self obliged to demonstrate every Thing strictly, and am resolved to use my utmost Endeavours, to trace back those very *Motives*, which induced the Ancient Sovereigns of *Germany*, and those of the last Century, to desire an unalterable Peace; and shall try to find out Methods, better than theirs, to form a more important Establishment.

As for *sufficient Motives*, I believe that if any one could propose a Treaty which might render the Union solid and unalterable, and so give every one a *sufficient Security* for the Perpetuity of the Peace, the Princes would find therein much fewer Inconveniencies, and those much less great, a greater Number of Advantages, and those much more great, than in the present System of War; that a great many Sovereigns, especially the least powerful, would begin by Signing it, and afterwards would present it to others to Sign; and that even the most powerful, if they examined it thoroughly, would soon find they could never embrace any Resolution, nor sign any Treaty, near so Advantageous as this would be.

As for *practicable and sufficient Means*, which consist in the Articles of a Treaty of Union, made to be to every one a *sufficient Security* for the Perpetuity of the Peace, I have spared no Pains to invent them, and I believe I have done it.

Now, as on the one side, those who have read the first Sketches of the fourth Discourse agree, that a Treaty which should be composed of such Articles, would form that *sufficient Security*, so sought after by Politicians; and as, on the other side, the signing of those Articles depends solely *upon the Will* of the Sovereigns, and all those Princes would be so much the more inclined to be *willing* to Sign them, and to procure the Execution of them, the more evidently they shall have seen the Greatness of the Advantages they may reap from them: We may conclude, that on their side there will be no Impossibility found in the Execution of the Project; and that the more they shall be convinc'd of this Security, and these Advantages, the more easily they will be brought to execute it. The whole Project then is contain'd in this single Argument.

If the European Society, *which is propos'd, can procure for all the Christian Princes a* sufficient Security *for the Perpetuity of the Peace, both without and within their Dominions, there is none of them that will not find it more advantageous to sign the Treaty for the Establishment of that Society, than not to sign it.*

Now the European Society, *which is propos'd, can procure, for all the Christian Princes, a* sufficient Security *for the Perpetuity of the Peace both within and without their Dominions.*

Therefore there will be none of them but what will find it much more advantageous to sign the Treaty for the Establishment of that Society, than not to sign it.

The Major or the first Proposition, contains *the Motives*, and the Proof of it may be found in the third Discourse after the Preliminary Discourse, which I thought necessary, in order to dispose the Mind of the Reader to conceive the Force of the Demonstration. The Minor, or the second Proposition, contains the Means; the Proof of it may be found in the fourth Discourse. As for the last Proposition, or the Conclusion, that is the End that I propos'd to my self in this Work.

As this Project may begin to be known in the Courts of *Europe*, either in the middle, or towards the end of a War, or in the Conferences, or after the Conclusion of a Peace, or even in the midst of a profound Peace, it was necessary to shew compendiously in the fifth Discourse, that upon any of those Occasions it would produce both a great Facility in concluding the Peace, and a great desire to render it perpetual, if it was concluded.

Having observ'd that several were of Opinion, that even though the Sovereigns of *Europe* should one by one have sign'd the Treaty of Union, yet there would, in all appearance, remain some Difficulties, almost insurmountable, in the Formation of the Congress, and in *the Means* how to begin and maintain such an Establishment: I was oblig'd in order to remove this

Doubt, to propose, in the Sixth Discourse, several Articles, to which the Sovereigns *may agree*: Not that I thought there could be none propos'd more useful, for the rendring the Establishment more solid in it self, and more convenient for each Member. All I pretend to prove is, that those feign'd Difficulties, which Men may form to themselves, with respect to the Execution of the Establishment, are very far from being insurmountable, since even the Articles that I propose are *sufficient* for that Execution, and that nothing hinders the Sovereigns from agreeing to them.

Such is the Analysis, such the Order I have follow'd in this Work; this is the Fruit I have gather'd from my Meditations for above four Years; this is the Use I have made of the judicious Criticisms of my Friends; and now, if ever any Body propos'd a Subject worthy to be attentively examin'd by the most excellent Wits, and especially by the wisest Ministers and the best Princes, it may be said, that this is it; since it treats of no less than of the Means how to procure to all the Sovereigns and Nations of *Europe*, the greatest Felicity that a new Establishment can possibly ever procure them.

It is easie to comprehend, that the more Methods this Project shall carry in it, for rendring the Peace of *Europe* unalterable, the more it may contribute to facilitate the Conclusion of that which is now treating at *Utrecht*: For the Allies of the House of *Austria* desire Peace as much as we do; but they do not care for it, without *sufficient Security* for its Duration. And indeed, if we were to examin the Interest of those Allies in the present War, we should find, that it all turns upon two principal Heads: The First is a *sufficient Security* for the Preservation of their Dominions against the great Power of the House of *France*, which may, in time, find specious Pretences and favourable Opportunities to make Conquests upon them, and to introduce into their Country a Religion and Government for which they have a very great Aversion. The other Head is, a *sufficient Security* for Liberty of Commerce; whether that of *America*, or that of the *Mediterranean*; in those two Commerces consists above half the Revenue of *England* and *Holland*.

But what *sufficient Securities* can be found for the Weakest against the Strongest? There are but two Systems for this; the first is, if it can be done, *sufficiently* to weaken the Strongest; which is either impossible, or ruinous; though it is that which the Allies follow in the present War, to arrive at their Chimerical *Equilibrium*. The second is, *sufficiently* to fortifie the Weaker, and to give him a Force sufficiently superior, without depriving the Stronger of any of his Force; which is what I propose to do by a Treaty of Society, that might give to the Weaker a new Augmentation of very strong Allies, and who would be so much the stronger, as they would be much more closely united;

not to deprive the Stronger of any thing he possesses, but to take from him the Power of ever disturbing the others, either in their Possessions at home, or in their Commerce abroad.

In my second Draught I took in all the Kingdoms of the World; but my Friends observ'd to me, that even though in following Ages most of the Sovereigns of *Asia* and *Africa* might desire to be receiv'd into the Union, yet this Prospect would seem so remote and so full of Difficulties, that it would cast an Air of Impossibility upon the whole Project; which would disgust all the Readers, and make some believe, that tho' it were even restrain'd only to the Christian part of *Europe*, the Execution of it would be still impossible; therefore I subscribed to their Opinion, and that the more willingly, considering, that the Union of *Europe* would suffice to preserve *Europe* always in Peace; and that it would be powerful enough to maintain its Frontiers and Commerce, in spight of those who should endeavour to disturb it. The General Council It might establish in the *Indies,* would soon become the Arbiter of the Sovereigns of that Country, and, by its Authority, hinder them from taking up Arms; the Credit of the Union would be much the greater amongst them, as they would be assur'd, that it only desired Securities for its Commerce; that that Commerce cannot but be very advantageous to them; that it does not aim at any Conquests; and that it will never look upon any as Enemies, but those who were Enemies to Peace.

If the Reader is willing to form a sound Judgment of the Work, it is, in my Opinion, necessary that he should make a stop at the end of every Discourse, and ask himself what Effect the Proofs I bring have upon him. If he thinks them sufficient, he may go on; but if he does not think them so, That may proceed, either from his still meeting with Difficulties, or from his not having read some Passages with Attention enough; and nothing is more common, even with the most thoughtful Readers, than sometimes to want Attention. In the first Case he need only make a Note of his Doubts, and observe, whether they be not sufficiently clear'd up in the following part of the Work. In the second Case, the only Remedy is, to read over again the Passages he did not well understand; otherwise he would act like a Judge, that should report and make a Judgment after a superficial Reading, and without having given sufficient Attention to the principal Evidences of the Cause. I have endeavour'd to make a Concatenation between the Thoughts, that the Mind might the more easily comprehend them. Now those who are not attentive enough to perceive this Concatenation, can never be sensible of the Force of particular Arguments, and much less of the Force of a Demonstration, which results from the Assemblage of those Arguments.

I own the Title gives a Prejudice to the Work; but as I am persuaded, that it is not impossible to find out Means sufficient and practicable to settle an Everlasting Peace among Christians; and even believe, that the Means which I have thought of are of that Nature; I imagin'd, that if I my self first seem'd to be uncertain, as to the Solidity of those Means, and doubtful of the Possibility of executing them, the Readers, tho' never so well dispos'd in favour of the System, might really doubt of it too, and that their real Doubtfulness might, perhaps, go further than my affected Doubtfulness. It is not with things, in which the Design is to persuade Men to Action, as it is with things of pure Speculation; the Pilot who himself seems uncertain of the Success of his Voyage, is not likely to persuade the Passenger to imbark; the Undertaker who himself seems to doubt of the Solidity of an important Work which he proposed to undertake, is not at all likely to persuade others to join in the Enterprize. Therefore I chose rather to venture being thought ridiculous in assuming an affirmative Stile, and promising in the Title all that I hope to make good in the Body of the Work, than to run the risque, by a false Air of Modesty and Uncertainty, of doing the least wrong to the Publick, by making Men of Sense look upon this Project as whimsical and impossible to be put in execution, when I, my self, form'd it, in full Expectation to see it one Day executed.

Nature's Domain

In French eighteenth-century thought, Morelly was long a cipher whose very existence was doubted and whose works were ascribed to Diderot and other *philosophes*. Though his identity is shadowy, his ideas had a powerful impact on utopian thinkers like Babeuf, Fourier, and, further afield, the founders of Brook Farm in Massachusetts. Morelly was the author of a number of treatises, among them *Essay on the Human Mind* (1743), *Essay on the Human Heart* (1745), *The Prince, the Delights of the Heart or Treatise on the Qualities of a Great King* (1751), and of a two-volume *Basiliade* (1753). This last, pretending to be a manuscript of the celebrated Brahman philosopher Pilpai, described in purple phrases an egalitarian, vegetarian, utilitarian, and sexually free society under a wise and benevolent autocrat. Two years later, Morelly published his most famous and influential book, *Nature's Code* (1755). There he expounded the doctrine that moral evil was not inherent in man but was the consequence of maleficent institutions. Renouncing the poetic fictions of his earlier work, he drafted a set of laws for an ideal and virtuous communist society. Private property is banished in the *Basiliade* as well as in *Nature's Code*; but the later book substituted representative government for enlightened despotism, and a certain austerity for the bounties of a tropical paradise.

Engraving from *Naufrage des Isles Flottantes*, Paris, 1753.

The Abundant Life*

In the bosom of a vast sea, mirror of that profound wisdom which embraces and rules the universe, in the bosom, I say, of a vast beach, forever calm, free of threatening reefs, there lies a rich and fertile continent. There, under a pure and serene sky, nature spreads out her most precious treasures. There she has not, as in our sad parts, locked them away in the bowels of the earth, from which insatiable greed tries to wrest them without ever having a chance to enjoy them. There lie fertile and broad fields which, with the help of light cultivation, bring forth from their bosom all that can render this life delightful. The plains are embellished with the most magnificent carpets of abundance. They are cut by mountains whose aspect is no less agreeable and whose slopes are covered with trees ever green, laden with delicious fruits, ever reborn and ever heralded by flowers. On the summit of these mountains there rise with majesty the incorruptible cedar and the towering pine. Their lofty heads seem to hold up the vault of the heavens, as though they were so many columns on which rests a ceiling decorated with azurite and gems. At the foot of this resplendent scenery there flow abundant reservoirs, a multitude of brooks and rivers. Their limpid waters with a gentle murmur lave the sands of gold and pearls whose brilliance they enhance. These pure waters are laden with aromatic and perfumed essences. Through an infinity of secret canals they bear the source of their fecundity toward the roots of the plants. Their creations nourished by these pleasant perfumes diffuse them in a salubrious atmosphere uncorrupted by those malignant influences, baleful vessels of infirmities, of painful maladies that are harbingers of death. This fortunate site was the habitation of a people whose innocent ways made them worthy of their rich possession. Pitiless Property, mother of all the crimes that inundate the rest of the world, was unknown to them. They regarded the earth as a nursing mother to all, who presents her breast without distinction to those of her children who feel the pangs of hunger. All consider themselves obligated to participate in making her fertile, but no one would say: "Here

*From Morelly, *Naufrage des Isles Flottantes, ou Basiliade du Célébre Pilpai. Poëme Heroique, Traduit de l'Indien par Mr. M******* (Messina, *i.e.* Paris, 1753), I, pp. 4–7, 8–11, 17–20, 32–3, 37–43; translated by the editors.

is my field, my ox, my house." The laborer looks on serenely as another harvests what he had planted, and he will find elsewhere the abundant satisfaction of his needs.

God, they say, created many men only that they might help one another. If he had intended them to be isolated one from another, like trees and plants, they too would draw their nourishing juices directly from the earth. Providence would not have left them deprived of anything. The son would not have needed the help of the father and the father would not feel for his son that tender solicitude which nature prompts in him. Finally, all men would have been born armed with everything needed for their preservation, and instinct would have immediately showed them its use.

The intentions of the Deity are not at all equivocal. He has enclosed all His bounties in the same treasury. All hasten, all are eager to open it. Each one draws there according to his needs, without worrying about whether another takes more than he does. Travelers who quench their thirst at a spring are not jealous of one who, more parched, swallows in great draughts many glassfuls of the refreshing liquid. Does one want to broaden the banks of this precious spring? Many arms are joined to carry out the task painlessly and their work is liberally rewarded. The same is true of Nature's gifts.

Such were the first and enduring maxims of this happy society. No one believed himself exempt from labor which, undertaken in concert by everybody, was thus rendered gay and easy. . . .

When Spring returned, one saw these people joyously flock to increase the fertility of their fields. Stimulated by friendly rivalry, he considered himself happy who traced the greatest number of furrows. "How pleased I am, my friends, that I have contributed most to the common utility!" Was the time come to gather in the fruits of an abundant harvest? Countless hands piled up the treasured crops into enormous mountains. All these labors were followed by games, dances, country feasts. The succulent meals consisted of a copious variety of delicious fruits. Keen appetite greatly enhanced enjoyment of them. Finally, the days devoted to these occupations were days of merrymaking and rejoicing, succeeded by a sweet repose which we, after our riotous and gaudy pleasures, have never tasted.

In exchange for the aid he gave the laborer, the ox received full recompense and seemed to share with his master the fruits of his toil. Free after his services, he did not have to fear that, with black ingratitude, a barbarous knife would spill his blood to thank the Deity for an abundant harvest. No, it never occurred to these people that one could honor the Author of life by the cruel destruction of some living being. Their pure and innocent customs did not allow them to entertain the notion that the Supreme Being would ever be angered against humans. The terrible noise of thunder, which everywhere else brings fear and spreads terror in guilty hearts, was heard not as the voice of an irate Power, but as the majestic resonance of a beneficent Sovereign who sometimes manifested His grandeur.

These gentle and truly human people were also ignorant of the savage custom of feeding on the flesh of animals. In their veins never flowed, along with the fatal elements of corruption and death, that furious passion that incites man against man himself. The heifer paying tribute with its milk and the timid ewe furnishing its wool not for useless adornment but to contribute to the sweetness and comfort of repose, did not fear that they and their tender nurslings were fated to become the prey of a cruel voracity. The birds whose varied song charms away the fatigue of many labors, the birds whose loves and industry herald the seasons, did not have to dread the attacks of those terrible machines for which ingenious wickedness has invented wings. Iron was never sharpened for these murderous purposes. It became an instrument for life's commodiousness, not for its destruction. The tender nightingale, which tries to please us with the sweetness of its melody, could busy itself with obliging us and did not have to tremble that its dear little ones would be torn from it. The dog, that affectionate and faithful animal, was not trained to afford his master the frightful spectacle of innocence crushed by the efforts of an unjust fury. Even the fiercest animals seemed to imitate the peaceful humans and to expect from their generosity what the weakness of their own instinct denied them.

The precious essence embedded in the wheat, prepared in a thousand different ways with milk and honey, fruits, and the most succulent vegetables formed the nourishment of these happy people. Their organs lubricated by gentle and soothing liquids preserved their vigor and their suppleness until an extreme old age, without a trace of wrinkles. We depopulate the earth and the sea to satisfy our taste depraved by intemperance. Greed drives us to seek at the far corners of the world pernicious and subtle poisons, which we swallow in deep draughts. We enjoy a treacherous sensuality that hides beneath its flowers the precipitate strides toward death, whose course it hastens. Furious against ourselves, we are heedlessly tearing at our own entrails. Thus the merciless Destroyer comes to attack us, announced by agonizing pains. But among these wise mortals, the approaches of death are like the gentle relaxation of sleep. And so the passage into death does not frighten them.

*   *   *

O Love, these peoples gave themselves over without fear or sense of crime to your delightful transports. Other nations pay homage to their ferocious divinities by spilling the blood of victims. These people honored the Generative Power of the universe by augmenting the number of its worshipers.

It is true, they concealed your sweet mysteries during years too tender for initiation into them. But as soon as they reached that springtime when you begin to make your first ardors felt, young hearts stirred with your fires, and no one treated their desires as criminal. A loving mother was pleased to recognize in her daughter the first uneasiness of an onrush of feeling hitherto unknown. A father regarded with the same satisfaction the first impressions that the charms of beauty made on his son.

Both of them secretly watched these lovers, not to restrain them but to enjoy the sight of their innocent and naive caresses, their tender speeches, and finally the touching spectacle of their mutual transports. Neither the arrogance of a chimerical aristocracy nor the interests of avarice fixed distinctions of status. Neither hypocritical modesty nor an elaborate decorum disfigured the charms of beauty with a pile of ornate rags. Beauty gloried in appearing stark naked, embellished only with the adornments of nature. When struck by its nascent charms, two young hearts felt taken with each other. They did not blush to survey with eager eyes all of the wonders that nature, prompted by love, led them to notice for the first time. "Whence comes," said a lover, "this sudden change that I feel? Why at the sight of this lovely girl should I feel so powerfully moved? Why do my eyes, accustomed to seeing her without astonishment, suddenly notice so many attractions? Why are my eyes filled with a fire that spreads so sweet an emotion through my senses?" The astonished girl asked the same questions of the author of her perturbation. "Why," she says to him with a tender smile, "do I feel such joy at your appearance wherever I may turn my steps—when I am diverting myself with my companions, when, excited by a reverie whose cause I know not, I go to muse in this grove or near that fountain? Why, as I look at myself in the crystal of its waters, am I so pleased to find myself pretty because of what is between us? Whence comes this sweet seizure that I feel when, as you amble past these bushes, you suddenly surprise me at the moment when I long for your return? By what secret charm do our two hearts seem to move together?" At these delightful notes, the lover flies into the arms of his beloved. He covers her with ardent kisses. He tenderly presses her against his heart. Their lips blending, they breathe sighs softer than the most exquisite perfume. It seems that their souls seek to exchange their abodes. "Stop!" cries the beloved with a weak and faltering voice, "Do not let your transports interrupt the joy that I feel in conversing with you. Satisfy my curiosity. I was about to ask you why this difference that Nature . . . But oh! you redouble your caresses . . . Ah, desist or I shall expire. I feel pleasures I have never known before. They are so violent they have an admixture of pain. A secret ardor spreads through my veins. Cease kindling a fire that will become a torment. But what are you doing, cruel one? . . . Your frenzy frightens me. Do you seek to rob me of my life? Do you wish to devour the one who loves you? Ah, I am dying. What bewitching delights . . . Renew your caresses, dearly beloved. Oh, that these tender ties might be everlasting! But you love me no more. You have brought me these delights only to deprive me of them in a moment. Oh! You are aroused again. My joy is utter. Continue, dear lover, but slacken the pace of your transports. Savor these precious moments. Ah . . . Ah . . . I myself . . . Go on, and let our two souls merge."

*   *   *

Never did a young beauty blush at becoming a mother, or do criminal deeds to avoid the appearance of it. She considered herself fortunate to give a citizen to the fatherland, and gloried in recognizing the true author of that cherished proof of her first love. Her lover was no less pleased with this precious gift. Either he became her husband, or, his passion subsided, he looked on calmly as his mistress passed into another's arms.

The children of several mothers were equally loved by their father. The one to whom he was in fact wed cherished them as though they were her own flesh and blood. She was devoted to the sons of those who had preceded her in the affections of a husband now entirely hers. She considered herself heiress to the glorious title of mother and the privileges attaching to it. She took care that she should be worthy of the tender devotion and gratitude of the foster children that she adopted. The baneful reasons for hating a stepmother and for discord among brothers had no place in these happy families.

The infamous terms incest, adultery, and prostitution were unknown. These nations had no idea of such crimes. A sister received her brother's tender embraces without conceiving any horror of them. Sometimes they strengthened the ties of blood with those of love. Age, respect, desires appeased or abated, and not fear of punishment, prevented a widow from accepting the caresses of her son—caresses of which she had been deprived by the death of her husband. Fathers were not smitten with the growing charms of their daughters. They preferred to see their dear offspring form new branches, and to recount to them the pleasures of their first years, than to tie them again onto a trunk already grown feeble with age.

*   *   *

Although there reigned among these peoples the equilibrium of perfect equality, nevertheless, a son recognizing his father as the source of his existence and the protector of his tender years, feeling himself indebted for the development of his intellect to the wise precepts of this benefactor, requited this gentle solicitude with a respectful love. A wife, submissive to the worshiper of her charms, did not feel she had discharged all her obligations even with the most ardent caresses, the most assiduous attention, to the author of her happiness. As for the husband, he was the most esteemed among his fellow citizens who suggested a better way of procuring for the nation the comforts of life, and whose fertile genius invented the swiftest expedients. In short, good deeds were the only titles of nobility. Gratitude, friendship, admiration, respect, and esteem were the kinds of homage paid that true grandeur.

Nevertheless, the first rank was yielded in those countries to an ancient family which had preserved a paternal authority over all the rest. From it stemmed this numerous people. The branches of that prolific trunk respected the antiquity of their stock, not with the absurd prejudice that among other peoples pays deference to an obscure and legendary past going back through the centuries, but because the whole nation was also indebted to that family for many men of skill and genius, innovators of practices most useful to society.

Thus it was not any fancied birthright, or pretended uninterrupted succession, that entitled this family to preeminence. Only its benevolence, wisdom, prudence, love of the people, were the unshakable foundations of its supreme power. These admirable qualities, always jealously preserved, alone gave it luster. And the art of winning the hearts of the people was all of its statecraft.

The heroes of this line transmitted from father to son the seductive secrets of this beguiling art, and added to the discoveries of their ancestors what they culled from their own experience. They did not look upon their peoples as a heritage of a throng of slaves that had fallen to the lot of one master to serve humbly his arrogant caprices. They believed themselves, on the contrary, to be the legacy of their peoples. The Prince called himself the immortal father of his country. Indeed, the ties of blood have no greater strength than the affection linking this monarch and his subjects. That happy predilection had roots in their hearts as deep as those of paternal and filial love. The Prince, then, not by vain ostentation or the heedless activity of a short-lived benevolence, but by principle and almost innate habit, was the most accessible and most human of all mortals. His solicitude, his attention, his favor were not limited to a few hundred base flatterers. He would have considered himself only half a monarch, if but one member of the family he headed had not felt the effect of his goodness. To inspire respect he had no need to see parade before him the dazzling and tumultuous pomp of the other kings of the earth, or to hide his weaknesses or vices in the solitude of those cavernous tombs called palaces. He did not have to inculcate, by fear or the sophistical maxims of a tyrannical morality, the notion that princes are the images of a Deity terrible and dreadful rather than beneficent. To have his orders executed with despatch, he had only to couch them in these terms: "They are useful to you, dear children of my ancestors and myself." There was no need to employ violence where crime was unknown and where obedience was the outcome of desire quickened by zeal.

The functions of the monarchy were to indicate what measures should be taken, and at what times, for the public good. It was only a question of regulating activities of people among whom constancy and unanimity always prevailed. These peoples knew the importance of this truth: All the parts of the same body love one another; but when it is a matter of helping one another, if they could act without the directions of the head, they would do so neither usefully nor opportunely. The hand would fidget as it came to the foot to perform that function; and the eye would close when it had to guide the hand. No balance, no accord, no order in the animal functions. And so it would be, they said, among a people without a chief.

Thus, just as one sees the rigging of a vessel move, as if enchanted, at the command of a knowing pilot, so, responding to the voice of the Prince, this body so well organized, animated with the same spirit, worked in admirable unison for the common good. Was it time to reap an abundant harvest, to cultivate or sow some field? Was it the moment to gather certain fruits, to adopt some new means of mitigating the difficulties of these tasks, of regulating the number of those who had to be assigned to each occupation? The decisions of the Prince were religiously observed. His orders were respected and carried by word of mouth to the outermost limits of the empire. As he was the moving spirit of every work plan, every regulation, every improvement, so was it also with all sports, rejoicings, pleasures. He decreed the time of their celebration and their duration; he prescribed the means of making them pleasant, imaginative, and diverting through varied and impressive spectacles.

Did some one have a useful opinion to propose? He was listened to with kindness. The praise and approval of the Prince, in the presence of the nation, were an inestimable prize for him who was thus honored. That sign of favor was the more remarkable for being limited to him who deserved it, and it inspired the onlookers to make themselves worthy of it by their zeal for the public good.

These happy kings were not surrounded by a crowd of slaves, or importunate flatterers. The anxieties, the black chagrin, created by constant
efforts of a power that can only force people to obey and respect it, the
troubles of a lofty station that seems bent on violating all the natural inclinations of humanity, the fear of a sword wielded or a poison poured by the hand
of a criminal never ruffled the calm of their brows. Their cherished persons
were not escorted by a numerous guard, who could not hinder death from
toppling their thrones.

———————◆———————

A Model Code of Laws*

SOURCE OF THE ERRORS OF MORALISTS ANCIENT AND MODERN; HOW THEY COULD HAVE RECOGNIZED AND AVOIDED THEM

I have tried to reveal this first link in the chain of error, and to make evident
this first point of deviation which has always kept our moralists and law-
makers distant from the truth. Listen to the lot of them, they will posit for
you as an indisputable principle and the foundation of all their systems the
following important proposition: *Man is born vicious and wicked*. Not quite,
some of them say, *but the circumstances of life in this world, his very make-up,
inevitably predispose him to perverseness*. Accepting this in its most literal sense,
none of them imagined that it could be otherwise; thus it did not occur to
anyone to propound and resolve this crucial problem:

*TO FIND A SITUATION IN WHICH IT WOULD BE ALMOST
IMPOSSIBLE FOR MAN TO BE DEPRAVED, OR WICKED, OR AT
LEAST WHERE THERE WOULD BE AS LITTLE EVIL AS POSSIBLE*

Failing to formulate or solve this problem, our instructors among the ancients
lost sight of the one first cause of all evil, the one obvious means which
would have disclosed an initial error. Proceeding along the same path, our
moderns found themselves still further from a first truth which would have

*From Morelly, *Code de la nature*, ed. Gilbert Chinard (Paris: Raymond Clavreuil, 1950), pp.
159–62, 285–328; translated by the editors.

made them perceive clearly the real origin, nature, and lineage of the vices, and the ineffectiveness of the remedies which common morality claims to apply to them. With the aid of this insight, I say, they could easily have dissected the official morality, and proved that its hypotheses were false, its precepts ineffectual, its maxims contradictory, and its means opposed to their avowed ends; in short, demonstrated in detail the flaws in every portion of this monstrous corpus.

As with mathematical equations, such reasoning, by avoiding and eliminating the false and the dubious, would finally make the *unknown quantity* emerge, that is, a system of ethics truly susceptible of the clearest proofs.

Following this method, I found that in every age our wise men, who sought a cure for the corruption which they, alas, regarded as an inevitable attribute of the human condition, have begun by imagining the cause of that decay where it never resided, and should have taken as a remedy for the evil precisely that poison which they claimed was its cause.

None of these chatterboxes, who repeated themselves endlessly, ever thought of suspecting that the cause of man's corruption was in fact one of their first lessons; the substance appeared to them too pure, too noble for that; their laws, their regulations, too wise and estimable for anyone to dare lay this profound grievance at their door; they preferred to throw the blame on nature. And so man as they fashioned him, completely wanting in metaphysical and moral ideas alike and simply equipped with the proper faculties to receive these ideas, man in the first moments of his existence, in truth totally insensitive to every impulse rather than excited to some impetuous passion, is, according to most of our philosophers, pretty well endowed with a number of vices mixed with a few *innate* virtues along with ideas of the same ilk. Even before seeing the light of day, he carries in his breast the fatal seeds of corruption which will move him to seek his own good at the expense of the whole species and the entire universe if possible.

Were I to overlook that specious absurdity, I would still be right to point out that, far from seeking means to uproot or repress these wicked proclivities and so permit the burgeoning of a few fragile virtues whose roots, according to the learned doctors, are not completely rotten; far, I say, from encouraging these wholesome inclinations, they have done precisely everything needed to plant the seed of vice in the heart of man and make it sprout—vice that was never there—and to suffocate in him the bit of virtue that they fancy they are cultivating.

* * *

MODEL LEGISLATION IN ACCORD WITH NATURE'S DESIGN

I am giving this outline of laws by way of an appendix and as an excursus, since unfortunately it is only too true that in our day it would be practically impossible to establish such a Republic.

On the basis of this text, which needs no long commentaries, every intelligent reader will be able to judge from how much distress these laws would deliver men. I have just shown that it would have been easy for the first legislators to act so that the peoples of the earth knew no other laws: if my proofs are convincing my object is achieved.

I am not so rash as to pretend to reform human-kind; but I have courage enough to tell the truth, without concerning myself over the outcries of those who are afraid of it because they are interested in deluding our species or in abandoning it to the errors by which they themselves have been duped.

FUNDAMENTAL AND INVIOLABLE LAWS
Which would cut off at the root the vices and all the evils of society.

I
Nobody will own anything in the society individually or as a landlord except the things which he is currently using for his needs, his pleasures, or his daily work.

II
Every Citizen will be a public person, supported, maintained, and employed at public expense.

III
For his part every Citizen will contribute to the public weal in accordance with his strength, his talents, and his age; these will determine his obligations, in conformity with the *Distributive Laws*.

DISTRIBUTIVE OR ECONOMIC LAWS

I
In order that everything may be carried out in an orderly fashion, without confusion or dispute, an entire Nation will be counted and divided into Families, Tribes, and Cities, and if its population is very large, into Provinces.

II
Each Tribe will consist of the same number of Families, each City of the same number of Tribes, and so on.

III
As the Nation grows in population, the Tribes and Cities will be proportionately increased, but only until the increment is sufficient to form new Cities with as many persons as the others. SEE *V of the Edile and XII of the Conjugal Laws*.

IV

All civil divisions involving things or persons will be made in terms of the number *ten* and its multiples; that is to say, all enumerations, every distribution by groups, every distributive measurement, and so on, will consist of decimal parts.

V

On the basis of *tens* or *hundreds*, and so on, of Citizens, there will be in each occupation workers whose number is in proportion to the difficulty of their labor and what they are obliged to supply to the people of each City, without wearing themselves out.

VI

To regulate the distribution of the products of nature and art, it will be noted first that there are some *durable* things, that is, those which can be preserved or used a long time, and that among all the products of that sort there are: (1) Those of daily and universal use; (2) Those of universal, but not continual use; (3) Some that are continually necessary only to someone, and from time to time to everyone; (4) Others that are never of continual or general use, such as those catering simply to pleasure or individual taste. Now, all these durable products will be collected in public warehouses for distribution, some daily or at stated times to all Citizens, for the ordinary needs of life and for carrying on their various occupations, others to people who make use of them.

VII

It will be noted in the second place that there are products of nature or art which are nondurable; these things will be brought to the marketplace and distributed by those who are in charge of cultivating or preparing them.

VIII

These products of every kind will be counted, and their quantities will be regulated in accordance with the number of Citizens in each City, or the number of those who use them. Among the various products, those which can be preserved will, according to the same rules, be publicly allotted, and their surplus held in reserve.

IX

If there should be a deficit of luxury items of universal or particular use, so that a single Citizen would be deprived, all distribution will be suspended, or else such items will be supplied only in the tiniest amount, until the shortage will have been remedied; but great care will be exercised that such accidents do not befall things which are universally necessary.

X

The surplus provisions of each City, of each Province, will be channeled into those that are threatened by a dearth, or will be reserved for future needs.

XI

According to the *Inviolable Laws*, nothing will be sold or bartered among Fellow-Citizens; thus, if anyone needs some herbs, vegetables, or fruits, he will go and take what he requires for one day only at the marketplace, where things are brought by those who grow them. If someone needs bread, he will go and get a supply sufficient for a certain length of time from the man who makes it, and the latter will find in the public warehouse the flour he needs for the amount of bread he is obliged to prepare for one or several days. The person who needs a piece of clothing will get it from him who fashions it, and he in turn will take the fabric from the one who makes it, and he will get the raw material from the warehouse where it has been brought by those who gather it. And thus with everything else which will be distributed to each Head of a Family for his use and that of his children.

XII

If a Nation succours a neighboring or foreign Nation with the products of its countryside, this commerce alone will be effected through exchange and through the intermediary of Citizens who will declare everything publicly; but scrupulous care will be taken to see that such commerce does not introduce any private property into the Republic, even the slightest amount.

AGRARIAN LAWS

I

The territory of each city will be as compact and regular as possible, not held as a landed estate, but just adequate for the subsistence of its inhabitants and the employment of those responsible for cultivating the soil.

II

If a City happens to be located on barren land, only the arts will be practiced there, and neighboring Cities will provide sustenance for its inhabitants. Nevertheless that City, like the others, will have its *Farm Corps,* either to make its land yield as much as possible, or to help in cultivating the lands of neighbor Cities.

III

Every Citizen, without exception, from the age of twenty to twenty-five, will be obliged to work at farming, unless some infirmity excuses him from it.

IV

In each City this Agricultural Youth Corps will be composed of Laborers, Gardeners, Shepherds, Woodcutters, Pioneers, Wagoners and Boatmen, Carpenters, Masons, Blacksmiths, and other workmen in Building Trades. Young people who have worked in one of the first six capacities will be able to quit after a stated period and resume whatever they had previously been trained for, or remain in agriculture as long as their strength permits. SEE *Police Laws III and V.*

EDILE LAWS

I

As in each City the Tribes will hardly exceed, if at all, a certain number of Families, and as the Tribes will never exceed a certain number by more than one, all the Cities will have about the same extent, in accordance with *Distributive Law II.*

II

Around a great square of regular shape, buildings of uniform and attractive style will be erected; these will be the public warehouses for all provisions and the public meeting halls.

III

The quarters of the City will extend in regular fashion from this enclosure; they will be of equal dimensions and shape, and regularly divided by streets.

IV

Each Tribe will occupy a quarter, and each Family a spacious and comfortable dwelling; all these buildings will be alike.

V

All the quarters of a City will be so arranged that they can be enlarged if necessary without disturbing the regularity; such increases will not exceed definite limits.

VI

Some distance away and forming galleries around the quarters of the City will be the workshops in all the mechanical trades for all work corps whose number is greater than ten; for it was provided in *Distributive Law V* that in each City there would be only a sufficient number of workers for every mechanical trade.

VII

Outside this ring of workshops will be constructed another row of buildings designed to house persons employed in agriculture and its dependent occupations. The buildings will also be used as workshops for these occupations, as barns, storerooms, mangers, toolsheds, always accommodated to the needs of the particular City.

VIII

At some distance beyond all these circles, a spacious and commodious building will be put up on the most healthful site. In it any sick Citizen will find lodging and care.

IX

On another side there will be a comfortable shelter for all infirm and decrepit Citizens.

X

On another side, in the least agreeable and most deserted spot, a building will be constructed that is surrounded by high walls and is divided into several small rooms, closed with iron railings. Here will be locked up those who deserve to be isolated from society for a time. SEE *the Penal Laws.*

XI

Nearby will be the walled cemetery, which will hold individual buildings of very strong stonework, cavernous structures that are rather spacious and heavily barred, to shut in forever and finally entomb Citizens who deserve civil death, that is, to be forever excluded from society. SEE *the Penal Laws.*

XII

In each City all buildings in general will be constructed, maintained, or rebuilt by the Work Corps assigned to Architecture.

XIII

The cleanliness of the Cities and of the public thoroughfares will ordinarily be maintained by the Pioneer and Driver Corps; they will also be responsible for provisioning the warehouses and arranging their goods. When there is some extraordinary need, all those who are occupied strictly with tilling the soil help out the others by putting in some work on the construction or repair of the public roads and on the aqueducts.

POLICE LAWS

I

In all occupations the oldest and at the same time most experienced will take their turn in accordance with seniority in directing five or ten of their comrades for five days; and these supervisors will distribute their own work load fairly among the others.

II

In each occupational corps there will be a Master for ten or twenty workers, whose task it will be to train them, to inspect their work, and to report on their diligence and conduct to the Corps Chief, who will hold office for a year; the Masters will be permanent, and will take turns at being Corps Chief.

III

No one can be a Master until a year has elapsed after he finishes his agricultural service and returns to his first occupation, in other words, until the end of his twenty-sixth year.

IV

In any occupation, a person who makes an important discovery will share it with all the members of his Corps, and thenceforward he will be a Master even if he has not yet reached the proper age, and he will be designated Corps Chief for the following year; the rotation will be interrupted only in this case and will be resumed thereafter.

V

At the age of ten, every Citizen will begin to learn the occupation for which he feels some inclination and which he seems capable of performing, without being pushed into it; at fifteen or eighteen he will marry; from twenty to twenty-five he will be engaged in some branch of farming; at twenty-six he will be a Master, in his first trade if he resumes it, or, if he remains in agriculture, in some craft connected with it; SEE *Agrarian Laws III and IV*. But if he happens to embrace any other sort of occupation, then he can be a Master only at the age of thirty. At forty, every Citizen who has never been convicted of an offense will become a Worker-at-Will; that is, without being exempt from work, he will be able to choose to whom he is subordinate, and will perform only the tasks which he sets for himself; he will be master of his hours of repose.

VI

The infirm and decrepit aged will be comfortably lodged, fed, and maintained in the public shelter provided for that purpose in each City according to *Edile Law IX*. All sick Citizens, without exception, will also be moved to the common residence that has been reserved for them, and will be cared for with the same meticulousness and cleanliness as in the bosom of their Families, and without distinction or preference. The Senate of each Town will be particularly concerned with proper management and service in these houses, and will see to it that they are not wanting in anything necessary or agreeable, whether for the restoration of health, the progress of convalescence, or finally to while away the tedium of infirmity.

VII

The Chiefs of all the Trades will fix the hours of rest and of work, and will prescribe what is to be done.

VIII

Every fifth day will be set aside as a public day of rest; for that purpose the year will be divided into seventy-three equal parts; there will be a double day of rest only once in the year, to which a day should be added. SEE *Distributive Law IV*.

IX

Public celebrations will always begin on a public restday and will last a total of six days.

X

These celebrations will take place just before ploughing begins, before the harvest starts, after the gathering and stacking of fruits of all sorts, and at New Year's; on this last occasion marriages will be solemnized, and City and Corps Chiefs will take office. SEE *the Laws of Government*.

SUMPTUARY LAWS

I

Every Citizen at the age of thirty will dress as he pleases but without great ostentation; similarly he will be fed in the bosom of his Family, neither intemperately nor lavishly; this law imposes on Senators and Chiefs the duty of strictly repressing any excess, and of setting an example of moderation themselves.

II

From ten to thirty years of age, young people of each trade will be clad alike in the same materials, in outfits that are clean, but ordinary and appropriate for their work. Each Corps will be distinguished by a color associated with its principal product, or by some other mark.

III

Every Citizen will have a work outfit, and party attire that is modest and becoming, all of it in accordance with what the Republic can afford, without anyone's getting ornaments which might win him favor or attention; all vanity will be curbed by the Chiefs and Heads of Families.

LAWS ON THE FORM OF GOVERNMENT
Which would prevent all tyrannical domination.

I

Every Head of a Family at the age of fifty will be a Senator, and will have a voice in the deliberations as well as a vote on all regulations to carry out the intent of the laws, whose guardian is the Senate.

II

Other Heads of Families or Work Corps Chiefs will be consulted when matters affecting their occupations are involved.

III

Within each Tribe, every Family in its turn will provide a Tribal Chief, who will occupy that position throughout his life.

IV

The Tribal Chiefs will take turns at the office of City Chief for one year.

V

Each City in turn will provide a Chief for the Province; his term will be one year; he will be chosen among the Tribal Chiefs of the City, who will also take turns at the office; the Tribe from which he comes will name a substitute Chief.

VI

All the Provinces will take turns at providing a permanent Chief of State; he will be by right the Provincial Chief actually incumbent at the time of the General's death, or just about to take office; but in the latter case, since he becomes General, he will be replaced in his Province by the man who would normally have succeeded him according to the preceding law.

VII

If the Nation is not sufficiently populous to include more than one Province, its annual Chief will be General for a year. If the National Body should be only one City, the annual Chief of that City would be Chief of the whole State for one year only. In either case, there will be no change in the order for conferring these dignities as set forth in Law V.

VIII

As heretofore provided in Law III, Chiefs of Tribes are to be permanent; hence those who serve their term as annual Chief of the City or Province will, on leaving that office, once more occupy their former positions; those who, in accordance with Law V, will have substituted for them during their Generalship will become once more simple Heads of Families, to await their succession as Tribal Chiefs.

IX

Every person who becomes a Tribal Chief, whether before or after the *senatorial* age, will no longer be or can no longer be a Senator, and if he attains to any annual or permanent office, neither during nor after his term will he be a member of any Senate, but only of the Council.

X

There will be a supreme National Senate renewed annually and composed of two or several Deputies of the Senate of each City, and each Senator will take his turn at becoming a Deputy. There will also be a supreme National Council subordinate to this great Senate and superior to the other Councils; it will be similarly composed of the Deputies of the City Councils, etc.

XI

If the State consists of only one City, its Senate will be supreme; its members will be persons aged fifty, and will perform the duties of the National Senate. Heads of Families aged forty make up the local Senate.

XII

Since Law IX on the form of Government stipulates that Tribal Chiefs shall be thereafter excluded from the Senatorial Body, they will form the Council of each City, along with Corps Chiefs and Master Artists who are not of senatorial age.

XIII

Every member of a Senate or a Council will take his turn at presiding for five days, to poll opinions and announce decisions on the basis of a plurality of votes.

LAWS ON GOVERNMENT ADMINISTRATION

I

The functions of the Supreme Senate will be to examine the decisions and regulations of the Senates of each City and to see whether they contain anything which can in the present or future contradict the laws of the State, whether economic and police measures wisely conform to the intent of the distributive and other laws; in consequence of this examination, the Supreme Senate will confirm or reject specific regulations in toto or only partially; what is thus enacted for one City will be observed in all the rest for the same purpose, and will have the force of law after the acquiescence of the local Senates.

II

Each Senate will seek the advice of its Council, and will heed its representations, with power to reject them only in the event that what the Council proposes is found to be directly or indirectly contrary to the intent of the laws and that there is a better alternative.

III

City Chiefs, under the orders of the General, will execute the decisions of the local Senate that have been approved by the Supreme Body.

IV

In the local Senates and the Supreme Senate will be vested all political authority, subject to that of the laws; that is, they will order definitively and without discussion everything that is formally prescribed by the laws; they will have the power to implement and apply to the business of government the provisions of these laws, which are expressed only in general terms, after deliberating and legislating on the means.

V

The functions of Chief of the Nation will be in general to act under the orders of the Supreme Senate and see that the laws and decisions relating to them are observed. In particular, he will have general command over all the State Corps engaged in agriculture or work connected with it; he will have oversight of all kinds of warehouses and the work of all the Trade Corps. If the State covers an extensive area, he will make a tour of all its Provinces, to see whether everything is timely carried out, whether everywhere there is as much uniformity as possible in customs and practices.

VI

Chiefs of Cities, under the authority of Provincial Chiefs, and these latter under the orders of the General, will perform the same functions for their districts as the General does for the whole State.

VII

All Chiefs, in accordance with their ranks and in their own sphere, will have the power, in special and unforeseen cases involving the organization and execution of some useful project, to put into effect means at their discretion. Their orders will always be absolute when there is a question of a greater good. In less urgent cases they will take the advice of their equals or of experienced people; they will account for and justify their conduct to their own Senate and to any Chiefs to whom they are subordinate, and these in turn to the General and the General to the Supreme Senate.

VIII

Chiefs of Tribes (and for that reason they are permanent) will have charge of inspecting the organization and supply of the warehouses, and the distribution of provisions, which will be carried out by Workers-at-Will, that is, by those who have reached the age for choosing their own employment; they will be assisted when necessary by persons detailed from the Farmers' Corps. As for products of daily manufacture and use, they will be distributed, as set forth in *Distributive Law IV*, to each Citizen by those who grow, prepare, or fashion these commodities.

IX

The annual City and Provincial Chiefs will occupy themselves only with the duties of office; after their terms have expired, they will be free to engage at will in whatever occupation they please. Every Artisan Corps Chief will also enter the ranks of the Workers-at-Will when he has finished his year of service.

X

All Senators, Political Chiefs, Chiefs of Workshops, and Master Artisans will be respected and obeyed for the common good of the fatherland just as Heads of Families are revered by their children.

XI

The formula for every public order will be: *willed by Reason, prescribed by Law*.

XII

All these government laws, like the *Fundamental Laws*, will be held sacred and inviolable; they cannot be changed or abrogated by anyone whomsoever, under penalties, etc. SEE *the Penal Laws*.

CONJUGAL LAWS
Which would prevent all debauchery.

I

Every Citizen, as soon as he has reached marriageable age, will be wed; nobody will be granted dispensation unless nature or his health interposes an obstacle. Celibacy will not be allowed anyone under forty.

II

At the beginning of each year, marriages will be publicly celebrated. The young people of both sexes will be assembled; in the presence of the City Senate, each boy will choose the girl who pleases him, and, with her consent, will take her to wife.

III

First marriages will be indissoluble for ten years, after which divorce will be permitted either with the consent of both parties or only of one.

IV

The reasons for divorce will be stated before the assembled Heads of Families of the Tribe, who will try to present arguments for reconciliation.

V

Once divorce has been declared, the separated persons may be reunited only after six months; but before that time, they may not see each other or speak to each other; the husband will remain with his Tribe or Family, and his wife will return to hers; they will be able to arrange their reconciliation only through the intermediary of common friends.

VI

Divorced persons may not take new marriage partners until a year has elapsed; after the second marriage, they will not be permitted to wed again.

VII

Persons who have separated cannot marry others younger than themselves, nor younger than the spouse they have left. Only the widowed will have that liberty.

VIII

Persons of one or the other sex who have been married will not be able to marry young persons who have not.

IX

Every Citizen will be able to marry into whatever Tribe, City, or Province he wishes; but the wife and the children will belong to the husband's Tribe.

X

Children of either sex will remain with the father in case of divorce, and his second wife will alone be considered their mother; none of her predecessors will be able to take this title with respect to her husband's children.

XI

Sons of the same father, though married and having children of their own, will be Heads of Families only after the death of their common father.

XII

At the time that marriages are publicly celebrated, there will be an annual census of the Citizens of each City. The Senate will keep an exact record of the number of persons of different ages and occupations by Tribe and Family. The number of Families composing the Tribes will be as nearly equal as possible; new Tribes will be formed and, if necessary, new Cities, when there is an excess number of Tribes sufficient for that purpose; or else Tribes and Cities which have dwindled through some accident will be repopulated.

XIII

When the Nation has reached a point of development where the number of births among the Citizenry is about equal to the number of deaths, the Tribes, Cities, etc. will remain and be kept almost equal. SEE *Economic Law III.*

EDUCATION LAWS
Which would prevent the consequences of blind paternal indulgence toward children.

I
Mothers themselves will nurse their children, if their health permits, and will not be excused without proof of illness.

II
Women who are separated from their husbands and who have children at their breasts will nevertheless be sure to nurse them during the year after their divorce.

III
Tribal Chiefs will exercise vigilance over the care given young children by their mothers and fathers.

IV
At the age of five, all the children of the Tribe will be gathered up, and the two sexes will be separately lodged and fed in a boarding-school designed for that purpose; their food, clothing, and primary education will be everywhere the same, without distinction, according to the regulations prescribed by the Senate.

V
A certain number of fathers and mothers, under the surveillance of the Tribal Chief, will take care of these children as they would their own for five days, and will be relieved in their turn by the next group. They will apply themselves to instilling in their pupils moderation and gentleness, to preventing by tact or mild punishment all quarreling, capriciousness, bad habits; they will treat them all with perfect impartiality.

VI
As their minds begin to develop, these children will be taught the laws of the fatherland. They will learn to respect them, to obey their parents, Chiefs, and other adults. They will be trained to behave good-naturedly toward their fellows, to seek their friendship, and never to lie. They will practice some simple task suitable to their age, and, from time to time, will participate in games to develop their bodies and prepare them for work. Nothing will be prescribed for them without explaining to them its reason. This primary instruction will be continued by the Masters to whose care they will be confided upon emerging from early childhood.

VII
Those children who before the age of ten are sufficiently robust to learn the first elements of the occupation for which they are deemed fit will be sent to the public workshops for a few hours every day to begin their apprenticeship.

VIII
At the age of ten, all the children will leave this common paternal residence to go into the workshops, where they will then be lodged, fed, clad, and trained by the Masters and Chiefs of each occupation, whom they will obey as their own Parents; everything will be done in common in each Corps and in each workshop, where the two sexes will be separately trained, each in the work that is appropriate for it.

IX
The Masters and Mistresses, as well as the Occupational Chiefs, will combine work practice with moral instruction. As the children's reason begins to develop, one of

them is bound to understand that there is a Deity, and, having heard talk about it, they will begin to ask questions about this Supreme Being. It will then be explained to them that He is the first and beneficent cause of all that they marvel at or find agreeable and good. Great care will be taken not to give them vague ideas of this ineffable being, nor to pretend to explain nature to them in terms devoid of meaning. They will be told quite bluntly that the Creator of the Universe cannot be known otherwise than through His works, which proclaim Him only as a Being infinitely good and wise, not comparable with anything mortal. The young people will be made to understand that the feelings of sociability in man are the only oracles through which the Deity's purposes are known; and that in observing them one succeeds in understanding what God is. The youth will be told that the laws are made to develop these sentiments and to apply their dictates in an orderly way to the good of society.

X

All precepts, maxims, moral reflections will be derived from the *Fundamental and Inviolable Laws,* and always related to harmony and social sympathy. The theme of the preaching will be individual happiness indissolubly linked to the common good, and the incentives cited to encourage the youth will be the esteem and friendship of their kin, Fellow-Citizens, and Chiefs.

XI

Chiefs and Senators will be on their guard to see that the laws and regulations for the education of children are everywhere precisely and uniformly observed, and especially that childish faults that could develop into the *proprietary spirit* are prudently corrected and forestalled. They will also prevent tender young minds from being filled with fables, tales, or absurd fictions.

XII

At fifteen or sixteen, when the young people are married, they will leave the public academies to return to the paternal roof, whence they will sally forth each day at certain times to ply their trades in the workshops, until they reach the age for practicing farming; at that time they will move into the houses specially built for that calling.

LAWS ON STUDIES

Which would prevent aberrations of the human mind and all metaphysical dreams.

I

The number of persons who apply themselves to the arts and sciences, which require more wisdom, perception, skill, diligence, and talent than physical strength, will be fixed for each type of study as well as for each City. Training will begin early for those Citizens who have the greatest inclination, without this type of study or practice excusing them from engaging in some branch of farming when they have reached the proper age. No one, except a number of masters and pupils prescribed for the arts and sciences, can embark on this course of study before the age of thirty, *according to Police Law V.* Then those whose experience has given them greater understanding and has strengthened the inclination for some profession more exalted than what they practiced before may thus occupy themselves.

II

There will be absolutely no other moral philosophy than that concerned with the plan and system of the laws; the observations and precepts of that science will only lay stress on the utility and wisdom of these laws, on the tender bonds of blood and friendship, the pleasures of service and gratitude which unite the Citizenry, the love and usefulness of work, the general and specific rules for the good order and for perfect harmony. This science will be studied by all the Citizens.

III

All metaphysics will be reduced to what has previously been said about the Deity. As to the question of man, one will add that he is endowed with reason designed to make him a social being; that the nature of his faculties, as well as the natural principles by which they operate, are unknown to us; that only the processes of reason can be followed and observed by the careful attention of that same faculty; that we do not know what in man is the foundation and support of that faculty, even as we do not know what happens to this Principle at death; one will say that perhaps this intelligent Principle continues to exist after life is over, but that it is useless to try to understand a state of being about which the Author of Nature gives us no inkling through any phenomenon whatever. Such will be the limits prescribed for speculation of this character.

IV

The wisdom and perceptiveness of the human mind will be entirely free when it comes to the theoretical and experimental sciences, whose object is to explore Nature's secrets or perfect the arts that are useful to society.

V

There will be a kind of public digest of all the sciences, and no metaphysics or morals beyond the bounds fixed by the laws will ever go into it; only discoveries in physical science, mathematics, or mechanics that are confirmed by experiment and reasoning will be added to it.

VI

The moral and physical beauties of nature, scientific subjects, the comforts and pleasures of society, as well as the Citizens who have made distinguished contributions to the perfection of all these things, will be celebrated in oratory, poetry, and painting.

VII

Every individual Senate will have drawn up in writing those deeds of the Chiefs and Citizens that are worthy of commemoration; but care will be taken to keep these histories free from all exaggeration, flattery, and, even more strictly, fable. The Supreme Senate will supervise the composition of an official history of the whole Nation.

VIII

Each chapter of these laws will be incised on a separate column or pyramid erected in the public square of every City, and the proper, direct, and literal meaning of their texts will always be followed; not the slightest change or alteration will ever be permitted. If something ambiguous or obscure crops up in a law, effort should be made either to explain it by reference to some other law, or to fix once and for all the meaning of that law in terms most consonant with the Fundamental and Inviolable Laws.

PENAL LAWS

As few as there are falsehoods, as mild as they are effective.

I

Every Citizen, no matter what his rank or office, even the General-in-Chief of the Nation, who might be—which is scarcely credible—so unnatural as to take someone's life or wound him mortally, who might try through a plot or otherwise to abrogate the inviolable laws in order to introduce hateful private property, after trial and judgment by the Supreme Senate, will be imprisoned for life. Like a dangerous madman and enemy of humanity, he will be shut away in a cavern constructed, as set forth in *Edile Law XI*, in the public cemetery. His name will be forever erased from the census of Citizens, his children and his whole Family will abandon his name, and they will be individually assimilated into other Tribes, Cities, or Provinces, where no one will be allowed to snub them or to reproach them with the wrong committed by their kin under penalty of being banished from society for two years.

II

Those who would dare to intercede for the guilty; those who are sorely wanting in respect or obedience to their Chiefs or Senators, to Fathers of Families or their kinfolk; those who have abused by insult or injury any of their fellows—will be imprisoned in places reserved for punishing these kinds of offenses, for one or several days, months, or years. The National Senate will once and for all set the terms, in accordance with the seriousness of the crimes; never will there be a reduction in the sentence to be served for an offense.

III

Adulterers will be imprisoned for a year; after that a husband or a wife may take the guilty one back, if he has not been repudiated immediately after the infidelity; and the offender can never marry his partner in adultery.

IV

Any person of either sex who has commerce with anyone during the year his divorce is in process will be punished as an adulterer.

V

Anyone who has deserved to be excluded from society for one or several years can never be a Senator or Tribal Chief.

VI

All persons entrusted with the education and care of children, who are grossly negligent and, instead of correcting and instructing their charges, allow them to acquire some vice or contract some bad habit that is anti-social, will be deprived of the honor of that occupation for a period or forever, in accordance with the judgment of guilt.

VII

All those cut off from society and imprisoned for life or only for a period, will be deprived of all amusement or occupation; they will be fed alike on good food, but of the plainest sort, and similarly clad; they will be served by young people who have confessed to minor offenses of laziness, recalcitrance, or lying; they will perform this function for several days, and, if they are unavailable, this duty will devolve on a certain number of the young apprentices in each occupation, who will alternate daily.

VIII

Other less serious offenses, like certain acts of negligence or carelessness, will be punished at the discretion of the Chiefs or Masters in each occupation, either by requiring the service just mentioned in the preceding law, or through the deprivation of all work and all amusement for several hours or days, in order to punish idleness with idleness.

IX

As it is not the punishment but the offense which is dishonorable, after a sentence has been served, all Citizens will be forbidden to make the slightest reproach to one who has expiated his crime according to the law, or to any of his relatives, or to inform anybody who was not aware of it, or to show the slightest contempt for such persons in their presence or absence, under pain of undergoing the same punishment. Only Chiefs will be permitted to warn them, with the voice of authority, about their obligations, without ever mentioning their past mistakes or chastisement.

X

Once a penalty has been imposed by law and defined for each type of offense, it can never be remitted, reduced, or commuted by any pardon whatsoever, nor for any consideration, except in case of sickness.

XI

The Senate of each City will alone have the power to impose penalties of isolation from society, upon the deposition of Chiefs of Tribes, Families, or Professional Corps; and these last will impose civil penalties.

XII

Every false accusation of a crime which would earn permanent isolation from society will be subject to the same punishment; in every other case, the false accuser will be subject to a penalty double that which the accused would have incurred.

XIII

Accusations by persons who are not endowed with civil or natural authority will not be heard or received by the Senate.

XIV

Persons who hold office will be obliged themselves to exercise vigilance over their subordinates, to reprimand or punish them in cases over which they have jurisdiction, to report them to a higher authority for graver offenses, without any leniency, under penalty of being relieved of office for a period or forever according to the importance of their oversight.

JEAN-JACQUES ROUSSEAU
(1712–1778)

The People of the Ideal Commonwealth and the Expression of their General Will*

Rousseau was born in Calvinist Geneva, the son of a watchmaker of French descent. After a stormy youth marked by strange amorous episodes, wanderings about Europe, and a miscellany of occupations from lackey to music teacher and secretary to an ambassador, he settled in Paris and joined the ranks of the Encyclopedists. Rousseau gained fame with his *Discourse on the Arts and Sciences* (1750) and *Discourse on the Origin of Inequality* (1755). There he maintained that man had deteriorated morally as civilization advanced, and, without advocating a return to the state of nature, he called for a reshaping of society in harmony with nature's laws. Though Rousseau's brilliance won him the friendship of the greatest intellects of his day, his exigent and paranoid character later alienated them and left him isolated. A dispute with Diderot and Grimm was followed a few years later by a rupture with David Hume, who had given him refuge in England when he was attacked for the deism of the *Emile* (1762). The *Contrat Social* (1762), or *Social Compact*, as the earliest translations called it, where Rousseau defined the relationships in an ideal government based on popular sovereignty, also brought him into conflict with the authorities. When the work was condemned and burned in theocratic Geneva, he angrily renounced his citizenship. Rousseau spent the last years of his life in France, a solitary who had broken with the philosophical and literary coteries.

*From Jean-Jacques Rousseau, *A Treatise on the Social Compact; or The Principles of Politic Law* (London: T. Becket, 1764), pp. 69–83, 179–93.

Rousseau, 1766, engraving by David Martin after the painting by Allan
Ramsay in the National Gallery, Edinburgh.

Of the People

As the architect, before he begins to raise an edifice, examines into the ground where he is to lay the foundation, that he may be able to judge whether it will bear the weight of the superstructure; so the prudent legislator does not begin by making a digest of salutary laws, but examines first whether the people for whom such laws are designed, are capable of supporting them. It was for this reason Plato refused to give laws to the Arcadians and Cyrenians, knowing they were rich and luxurious, and could not admit of the introduction of equality among them. It was for this reason that Crete, though it boasted good laws, was inhabited by such bad men; Minos had only endeavoured to govern a people already depraved by vice. Various have been the nations that have made a distinguished figure in the world, and yet have not been capable of being governed by good laws; and even those who were capable of being so governed, continued so but a short time. Nations, as well as individuals, are docile only in their infancy: they become incorrigible as they grow old. When customs are once established and prejudices have taken root among them, it is a dangerous and fruitless enterprize to attempt to reform them. A people cannot even bear to have their wounds probed, though in order to be cured; but resemble those weak and cowardly patients who shudder at the sight of their physician. Not, but that sometimes, as there are distempers which affect the brain of individuals and deprive them of the capacity of remembering what is past, there happen in states such revolutions as produce the same effect on a people, when the horror of the past supplies the place of oblivion, and the state, inflamed and exhausted by civil wars, rises again, if I may so express myself, out of its own ashes, and reassumes the vigour of youth in forsaking the arms of death. This was the case with Sparta in the time of Lycurgus, and of Rome after the Tarquins; and such hath been the case in modern times with Holland and Switzerland after the expulsion of their tyrants. But these events are rare; and are such exceptions as have their cause in the particular constitution of the state excepted. They cannot even take place twice among the same people: for though they may be made free when they are only barbarous and uncivilized; yet, when the resources of society are exhausted, they cannot be renewed.

In that case, faction may destroy, but revolutions cannot re-establish their freedom; they require for ever after a master, and not a deliverer. Every free people, therefore, should remember this maxim, that tho' nations may acquire liberty, yet if once this inestimable acquisition is lost, it is absolutely irrecoverable.

There is in nations, as well as individuals, a term of maturity, at which they should be permitted to arrive before they are subjected to laws. This term, however, is not always easy to be known; and yet if it be anticipated it may be of dangerous consequence. Again, one people may be formed to discipline in their infancy; while another may not be ripened for subjection till after many centuries. The Russians, for instance, will never be truly polished because they were disciplined too soon. Peter had only an imitative turn; he had nothing of that true genius, whose creative power forms things out of nothing. Some of his measures, indeed, were proper enough, but most of them were ill-timed or ill-placed. He saw that his subjects were mere barbarians, but he did not see that they were not ripe for being made polite. He wanted to civilize them, when he should only have checked their brutality. He wanted to make them, at once, Germans and Englishmen, whereas he ought to have begun by making them first Russians; and thus he prevented his subjects from ever becoming what otherwise they might have been, by persuading them they were such as they were not. It is thus a French tutor forms his pupil to make a figure in his child-hood, and to make none for ever afterwards. The Empire of Russia, while it is ambitious of reducing all Europe to its subjection, will be subjected itself. Its neighbours, the Tartars, will in time become both its masters and ours. This event seems to me inevitable; all the monarchs in Europe seeming to act, in concert, to accelerate such a revolution.

In the same manner as nature hath limited the dimensions of a well-formed human body, beyond which she produces only giants or dwarfs, so in the body politic there are limits, within or beyond which a state ought not to be confined or extended; to the end that it may not be too big to be well governed, nor too little to maintain its own independency. There is in every body politic a *maximum* of force which it cannot exceed, and from which it often recedes by extending its dominion. The more the social knot is extended, the more lax it grows; and in general, a little state is always proportionably stronger than a great one.

A thousand reasons might be given in support of this maxim. In the first place, the administration of government becomes always more difficult as the distance from the seat of it increases, even as a body has the greatest weight at the end of the longest lever. It becomes also more burthensome in proportion as it is divided into parts; for every town hath first its own particular government to pay; that of each district again is paid by the same people; next that of the province, then that of particular governments with their viceroys, all of whom are to be paid as they rise in dignity, and always at the expence of the unhappy people; whom, last of all, the supreme administration itself crushes with the whole weight of its oppression. It is impossible so many needless charges should not tend continually to impoverish the people; who, so far from being better governed by these different ranks of superiors, are much worse so, than if they had but one order of governors in the state. And yet with this multiplicity of rulers, they are far from being furnished with proper resources for extraordinary occasions; but, on the contrary, when they have occasion to recur to them, the state is always on the brink of ruin.

Nor is this all; the government not only becomes less vigorous and active in putting the laws in execution, removing private oppression, correcting abuses or preventing the seditious enterprises of rebellion in distant provinces; but the people have less affection for their chiefs, whom they never have an opportunity to see; for their country, which to them is like the whole world; and for their fellow-subjects, of which the greater part are utter strangers. The same laws cannot be convenient for so many various people of different manners, and climates, and who cannot be supposed to live equally happy under the same form of government. And yet different laws must occasion much trouble and confusion among people, who, living under the same administration, and carrying on a perpetual intercourse, frequently change their habitations, inter marry with each other, and, being educated under different customs, hardly ever know when their property is secure. Great talents lie buried, virtue lives obscured, and vice prevails with impunity, amidst that multitude of strangers, which flock together round the chief seat of administration. The principals, overwhelmed with a multiplicity of business, can look into nothing themselves; the government of the state being left to their deputies and clerks. In a word, the measures to be taken, in order to maintain the general authority, on which so many distant officers are ever ready to encroach or impose, engross the public attention; there is none of it left to be employed about the happiness of the people, and indeed hardly any for their defence in case of need: thus it is, that a body too unwieldy for its constitution grows debilitated and sinks under its own weight.

On the other hand, a state ought to be fixed on some basis, to secure its solidity, to be able to resist those shocks which it will not fail to encounter, and to make those efforts which it will find necessary to maintain its independence. Nations have all a kind of centrifugal force by which they act continually against each other, and tend, like the vortices of Descartes, to aggrandize themselves at the expence of their neighbours. Thus the weak run in danger of being presently swallowed up by the strong; nor is there any security for them, but by keeping themselves in equilibrio with the rest, and making the compression on every side equal.

Hence we see it is prudent in some cases to extend, and in others to restrain, the limits of a state; nor is it one of the least arts in civil polity to distinguish between one and the other, and to fix on that advantageous proportion which tends most to the preservation of the state. It may be observed in general, that the reasons for extending dominion, relating to objects external and relative, ought to be subordinate to those for contracting it, whose objects are internal and absolute. A sound and vigorous constitution is the first thing to be considered, and a much greater reliance is to be made on a good government, than on the resources which are to be drawn from an extensive territory.

Not but that there have been instances of states so constituted, that the necessity of their making conquests hath been essential to their very constitution. It is possible also they might felicitate themselves on that happy necessity, which pointed out, nevertheless, with the summit of their grandeur, the inevitable moment of their fall.

The magnitude of a body politic may be taken two ways; viz. by the extent of territory, and the number of the people; a certain proportional relation between them constituting the real greatness of a state. It is the people which form the state, and the territory which affords subsistence to the people; this relation, therefore, exists when the territory is sufficient for the subsistence of the inhabitants, and the inhabitants are as numerous as the territory can maintain. In this proportion consists the *maximum* of the force of any given number of people; for if the territory be too extensive, the defence of it is burthensome, the cultivation insufficient, and the produce superfluous; hence the proximate causes of defensive war. If, on the other hand, the territory be too small, the state is under the necessity of being obliged for part of its subsistence to its neighbours; hence the proximate causes of offensive war. Every people who, by their situation, have no other alternative than commerce or war, must be necessarily feeble: they must depend on their neighbours, on adventitious circumstances, and can only have a short and uncertain existence. They must conquer others, and thereby change their situation, or be conquered themselves, and thence be reduced to nothing. It is impossible such a state can preserve its independency but by its insignificancy or its greatness.

It is not easy to calculate the determinate relation between the extent of territory and number of inhabitants, sufficient for each other; not only on account of the difference in the qualities of the soil, in its degrees of fertility, in the nature of its productions, and in the influence of climate, but also on account of the remarkable difference in the temperament and constitution of the inhabitants; some consuming but little in a fertile country, and others a great deal on a barren soil. Regard must also be had to the degree of fecundity among the females, to the circumstances favourable or destructive to population, and to the number of people which the legislator may hope to draw from other countries by the advantages attending his scheme of government; so that he ought not to found his judgment on what actually exists; but on what he foresees may exist hereafter; not on the present state of population, but on that which will naturally succeed. In fine, there are a thousand occasions, on which local accidents acquire, or permit, a state to possess a larger share of territory than may appear actually necessary for present use. Thus a people may spread themselves over a large spot in a mountainous country, whose natural produce, of wood or pasture, requires less labour of cultivation; where experience teaches us that women are more fruitful than in the flat countries; and in which a large inclined superficies gives but a small horizontal base, by which only the land must be estimated in the affair of vegetation. A people, on the contrary, may inhabit a less space on the sea-shore, or even among rocks and almost barren sands; because the fishery supplies them with sustenance, instead of the produce of the earth; they can easily disburthen their community by sending out colonies of its supernumerary inhabitants; and lastly, because it is necessary for them in such a case to live near to each other, in order to repel the invasions of pyrates.

We may add to these conditional precautions, respecting the formation of a people, one that can be supplied by no other, but without which all the rest are useless: this is, that they should enjoy peace and plenty. For the time in which a state is forming, resembles that in which soldiers are forming a battalion; it is the moment in which they are least capable of resistance, and the most easily defeated. They would even make a greater resistance when put into absolute disorder afterwards, than during the interval of their first fermentation, when each is taken up more about his own particular rank than the common danger. Should a war, a famine, or a rebellion, break out at such a crisis, the state would be infallibly subverted.

Not but there have been many governments established in times of disorder and confusion: in such cases, however, those very governments subverted the state. Usurpers have always given rise to, or took the advantage of, those times of general confusion, in order to procure such destructive laws, which the people never could have been prevailed on to pass at a more dispassionate season. The choice of the proper time for the institution of laws, is one of the most certain tokens by which we may distinguish the design of a legislator from that of a tyrant.

If it be asked then, what people are in a situation to receive a system of laws? I answer, those who, though connected by some primitive union either of interest or compact, are not yet truly subjected to regular laws; those whose customs and prejudices are not deeply rooted; those who are under no fear of being swallowed up by a sudden invasion, and who, without entering into the quarrels of their neighbours, are able to encounter separately with each, or to engage the assistance of one to repel the other; a people whose individuals may be known to each other, and among whom it is not necessary to charge a man with a greater burthen than it is possible for him to bear; a people who can subsist without others, and without whom all others might subsist,[1] a people neither rich nor poor, but possessed of a competence within themselves; a people, in short, who possess at once the consistency of an ancient nation, and the docility of a newly-created one. The great difficulty in legislation, consists less in knowing what ought to be established than what ought to be eradicated; and what renders it so seldom successful, is the impossibility of finding the simplicity of nature in the wants of society. It is true that all these circumstances are very rarely united; and it is for this reason that so few states have much to boast of, in their constitution. There is still one country in Europe capable of receiving laws: this is the island of Corsica. The valour and constancy, with which those brave people recovered, and have defended their liberty, might deservedly excite some wise man to teach them how to preserve it. I cannot help surmising, that this little island will, one day or other, be the astonishment of Europe.

*　　*　　*

1. If two neighbouring people were so situated that one could not subsist without the other, the circumstances of the first would be very hard, and of the latter very dangerous. Every wise nation, in such a case, would extricate itself as soon as possible from such a state of dependence. The republic of Thlascala, situated in the heart of the Mexican empire, chose rather to be without salt than purchase it, or even receive it gratis of the Mexicans. The prudent Thlascalans saw through the snare of such liberality. Thus they preserved their liberty; this petty state, included within that great empire, being, in the end, the cause of its ruin.

THAT THE GENERAL WILL CANNOT BE ANNIHILATED

So long as a number of individuals remain perfectly united and consider themselves as one body, they can have but one will; which relates to their common preservation and welfare. All the resources of the state, are then simple and vigorous, its political maxims clear and obvious; it comprehends no intricate and opposite interests; but that of the public is demonstrably evident to all, and requires only the gift of common-sense to understand it. Peace, concord, and equality are enemies to political refinements. When men are honest, and simple, their very simplicity prevents their deception; they are not to be imposed on by sophistry, but are too artless even to be duped. When it is known, that, among the happiest people in the world, a number of peasants meet together under the shade of an oak, and regulate the affairs of state, with the most prudential economy, is it possible to forbear despising the refinements of other nations, who employ so much artifice and mystery to render themselves splendidly miserable?

A state thus simply governed hath need of but few laws, while in proportion as it becomes necessary to promulgate new ones, that necessity is universally apparent. The first person who proposes them, takes on himself to speak only what every one hath already thought; and neither eloquence nor intrigue is requisite to make that pass into a law, which every one had already resolved to do, as soon as he should be assured others would do the same.

That which deceives our reasoners on this subject, is, that, seeing none but such states as were badly constituted at their beginning, they are struck with the impossibility of maintaining such a policy in them. They smile to think of the absurdities, into which a designing knave or insinuating orator might lead the people of Paris and London. They are not apprized that a Cromwell, and a Beaufort, would have been treated as incendiaries at Berne and Geneva, and have underwent the discipline due to their demerit.

But when the bonds of society begin to relax, and the state to grow weak; when the private interests of individuals begin to appear, and that of parties to influence the state, the objects of public good meet with opposition; unanimity no longer presides in the assemblies of the people; the general will is no longer the will of all; contradictions and debates arise, and the most salutary counsel is not adopted without dispute.

Again, when the state is bordering on ruin, and exists only in empty form, when the social tie no longer connects the hearts of the people, when the basest motives of interest impudently assume the sacred name of the public good; then is the general will altogether silent; individuals, actuated by private motives, cherish no more the sentiments of citizens, than if the state had never existed, while the mock legislature pass, under the name of laws, those iniquitous decrees which have no other end than private interest.

Doth it follow from hence, however, that the general will is annihilated or corrupted? No. This remains ever constant, invariable, and pure; though it is subjected to that of party. There is not an individual who doth not see, while he detaches his own interest from that of the public, that he cannot separate himself from it entirely: but his share in the common evil seems nothing in comparison to the good which he proposes to secure exclusively to himself. Setting this motive aside, he is as ready to concur in measures for the good of the public, and that even for his own sake as any one. Nay, even in selling his vote, he doth not lose all sense of the general will; he only eludes it. The fault he is guilty of, lies in changing the state of the question, and making an answer to what is not asked him; so that, instead of admitting by his vote, *that it is to the interest of the state*, he says, *it is to the interest of such an individual or such a party, that this or that law should pass.* Thus the order which should prevail in the public assemblies of the state, should not be calculated so much to preserve the general will inviolate, as to cause it to be always interrogated, and to make it answer.

I might here make a variety of reflections on the simple right of voting in every act of the sovereignty; a right which the citizens cannot be deprived of: as also on the rights of thinking, proposing and debating on public matters; privileges which government is ever solicitous enough to confine to its own members. This subject, however, is of importance enough to deserve a whole treatise of itself; and it is impossible for me to say every thing in the present.

On Votes

It is evident, from what hath been said in the preceding chapter, that the manner in which public affairs are carried on, may afford a sure indication of the actual state of manners, and the health of the body politic. The more concord there is in public assemblies, that is to say, the nearer the members approach to unanimity in giving their votes, the more prevalent is the general will among them: but long debates, dissentions and commotions, evince the ascendency of particular interests and the decline of the state.

This appears less evident, indeed, when two or more orders of men, enter into the constitution; as at Rome, where the quarrels of the Patricians and Plebeians occasioned frequent disturbances in the *Comitia*, even in the most flourishing times of the republic. This exception however, is more apparent than real: as in that case there exists, by a defect inherent in the body politic, two states in one; and that which is not true of both together, may nevertheless be true of each apart. It is also true in fact that, even during the most turbulent times of the republic, the decrees of the Plebeians, when the Senate did not intermeddle, were passed with great tranquillity agreeable to the plurality of voices. The citizens having but one common interest, the people could have but one will.

Unanimity returns again at the opposite extremity of the circle; and this is where the citizens, reduced to slavery, have neither liberty nor will. In such a situation, fear and flattery pervert their votes into acclamations; they no longer deliberate among themselves; but either adore or curse their tyrants. Such were the debased principles of the Senate under the Roman emperors. Under these circumstances also, the sentiments of the public were frequently expressed, with the most ridiculous precaution; Tacitus observing that, under Otho, the Senators, while they loaded Vitellius with execrations, they affected at the same time to make a confused and clamorous noise, in order to prevent his knowing, should he become their master, what any individual had said.

From these considerations may be deduced the maxims, on which the manner of counting votes, and comparing different suffrages, should be regulated, according as the general will is more or less easy to be discovered, and the state more or less advanced towards its decline. There is but one law, which in its own nature, requires unanimous consent: and this is the social compact. For civil association is the most voluntary act in the world: every man being born free, and master of himself, no one can lay him under restraint, on any pretence whatever, without his own consent. To affirm that the son of a slave is born a slave, is to affirm he is not born a man.

If there be any persons, however, who oppose this contract itself, their opposition does not invalidate that contract; it only hinders their being comprehended therein; and they remain aliens in the midst of citizens. When a state is formed, a consent to its institution is inferred by the residence of the party: to submit to residence in any country is to submit to its sovereignty.[2]

---

2. This must always be understood, however, of a free state, from which people have the liberty to depart with their effects at pleasure. For in others the consideration of their family, their property, the want of an asylum, necessity or violence, may detain an inhabitant in a country contrary to his will; in which case, his simple residence neither implies his consent to the contract, nor his violation of it.

If we except this primitive contract, the determination of the majority is always obligatory on the rest: this is a necessary consequence of the contract itself. But it may be asked, how can a man be free, and yet be obliged to conform to the will of others. How can the members of an opposition be called free-men, who are compelled to submit to laws which they have not consented to? I answer that this question is not properly stated. The citizen consents to all laws passed by a majority, though some of them in particular may have passed contrary to his inclination; nay be consents to those by which he is punishable for the breach of any one. The constant will of all the members of a state, is the general will; and it is this alone that makes them either citizens or freemen.[3] When a law is proposed in the assembly of the people, they are not precisely demanded, whether they severally approve or reject the proposition; but whether it be conformable or not to the general will, which is theirs as a collective body; each person, therefore, in giving his vote declares his opinion on this head, and on counting the votes, the declaration of the general will, is inferred from the majority. When a law thus passes contrary to my opinion, it proves nothing more than that I was mistaken, and that I concluded the general will to be what it really was not. So that, if my particular advice had been followed, it would have been contrary to my will, which as a citizen is the same as the general, and in that case I should not have been free.

This argument supposes, indeed, that all the characteristics of the general will, are contained in the plurality of votes: and when this ceases to be the case, take what course you will, there is an end of liberty.

In having shewn how the will of particulars and parties is substituted for the general, in public deliberations, I have already sufficiently pointed out the practicable means of preventing such abuses; of this, however, I shall speak further hereafter. With regard to the proportional number of votes that indicate this general will, I have also laid down the principles on which it may be determined. The difference of a single voice is enough to break the unanimity; but between unanimity and an equality there is a variety of proportions; to each of which the number in question may be applied, according to the circumstances of the body politic.

There are two general maxims, which may serve to regulate these proportions: the one is, that the more grave and important the deliberations, the

---

3. At Genoa we see the word *Libertas* inscribed on the chains of the galley slaves, and on the doors of the prisoners: the application of which device is beautiful and just; as it is in fact only the criminals of all states that infringe the liberty of the citizen. A country, whose malefactors should be all actually chained to the oar, would be a country of the most perfect liberty.

nearer ought the determination to approach to unanimity: the other is, that the more expedition the affair requires, the less should unanimity be insisted on. In deliberations where the matter should be immediately determined, the majority of a single vote should be sufficient. The first of these maxims seems most applicable to permanent laws, and the second to matters of business. But be this as it may, it is from their judicious combination, that the best proportions must be deduced, concerning that plurality in whose votes should be supposed to consist the general will.

Of Elections

With regard to the election of a prince or of magistrates, which, as I before observed is a complicated act; there are two methods of proceeding; viz. by choice and by lot. They have each been made use of in different republics; and we see in our own times, a very intricate mixture of both in the election of the doge of Venice.

The preference by lot, says Montesquieu, *is of the nature of a democracy.* This I admit, but not for the reasons given. *The choice by lot,* says he, *is a method which offends no-body; by permitting each citizen to entertain the reasonable hope of being preferred to the service of his country.*

This, however, is not the true reason. If we reflect that the election of chiefs is a function of government and not of the sovereignty, we shall see the reason why this method is of the nature of a democracy, in which the administration is so much the better, as its acts are fewer.

In every real democracy the office of magistrate is not advantageous but expensive and burthensome, so that it were unjust to impose it on one person rather than another. The law, therefore, imposes that charge on him, to whose lot it falls. For in this case, all standing an equal chance, the choice doth not depend on human will, nor can any particular application change the universality of the law.

In an aristocracy the prince makes choice of the prince; and, the government providing for itself, here it is that votes are properly applicable. The apparent exception, in the election of the doge of Venice, confirms this distinction, instead of destroying it: such a mixt form as is used by the

Venetians is adapted to a mixt government. For it is a mistake to suppose the government of Venice a true aristocracy. If the lower order of people, indeed, have no share in the government, the nobility stand in their place, and become the people in respect to the administration. What a number is there of the inferior order of nobles, who stand no chance of ever getting into the magistracy, and reap no other advantage from their rank than the empty title of Excellency, and the privilege of sitting in the great Council. This great council being as numerous as our general council at Geneva, its illustrious members have no greater privileges therefore than our ordinary citizens. It is certain, that setting aside the extreme disparity of the two republics, the burghers of Geneva represent exactly the Patricians of Venice; our natives and sojourners represent the citizens and people, and our peasants the inhabitants of the *terra firma* belonging to that state. In a word, consider their Venetian republic in what light you will, abstracted from its grandeur, its government, is no more aristocratical than that of Geneva. All the difference is that we have no occasion for this kind of election.

The choice by lot, is attended with very little inconvenience in a real democracy, when all men being nearly on an equality, as well with regard to manners and abilities, as to sentiments and fortune, the matter of choice is indifferent. But I have already observed a true democracy is only imaginary.

When the election is of a mixt form, viz. by vote and by lot, the first ought to provide for those officers which require proper talents, as in military affairs; the other being best adapted to those which require only common sense, honesty and integrity; such as the offices of judicature; because in a well-formed state, those qualities are possessed by all the citizens in common.

No election either by vote or lot, hath place under a monarchical government; the monarch himself being the only rightful prince and legal magistrate, the choice of his substitute is vested in him alone. When the Abbé de St. Pierre, therefore, proposed to increase the number of the king's councils in France, and to elect their members by ballot, he was not aware that he proposed to change the form of the French government.

LOUIS SÉBASTIEN MERCIER
(1740–1814)

In the Year 2500[*]

In the last decades of the *ancien régime,* Mercier was a typical Parisian litterateur not far above the Grub Street level. He taught rhetoric and later history, and during the period of the Revolution served in the Convention and in the Council of Five Hundred. Though a member of Napoleon's Institute, he remained a republican throughout the Empire. As a dramatist he demanded liberation from the forms and subject matter of classical art, and urged that the theater concern itself with modern society and ordinary men. The work here excerpted, originally published in 1771 and entitled *L'An 2440,* laments the intellectual debasement that tyranny has fostered in France, and envisions a future society where justice is enthroned and the arts and sciences flourish.

[*]From Louis Sébastien Mercier, *Memoirs of the Year Two Thousand Five Hundred,* trans. W. Hooper, M.D. (Dublin: W. Wilson, 1772), I, pp. i–iii; II, pp. 34–49; I, pp. 81–95.

J'ai sept cent ans,

Engraving from *L'An 2440*, Paris, 1786.

Epistle Dedicatory to the Year 2500

August and venerable Year! thou who art to bring felicity upon the earth! thou, alas! that I have only in a dream beheld, when thou shalt rise from out the bosom of eternity, thy sun shall enlighten them who will tread upon my ashes, and upon those of thirty generations, successively cut off, and plunged in the profound abyss of death. The kings that now sit upon the throne shall be no more; their posterity shall be no more. Then shalt thou judge the departed monarch, and the writer who lived in subjection to his power. The names of the friends, the defenders of humanity, shall live and be honoured, their glory shall be pure and radiant; but that vile herd of kings, who have been, in every sense, the tormentors of mankind, still more deeply plunged in oblivion than in the regions of death, can only escape from infamy by the favour of inanity.

The thought survives the man, and forms his most glorious possession; the thought rises from his tomb, assumes an immutable body, becomes immortal. While the thunders of despotism fall and vanish, the pen of the writer, bounding over the interval of time, absolves or punishes the masters of the universe.

I have exercised that authority which nature gave me; I have cited before my solitary reason the laws, the customs, and abuses of the country in which I have lived obscure and unknown. I have felt that virtuous hatred which is due to oppression from a being of humanity; I have detested, pursued with infamy, to the utmost of my power, opposed all tyranny. But, alas! August and Venerable Year, perhaps to little purpose, when contemplating thee, have I animated, exalted my ideas; they may appear in thy eyes the mere conceptions of servitude. Forgive me; the genius of my age surrounds and oppresses me. Stupidity now reigns; the tranquility of my country resembles that of the grave. I see nought around me but coloured carcases, who move and talk, but in whom the active principle of life has never produced the least emotion. Even now, the voice of philosophy, wearied and dejected, cries in the midst of mankind as in the center of a boundless desert.

Oh! could I but divide the term of my existence, with what pleasure would I instantly descend to the grave! with what joy should I part from the gloomy, wretched aspects of my co-temporaries, to awake in the midst of those fair days that thou shalt bring forth; that blissful period, when man shall have regained his courage, his liberty, his independence, and his virtue! How happy, could I but behold thee otherwise than in a dream! Haste! thou age so desired, thou object of my earnest wishes! Come, and pour down happiness upon the earth! But what do I say? Delivered from the illusions of a pleasing dream, I fear, alas! I fear, that thy sun is more like to cast a gloomy light on a formless mass of ashes, and of ruins.

The Academy of Science

We advanced toward the academy. It still preserved that name; but how different its situation from that where it was formerly held! It no longer made a part of the palace of a king. How wonderful are the revolutions of ages! A pope now sits in the place of the Caesars! ignorance and superstition inhabit Athens! the fine arts have flown to Russia! Would it have been believed in my time, that a mountain marked with ridicule for merely affording nurture to a few asses by its thistles, should become the just image of the ancient Parnassus, the seat of genius, the habitation of renowned writers? They would have abolished the name of Montmartre, but from a complaisance to received prejudices.

This august spot, cloathed on all sides by venerable woods, is consecrated to solitude; an express law forbids the approach of all discordant noise. The earth has produced fresh beds of stone to form the foundations of this noble asylum. On this mount, blessed with the most genial rays of the sun, are nourished fair trees, whose towering summits sometimes embrace each other, and sometimes at distance keep, to afford the exploring eye a prospect of the face of heaven.

As I mounted with my guide, I observed, here and there, elegant hermitages, distinct from each other. I asked who inhabited those flowery spots, half concealed by the woods, and half exposed to view, whose aspect appeared so engaging.—"You shall soon know," was replied; "let us now hasten; the hour approaches." In fact, I saw a great number of persons arrive from every side, not in coaches, but on foot. Their conversation seemed to be highly pleasing and animated. We entered an edifice sufficiently large, but decorated with great simplicity. I observed no Swiss, armed with a heavy halberd, at the door of the tranquil sanctuary of the Muses; there was nothing to forbid entrance amidst a crowd of worthy men.[1]

The hall was remarkably sonorous; so that the most feeble academic voice might be heard at the greatest distance. The order that there reigned was not less remarkable; several rows of benches surrounded the hall; for they knew that the ear should be at its ease in an academy, as the eye in the saloon of a painter. I considered every object at my leisure. The number of academics seats was not ridiculously fixed; but what seemed most singular was, that, on the back of every chair, a scroll was displayed, on which were distinctly wrote the titles of that academician who chose it for his seat; every one might place himself in an armed chair without any other previous ceremony than that of displaying the scroll that contained the title of his works. It is easy to conceive, that no one offered to display a charte blanche, as was done in my day, by bishops, marshals, and preceptors;[2] still less would they dare to expose to the severe public eye the title of a work of mean merit, or a servile imitation; it must be a work that points out some new discovery in the arts, or, at least, that excels all others on the same subject.[3]

My guide pulled me by the sleeve—"You seem astonished; let me increase your wonder. Those charming habitations which you observed on ascending the mountain, form the retreats of those who are struck by an unknown power that commands them to write. Our academicians are Carthusians;[4] it is in solitude that genius displays its powers, forsakes the beaten path, and discovers unknown regions. When does enthusiasm spring forth? When the author descends into himself, when he investigates his own soul, that profound mine, of whose value the possessor is not unfrequently ignorant. What inspirers are retreat and friendship![5] What more is necessary to those who

1. I have ever been highly curious to see a man of genius, and have thought that I discovered in his port, his actions, the air of his head, his countenance, and aspect, something that distinguished him from the common race of men. The science of physiognomy still remains to be properly investigated.

2. We have seen on the Boulevards an automaton that articulated sounds, and the people flock to admire it. How many automata, with human faces, do we see at court, at the bar, in the academies, who owe their speech to the breath of invisible agents; when they cease, the machines remain dumb.

3. There are no longer any means left to distinguish ourselves, they say. Wretches! that hunt after smoke, the path of virtue still lies before you; there you will find but few competitors; but that is not the sort of glory that you seek. I understand you; you would become the subject of popular discourse. I sigh for you, and for the human race.

4. Let him who would acquire a strength of mind, assiduously exert its powers; the greatest sluggard is ever the greatest slave.

5. Man has much longer time to live with the mind than with the senses; he would therefore act wisely to depend for his pleasures on the former rather than on the latter.

search for nature and truth? Where do we hear their sublime voice? In the tumult of cities, amidst that crowd of low pursuits, that, unknown to ourselves, besiege the heart? No; it is amidst the rural scenes that the soul rejuvenates; it is there that it contemplates the majesty of the universe, that majesty eloquent and all-gracious; the thought strikes, the expression glows; the image and its splendor become widely extended, like the horizon that surrounds us.

"In your days, the men of letters frequented the circles to amuse the coquettes, and obtain an equivocal smile; they sacrificed all that was bold and manly to the superstitious empire of fashion; they divested the soul of its real nature, to please the age. Instead of looking forward to an august series of ages, they rendered themselves slaves to a momentary taste. In a word, they pursued ingenious falshoods; they stifled that inward voice which cries, *Be severe as the time that flies; be inexorable as posterity.*

"These academics, moreover, here enjoy that happy mediocrity,[6] which, amongst us, constitutes sovereign wealth. We do not offer to interrupt them, either with a desire to discover the least movements of their minds, or from a vanity of being admitted to their company. We revere their time, as we do the hallowed bread of the indigent; but attentive to their desires, at the least signal they find them gratified."—If that be the case, you must have sufficient employment. Are there not those who assume the rank to cover their idleness or real weakness?—"No; this region is so strongly illuminated, that the least spot is easily discovered. Imposture dare not here intrude; it can never bear the look of a man of genius, whose piercing eye nought can deceive. For those whom presumption may bring hither,[7] there are persons of a benign temper, who effectually dissuade them from a project that cannot redound to their honour. In a word, the law enjoins. . . ."—Our conversation was interrupted by a sudden general silence in the assembly. My whole soul flew to my ear, when I beheld one of the academicians prepare to read a manuscript which he held in his hand, and with a grace by no means insignificant.

O ungrateful memory, how could I reproach thee? Why didst thou desert me? Would that I could repeat the persuasive discourse pronounced by that academic! The force, the method, the flowing periods have escaped me; but the impression on my mind can never be effaced. No; never was I so enraptured. The visage of each auditor reflected those sentiments with which I

6. The great man is modest; the man of mediocrity displays his indifferent advantages; so the majestic river glides silently along, while the rivulet runs chattering over the rugged pebbles.

7. There is no object that may not be viewed from a hundred different stations; but there is only one from whence it can be justly beheld; and if that is not chosen, genius and labour become useless.

was agitated; it was one of the most delicious enjoyments my heart ever felt. What depths! what images! what truths! what a noble flame! how sublime a tone! The orator declaimed against envy,[8] described the sources of that fatal passion, its horrible effects, the infamy it has cast on the laurels that have crowned many great men; all its vile, unjust, detestable qualities were so strongly painted, that while we deplored the fate of its blind, unhappy victims, we trembled lest our own hearts should be infected by its poison. The mirror was so properly presented before each particular character, their meanness exposed in such various and ridiculous lights, the human heart displayed in a manner so new, so refined, so striking, that it was impossible not to know them; and when knowing, not to form the design of abjuring that miserable weakness. The fear of bearing some resemblance to that frightful monster, envy, produced a happy effect. I saw, O instructive sight! O moment unheard of in the annals of literature! I saw the members of that assembly regard each other with a tender and sympathizing look; I saw them mutually open their arms, embrace, and cry with joy; their bosoms resting and panting against each other; I saw (will it be believed?) the authors dispersed about the room imitate the affectionate transports of the academicians, and convinced of the talents of their brethren, swear an unalterable, eternal friendship; I saw the tears of affection and benevolence flow from every eye. They were a company of brothers, who substituted that honourable applause in the room of our stupid clapping of hands.[9]

After the full enjoyment of those delicious moments; after each one had expressed the various sensations that he had felt, and those strokes by which he was most strongly affected; and after frequently repeating the vows of endless friendship, another member of this august society arose with a smiling air; an applauding murmur ran through the hall, for he was esteemed a Socratic railer.[10] He raised his voice, and said,

"Gentlemen, Many reasons have induced me to offer you to day a short, but, I think, curious extract of what our academy was in its infancy, that is,

8. How I pity the envious and jealous mind, that glances over the valuable parts of a work, and knows not how to enjoy them. By analogy it dwells on those parts only that are imperfect. The man of letters who by an habitual exercise of reason and taste, improves the one and the other, and incessantly creates to himself new joys, is of all men the most happy—if he can divest himself of jealousy or of an over sensibility.

9. When, at the theatre or the academy, an affecting or sublime passage strikes the assembly, instead of that sigh from the bottom of the heart, and the silent emotions, I hear those clappings redoubled till they shake the roof, I say to myself, these people have no feeling; they are men of wood that strike two boards together.

10. As a malignant raillery is the fruit of an iniquitous disposition, so an ingenious pleasantry is the fruit of wisdom. A sprightly temper and graceful manner were the most triumphant arms of Socrates.

about the eighteenth century. The cardinal who was our founder, and whom our predecessors have so extravagantly extolled, and to whom they attributed, in our establishment, the most profound designs, would never have formed this institution, (let us confess it) if he had not himself made wretched verses which he idolized, and which he was desirous that we should celebrate. That cardinal, I say, at the time he invited the authors to form one body, discovered his despotic temper, when he made them subject to rules ever unknown to genius. Our founder had so imperfect an idea of what such a society ought to be, that he limited the number of members to forty; so that Corneille and Montesquieu might have waited at the door to the end of their days. This cardinal imagined, moreover, that genius would naturally remain in obscurity, if titles and dignities did not rouse it from its inanity. When he formed this strange judgment, surely, he could think of such rhimers only as Colletet and his colleagues, whom he supported out of mere vanity.

"From thence it became an established custom, that they who had money in the room of merit, and titles instead of genius, seated themselves by those whose names had been celebrated by fame throughout all Europe. He was himself the first example, and he was but too well imitated. When those great men who drew the attention of their own age, and whose regards were fixed on that of posterity, had covered with glory the place where they held their assemblies, the gilt and titled idiots besieged the door; nay, almost presumed to declare, that they reflected honour on the society by their paltry ribbons, and, in fact, believed, or pretended to believe, that, by seating themselves by men of genius, they actually resembled them.

"Then were seen marshals, as well victorious as beaten, mitred heads that had never made a mandate, men of the long robe, preceptors, and financiers, who pretended to the title of men of genius; and though they were nothing more than the decorations of the theatre, really believed themselves to be capital performers. Some eight or ten among the forty shone by their own lustre; the rest had only a borrowed light; yet it was necessary to wait for the death of an academician in order to fill his place, and which, nevertheless, for the most part, still remained empty.

"What could be more ludicrous than to see that academy, whose renown was spread over all the capital, hold its assemblies in a small, close, mean room? There, in several armed chairs, that were formerly red, were seen, from time to time, a number of indolent wretches, carelessly seated, weighing of syllables, or carefully culling the words out of some piece of prose or poetry, in order, at last, to applaud the most unmeaning among them. But, on the other hand, pray remark it, gentlemen, they never erred in calculating the number of counters that each gained by the absence of his brethren. Can you believe that they gave the conqueror a gold medal in the room of a branch of oak, and that on it there was engraved this ridiculous inscription: *A l'imortalité?* Alas! that immortality passed the next day into the goldsmith's crucible; and that was the most real advantage the victorious champion obtained.

"Could you imagine, that those little victories sometimes turned the conquerors brains, so great was their ridiculous vanity?[11] and that the judges exercised scarce any other function than that of distributing those useless prizes, about which no one even ever made inquiry?

"The place of their assembly was open to none but authors; and they were admitted by tickets only. In the morning was performed a musical mass; then a trembling priest pronounced the panegyric of Lewis IX. (I know not very well why) extolling him for more than an hour, though he was certainly a bad sovereign.[12] Then the orator declaimed on the croisades, which highly inflamed the archbishop's bile, who interdicted the priestly orator, for his temerity in displaying good sense. In the evening was another eulogy; but as that was on a profane subject the archbishop happily did not concern himself with the doctrine it contained.

"It is proper to remark, that the place where they displayed their wit was guarded by fusileers and gigantic Swiss, who understood no French. Nothing was more comic than the contrast between the meagre figure of the man of letters, and the enormous blustering stature of the Swiss. This was called *a public assembly*. The public, it is true, were there; but it was at the door; a poor acknowledgement for their complaisance. In the mean time, the sole liberty that remained to the nation was to pronounce absolutely on prose or verse, to condemn one author, applaud another, and sometimes laugh at them all.

"The academic rage, however, possessed every brain; every one would be a royal censor,[13] and then an academician. They calculated the lives of all the

11. Except the university prizes, which give rise to a foolish pride in childish heads, I know of nothing more pernicious than the medals of our literary academies. The conqueror really thinks himself a person of consequence, and is ruined for the remainder of his days; he disdains every one who has not been crowned with so rare and illustrious a laurel. See in the Mercure de France, for the month of September, 1769, page 184, an instance of the most ridiculous egotism. A very diminutive author informs the publick, that when he was at college, he performed his theme better than his colleagues; he glories in it, and imagines that he maintains the same rank in the republic of letters.—*Risum teneatis, amici?*

12. The first penal edict against particular sentiments or opinions was denounced by Lewis IX. vulgarly called St. Lewis.

13. Royal censor! I never hear that word without laughter. We Frenchmen know not how ridiculous we are, nor what right we give posterity to regard us with pity.

members of the academy, remarked the degree of vigour that their stomachs discovered at table; death seemed to the candidates to be slow in his approach; the cry was, They are immortal! When a new member was chosen, some one muttered softly, Ah! when shall I make thy eulogy at the bottom of the long table, standing with my hat on, and declare thee to be a great man, as well as Lewis XIV. and the chancellor Seguier, while you sleep profoundly under your tomb-stone decorated with a curious epitaph.

"The men of money at last so far prevailed in a golden age, that they completely banished the men of letters; so that in the following generation, messieurs the farmers-general, were in possession of the forty armed chairs, where they snored as much at their ease as their predecessors; and were still more dextrous in dividing the counters. From thence it was that the old proverb arose, *There is no entering the academy without an equipage.*

"The men of letters, unable to regain their usurped dominion, and drove to despair, conspired in form. They had recourse to their usual weapons, epigrams, songs, and vaudevilles;[14] they exhausted all the arrows from the quiver of satire; but, alas! all their attacks were fruitless; the hearts of their adversaries were become so callous as to be no longer penetrable, even by the piercing strokes of ridicule; all the bon mots of messieurs the authors would have been thrown away but for the aid of a violent indigestion, that surprised the academicians on a certain day, when assembled at a splendid feast. Those three divinities, Apollo, Pluto, and the god of the digestive faculty, quarrelled with each other; Indigestion attacking them under the double title of financiers and academics, destroyed them almost all; the men of letters again entered their ancient dominion, and the academy was saved . . ."

There was an universal burst of laughter in the assembly. Some of them asked me, in a low voice, if the account was just. Yes, I replied, for the most part; but when we look down on past times from the summit of seven hundred years, it is doubtless easy to give a ridiculous turn to what then existed. For the rest, the academy agreed, even in my time, that each member who composed it was of more worth than the institution itself. Nothing can be added to that confession. The misfortune is, that when men meet in assemblies, their heads contract, as Montesquieu said, who ought to know.

I passed into an apartment that contained the portraits of the academicians, as well ancient as modern; I took particular notice of those that succeeded the academics now living; but, to avoid offence, I shall not name them.

---

14. Poor arms! which even are now prohibited, and which the insolent pride of the great at once seeks after and dreads.

Hélas! la vérité si souvent est cruelle,
On l' aime, et les humains sont malheureux par elle.
                                        VOLT.

Alas! the truth we love, though oft we find
Her cruel, and a foe to human kind.

I cannot, however, refrain from relating a fact that will certainly give
great pleasure to every generous mind, that loves justice and detests tyranny;
which is, that the portrait of the abbé St. Pierre was reinstated in its rank with
all the honours due to such exemplary virtue. They had effaced the turpitude
of which the academy had rendered itself culpable, while it bowed the neck
to a yoke of a servitude it ought never to have known. They had placed this
inestimable and virtuous writer between Fénelon and Montesquieu. I gave
the praises due to this noble equity. I saw no portrait of Richelieu, nor of
Christina, nor of ——, nor ——, nor ——, which, though but paintings, had
been for ever discarded.

As I descended the mountain, I cast my eyes many times on those lovely
groves where dwelt the men of brilliant genius, who, in silence, and in the
contemplation of nature, laboured to form the hearts of their countrymen to
virtue, to the love of the true and beautiful; when softly I said: Would that
I could render myself worthy of this academy!

Execution of a Criminal

The repeated mournful sounds of a dreadful clarion suddenly struck my ear,
and seemed to murmur to the air the names of misery and death; the drums
of the city guards went slowly round, beating the alarm; and these ominous
sounds, repeated by the mind, filled it with a profound horror. I saw the
citizens come forth with doleful aspects; each one addressed his neighbour,
and lifting his eyes to heaven, wept, and showed all the tokens of the most
piercing grief. I asked one of them, why tolled the funeral bells, and what
accident had happened?

"One that is most terrible," he replied, with a groan. "Justice this day is
forced to condemn a citizen to lose his life, of which he has rendered himself
unworthy, by embruing his murdering hands in his brother's blood. More

than thirty years have passed since the sun beheld a crime like this. Before the day is finished, he must expire. O, what tears have I shed for the fury that drove him to such a blind vengeance! Have you heard the particulars of the crime that was committed the night before last? O grief! is it not enough that we have lost one worthy citizen; but must another suffer death?"—He sighed bitterly.—"Hear, hear the story of that direful event, which has spread over us an universal lamentation.

"One of our fellow-citizens, of a fiery disposition, from his birth remarkable for passion, though otherwise a man of merit, was on the point of being married to a young woman whom he loved to distraction. Her temper was as gentle as that of her lover was impetuous; she flattered herself, however, with being able to soften his manners; but the many sallies of wrath that escaped him, notwithstanding all his care to conceal them, made her tremble for the direful consequences that might proceed from a union with a man of his violent temper. Every woman, by our law, is absolute mistress of her person; she therefore determined, from a fear of being miserable, to marry another, who was of a character more conformable to her own. The torch of these nuptials set fire to the rage of an implacable heart, which in the tenderest years had never known moderation. He gave many private challenges to his happy rival, who despised them; for he knew there was more bravery in disdaining an insult, and in stifling a resentment, than in yielding to the impulse of passion, in a manner that both our laws and reason proscribe. The enraged man, listening to nothing but jealousy, rencountered the other, the day before yesterday, in a private path without the city, and on his refusing again to combat with him, he seized a branch of a tree, and laid him dead at his feet. After this horrid act, the inhuman wretch dared to come amongst us; but his crime was already engraved on his front; we no sooner saw him, than we discovered that he was criminal, though then ignorant of the nature of his offence. But soon we saw several citizens, their cheeks wet with tears, who bore, with solemn steps, to the foot of the throne of justice, the bloody corpse that cried for vengeance.

"At the age of fourteen, they read to us the laws of our country. Every one is obliged to write them with his own hand, and to make oath that he will observe them.[1] These laws command us to inform the police of all those

---

1. It is scarce to be believed, that the most important of our laws, as well civil as criminal, are unknown to the greatest part of the nation. It would be extremely easy to imprint them with a character of majesty; but they are only published to thunder on the guilty, and not to excite the citizen to virtue. The sacred code of the laws is wrote in a dry and barbarous language, and sleeps among the dust of the rolls. Would it not be proper to clothe it with the charms of eloquence, and by that means render it respectable to the multitude?

infractions that offend against the order of society; but they intend those matters only that cause a real detriment. We renew this sacred oath every ten years; and without being busy informers, religiously watch over the preservation of our venerable laws.

"Yesterday they published the monitory, which is an act entirely civil. Whoever should delay to declare what he knew would be branded with infamy. By this means it is that homicide is soon discovered. None but a villain, for a long time familiarized with guilt, can cooly deny the crime he has just committed; and of this sort of monsters our nation is purged; they no longer terrify us, but in the histories of past ages.

"Obey, with me, the voice of justice, that calls all the people to be witness of its awful decrees. It is the day of its triumph; and, fatal as it is, we receive it with applause. You will not see a wretch who has been plunged for six months in a dungeon, his eyes dazzled by the light of the sun, his bones broken by a previous and secret punishment more horrible than that he is going to suffer,[2] advance with hideous and dying looks, towards a scaffold erected in an obscure nook. In your time, the criminal, judged in the secrecy of a prison, was sometimes broke on the wheel in the silence of the night, at the door of some sleeping citizen; who waking with terror at the cries of the excruciated wretch, was uncertain whether he was suffering under the iron bar of an executioner, or the sword of an assassin. We have none of those tortures that are shocking to nature; we have a regard to humanity even with them who have offended against it. In your age, they seemed not to be content with merely putting a man to death, so little effect the tragic scenes had upon you, all horrible as they were, and multiplied in cold blood. The guilty, far from being dragged along in a manner that is disgraceful to justice, is not even fettered. Alas! why should he be loaded with chains, when he freely delivers himself up to death? Justice has full power to condemn him to death, but not to charge him with marks of slavery. You will see him walk freely in the midst of some soldiers, who surround him merely to keep off the multitude. We have no fear that he will a second time disgrace himself by endeavouring to fly from the terrible voice that accuses him. Whither should he fly? What country, what people would receive among them an

---

2. Wretched is the state that refines on its penal laws. Is not the punishment of death sufficient; but must man add to its horror? Can I e be called a magistrate who interrogates with torturing machines, and gradually crushes a wretch by a slow progression of the most horrid pangs? who, ingenious in his tortures, stops death, when, gentle and charitable, it advances to deliver the victim? Here nature revolts. But if you would be more fully convinced of the inutility of the torture, see the admirable Treatise on Crimes and Punishments. I defy any man to produce one solid reason in favour of that barbarous law.

assassin?[3] and how could he ever efface that horrid mark which the hand of the Divinity imprints on the front of a murderer; the tempest of remorse is there painted in glaring characters; and the eye accustomed to the aspect of virtue will easily distinguish the physiognomy of guilt. How, in short, can he ever be free who feels the immense weight that presses upon his heart!"

We arrived at a spacious place that surrounded the palace of justice. Along the front of the hall of audience there ran a large flight of steps. It was on this kind of amphitheatre that the senate assembled on public affairs, in the sight of the people; it was under their inspection that it chose to transact the most important affairs of the nation; the numerous body of citizens there assembled inspired them with sentiments worthy of the august concerns committed to their care. The death of a citizen was a calamity to the state. The judges failed not to give their sentence all that solemnity, all that importance it deserved. The order of advocates were on one side, constantly ready to plead for the innocent, but silent in the cause of the guilty. On the other side, the prelate, accompanied by the pastors, bare-headed, silently invoked the God of Mercy, and edified the people, spread in crowds over all the place.[4]

The criminal appeared; he was dressed in a bloody shirt; he beat his breast, and shewed all the marks of a sincere repentance. His visage, however, expressed nothing of that dreadful embarrassment so unbecoming a man, who

---

3. They say that Europe is civilized; and yet a man who has committed a murder, or made a fraudulent bankruptcy, can retire to London, Madrid, Lisbon, Vienna, etc., and there peaceably enjoy the fruits of his iniquity. Among so many puerile treaties, can they not stipulate, that the murderer shall no where find an asylum? Is not every state and every man interested in his punishment? But monarchs will as soon agree on the destruction of the Jesuits.

4. Our form of justice does not command awe, but excites disgust. It is an odious and shocking sight to see a man take off his laced hat, lay down his sword on the scaffold, mount the ladder in a suit of silk or lace, and dance indecently on the body of the wretch that is hanging. Why not give the executioner that formidable aspect he ought to shew? To what purpose is this cold barbarity? The laws thereby lose their dignity, and the punishment its terror. The judge is still more sprucely powdered than the hangman. Shall I here declare the sensations that I have felt? I have trembled, not for the criminal's offence, but for the horrid unconcern of all those that surrounded him. There has been none but that generous man who reconciled the unfortunate sinner to the Supreme Being, who assisted him in drinking the cup of death, that appeared to me to have any remains of humanity. Do we only wish to destroy mankind? Are we ignorant of the art of terrifying the imagination without violence to humanity? Learn at length, thoughtless and cruel men, learn to be judges, learn how to prevent crimes; conciliate what is owing to the law with what is owing to man. I have not the power to speak here of those artful tortures that some criminals have suffered, who seem to have been reserved, so to say, for a privileged punishment. O disgrace to my country! the eyes of that sex which seems made for pity remained the longest fixed on that scene of horrors. Let us draw the curtain. What can I say to those who understand me not?

ought to know how to die when necessity calls, and especially when he merits death. They made him pass by a sort of cage, where, they told me, the body of the murdered man was exposed. On his near approach, he was seized with such violent remorse, that they suffered him to retire. He approached the judges, and put one knee to the ground, to kiss the sacred volume of the law. It was then opened to him, and they read, with a loud voice, the sentence relative to homicides; they placed the book before him, that he might read it; he then fell on his knees, and confessed his guilt. The head of the senate, mounting a platform that was prepared for him, read his condemnation with a strong and majestic voice. All the counsellors, as well as the advocates, who were standing, then sat down, by which they declared that no one of them would undertake his defence.

When the head of the senate had done reading, he deigned to stretch out his hand to the criminal, and raise him up; he then said, "nothing now remains for you but to die with firmness, and obtain your pardon of God and of men. We do not hate you; we grieve for you, and your memory will not be held in detestation by us. Obey the law with chearfulness, and revere its salutary rigour. Our tears bear witness that affection will take place in our hearts, when justice shall have accomplished her fatal decrees. Death is less dreadful than ignominy. Submit to the one, to avoid the other. It is still in your power to choose. If you will live, you may; but it must be in disgrace, and loaded with our indignation. You will behold the sun constantly upbraiding you with having deprived your fellow-being of his genial and brilliant rays; to you they will be hateful, as they will only discover those disdainful looks with which all men regard an assassin. You will bear about with you every where the load of your remorse, and the eternal shame of having refused to submit to that just law which has condemned you. Do justice to society, and condemn yourself."[5]

The criminal bowed his head; by which he declared that he judged himself deserving of death.[6] He immediately prepared to submit with constancy, and

5. They who are invested with a power that gives them authority over mankind ought to take great heed how they treat them merely according to their own demerits; they should regard every criminal as a wretch more or less insane; they should therefore treat them as beings who, by some unknown cause, have been led out of the right path. Even when the judge pronounces condemnation with majesty, he should secretly lament that he cannot screen the criminal from punishment. To terrify vice by the most awful apparatus of justice, and privately to reclaim the guilty, should be the two grand points of criminal jurisprudence.

6. Propitious conscience, thou equitable and ready judge, be never absent from me! Tell me constantly, that I cannot do the least injury to another without receiving the counter-stroke; that I must necessarily wound myself, when I wound another.

with that resignation which, in our last moments, is so highly becoming of humanity.[7] He was no longer regarded as guilty; the body of pastors surrounded him; the prelate, taking off the bloody shirt, clothed him in a white vestment, which was the token of his reconciliation with mankind, and gave him the kiss of peace. His friends and relations crowded to embrace him; he appeared satisfied by receiving their caresses, and by being vested with that garment, which was a proof of the pardon he received from his country. Those testimonies of friendship took from him the horrors of approaching death. The prelate, advancing toward the people, seized that moment to make a nervous and pathetic discourse on the danger of passion; it was so eloquent, so just and affecting, that every heart was filled with admiration and terror. Each one resolved to watch carefully over his temper, and to stifle those seeds of resentment, which increase in a manner unknown to ourselves, and soon produce the most unbridled passions.

During this interval, a deputy from the senate bore the sentence of death to the monarch, that he might sign it with his own hand; for no one could be put to death without his consent, as in him resided the power of the sword. That good father would gladly have spared the life of the criminal;[8] but, in that moment, he sacrificed the earnest desire of his heart to the necessity of an exemplary justice.

The deputy returned. Then again the bells of the city began their funeral tolls, the drums repeated their mournful march, and those deploring sounds meeting in the air with the groans of the numerous people, one would have thought that the city was on the brink of an universal destruction. The friends and relations of the unfortunate man going to meet his death gave him the last embrace; the prelate invoked, with a loud voice, the forgiveness of the Supreme Being, and the vaulted roof of heaven resounded with the supplications of the whole people, who cried, with one mighty voice, "*O Almighty God, receive his soul! O God of Mercy, forgive him, even as we forgive him!*"

They conducted him, with slow steps, to the cage I have mentioned, still surrounded by his friends. Six fusileers, their faces covered with crape, advanced; the head of the senate gave the signal, by holding up the book of the law; they fired, and the soul disappeared.[9] They took up the dead body.

7. Agesilaus seeing a malefactor endure punishment with unconcern, "O wicked man," he said, "to make so bad a use of fortitude."

8. I am sorry that our kings have renounced that ancient and wise custom. When they sign so many papers, why should they neglect one of the most august privileges of their crown?

9. I have frequently heard it debated, whether the person of an executioner be infamous. I have always been concerned when they have given it in his favour, and could never have a respect for those who ranked him with the class of other citizens. I may be wrong; but such is my opinion.

His crime being fully expiated by his punishment, he was again received into the class of citizens; his name, that had been effaced, was inscribed again in the public register, with the names of those who had died the same day. This people had not the cruelty to pursue the memory of a man even to his tomb; and to reflect on a whole innocent family the crime of an individual;[10] they did not find pleasure in dishonouring, without cause, useful citizens, and make men miserable, for the satisfaction of making them humble. His body was carried to be burned without the city, with his fellow-citizens, who, the preceding day, had paid the inevitable debt to nature; his relations had no other grief to encounter than that which arose from the loss of a friend. The same evening, a place of trust and honour becoming vacant, the king conferred it on the brother of the criminal; and every one applauded a choice that was dictated by equity and beneficence.

With a heart full of tenderness and commiseration, I said, O, how is humanity respected among you! The death of a citizen is the cause of universal mourning to his country.—"It is because our laws," they replied, "are wise and humane; they are calculated more for reformation than for chastisement; the way to intimidate vice is not to render punishment common, but formidable; it is our study to prevent crimes; we send the refractory to places of solitude, where they are attended by those who endeavour to bring them to repentance, who operate by degrees on their hardened hearts, and gradually display the refined charms of virtue, to whose attractions the most depraved of mortals are not insensible. Does the physician at the first attack of a violent fever abandon his patient? Why, therefore, should we desert the guilty, who may yet be recovered? There are few hearts so corrupted, as not to be restored by perseverance; and a little blood, properly poured forth, cements our tranquility and our happiness.

"Your penal laws were all made in favour of the rich; all fell on the head of the poor; gold was become the god of nations; edicts and gibbets surrounded all possessions; and tyranny, with sword in hand, bartered the days, the sweat and blood of the unfortunate; it made no distinction in chastisements, and thereby taught the people to make none in crimes; it punished the least offence as the most infamous villainy. What was the consequence? The multiplying of laws multiplied crimes, and the offenders became as inhuman as their judges. Legislation, when it attempted to unite the members of society, drew the bands so tight as to throw it into convulsions; and, instead of maintaining, destroyed the connections; mournful humanity sent forth the

10. Base and despicable prejudice, that confounds all notions of justice, is contrary to reason, and only calculated for a weak or wicked people.

cry of grief, and saw too late, that the tortures of the executioner never inspire virtue."[11]

11. When we examine the validity of that right which human societies have assumed of punishing with death, we are terrified at the imperceptible point which separates equity from injustice. It is to little purpose here that we accumulate arguments; all our lights serve but to lead us astray; we must return to the law of nature only, which has far more regard than our institutions, for the life of a man; that teaches us, that the law of retaliation is, of all others, the most conformable to right reason. Among rising governments, which have yet the signature of nature, there is scarce any crime punished with death. In the case of murder there is no doubt; for nature tells us, that we should arm ourselves against assassins. . . .

DENIS DIDEROT

(1713–1784)

Love in Tahiti*

Diderot was the son of a prosperous cutler of Langres. After attending Jesuit schools in his native city and in Paris, to his father's dismay he turned his back on the more "respectable" professions and became a bookseller's hack, writing, among other pieces, sermons for missionaries. Diderot's talented and prolific pen gained him entree to the literary and artistic circles of the capital. His reputation as a *philosophe* was largely earned as principal editor and author of the *Encyclopedia*, a titanic effort that consumed his mature years but left him in straitened circumstances. He was rescued from his financial plight by Catherine the Great, who purchased his library and allowed him to keep it in Paris, appointing him her librarian at an annual stipend. Many of Diderot's works remained in manuscript during his lifetime. The dialogue reprinted here, in which he used the imagined felicity of the South Seas as a foil for the unnatural and corrupt mores of his own society, is part of the *Supplement to Bougainville's Voyage*. Written in 1772 as the expansion of a sympathetic book review of Bougainville's account, the work was posthumously published (1796) by an abbé with the intention of exposing its author as the founder of sansculottism.

*From Denis Diderot, *Rameau's Nephew and Other Works*, translated by Jacques Barzun and Ralph H. Bowen (Garden City, N.Y.: Doubleday, 1956), pp. 202–23. Copyright © 1956 by Jacques Barzun and Ralph H. Bowen. Reprinted by permission of Doubleday and Company, Inc.

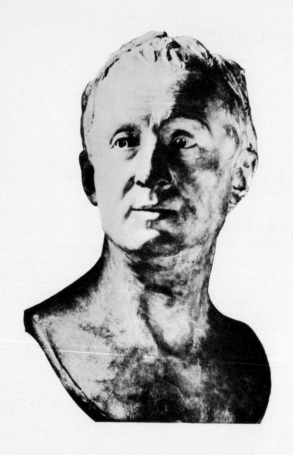

Bust of Diderot by Jean-Antoine Houdon, plaster, 1771. (Paris, Louvre.)

Orou and the Chaplain

B.—When the members of Bougainville's expedition were shared out among the native families, the ship's chaplain fell to the lot of Orou. The Tahitian and the chaplain were men of about the same age, that is, about thirty-five years old. At that time, Orou's family consisted of his wife and three daughters, who were called Asto, Palli and Thia. The women undressed their guest, washed his face, hands and feet, and put before him a wholesome though frugal meal. When he was about to go to bed, Orou, who had stepped outside with his family, reappeared and presented to him his wife and three girls— all naked as Eve—and said to him:

"You are young and healthy and you have just had a good supper. He who sleeps alone, sleeps badly; at night a man needs a woman at his side. Here is my wife and here are my daughters. Choose whichever one pleases you most, but if you would like to do me a favor, you will give your preference to my youngest girl, who has not yet had any children."

The mother said: "Poor girl! I don't hold it against her. It's no fault of hers."

The chaplain replied that his religion, his holy orders, his moral standards and his sense of decency all prevented him from accepting Orou's invitation.

Orou answered: "I don't know what this thing is that you call 'religion,' but I can only have a low opinion of it because it forbids you to partake of an innocent pleasure to which Nature, the sovereign mistress of us all, invites everybody. It seems to prevent you from bringing one of your fellow creatures into the world, from doing a favor asked of you by a father, a mother and their children, from repaying the kindness of a host, and from enriching a nation by giving it an additional citizen. I don't know what it is that you call 'holy orders,' but your chief duty is to be a man and to show gratitude. I am not asking you to take my moral standards back with you to your own country, but Orou, your host and your friend, begs you merely to lend yourself to the morality of Tahiti. Is our moral code a better or a worse one than your own? This is an easy question to answer. Does the country you were born in have more people than it can support? If it does, then your morals are neither better nor worse than ours. Or can it feed more people than it now has?

Then our morals are better than yours. As for the sense of propriety that leads you to object to my proposal, that I understand, and I freely admit that I am in the wrong. I ask your pardon. I cannot ask you to do anything that might harm your health; if you are too tired, you should by all means go to sleep at once. But I hope that you will not persist in disappointing us. Look at the distress you have caused to appear on the faces of these four women— they are afraid you have noticed some defect in them that arouses your distaste. But even if that were so, would it not be possible for you to do a good deed and have the pleasure of honoring one of my daughters in the sight of her sisters and friends? Come, be generous!"

THE CHAPLAIN.—"You don't understand—it's not that. They are all four of them equally beautiful. But there is my religion! My holy orders!"

OROU.—"They are mine and I offer them to you; they are all of age and they give themselves to you. However clear a conscience may be demanded of you by this thing, 'religion,' or by those 'holy orders' of yours, you need have no scruples about accepting these women. I am making no abuse of my paternal authority, and you may be sure that I recognize and respect the rights of individuals to their own persons."

At this point in his account, the truthful chaplain has to admit that up to that moment Providence had never exposed him to such strong temptation. He was young, he was excited, he was in torment. He turned his eyes away from the four lovely suppliants, then let his gaze wander back to them again. He lifted his hands and his countenance to Heaven. Thia, the youngest of the three girls, threw her arms around his knees and said to him: "Stranger, do not disappoint my father and mother. Do not disappoint me! Honor me in this hut and among my own family! Raise me to the dignity enjoyed by my sisters, for they make fun of me. Asto, my eldest sister, already has three children; Palli, the second oldest of us, has two; and Thia has none! Stranger, good stranger, do not reject me! Make me a mother! Give me a child whom I can some day lead by the hand as he walks at my side, to be seen by all Tahiti—a little one to nurse at my breast nine months from now, a child of whom I can be proud, and who will be part of my dowry when I go from my father's hut into that of another. Perhaps I shall be more fortunate with you than I have been with our Tahitian young men. If you will only grant me this favor, I will never forget you; I will bless you all my life; I will write your name on my arm and on that of my child; we will always pronounce it with joy; and when you leave this shore, my prayers will go with you across the seas all the way to your own country."

The poor chaplain records that she pressed his hands, that she fastened her eyes on his with the most expressive and touching gaze, that she wept, that her father, mother and sisters went out, leaving him alone with her, and that despite his repetition of "But there is my religion and my holy orders," he awoke the next morning to find the young girl lying at his side. She overwhelmed him with more caresses, and when her father, mother and sisters came in, she called upon them to add their gratitude to hers.

Asto and Palli, who had left the room briefly, soon returned bearing native food, drink and fruits. They embraced their sister and wished her good fortune. They all ate breakfast together; then, when Orou was left alone with the chaplain, he said to him:

"I see that my daughter is pleased with you, and I thank you. But would you be good enough to tell me the meaning of this word, 'religion,' which you have spoken so frequently and so mournfully?"

After considering for a moment what to say, the chaplain replied:

"Who made your hut and all the furnishings in it?"

Orou.—I did.

The Chaplain.—Well, we believe that this world and everything in it is the work of a maker.

Orou.—Then he must have hands and feet, and a head.

The Chaplain.—No.

Orou.—Where is his dwelling place?

The Chaplain.—Everywhere.

Orou.—In this place too?

The Chaplain.—In this place too.

Orou.—But we have never seen him.

The Chaplain.—He cannot be seen.

Orou.—He sounds to me like a father that doesn't care very much for his children. He must be an old man, because he must be at least as old as the things he made.

The Chaplain.—No, he never grows old. He spoke to our ancestors and gave them laws; he prescribed to them the way in which he wishes to be honored; he ordained that certain actions are good and others he forbade them to do as being evil.

Orou.—I see. And one of these evil actions which he has forbidden is that of a man who goes to bed with a woman or girl. But in that case, why did he make two sexes?

The Chaplain.—In order that they might come together—but only when certain conditions are satisfied and only after certain initial ceremonies have been performed. By virtue of these ceremonies one man belongs to one woman and only to her; one woman belongs to one man and only to him.

OROU.—For their whole lives?

THE CHAPLAIN.—For their whole lives.

OROU.—So that if it should happen that a woman should go to bed with some man who was not her husband, or some man should go to bed with a woman that was not his wife . . . but that could never happen because the workman would know what was going on, and since he doesn't like that sort of thing, he wouldn't let it occur.

THE CHAPLAIN.—No. He lets them do as they will, and they sin against the law of God (for that is the name by which we call the great workman) and against the law of the country; they commit a crime.

OROU.—I should be sorry to give offense by anything I might say, but if you don't mind, I'll tell you what I think.

THE CHAPLAIN.—Go ahead.

OROU.—I find these strange precepts contrary to nature, and contrary to reason. I think they are admirably calculated to increase the number of crimes and to give endless annoyance to the old workman—who made everything without hands, head or tools, who is everywhere but can be seen nowhere, who exists today and tomorrow but grows not a day older, who gives commands and is not obeyed, who can prevent what he dislikes but fails to do so. His commands are contrary to nature because they assume that a thinking being, one that has feelings and a sense of freedom, can be the property of another being like himself. On what could such a right of ownership be founded? Do you not see that in your country you have confused things that have no feelings, thoughts, desires or wills—things one takes or leaves, keeps or sells, without them suffering or complaining—with things that can neither be bought nor sold, which have freedom, volition, and desires of their own, which have the ability to give or to withhold themselves for a moment or forever, which suffer and complain? These latter things can never be treated like a trader's stock of goods unless one forgets what their true character is and does violence to nature. Furthermore, your laws seem to me to be contrary to the general order of things. For in truth is there anything so senseless as a precept that forbids us to heed the changing impulses that are inherent in our being, or commands that require a degree of constancy which is not possible, that violate the liberty of both male and female by chaining them perpetually to one another? Is there anything more unreasonable than this perfect fidelity that would restrict us, for the enjoyment of pleasures so capricious, to a single partner—than an oath of immutability taken by two individuals made of flesh and blood under a sky that is not the same for a moment, in a cavern that threatens to collapse upon them, at the foot of a cliff that is crumbling into dust, under a tree that is withering, on a bench of stone that is being worn away? Take my word for it, you have reduced human beings to a worse condition that that of the animals. I don't know what your great workman is, but I am very happy that he never spoke to our forefathers, and I hope that he never speaks to our children, for if he does, he may tell them the same foolishness, and they may be foolish enough to believe it. Yesterday, as we were having supper, you told us all about your "magistrates" and "priests." I do not know who these characters are whom you call Magistrates and Priests and who have the authority to govern your conduct—but tell me, are they really masters of good and evil? Can they transform justice into injustice and contrariwise? Is it within their power to attach the name of "good" to harmful action or the name of "evil" to harmless or useful deeds? One can hardly think so because in that case there would no longer be any difference between true and false, between good and bad, between beautiful and ugly—only such differences as it pleased your great workman, your magistrates or your priests to define as such. You would then have to change your ideas and behavior from one moment to the next. One day you would be told, on behalf of one of your three masters: "Kill", and in all good conscience you would be obliged to kill. Another day they might say: "Steal," and you would be bound to steal. Or: "Do not eat of this fruit," and you would not dare to eat of it; "I forbid you to eat this vegetable or this meat," and you would be careful never to touch them. There is not a single good thing they could not forbid you to enjoy, and no wickedness they could not order you to commit. And where would you be if your three masters, disagreeing among themselves, took it into their heads to permit, enjoin and forbid you to do the same thing, as I am sure must occasionally happen? Then, in order to please your priest, you would have to get yourself into hot water with the magistrate; to satisfy the magistrate, you would have to risk the displeasure of the great workman; and to make yourself agreeable to the great workman, you would have to fly in the face of your own nature. And do you know what will finally happen? You will come to despise all three, and you will be neither man, nor citizen nor pious believer; you will be nothing at all; you will be at odds with all the authorities, at odds with yourself, malicious, disturbed by your own conscience, persecuted by your witless masters, and miserable, as you were yesterday evening when I offered you my wife and daughters and you could only wail: "What about my religion? What about my holy orders?" Would you like to know what is good and what is bad in all times and places? Pay close attention to the nature of things and actions, to your relations with your fellow creatures, to the effect of your behavior on your own well-being and on the general welfare. You are mad if you believe that there is anything in the universe, high or low, that can add or subtract from the laws of nature. Her eternal will is that good shall be chosen rather than evil, and the general welfare rather than the individual's well-being. You may decree the opposite, but you will not be obeyed. By threats, punishment and guilt, you can make more wretches and rascals, make more depraved consciences and more corrupted characters. People will no longer know what they ought or ought not to do. They will feel guilty when they are doing nothing wrong and proud of themselves in the midst of crime; they will have lost the North Star that should guide their course. Give me an honest answer—in spite of the express commands of your three legislators, do the young men in your country never go to bed with a young woman without having received permission?

THE CHAPLAIN.—I would be lying if I said they never do.

OROU.—And the women, once they have sworn an oath to belong to only one husband, do they never give themselves to another man?

THE CHAPLAIN.—Nothing happens more often.

OROU.—And are your legislators severe in handing out punishment to such disobedient people, or are they not? If they are, then they are wild animals who make war against nature; if they are not severe, they are fools who risk bringing their authority into contempt by issuing futile prohibitions.

THE CHAPLAIN.—The guilty ones, if they escape the rigor of the laws, are punished by public opinion.

OROU.—That's like saying that justice is done by means of the whole nation's lack of common sense, and that public folly is the substitute for law.

THE CHAPLAIN.—A girl who has lost her honor cannot find a husband.

OROU.—Lost her honor! And for what cause?

THE CHAPLAIN.—An unfaithful woman is more or less despised.

OROU.—Despised! Why should that be?

THE CHAPLAIN.—And the young man is called a cowardly seducer.

OROU.—Coward? Seducer? Why that?

THE CHAPLAIN.—The father and mother and their dishonored child are desolate. An erring husband is called a libertine; a husband who has been betrayed shares the shame of his wife.

OROU.—What monstrous foolishness you're talking! And still you must be holding something back, because when people take it upon themselves to rearrange all ideas of justice and propriety to suit their own whims, to apply or remove the names of things in a completely arbitrary manner, to associate the ideas of good and evil with certain actions or to dissociate them for no reason save caprice—then of course people will blame each other, accuse each other, suspect each other, tyrannize, become jealous and envious, deceive and wound one another, conceal, dissimulate, and spy on one another, catch each other out, quarrel and tell lies. Girls deceive their parents, husbands their wives and wives their husbands. Unmarried girls—yes, I am sure of it—unmarried girls will suffocate their babies; suspicious fathers will neglect or show contempt for their own rightful children; mothers will abandon their infants and leave them to the mercy of fate. Crime and debauchery will appear in every imaginable shape and form. I see all that as plainly as if I had lived among you. These things are so because they must be so, and your society, whose well-ordered ways your chief boasts to you about, can't be anything but a swarm of hypocrites who secretly trample the laws under foot, or a multitude of wretched beings who serve as instruments for inflicting willing torture upon themselves; or imbeciles in whom prejudice has utterly silenced the voice of nature, or ill-fashioned creatures in whom nature cannot claim her rights.

THE CHAPLAIN.—That is a close likeness. But do you never marry?

OROU.—Oh yes, we marry.

THE CHAPLAIN.—Well, how does it work?

OROU.—It consists only of an agreement to occupy the same hut and to sleep in the same bed for so long as both partners find the arrangement good.

THE CHAPLAIN.—And when they find it bad?

OROU.—Then they separate.

THE CHAPLAIN.—But what becomes of the children?

OROU.—Oh Stranger! That last question of yours finally reveals to me the last depths of your country's wretchedness. Let me tell you, my friend, that the birth of a child is always a happy event, and its death is an occasion for weeping and sorrow. A child is a precious thing because it will grow up to be a man or a woman. Therefore we take infinitely better care of our children than of our plants and animals. The birth of a child is the occasion for public celebration and a source of joy for its entire family. For the hut it means an increase in wealth, while for the nation it signifies additional strength. It means another pair of hands and arms for Tahiti—we see in the newborn baby a future farmer, fisherman, hunter, soldier, husband or father. When a woman goes from her husband's hut back to that of her family, she takes with her all the children she had brought with her as her dowry; those born during the marriage are divided equally between the two spouses, and care is taken to give each an equal number of boys and girls whenever possible.

THE CHAPLAIN.—But children are a burden for many years before they are old enough to make themselves useful.

OROU.—We set aside for them and for the support of the aged one part in six of all our harvests; wherever the child goes, this support follows him. And so, you see, the larger the family a Tahitian has, the richer he is.

THE CHAPLAIN.—One part in six!

OROU.—Yes. It's a dependable method for encouraging the growth of population, for promoting respect for our old people and for safeguarding the welfare of our children.

THE CHAPLAIN.—And does it ever happen that a couple who have separated decide to live together again?

OROU.—Oh, yes. It happens fairly often. Also, the shortest time any marriage can last is one month.

THE CHAPLAIN.—Assuming, of course, that the wife is not with child, for in that case, wouldn't the marriage have to last at least nine months?

OROU.—Not at all. The child keeps the name of its mother's husband at the time it was conceived, and its paternity, like its means of support, follows it wherever it goes.

THE CHAPLAIN.—You spoke about the children that a wife brings to her husband as dowry.

OROU.—To be sure. Take my eldest daughter, who has three children. They are able to walk, they are healthy and attractive, and they promise to be strong when they are grown up. If she should take it into her head to get married, she would take them along, for they belong to her, and her husband would be extremely happy to have them in his hut. He would think all the better of his wife if she were carrying still a fourth child at the time of her wedding.

THE CHAPLAIN.—*His* child?

OROU.—His or another's. The more children our young women have had, the more desirable they are as wives. The stronger and lustier our young men are, the richer they become. Therefore, careful as we are to protect our young girls from male advances, and our young boys from intercourse with women, before they reach sexual maturity, once they have passed the age of puberty we exhort them all the more strongly to have as many children as possible. You probably haven't fully realized what an important service you will have rendered my daughter Thia if you have succeeded in getting her with child. Her mother will no longer plague her every month by saying,

"But Thia, what is the matter with you? You never get pregnant, and here you are nineteen years old. You should have had at least a couple of babies by this time, and you have none. Who is going to look after you in your old age if you throw away your youth in this way? Thia, I begin to think there is something wrong with you, some defect that puts men off. Find out what it is, my child, and correct it if you can. At your age, I was already three times a mother!"

THE CHAPLAIN.—What precautions do you take to safeguard your boys and girls before they reach maturity?

OROU.—That's the main object of our children's education within the family circle, and it's the most important point in our code of public morality. Our boys, until the age of twenty-two, that is for two to three years after they reach maturity, must wear a long tunic that covers their bodies completely, and they must wear a little chain around their loins. Before they reach nubile age, our girls would not dare to go out without white veils. The two misdeeds of taking off one's chain or raising one's veil are rarely met with because we teach our children at a very early age what harmful results will ensue. But when the proper time comes—when the male has attained his full strength, when the principal indication of virility lasts for a sufficient time, and when we are confirmed in our judgment by the quality and by the frequent emission of the seminal fluid—and when the young girl seems wilted and suffers from boredom, when she seems mature enough to feel passion, to inspire it and to satisfy it—then the father unfastens his son's chain and cuts the nail on the middle finger of the boy's right hand. The mother removes her daughter's veil. The young man can now ask a woman for her favors or be asked by her to grant his. The girl may walk about freely in public places with her face and breast uncovered; she may accept or reject men's caresses. All we do is to point out in advance to the boy certain girls and to the girl certain boys that they might well choose as partners. The day when a boy or girl is emancipated is a gala holiday. In the case of a girl, the young men assemble the night before around her hut and the air is filled all night long with singing and the sound of musical instruments. When the sun has risen, she is led by her father and mother into an enclosure where dancing is going on and where games of wrestling, running and jumping are in progress. A naked man is paraded in front of her, allowing her to examine his body from all aspects and in all sorts of attitudes. For a young man's initiation, the young girls do the honors of the occasion by letting him look at the nude female body unadorned and unconcealed. The remainder of the ceremony is enacted on a bed of leaves, just as you saw it on your arrival here. At sunset the girl returns to her parents' hut or else moves to the hut of the young man she has chosen and remains there as long as she pleases.

THE CHAPLAIN.—But is this celebration a marriage ceremony or is it not?

OROU.—Well, as you have said . . .

A.—What do I see written there in the margin?

B.—It is a note in which the good chaplain says that the parents' advice on how to choose wives and husbands was full of common sense and contained many acute and useful observations, but that he could not bring himself to quote the catechism itself because it would have seemed intolerably licentious to corrupt, superstitious people like us. He adds, nevertheless, that he was sorry to have left out certain details that would have shown, in the first place, what vast progress a nation can make in some important matter without the assistance of physics and anatomy, if it busies itself continually with it, and in the second place, the different ideals of beauty that prevail in a country where one judges forms in the light of momentary pleasures, as contrasted with a nation where they are appreciated for their usefulness over a longer period of time. To be considered beautiful in the former country a woman must have a high color, a wide forehead, a small mouth, large eyes, finely modeled features, a narrow waist, and small hands and feet. . . . With the Tahitians, however, scarcely one of these things is of any account. The woman who attracts the most admirers and the most lovers is the one who seems most likely to bear many children (like the wife of Cardinal d'Ossat) and whose children seem likely to be active, intelligent, brave, healthy and strong. The Athenian Venus has next to nothing in common with the Venus of Tahiti —the former is a flirtatious Venus, the latter a fertile Venus. A woman of Tahiti said scornfully one day to a woman of her acquaintance: "You are beautiful enough, but the children you bear are ugly; I am ugly, but my children are beautiful, so the men prefer me."

Following this note by the chaplain, Orou continues:

OROU.—What a happy moment it is for a young girl and her parents when it is discovered that she is with child! She jumps up and runs about, she throws her arms around her father's and mother's necks. She tells them the wonderful news amidst outcries of mutual joy. "Mother! Father! kiss me! I am pregnant!" "Is it really true?" "Really and truly!" "And who got you with child?" "Such-and-such a one."

THE CHAPLAIN.—How can she know who the father of her child is?

OROU.—How could she not know? With us the same rule that applies to marriage applies also to love affairs—each lasts at least from one moon to the next.

THE CHAPLAIN.—And is the rule strictly observed?

OROU.—You can judge for yourself. First, the interval between two moons isn't long, but when it appears that two men have well-founded claims to be the father of a child, it no longer belongs to the mother.

THE CHAPLAIN.—To whom does it belong?

OROU.—To whichever of the two men the mother chooses to give it. This is the only right she has, and since a child is an object of both interest and value, you can understand that among us loose women are rare and that our young men keep away from them.

THE CHAPLAIN.—Then you do have a few licentious women? That makes me feel better.

OROU.—Yes, we have some, and more than one kind—but that is another subject. When one of our girls gets pregnant, she is twice as pleased with herself if the child's father is a handsome, well-built, brave, intelligent, industrious young man, because she has reason to hope that the child will inherit its father's good qualities. The only thing a girl would be ashamed of would be a bad choice. You have no idea how much store we set by good health, beauty, strength, industry and courage; you have no notion what a tendency there is, even without our having to pay any particular attention to it, for good physical inheritance to be passed on from generation to generation among us. You are a person who has traveled in all sorts of countries —tell me if you have seen anywhere else so many handsome men and beautiful women as in Tahiti. Look at me. What do you think of me? Well, there are ten thousand men on this island who are taller than I am and just as strong; but there is none braver, and for that reason mothers very often point me out to their girls as a good father for their children.

THE CHAPLAIN.—And out of all these children you have sired outside your own hut, how many fall to your share?

OROU.—Every fourth, be it a boy or a girl. You see, we have developed a kind of circulation of men, women and children—that is, of able-bodied workers of all ages and occupations—which is much more important than trade in foodstuffs (which are only the products of human labor) in your country.

THE CHAPLAIN.—I can easily believe it. What is the significance of those black veils that I have seen a few persons wearing?

OROU.—They indicate barrenness, either congenital or that which comes with advanced age. Any woman who lays aside such a veil and mingles with men is considered dissolute, and so is any man who raises such a veil and has commerce with a barren woman.

THE CHAPLAIN.—And the gray veils?

OROU.—That shows that the woman is having her monthly period. Failure to wear this veil when it should be worn also stigmatizes a woman as dissolute if she has relations with men during that time, and likewise the man who has relations with her.

THE CHAPLAIN.—Do you punish this libertinism?

OROU.—Only with public disapproval.

THE CHAPLAIN.—May a father sleep with his daughter, a mother with her son, a brother with his sister, a husband with someone else's wife?

OROU.—Why not?

THE CHAPLAIN.—Well! To say nothing of the fornication, what of the incest, the adultery?

OROU.—What do you mean by those words, *fornication, incest,* and *adultery?*

THE CHAPLAIN.—They are crimes, horrible crimes for which people are burned at the stake in my country.

OROU.—Well, whether they burn or don't burn in your country is nothing to me. But you cannot condemn the morals of Europe for not being those of Tahiti, nor our morals for not being those of Europe. You need a more dependable rule of judgment than that. And what shall it be? Do you know a better one than general welfare and individual utility? Well, now, tell me in what way your crime of *incest* is contrary to the two aims of our conduct; if you think that everything is settled once and for all because a law has been promulgated, a derogatory word invented, and a punishment established. Why don't you tell me what you mean by *incest.*

THE CHAPLAIN.—Why, *incest* . . .

OROU.—Yes, incest . . . ? Has it been a long time since your great workman without hands, head or tools made the world?

THE CHAPLAIN.—No.

OROU.—Did he make the whole human race at one time?

THE CHAPLAIN.—No, he made only one man and one woman.

OROU.—Had they children?

THE CHAPLAIN.—Of course.

OROU.—Let's suppose that these two original parents had no sons—only daughters—and that the mother was the first to die. Or that they had only sons and that the wife lost her husband.

THE CHAPLAIN.—You embarrass me. But in spite of anything you may say, incest is a horrible crime, so let's talk about something else.

OROU.—That's all very well for you to say. But as for me, I won't speak another word until you tell me why incest is such a horrible crime.

THE CHAPLAIN.—All right, I'll grant you that perhaps incest does not offend nature, but isn't it objection enough that it threatens the political order? What would happen to the security of the chief of state, and what would become of a nation's tranquillity, if millions of people should come to be under the thumbs of fifty or so fathers of families?

OROU.—That would be the lesser of two evils: There would be no single great society but fifty or so little ones, more happiness and one crime the less.

THE CHAPLAIN.—I should think, though, that even here, it must not be very common for a son to sleep with his mother.

OROU.—No, not unless he has a great deal of respect for her, or a degree of tenderness that makes him forget the disparity in their ages and prefer a woman of forty to a girl of nineteen.

THE CHAPLAIN.—What about intercourse between fathers and daughters?

OROU.—Hardly more frequent, unless the girl is ugly and little sought after. If her father has a great deal of affection for her, he helps her in getting ready her dowry of children.

THE CHAPLAIN.—What you say suggests to me that in Tahiti the women on whom nature has not smiled have a rather hard time of it.

OROU.—What you say only shows that you haven't a high opinion of the generosity of our young men.

THE CHAPLAIN.—As for unions between brothers and sisters, I imagine they are very common.

OROU.—Yes, and very strongly approved of.

THE CHAPLAIN.—According to you, the same passion that gives rise to so many evils and crimes in our countries is completely innocent here.

OROU.—Stranger, you have poor judgment and a faulty memory. Poor judgment, because whenever something is forbidden, it is inevitable that people should be tempted to do that thing, and do it. Faulty memory, because you have already forgotten what I told you. We do have dissolute old women who sneak out at night without their black veils and offer themselves to men, even though nothing can come of it. If they are recognized or surprised, the punishment is either exile to the northern tip of the island or slavery. There are precocious girls who lift their white veils without their parents' knowledge—for them we have a locked room in the hut. There are young boys who take off their chain before the time established by nature and our laws—in that case the parents get a strong reprimand. There are women who find the nine months of pregnancy a long time; women and girls who are careless about wearing their gray veils—but as a matter of fact we attach little importance to all these lapses. You would find it hard to believe how much our morals have been improved on these points by the fact that we have come to identify in our minds the idea of public and private wealth with the idea of increasing the population.

THE CHAPLAIN.—But don't disturbances ever arise when two men have a passion for the same woman, or when two girls desire the same man?

OROU.—I haven't seen as many as four instances. The choice of the woman or man settles the matter. If a man should commit any act of violence, that would be a serious misdemeanor, but even then no one would take any notice unless the injured party were to make a public complaint, and it is almost unheard of for a girl or woman to do so. The only thing I have noticed is that our women are a little less considerate of homely men than our young men are of ill-favored women; but no one is worried with this state of affairs.

THE CHAPLAIN.—So far as I can see, jealousy is practically unknown here in Tahiti. But tenderness between husband and wife, and maternal love, which are strong, beautiful emotions—if they exist here at all, they must be fairly lukewarm.

OROU.—We have put in their place another impulse, which is more universal, powerful and lasting—self-interest. Examine your conscience in all candor, put aside the hypocritical parade of virtue which is always on the lips of your companions, though not in their hearts, and tell me, if there is anywhere on the face of the earth a man who, if he were not held back by shame, would not prefer to lose his child—a husband who would not prefer to lose his wife—rather than lose his fortune and all the amenities of life? You may be sure that if ever a man can be led to care as much about his fellow men as he does about his own bed, his own health, his leisure, his house, his harvests or his fields, he can be depended upon to do his utmost to look out for the well-being of other people. Then you will see him shedding tears over the bed of a sick child or taking care of a mother when she is ill. Then you will find fruitful women, nubile girls and handsome young men highly regarded. Then you will find a great deal of attention paid to the education of the young, because the nation grows stronger with their growth, and suffers a material loss if their well-being is impaired.

THE CHAPLAIN.—I am afraid there is some reason in what this savage says. The poor peasant of our European lands wears out his wife in order to spare his horse, lets his child die without help, and calls the veterinary to look after his ox.

OROU.—I didn't quite hear what you were just saying. But when you get back to your own country where everything is so well managed, try to teach them how well our method works. Then they will begin to realize how precious a newborn baby is and how important it is to increase the population. Shall I tell you a secret? But take care that you don't let it out. When you came, we let you do what you liked with our women and girls. You were astonished and your gratitude made us laugh. You thanked us, even though we were levying the heaviest of all taxes on you and your companions. We asked no money of you; we didn't loot your ship; we didn't give a hang for any of your stores of food—but our women and girls came to draw the blood out of your veins. When you go away, you will leave with us a brood of children. Do you think we could have extracted a more valuable tribute from you than this tax collected from your own bodies and from your own substance? If you would care to try and estimate its value, imagine that you have yet to sail along two hundred leagues of coastline, and that every twenty miles they collect the same tribute from you! We have vast areas of land yet to be put under the plow; we need workers, and we have tried to get you to give them to us. We have epidemics from time to time, and these losses must be made up; we have sought your aid to fill up the gaps in our population. We have external enemies to deal with, and for this we need soldiers, so we have allowed you to give them to us. We have a surplus of women and girls over men, and we have enlisted your services to help us out. Among these women and girls there are some with whom our men have thus far been unable to beget any children, and these were the ones we first assigned to receive your embraces. A neighboring nation holds us in vassalage, and we have to pay an annual tribute to them in men; you and your friends have helped us to pay off this debt, and in five or six years we shall send them your sons if they turn out to be inferior in some way to our own. Although we are stronger and healthier than you, we have observed that you have the edge on us when it comes to intelligence. So we immediately marked out some of our most beautiful women and girls to collect the seed of a race superior to ours. This is an experiment we have tried, and that we hope will succeed. We have taken from you and your fellows the only thing we could get from you. Just because we are savages, don't think we are incapable of calculating where our best advantage lies. Go wherever you will, and you will always find a man as shrewd as you are. He will give you what he has no use for, and he will always ask for something he has need of. If he offers to trade you a piece of gold for a scrap of iron, that is because he doesn't care a hang for gold, and desires iron. By the way, why is it that you are not dressed like the others? What is the significance of the long robe that covers you from head to foot, and what is that pointed bag that you let hang over your shoulders and sometimes draw up around your ears?

THE CHAPLAIN.—The reason I dress as I do is that I am a member of a society of men who are called monks in my country. The most sacred of their vows is never to have intercourse with any woman and never to beget any children.

OROU.—Then what kind of work do you do?

THE CHAPLAIN.—None.

OROU.—And your magistrates allow that sort of idleness—the worst of all?

THE CHAPLAIN.—They more than allow it: they honor it and make others do the same.

OROU.—My first thought was that nature, or some accident, or some cruel form of sorcery, had deprived you of the ability to reproduce your kind, and that out of pity they had let you go on living instead of killing you. But my daughter tells me that you are a man as robust as any Tahitian and that she has high hopes of getting good results from your repeated caresses. Well, at last I know why you kept mumbling yesterday evening, "But there's my religion, my holy orders!" Could you explain to me why it is that your magistrates show you such favor and treat you with so much respect?

THE CHAPLAIN.—I don't know.

OROU.—Still, you must know why it was that, although you are a man, you have condemned yourself of your own free will to be one no longer?

THE CHAPLAIN.—That's hard to explain, and it would take too long.

OROU.—Are monks faithful to their vows of sterility?

THE CHAPLAIN.—No.

OROU.—I was sure of it. Do you also have female monks?

THE CHAPLAIN.—Yes.

OROU.—As well behaved as the male monks?

THE CHAPLAIN.—They are kept more strictly in seclusion, they dry up from unhappiness and die of boredom.

OROU.—So nature is avenged for the injury done to her! Ugh! What a country! If everything is managed the way you say, you are more barbarous than we are.

The good chaplain tells us that he spent the rest of the day wandering about the island, visiting a number of huts, and that in the evening, after supper, the father and mother begged him to go to bed with Palli, the second eldest daughter. She offered herself in the same undress as Thia's, and he tells us that several times during the night he cried out, "My religion! My holy orders!" The third night he suffered the same guilty torments in the arms of Asto, the eldest, and the fourth night, not to be unfair, he devoted to his hostess.

NICOLAS-EDME RESTIF DE LA BRETONNE

(1734–1806)

The Pursuit of Happiness through Rules and Regulations

The printing press opened the way to a literary career for Restif de la Bretonne. This Burgundian peasant's son was apprenticed for a time to an Auxerre typographer, and was still a young man when he set up in the capital as a master printer. With presses at his disposal, in 1767 he began to write and print his works. He published nearly 300 volumes during the next 35 years. Restif was a rake who frequented high and low society, squandered his money, and ended up earning a pittance as an underling in the Napoleonic police bureau of intercepted letters. While his erotic and sometimes pornographic novels earned him the sobriquet of "Rousseau of the gutters," he also produced books of serious intent. In *The French Daedalus* (1781), he used the popular form of the imaginary voyage to introduce a tranquil, egalitarian society in Megapatagonia. *The Andrograph* (1782)—much praised by Benjamin Franklin—soberly advanced rigid and detailed proposals for a total reformation of society along communist lines through a minute regulation of every aspect of existence.

Victorin prenant son vol

Engraving from *La Découverte australe par un Homme-Volant*, Paris, 1781.

Megapatagonian Maxims*

Then the wise Teugnil spoke . . .

"When everybody works," he said, "the burden amounts to nothing at all. On the contrary, work is then only a pleasure, because no matter what each individual is obliged to do, he is never pushed to the point of fatigue. The work merely exercises his limbs and renders them more supple. It contributes to the development of his mind instead of stunting it. Among your Europeans, on the other hand, where inequality reigns, everybody must be unhappy—some because of overwork, others because of idleness. Everybody must become quite stupid. The workers are brutalized, the idlers become either torpid or feverish with bizarre passions. Doubtless they think only of nonsense and extravagant fancies. If some common sense is found among you, it is perhaps only in the middling estate. Moreover, such persons must be very rare, either because there are so many bad examples, or because most of the people are crushed by heavy work or drowned in idleness. Do I guess right?"

"Quite right, illustrious Megapatagon," answered Hermantin.

"Here, on the other hand, the faculties of each person are developed to the right degree. Among us, you will not find creatures who cannot understand at all what others comprehend easily. And although we have among us powerful geniuses who go further than others, they only surpass in the faculty of invention. Their ideas are readily understood by everybody, even in the most abstract matters.

"You have observed how we employ our days. All of them are similar to the one you witnessed upon your arrival here. The day is divided into two equal parts, twelve hours of sleep or total repose, and twelve hours of activity. In the twelve hours of rest is included the time men give to love, women, and living as private individuals in the bosom of their families. The other twelve hours are devoted to the public. They begin at six o'clock in the morning, at daybreak, and finish with the end of daylight at six in the evening. Tasks are

*From Nicolas-Edme Restif de la Bretonne, *La Découverte australe par un Homme-Volant, ou Le Dédale français; Nouvelle très-philosophique: Suivie de la Lettre d'un Singe*, etc. (Leipzig, *i.e.* Paris, 1781), III, pp. 496–505, 508–14, 520–3; translated by the editors.

distributed among all the citizens, in proportion to their strength and capacity, by the Venerable Syndic of each dwelling section. Every neighborhood has one hundred families and every section has twenty-five, at the head of which stands the oldest of the Venerables, who is called a Section-Head. In his absence, the next in line represents him. Venerables who have reached the age of 150 no longer work, but command. Children under 20 do not yet work, but a Venerable trains them to make different things as part of their play during recreation hours. In addition to their occupation, they learn to read and write, they are taught related languages, the true principles of their mother tongue, then morality, history, and physical science.

"The task each one has received from the Venerable Syndic is discharged carefully and without haste. One's whole mind is devoted to it. The work lasts four hours. Then everyone assembles in the commonroom of the neighborhood to take a meal, which has been prepared by fellow-citizens whose special responsibility it was during the four hours of general work. After the meal, all enjoy the rest necessary in these hot climates. They sleep for an hour and a half, and then they give themselves over to various diversions until supper. At the end of this period, everyone retires to his private quarters with his wife and children.

"One is not always obliged to take the same job. On the contrary, those who wish to change do not meet with the slightest objection on the part of the Venerable Syndics. The citizens are even encouraged to make such switches. And only those who absolutely insist upon it always perform the same task.

"The men do all the outside work and the rough work; the women, those tasks that are performed indoors, except such heavy work as might entail handling metals, copper, metal plates, or stone and wood. All needlework is done by women, except shoe-making, for we are very careful lest they engage in anything that might spoil their daintiness or involve them in unpleasant toil. Women are submissive and respectful toward men; in turn they are respected and honored by them as the repositories of the future generation. For why should anybody want to degrade or seduce a woman who might one day be his own? Our pleasures consist of games that exercise the body without tiring it and that require skill rather than strength. The only glory appreciated in a country such as ours is the victor's prize. Women amuse themselves with dances, which tend to give them attractive bearing, or with games of skill that have the same purpose, to make their movements easy and graceful. In addition, they occupy themselves with creating and trying on all sorts of finery; they unite their sweet and well-modulated voices either with the masculine sounds of the men or with instruments they play.

Besides, they have a sort of game they greatly enjoy, and that is, to practice among themselves seeing who can assume the most engaging manner, the most seductive smile, who will find the most effective means of pleasing men in all possible situations. For the idea is inculcated into them from childhood that they are made for man as man is for the fatherland. Thus, among us work is almost a game and games are a form of education. Every day is a holiday, but not as it would be with the Europeans, if they adopted our customs. For among them there would doubtless be one part of mankind who amused themselves without doing anything, while the other worked without amusing itself."

"Have you any plays," said Hermantin, "any dramatic presentations, illustrious Megapatagon?"

"These sorts of pleasures are only trifles worthy of a nation of children or a nation in its infancy," answered the wise Teugnil. "We want only the real, and we have time only for the enjoyment of true pleasures without going about inventing artificial ones."

"Do you not have the fine arts, such as painting, sculpture, music, poetry?"

"We despise painting. Our portraits are our handsome men and our beautiful women whom we see every day. If the human race were annihilated and only a single survivor were condemned to live eternally alone on the earth, we might find it pardonable that he should apply himself to the two arts of painting and sculpture in order to beguile his solitude with a deceptive image. Perhaps, too, if we had your way of living—leaving our country to travel for years on end—we might desire to paint cherished objects. But here, with our customs, painting and sculpture would only be child's play. We value necessary occupations more than useless arts. To be sure, we have some painters; these few are employed in depicting the splendid deeds of our most virtuous citizens, and the paintings are intended to adorn the apartments of the Venerables who performed these actions. As for music, I told you that we have it. It is one of the charms of life to listen to the cultivated sounds of the human voice, to sing of the great men, their pleasures and their loves. Poetry, the sister of music, is a livelier and more harmonious method of expression. But we adopt it only for joyful subjects; it is absurd in dreadful ones, harmful if used in education. In a word, we have only three kinds of poetic writing: that which celebrates the actions of heroes, benefactors of humanity, of whom one can speak only with enthusiasm; that which we call the ode; and songs. It is prohibited to versify any other work of the intellect."

* * *

"It is a principle among us that the sole end of society is to have men live together more agreeably. Do not imagine that such principles make us effeminate. First of all, work, to which we are all subject, does not stultify us, but strengthens us. Our games have as their purpose to make our limbs more supple and to avoid the laziness of the savages. We even train ourselves for war, because we might be attacked. And above all, we elevate the souls of our young people beyond the fear of death. With this end in view, we have fully persuaded them that all beings emanating from the sun and the earth, to become individuals distinct in appearance, are nevertheless not cut off from one another, but are forever linked together and that death only makes them change places so that they exist thereafter in another form. In truth, we do not retain the memory of our previous transformations. This is impossible since the organs of memory have disintegrated. But what of it? It is enough to feel one's present existence, to grasp the whole of it through memory and foresight. That is sufficient to occupy us agreeably. The memory of an almost infinite multitude of previous existences would only tax our brains, overload them, and destroy our attentiveness to things present. This memory would kill children by making them too rationalist. It would perpetuate hatreds and dissensions among vicious peoples, and so on. Wise nature did not wish it so. But through analogy we know that we are merely subject to decomposition, and that must be. Plants decompose and reproduce themselves. Each animal draws its life from the same source. It is the same intelligence and the same matter that constitute it. It is therefore as eternal as its Principle. This is so in despite of the death of planets and suns, because the death of these great Beings is no more an annihilation than is ours, or that of plants. These are the principles we inculcate in our youth. They are dedicated to the public good to the point of gladly sacrificing their lives because they are assured of existing again immediately after the dissolution of their bodies and of thus dwelling eternally in this beautiful land. We pay great heed to the immediate dissolution of dead bodies and we consider the speediest method to be the most pious. We burn them. To bury them in the earth is second best, but it retards somewhat the process of decomposition. To embalm them in order to preserve them is a sacrilege. If we had criminals here, we would have them embalmed as the most horrible disgrace with which they could be branded."

"This way of thinking is completely opposite to that of the Europeans," said Hermantin, "but it seems to me to be wiser."

"Our young men have no fear whatever of death and would make excellent soldiers if we were ever attacked by ambitious Europeans. Finally, we pay our dead great honor, and their names are preserved for many years. They are repeated from one generation to another in each family, along with accounts of one or two of their noblest and most remarkable exploits. . . . But to come back to your question about our morality, it consists solely in taking the shortest route and the one beset with least obstacles in order to be happy. And since sensuality uncontrolled would cause great trouble, you may imagine that this is not the path we choose. We know that deprivations season pleasure and generate a hunger for it, so to speak. Therefore we have deprivations. There is, similarly, a form and a moderation in our pleasures. We never carry them to the point of utter satiety. But what strengthens good morals among us is that they are never left—as you have told me the case is in Europe—to individual caprice. Through our sense of equality, our community feeling, moral behavior is uniform and public. We practice virtue in a body. We reject vice in a body. Laziness, uselessness, sumptuary excess, or luxury—all this becomes impossible among us. No man can gorge himself in a public assemblage of his fellow-citizens. Each one takes only what he needs. This fortunate habit has succeeded in eradicating among us guzzling and gluttonous temperaments, recognized by their foul breath and complexions in the isles of this hemisphere. A man will not commit excesses of debauch with his wife. A brother in the midst of brothers who are discharging their duties will not neglect his own. He will not be vagrant in a land where all about him are employed. As our ways are established forever, we had to make them mild. You see from our occupations and diversions that they could not be more so. I repeat to you, equality cuts all vices at the root. No more thieves or assassins or idlers or corrupters. Since among a people of equals mockery might have produced some abuses, it is prohibited. Every Megapatagon must abandon this wretched way of showing his wit. In its stead, an atmosphere of goodness and honesty prevails among us. Truth above all is so sacred that no one permits himself the least jest which might injure it, even where there is an intention of later producing an agreeable surprise. Only that which is comes forth from our mouths; that which is not—the ridiculous mask of myth and of allegory—is unworthy of the eldest son of nature. We leave it to those among the monkeys who are capable of reasoning, such as those you have discovered. This is one of the reasons why comedy and all drama are banished from our system. This sort of thing is good only for the people of the Monkey Isle and the flighty Europeans."

*   *   *

"Happy Megapatagons!" cried Hermantin. "Ah! that my revered ancestor might have had the pleasure of seeing and conversing with you! He would have admired above all the fact that you are the moral antipodes of his country even in a more perfect sense than you are antipodes by your situation on the globe. We shall soon rejoice his old age with the account of everything we have learned from you. It is not, most wise Megapatagons, that our revered ancestor does not know maxims as fine as yours. He has transplanted into your hemisphere, which is at present ours, a religion which teaches equality and fraternity, which makes a law of it, and which declares that without charity, that is to say, the virtue of loving our brothers, of cherishing them, we are only vile and wretched creatures. All the precepts of this religion tend toward disinterestedness, purity of manners, beneficence, modesty. All men of great wealth are accursed in this religion. It forbids anyone to call a person his Lord in the name of that principle which makes us all equally the sons of God. It enjoins brothers to share with one another their bread, their clothes, without regard to rank, nationality, religion, opinion . . ."

"And do not all the peoples of Europe then profess this religion?"

"Pardon me, illustrious son of the wisest of Venerables."

"But who then are they whose deeds are recorded in the history books you gave us in an upside-down language?"

"They are the same peoples."

"This time, illustrious Christinians, you are making fun of me, or these people are making fun of their legislator and of the great God whom you say they worship."

"They are not mocking him, wise Teugnil, but swept away by their passions, they follow hardly anything of their religion. Their priests are in this respect no more meticulous and they are the first to violate the religion in its most fundamental tenets, though they are the most careful of men to preserve the prerogatives this religion bestows upon them in the eyes of the people."

"I do not understand you, noble Christinians. Either they profess their religion or they do not."

"They profess it."

"Without obeying it?"

"That is so."

"You arouse in me incredible scorn for the Europeans. So noble a religion, dictated by the great God himself—I recognize it by the precepts that it teaches! To profess it without practicing it! Your Europeans are monsters."

On Marriage*

Art. XXXIV.   All young people of both sexes will be destined to wed, for matrimony is the state for which Nature, religion, and the social laws intended them. Every well-built individual will be obliged to marry, and to this end detailed procedures will be set forth in the following articles.

XXXV.   Only in cases of infirmity or deformity will exceptions be made. The sick, whatever their ailments may be, will not be required to marry at all. As for the deformed, if they are vigorous, they will only be prohibited from marrying virgins, but they will nevertheless be able to secure widows of thirty-five and over. Such widows, for their part, will not be able to marry well-formed young men, unless there are too many for the girls, in which case the magistrate will grant a license to the widows to marry the youngest and handsomest of the surplus youths. Deformed men, as a compensation for their handicap, will be favored for all positions where celibacy is a suitable qualification.

XXXVI.   In the future the choice of a mate will depend neither on caprice nor interest. The degree of merit of each presentable young man will give him the right to choose among all the girls, as set forth in Article XXX of the First Title. For this purpose, at the four great marriage festivals which will be fixed around the solstices and equinoxes, namely at the St. André, at Carnival, at the St. Jean, and on the ninth of September after harvest, all work will stop for three days throughout the nation. The whole population will assemble to witness the marriages and to participate in the joy of the newly weds. These three days will be preceded by a fortnight of preparation in families that have boys or girls to be married at the approaching festival. Their clothes will be got ready, and they will be given special instruction— the boys, as prescribed in Article XLI below, the girls, in Article LXV of the *Gynographs* regulation. Choosing will take place on the second of the three festival days, the first having been employed by the eligible young people in reading the moral register and in parading before one another. On selection day, all the girls will range themselves in a row or a number of rows in accordance with the locality, and the boys will be lined up separately. The first class will step forth and choose among the girls the ones who please them, in

*From Nicolas-Edme Restif de la Bretonne, *L'Andrographe, ou Idées d'un Honnête-Homme, sur un Projet de Règlement, Proposé à toutes les Nations de l'Europe, pour opérer une Réforme générale des moeurs, et, par elle, la bonheur du Genre-humain* (The Hague: Gosse and Pinet, 1782), pp. 53–65; translated by the editors.

the presence of their parents, who will speak with those of the girls. Then will come the second class, and so on through the sixth, who will choose last. Within the different classes of young men, those who have rather more merit will always take precedence (the drawing of lots, discussed in Article XXX, taking place only among those who are perfectly equal): in each class every lad will have a number beginning with one for the most deserving, and this system will be in force through the last members of class six. Each girl thus publicly chosen will modestly follow her future husband to the altar, where all the boys and girls will be forthwith united in a single general blessing. The parents have but to see to it that the couple related to them by blood pronounce the "yes." In making choices, relative age will be regulated as set forth in Article XXVIII of the *Gynographs,* and other conditions in accordance with Article XXIX of this regulation for girls. Immediately after the benediction, the newly weds will be separated, to be reunited only at intervals and in the manner prescribed by Article XLII. Every wife will have a ring inscribed with the class and rank of her husband.

XXXVII.   In the event that a girl chosen by a young man cannot bring herself to receive him as a husband, she will immediately make her opposition known through one of the matrons of the Committee of Ancient Dames established by Article LXXX of the *Gynographs* regulation. Then the reasons for the rejection will be examined in the open, not to determine their validity—there will always be some—but to inflict punishment on the girl if the reasons are to her discredit. In case of doubt, her marriage will be put off until the next festival; in case she is wrong and the reasons advanced are false, she will be cast into the lowest ranks, to be chosen in the future only by members of the class last in merit and good looks; in case she is right, she may that same day be rechosen by one of the substitute young men, who are ten in number, in place of the one whom she has justly rejected. (To the details of Article XII of the *Gynographs* should be added that girls of first merit will be placed in the front row, the more readily to be viewed and selected by the members of class one and class two and other young men of distinction. Note that in girls a degree of beauty, gentleness, or at least amiability must be joined to the virtues appropriate to their sex.)

XXXVIII.   Every boy who has some bodily defect will be excluded from the legitimate classes, and different classes of cripples will be constituted, in accordance with their degree of infirmity. (1) Those disabled by accident who can still work will have a choice of marriage or the ecclesiastical state, secular or regular, as with the following class. (2) The lame without any other deformity will form a second class who can be given young girls as wives if they are otherwise vigorous and healthy. (3) The bandy-legged will qualify only for widows. (4) Congenital hunchbacks and deformed men will only obtain women past forty. (5) The deaf and one-eyed will have as wives only rejected girls who have not been chosen at the marriage festivals. (6) The blind will have the ugliest girls who have not been able to find husbands. Selection among the malformed will have as many divisions as among the robust. Priority will be given to those uniting the least deformity with the greatest merit; the rest will be ranked in accordance with the merit which offsets their deformities, until that subject is reached who has the least merit and the greatest deformity. Finally, it should be observed that those whose illness is communicable, such as the scrofulous, the scorbutic, the herpetic, the syphilitic, and so on, will not be able to marry, or will be permitted to marry only women past fifty, who might be willing to expose themselves to the disease. This will apply also to those attacked by epilepsy, consumption, and so on.

XXXIX. The reasons for the rejection of a young man will have to be specific, since the Committee of Elders, who will be treated under Title Five, will have carefully excluded those who might fall under some general cause. Thus, (1) A specific and secret insult to a girl will be a cause of rejection; (2) A secret vice known to the girl; (3) An insult to her father, brother, uncle, male cousin germane, mother, sister, aunt, female cousin germane, teacher of either sex; (4) Mockery of the girl; (5) Refusal to do her a favor; (6) Having on some occasion demonstrably preferred someone else to her. With all these reasons, especially the last, the girl cannot be proved in the right and the boy put off to another festival and even cast into a lower class, unless the offense has been grave in nature.

XL. Even if the reasons are not legitimate, the rejection will be sustained, but then the girl will be punished in accordance with the circumstances. In case of failure to prove frivolous charges, her marriage will merely be postponed to another festival and the boy will no longer be able to choose her. But if the girl falsely made serious accusations, or if she gave illegitimate reasons for rejection such as the following: (1) That he is not handsome; (2) That he has no taste for light amusement, to which people apply the empty term agreeableness; (3) That he is serious and cold; (4) That he made errors when in fact he was right, such as having occasionally voiced correct observations about the real shortcomings of the young lady; (5) That he is too rigidly virtuous; (6) That his family is inferior—in such and similar instances the girl will be demoted to the lower classes, and in (4) and (5) she will be put in the last row. As for the boy who is rejected without cause, he may again choose that very day among all the girls who have not been taken, if there are any left; otherwise, among ten of the following class, who like the boys will always be kept in reserve as a supplement in case of a shortage.

XLI.   In addition to the sage counsel which has been given to the young people before marriage, the chief of the Committee of Elders will address them immediately after the celebration that forms part of the festival and he will recapitulate all the earlier instructions, to wit: (1) That marriage is a hallowed state and the act of marriage the most honorable and sacred of nature's mysteries; (2) That consequently one may permit oneself nothing which might profane it either by brutal transports of passion or indecent liberties, obscene speech, and so on; (3) That the delights with which nature accompanies the act of marriage are a beneficence for which thanks are due her; (4) That these delights should persuade a reasonable spirit to bear with resignation the pains attached to the conjugal bond; (5) That since a father's pleasure in the birth of his children is the tenderest that can be experienced, it should make a wife dearer to us and should commit us to bringing up the children well; (6) That the impatience of a husband with his wife, brutality, rage, and so on, are acts at once ferocious and puerile; (7) That for the sake of the children's constitution and the father's health, the taste for carnal pleasure inspired by a wife should cease to exercise the dominion and ardor of a novelty, since this taste might consume the husband's strength and give the fatherland children with weak bodies but violent passions, that is, disproportionate to their strength; (8) That there is among married couples a sort of gentle intimacy founded upon confidence and mutual need, which is preferable even to the tenderest love, since that can only be a detriment to the fulfillment of one's duties because it is too absorbing; (9) That one cannot master the art of inspiring love or prevent it from waning, but one can be adept at winning confidence, fostering mutual dependence, and these virtues are the foundation of happiness; (10) That spouses should be polite to each other, politeness being a kind of amiability which renders us agreeable, for no persons have more need to be agreeable one to another than spouses destined to live together; (11) That consequently they should not be exigent, captious, sensitive; sincerity, amiable candor, frankness should be the soul of their converse; (12) They will be warned that they should enjoy hymen's pleasures only in stealth until the age of 35; (13) That at this age they will be free, as mature men; (14) That it is low, criminal, and reprehensible to give a bad example to youth either by word or indecent action contrary to good morals; (15) That a good example set by one's conduct with one's spouse will be praised and there will be public rewards for those who have particularly distinguished themselves in this respect; (16) That the proper education of children is the principal responsibility of married people, in view of the fact that it serves the general good while accomplishing a private good; (17) That fathers of wicked children will not be esteemed, while good children of wicked parents will be considered doubly meritorious; (18) That the wicked father of a good son will nonetheless be punished and relegated to the last classes of men, as will be specified in Article LV of Title Three of this regulation, but that his good son may obtain his pardon once; (19) That a pusillanimous husband who lets himself in a cowardly manner be dominated, mastered, and led by his wife out of weakness or love will be publicly censured for the first offense; for further offenses he will be obliged to appear in the village or city assemblies with a little distaff and a little spindle in his hat; (20) That, on the other hand, every husband who preserves masculine dignity without harshness, who is the guide, protector, noble and upright defender of his spouse, will be lauded if he has these qualities to a notable degree, and in the event of exemplary conduct in this respect, he will be raised to a class above the one in which he stood at the time of his marriage; (21) That distinguished services rendered to the state, sublime moral virtues, an invention useful and rare, a splendid and superb system of bringing up children that has produced excellent results, will likewise raise a citizen in grade and might even elevate him to the level of top man in the top class, in accordance with his deserts; (22) Finally, that a bad husband, quarrelsome, drunk, brutal to the point of striking his wife, will be sequestered from society, confined to the class of the helpless deformed, and treated with terrible severity. Still further instructions might be added according to the time and circumstances.

XLII. The newly weds will see their wives only through the grillwork separating men and women in the common room set aside for meals and public diversions. Each evening the young man will return to his parents' home, and his wife's parents will take their daughter home, where she will live as before her marriage. But she will sleep alone, and if her husband is clever enough to get to her, joy will be with him. However, he will never be encouraged by the parents, who would otherwise be considered blameworthy. Until the age of 35, a husband cannot be seen with his wife anywhere without dishonor and without exposing himself to censure; but anything he does in secret and without being discovered, though the results may betray him, will be praised. And it will be a great achievement to have had several children by one's wife without ever having been caught by the parents or seen alone with one's wife. This virtue carried to the highest point of perfection will result in advancement by a degree to a higher class. And if it is joined to another cause of advancement the husband will be graded one number higher than his equals in merit.

XLIII.   Should it happen that a newly wed husband, in defiance of this wise regulation, presumes to behave freely with his wife in accordance with present abuses, he will be deported, that is to say, sent to the colonies until the age of 35, at which time he will be obliged to go back to his country, where he will be placed in the lowest class. His wife will then be returned to him and he will follow the common lot.

XLIV.   But if the young husband employs new and clever means to pass happy moments with his wife, he will be praised for it, whatever they are, provided that he uses no violence or firearms, only stratagems either to take the parents of his wife by surprise or to conceal himself from them and remain totally undiscovered. The law provides that in this case the young wife may not elude him or try to make her husband fail. If such a thing should happen, she would be punished as a felon by the Committee of Ancient Dames, even without her husband's filing complaint. There will be instances, however, when the young husbands will be warned by their families that nothing is to be attempted; and mothers especially will be authorized to keep the newly weds under their surveillance on those occasions.

XLV.   When brides become pregnant, their husbands will be allowed to see them every day and to spend one or two hours with them under the eyes of the mother and the whole household. For this purpose, mealtimes will be preferred. This indulgence is intended to instill a kind of contentment in the soul of the young wife, who will take care to inform her mother as soon as she believes herself pregnant. Until the pregnancy is confirmed, however, permission will be granted the husband only for a brief interview. Finally, in the last two months, the husband may remain much longer with his wife if his parents or the Elders judge he can do so without neglecting his duties. Otherwise this privilege will not be granted. The bad conduct of husbands or wives will deprive them of this advantage.

XLVI.   If, despite all the security which the regulation gives to the conjugal union, it should transpire that a woman commits an essential infidelity, a single eyewitness will suffice to convict her; for even if she has not committed the crime of adultery, an intimacy great enough to arouse suspicion will be enough to render her unworthy of her husband. If it is the husband himself who has seen it, his testimony will be irrefutable. The marriage will be broken, entirely annulled, if there are still no children; and the woman will be confined to outcasts disgraced in the eyes of nature in proportion to her transgression and the degree of its certainty. That is, if there is only one witness and consequently the consummation of the adultery is not completely proved, she will be put in the rank of the least deformed, and as such she might be given in marriage to a deformed young man from among those who can marry girls, as set forth in Article XXXVIII, or to a widower. If there is a clear-cut conviction either on the testimony of her husband or of two or more witnesses, the woman thus justly repudiated will be given to the most deformed blind men, and condemned to serve them and to lead them under pain of prison and flogging in case she fails to conduct herself well or to care for them. It should be noted that the guilty will always be sent to a different region, to places known only to the chief of the Committee of Elders, so that the deformed who marry them will be ignorant of their particular crime and will not be able to reproach them with it. For there are still other crimes for which girls will be cast into the deformed classes, such as indiscretion, indolence, inveterate slovenliness, base malice, habitual calumny, and so on. (This should serve as a supplement to Article XIX of the *Gynographs*.) When women are unfaithful after they have had children, the marriage will not be dissolved. If the charge is not completely proved, they will be deprived of the right to bring up their daughters. If the crime is certain, they will be treated as prescribed in Article XLIII of the *Gynographs*.

If it is the man who is unfaithful, it will be ascertained whether his partner was a girl or a widow or a deformed person or a guilty woman assimilated to the deformed. Then the circumstances will be examined to see whether the act occurred after he had long been unable to approach his wife or whether he lacked this excuse in his favor. And a decision will be made accordingly, to wit: (1) If it is a well-formed girl and one without reproach whom he has thus dishonored, he will not be obliged to pay damages; under the system of equal wealth established by this regulation such penalties could not be inflicted, and even under the present system they should not be imposed since they would hurt the family of the seducer, which is not guilty. But the seducer's punishment will be personal and will consist throughout his whole life of not being able to pass before the girl or her parents without falling on his knees and asking their pardon, even if he should meet them ten times a day. He would be forbidden to reply to anything they might say to him, or to complain, save to the Committee of Elders to put bounds to the matter on its own initiative. (2) If the man has seduced a married woman, the marriage of the adulterer will be broken if he has no children and his wife demands it. She will remain free to marry again anyone permitted by law to marry widows. But the two adulterers will not be able to marry each other under any circumstances. The woman will be consecrated to the blind, deformed ones, and the man obliged to take the hand of any blind girl who would condescend to receive him, with the injunction that he must treat her well, and so on. (3) If the husband has been adulterous with a widow, the marriage will not be dissolved, but the guilty one will be publicly stigmatized by the Committee and will be barred from amusements at the four marriage festivals. Instead of giving themselves over to pleasures like the rest on those days, the guilty of every description, especially the last group, will do the heavy work, will carry water, help in the kitchen, and so on. In case of repeated offenses, they will be condemned for life (see Article LXII on crimes and LXVIII on cooks under the following Title). (4) If the husband has forgotten his duty with a deformed person, he will only be subject to a reprimand and condemned to do the lighter work during the four festivals. (5) Finally, if it was with a guilty one assimilated to the deformed, the marriage would be dissolved if there were no children and the wife demanded it. And the husband condemned in the same sentence as the criminal woman would be obliged to marry her, the adultery in this case destroying the marriage as is written in the Gospel. (6) In conclusion, it should be observed that if the man has fornicated with women of the last three classes at a time when he was forced to abstain from his own wife, either because of her illness or absence, the punishment will be incomparably lighter and of the easiest kind, such as a reprimand and the least onerous service at the marriage festivals. If, of course, the laws of the several countries are absolutely opposed to the dissolution of the marriage bonds, it could be omitted. . . .

CONSTANTIN FRANÇOIS CHASSEBOEUF, COMTE DE VOLNEY

(1757–1820)

The End of Privilege*

After Volney had completed studies in law and medicine, his adventurous spirit took him to a Lebanese monastery, where he learned Arabic, to Egypt and Syria, and at the end of the century to the United States. He represented Anjou in the Estates-General of 1789, and in the following year became secretary of the Constituent Assembly. His attempt to run a Corsican estate according to novel political and economic theories was interrupted by imprisonment during the Terror. Volney escaped the guillotine and, after an interval in which he devoted himself to public education, re-entered active political life. He remained an outspoken champion of libertarian ideas even in the legislative bodies of the Empire and the Restoration. Though he wrote a number of works on languages, travel, and ancient history, Volney's fame rests principally on *The Ruins: or a Survey of the Revolutions of Empires* (1791), where he unveiled a future society founded on liberty, justice, and the general will.

*From Constantin François Chasseboeuf, Comte de Volney, *The Ruins: or A Survey of the Revolutions of Empires* (London: J. Johnson, 1792), pp. 117–31; translated from *Les Ruines, ou Méditations sur les révolutions des empires.*

Here an opulent City once flourished; this was the seat of a powerful Empire.—Yes these places now so desert, a living Multitude formerly animated &c. Chap.II.

Engraving by John Scoles, from *The Ruins*, New York, 1796.

The Grand Obstacle to Improvement

The Genius stopt. My mind however, preoccupied with gloomy forebodings, yielded not to persuasion; but fearful of offending him by opposition, I made no reply. After a short interval; fixing on me a look that transpierced my soul: You are silent, said he, and your heart is agitated with thoughts which it dares not utter!—Confused and terrified: O Genius, I made answer, pardon my weakness: truth alone has doubtless proceeded from your lips; but your celestial intelligence can distinguish its traits, where to my gross faculties there appear nothing but clouds. I acknowledge it, conviction has not penetrated my soul, and I feared that my doubts might give you offence.

And what is doubt, replied he, that it should be regarded as a crime? Has man the power of thinking contrary to the impressions that are made upon him? If a truth be palpable, and its observance important, let us pity the man who does not perceive it: his punishment will infallibly spring from his blindness. If it be uncertain and equivocal, how is he to find in it what does not exist? To believe without evidence and demonstration is an act of ignorance and folly. The credulous man involves himself in a labyrinth of contradictions; the man of sense examines and discusses every question, that he may be consistent in his opinions; he can endure contradiction, because from the collision evidence arises. Violence is the argument of falsehood; and to impose a creed authoritatively, is the index and proceeding of a tyrant.

Emboldened by these sentiments, I replied: O Genius, since my reason is free, I strive in vain to welcome the flattering hope with which you would console me. The sensible and virtuous soul is prone enough to be hurried away by dreams of fancied happiness; but a cruel reality incessantly recals its attention to suffering and wretchedness. The more I meditate on the nature of man, the more I examine the present state of society, the less possible does it appear to me that a world of wisdom and felicity should ever be realized. I survey the face of our whole hemisphere, and no where can I perceive the germ of a happy revolution. All Asia is buried in the most profound darkness. The Chinese, subjected to an insolent despotism, dependent for their fortune upon the decision of lots, and held in awe by strokes of the bamboo, enslaved by the immutability of their code, and by the irremediable vice of their

language, offer to my view an abortive civilization and a race of automata.
The Indian, fettered by prejudice, and manacled by the inviolable institution
of his casts, vegetates in an incurable apathy. The Tartar, wandering or
fixed, at all times ignorant and ferocious, lives in the barbarity of his ancestors.
The Arab, endowed with a happy genius, loses its force and the fruit of his
labour in the anarchy of his tribes, and the jealousy of his families. The
African, degraded from the state of man, seems irremediably devoted to
servitude. In the North I see nothing but serfs, reduced to the level of cattle,
the live stock of the estate upon which they live. Ignorance, tyranny, and
wretchedness have every where struck the nations with stupor; and vicious
habits, depraving the natural senses, have destroyed the very instinct of
happiness and truth. In some countries of Europe, indeed, reason begins to
expand its wings; but even there is the knowledge of individual minds common
to the nation? Has the superiority of the government been turned to the
advantage of the people? And these people, who call themselves polished,
are they not those who three centuries ago filled the earth with their injustice?
Are they not those who, under the pretext of commerce, laid India waste,
dispeopled a new continent, and who at present subject Africa to the most
inhuman slavery? Can liberty spring up out of the bosom of despots, and
justice be administered by the hands of rapacity and avarice? O Genius!
I have beheld civilized countries, and the illusion of their wisdom has vanished
from my sight. I saw riches accumulated in the hands of a few individuals,
and the multitude poor and destitute. I saw all right and power concentered
in certain classes, and the mass of the people passive and dependent. I saw
the palaces of princes, but no incorporation of individuals as such, no common-
hall of nations. I perceived the deep attention that was given to the interests
of government; but no public interest, no sympathetic spirit. I saw that the
whole science of those who command consisted in prudently oppressing; and
the refined servitude of polished nations only appeared to me the more
irremediable.

With one obstacle in particular my mind was sensibly struck. In surveying
the globe, I perceived that it was divided into twenty different systems of
religious worship. Each nation has received, or formed for itself, opposite
opinions, and ascribing to itself exclusively the truth, has imagined every
other to be in error. But if, as is the fact, in this discordance the majority
deceive themselves, and deceive themselves with sincerity, it follows that the
human mind as readily imbibes falsehood as truth; and in that case how is it
to be enlightened? How are prejudices to be extirpated that first take root
in the mind? How is the bandage to be removed from the eyes, when the

first article in every creed, the first dogma of all religions, is the proscription of doubt, of examination, and of the right of private judgment? How is truth to make itself known? If she resort to the demonstration of argument, pusillanimous man appeals against the evidence to his conscience. If she call in the aid of divine authority, already prepossessed, he opposes an authority of a similar kind, and treats all innovation as blasphemy. Thus, in his blindness, riveting the chains upon himself, does he become the sport of his ignorance and passions. To dissolve these fatal shackles, a miraculous concurrence of happy circumstances would be necessary. It would be necessary that a whole nation, cured of the delirium of superstition, should no longer be liable to the impressions of fanaticism; that, freed from the yoke of a false doctrine, it should voluntarily embrace the genuine system of morality and reason; that it should become at once courageous and prudent, wise and docile; that every individual, acquainted with his rights, should scrupulously observe their limits; that the poor should know how to resist seduction, and the rich the allurements of avarice; that there should be found upright and disinterested chiefs; that its tyrants should be seized with a spirit of madness and folly; that the people, recovering their powers, should perceive their inability to exercise them, and consent to appoint delegates; that having first created their magistrates, they should know both how to respect and how to judge them; that in the rapid renovation of a whole nation pervaded with abuse, each individual, removed from his former habits, should suffer patiently the pains and self-denials annexed; in fine, that the nation should have the courage to conquer its liberty, the wisdom to secure it, the power to defend it, and the generosity to communicate it. Can sober judgment expect this combination of circumstances? Should fortune in the infinite variety of her caprices produce them, is it likely that I should live to see that day? Will not this frame long before that have mouldered in the tomb?

Here, oppressed with sorrow, my heart deprived me of utterance. The Genius made no reply; but in a low tone of voice I heard him say to himself: "Let us revive the hope of this man; for if he who loves his fellowcreatures be suffered to despair, what is to become of nations? The past is perhaps but too much calculated to deject him. Let us then anticipate futurity; let us unveil the astonishing age that is about to arise, that virtue, seeing the end of its wishes, animated with new vigour, may redouble its efforts to hasten the accomplishment of it."

The New Age

Scarcely had the Genius uttered to himself these words than an immense noise proceeded from the West, and turning my eyes to that quarter, I perceived, at the extremity of the Mediterranean, in the country of one of the European nations, a prodigious movement, similar to what exists in the bosom of a large city when, pervaded with sedition, an innumerable people, like waves, fluctuate in the streets and public places. My ear, struck with their cries which ascended to the very heavens, distinguished at intervals these phrases:

"What is this new prodigy? What this cruel and mysterious scourge? We are a numerous people, and we want strength! We have an excellent soil, and we are destitute of provision! We are active and laborious, and we live in indigence! We pay enormous tributes, and we are told that they are not sufficient! We are at peace without, and our persons and property are not safe within! What then is the secret enemy that devours us?"

From the midst of the concourse, some individual voices replied: "Erect a standard of distinction, and let all those who, by useful labours, contribute to the support and maintenance of society, gather round it, and you will discover the enemy that preys on your vitals."

The standard being erected, the nation found itself suddenly divided into two bodies of unequal magnitude and dissimilar appearance: the one, innumerable and nearly integral, exhibited, in the general poverty of their dress, and in their meagre and sunburnt faces, the marks of toil and wretchedness; the other, a petty groupe, a valueless fraction, presented, in their rich attire, embroidered with gold and silver, and in their sleek and ruddy complexions, the symptoms of leisure and abundance. Considering these men more attentively, I perceived that the large body was constituted of labourers, artisans, tradesmen, and every profession useful to society; and that in the lesser groupe there were none but priests, courtiers, public accountants, commanders of troops, in short the civil, military, or religious agents of government.

The two bodies being front to front assembled, and having looked with astonishment at each other, I saw the feelings of indignation and resentment spring up in the one, and a sort of panic in the other; and the large said to the small body:

Why stand you apart? Are you not of our number?

No, replied the groupe; you are the people; we are a priviledged class; we have laws, customs, and rights peculiar to ourselves.

PEOPLE.—And what labour do you perform in the society?

PRIVILEGED CLASS.—None: we are not made to labour.

PEOPLE.—How then have you acquired your wealth?

PRIVILEGED CLASS.—By taking the pains to govern you.

PEOPLE.—To govern us! and is this what you call governing? We toil, and you enjoy; we produce, and you dissipate; wealth flows from us, and you absorb it. . . . Privileged men, class distinct from the people, form a nation apart, and govern yourselves.

Then, deliberating on their new situation, some among the groupe said: Let us join the people, and partake their burthens and cares; for they are men like ourselves. Others replied: To mix with the herd would be degrading and vile; they are born to serve us, who are men of a superior race. The civil governors said: the people are mild and naturally servile; let us speak to them in the name of the king and the law, and they will return to their duty. . . . People! the king decrees, the sovereign ordains.

PEOPLE.—The king cannot decree any thing which the safety of the people does not demand; the sovereign cannot ordain but according to law.

CIVIL GOVERNORS.—The law calls upon you for submission.

PEOPLE.—The law is the general will; and we will a new order.

CIVIL GOVERNORS.—You are in that case rebels.

PEOPLE.—A nation cannot be a rebel; tyrants only are rebels.

CIVIL GOVERNORS.—The king is on our side, and he enjoins you to submit.

PEOPLE.—Kings cannot be separated from the nation in which they reign. Our king cannot be on your side; you have only the phantom of his countenance.

Then the military governors advanced, and they said: The people are timorous; it is proper to threaten them; they will yield to the influence of force. . . . Soldiers, chastise this insolent multitude!

PEOPLE.—Soldiers, our blood flows in your veins! will you strike your brothers? If the people be destroyed, who will maintain the army?

And the soldiers, grounding their arms, said to their chiefs: We are a part of the people; we whom you call upon to fight against them.

Then the ecclesiastical governors said: There is but one resource left. The people are superstitious; it is proper to overawe them with the names of God and religion.

PRIESTS.—Our dear brethren, our children, God has appointed us to govern you.

PEOPLE.—Produce the patent of his commission.

PRIESTS.—You must have faith; reason leads men into guilt.

PEOPLE.—And would you govern us without reason?

PRIESTS.—God is the God of peace; religion enjoins you to obey.

PEOPLE.—No; justice goes before peace; obedience implies a law and renders necessary the cognizance of it.

PRIESTS.—This world was intended for trial and suffering.

PEOPLE.—Do you then show us the example of suffering.

PRIESTS.—Would you live without Gods or kings?

PEOPLE.—We abjure tyranny of every kind.

PRIESTS.—You must have mediators, persons who may act in your behalf.

PEOPLE.—Mediators with God, and mediators with the king! Courtiers and priests, your services are too expensive; henceforth we take our affairs into our own hands.

Then the smaller groupe exclaimed: It is over with us; the multitude are enlightened. And the people replied: You shall not be hurt; we are enlightened, and we will commit no violence. We desire nothing but our rights: resentment we cannot but feel, but we consent to pass it by: we were slaves, we might now command; but we ask only to be free, and free we are.

MARIE JEAN ANTOINE NICOLAS DE CARITAT, MARQUIS DE CONDORCET

(1743-1794)

The Future of Man[*]

Condorcet was born in Picardy of an ancient and noble line, and was rigorously educated at a Jesuit seminary. He won a reputation as an eminent mathematician, an elegant essayist, and a *philosophe*. As a reformer, he was linked with Voltaire and Turgot, whose biographies he wrote. He was permanent secretary of the Academy of Sciences, and a member of the French Academy, as well as the academies of Turin, Bologna, St. Petersburg, and Philadelphia. In middle life, he married the beautiful and talented young Sophie de Grouchy, who presided over his salon at the Mint, of which he was comptroller, and who shared her husband's philosophical and political views. Though an aristocrat, Condorcet welcomed the Revolution. He served as a deputy in the Legislative Assembly, and he drafted a scheme which later became the foundation of the French system of national education. He was subsequently elected to the National Convention, but his vote against the King's execution, his criticism of the new constitution, and his association with the Girondists made Robespierre his enemy. Condorcet's faith in the limitless progress of science and of man was invincible. Proscribed during the Terror, he wrote his *Outlines of an Historical View of the Progress of the Human Mind* (posthumously published in 1795) in a garret where he lay secreted from the police. Later he was apprehended as he tried to escape from Paris, and he died in a Jacobin detention cell.

[*]From Marie Jean Antoine Nicolas de Caritat, Marquis de Condorcet, *Outlines of an Historical View of the Progress of the Human Mind* (London: J. Johnson, 1795), pp. 316–72; translated from the *Esquisse d'un tableau historique des progrès de l'esprit humain.*

Marquis de Condorcet, lithograph by Joseph Bordes after A. de Saint-Aubin.

Tenth Epoch

FUTURE PROGRESS OF MANKIND

If man can predict, almost with certainty, those appearances of which he understands the laws; if, even when the laws are unknown to him, experience of the past enables him to foresee, with considerable probability, future appearances; why should we suppose it a chimerical undertaking to delineate, with some degree of truth, the picture of the future destiny of mankind from the results of its history? The only foundation of faith in the natural sciences is the principle, that the general laws, known or unknown, which regulate the phenomena of the universe, are regular and constant; and why should this principle, applicable to the other operations of nature, be less true when applied to the development of the intellectual and moral faculties of man? In short, as opinions formed from experience, relative to the same class of objects, are the only rule by which men of soundest understanding are governed in their conduct, why should the philosopher be proscribed from supporting his conjectures upon a similar basis, provided he attribute to them no greater certainty than the number, the consistency, and the accuracy of actual observations shall authorise?

Our hopes, as to the future condition of the human species, may be reduced to three points: the destruction of inequality between different nations; the progress of equality in one and the same nation; and lastly, the real improvement of man.

Will not every nation one day arrive at the state of civilization attained by those people who are most enlightened, most free, most exempt from prejudices, as the French, for instance, and the Anglo-Americans? Will not the slavery of countries subjected to kings, the barbarity of African tribes, and the ignorance of savages gradually vanish? Is there upon the face of the globe a single spot the inhabitants of which are condemned by nature never to enjoy liberty, never to exercise their reason?

Does the difference of knowledge, of means, and of wealth, observable hitherto in all civilized nations, between the classes into which the people constituting those nations are divided; does that inequality, which the earliest progress of society has augmented, or, to speak more properly, produced, belong to civilization itself, or to the imperfections of the social order? Must it not continually weaken, in order to give place to that actual equality, the chief end of the social art, which diminishing even the effects of the natural difference of the faculties, leaves no other inequality subsisting but what is useful to the interest of all, because it will favour civilization, instruction, and industry, without drawing after it either dependence, humiliation or poverty? In a word, will not men be continually verging towards that state, in which all will possess the requisite knowledge for conducting themselves in the common affairs of life by their own reason, and of maintaining that reason uncontaminated by prejudices; in which they will understand their rights, and exercise them according to their opinion and their conscience; in which all will be able, by the development of their faculties, to procure the certain means of providing for their wants; lastly, in which folly and wretchedness will be accidents, happening only now and then, and not the habitual lot of a considerable portion of society?

In fine, may it not be expected that the human race will be meliorated by new discoveries in the sciences and the arts, and, as an unavoidable consequence, in the means of individual and general prosperity; by farther progress in the principles of conduct, and in moral practice; and lastly, by the real improvement of our faculties, moral, intellectual and physical, which may be the result either of the improvement of the instruments which increase the power and direct the exercise of those faculties, or of the improvement of our natural organization itself?

In examining the three questions we have enumerated, we shall find the strongest reasons to believe, from past experience, from observation of the progress which the sciences and civilization have hitherto made, and from the analysis of the march of the human understanding, and the development of its faculties, that nature has fixed no limits to our hopes.

If we take a survey of the existing state of the globe, we shall perceive, in the first place, that in Europe the principles of the French constitution are those of every enlightened mind. We shall perceive that they are too widely disseminated, and too openly professed, for the efforts of tyrants and priests to prevent them from penetrating by degrees into the miserable cottages of their slaves, where they will soon revive those embers of good sense, and rouse that silent indignation which the habit of suffering and terror have failed totally to extinguish in the minds of the oppressed.

If we next look at the different nations, we shall observe in each, particular obstacles opposing, or certain dispositions favouring this revolution. We shall distinguish some in which it will be effected, perhaps slowly, by the wisdom of the respective governments; and others in which, rendered violent by resistance, the governments themselves will necessarily be involved in its terrible and rapid motions.

Can it be supposed that either the wisdom or the senseless feuds of European nations, co-operating with the slow but certain effects of the progress of their colonies, will not shortly produce the independence of the entire new world; and that then, European population, lending its aid, will fail to civilize or cause to disappear, even without conquest, those savage nations still occupying there immense tracts of country?

Run through the history of our projects and establishments in Africa or in Asia, and you will see our monopolies, our treachery, our sanguinary contempt for men of a different complexion or a different creed, and the proselyting fury or the intrigues of our priests, destroying that sentiment of respect and benevolence which the superiority of our information and the advantages of our commerce had at first obtained.

But the period is doubtless approaching, when, no longer exhibiting to the view of these people corruptors only or tyrants, we shall become to them instruments of benefit, and the generous champions of their redemption from bondage.

The cultivation of the sugar-cane, which is now establishing itself in Africa, will put an end to the shameful robbery by which, for two centuries, that country has been depopulated and depraved.

Already, in Great Britain, some friends of humanity have set the example; and if its Machiavelian government, forced to respect public reason, has not dared to oppose this measure, what may we not expect from the same spirit, when, after the reform of an abject and venal constitution, it shall become worthy of a humane and generous people? Will not France be eager to imitate enterprises which the philanthropy and the true interest of Europe will equally have dictated? Spices are already introduced into the French islands, Guiana, and some English settlements; and we shall soon witness the fall of that monopoly which the Dutch have supported by such a complication of perfidy, of oppression, and of crimes. The people of Europe will learn in time that exclusive and chartered companies are but a tax upon the respective nation, granted for the purpose of placing a new instrument in the hands of its government for the maintenance of tyranny.

Then will the inhabitants of the European quarter of the world, satisfied with an unrestricted commerce, too enlightened as to their own rights to sport with the rights of others, respect that independence which they have hitherto violated with such audacity. Then will their establishments, instead of being filled by the creatures of power, who, availing themselves of a place or a privilege, hasten, by rapine and perfidy, to amass wealth, in order to purchase, on their return, honours and titles, be peopled with industrious men, seeking in those happy climates that ease and comfort which in their native country eluded their pursuit. There will they be retained by liberty, ambition having lost its allurements; and those settlements of robbers will then become colonies of citizens, by whom will be planted in Africa and Asia the principles and example of the freedom, reason, and illumination of Europe. To those monks also, who inculcate in the natives of the countries in question the most shameful superstitions only, and who excite disgust by menacing them with a new tyranny, will succeed men of integrity and benevolence, anxious to spread among these people truths useful to their happiness, and to enlighten them upon their interests as well as their rights: for the love of truth is also a passion; and when it shall have at home no gross prejudices to combat, no degrading errors to dissipate, it will naturally extend its regards, and convey its efforts to remote and foreign climes.

These immense countries will afford ample scope for the gratification of this passion. In one place will be found a numerous people, who, to arrive at civilization, appear only to wait till we shall furnish them with the means; and who, treated as brothers by Europeans, would instantly become their friends and disciples. In another will be seen nations crouching under the yoke of sacred despots or stupid conquerors, and who, for so many ages, have looked for some friendly hand to deliver them: while a third will exhibit either tribes nearly savage, excluded from the benefits of superior civilization by the severity of their climate, which deters those who might otherwise be disposed to communicate these benefits from making the attempt; or else conquering hordes, knowing no law but force, no trade but robbery. The advances of these two last classes will be more slow, and accompanied with more frequent storms; it may even happen that, reduced in numbers in proportion as they see themselves repelled by civilized nations, they will in the end wholly disappear, or their scanty remains become blended with their neighbours.

We might shew that these events will be the inevitable consequence not only of the progress of Europe, but of that freedom which the republic of France, as well as of America, have it in their power, and feel it to be their interest, to restore to the commerce of Africa and Asia; and that they must also necessarily result alike, whether from the new policy of European nations, or their obstinate adherence to mercantile prejudices.

A single combination, a new invasion of Asia by the Tartars, might be sufficient to frustrate this revolution; but it may be shewn that such combination is henceforth impossible to be effected. Meanwhile every thing seems to be preparing the speedy downfal of the religions of the East, which, partaking of the abjectness of their ministers, left almost exclusively to the people, and, in the majority of countries, considered by powerful men as political institutions only, no longer threaten to retain human reason in a state of hopeless bondage, and in the eternal shackles of infancy.

The march of these people will be less slow and more sure than ours has been, because they will derive from us that light which we have been obliged to discover, and because for them to acquire the simple truths and infallible methods which we have obtained after long wandering in the mazes of error, it will be sufficient to seize upon their developements and proofs in our discourses and publications. If the progress of the Greeks was lost upon other nations, it was for want of a communication between the people; and to the tyrannical domination of the Romans must the whole blame be ascribed. But, when mutual wants shall have drawn closer the intercourse and ties of all mankind; when the most powerful nations shall have established into political principles equality between societies as between individuals, and respect for the independence of feeble states, as well as compassion for ignorance and wretchedness; when to the maxims which bear heavily upon the spring of the human faculties, those shall succeed which favour their action and energy, will there still be reason to fear that the globe will contain spaces inaccessible to knowledge, or that the pride of despotism will be able to oppose barriers to truth that will long be insurmountable?

Then will arrive the moment in which the sun will observe in its course free nations only, acknowledging no other master than their reason; in which tyrants and slaves, priests and their stupid or hypocritical instruments, will no longer exist but in history and upon the stage; in which our only concern will be to lament their past victims and dupes, and, by the recollection of their horrid enormities, to exercise a vigilant circumspection, that we may be able instantly to recognise and effectually to stifle by the force of reason, the seeds of superstition and tyranny, should they ever presume again to make their appearance upon the earth.

In tracing the history of societies we have had occasion to remark, that there frequently exists a considerable distinction between the rights which the law acknowledges in the citizens of a state, and those which they really enjoy; between the equality established by political institutions, and that which takes place between the individual members: and that to this disproportion was chiefly owing the destruction of liberty in the ancient republics, the storms which they had to encounter, and the weakness that surrendered them into the power of foreign tyrants.

Three principal causes may be assigned for these distinctions: inequality of wealth, inequality of condition between him whose resources of subsistance are secured to himself and descendable to his family, and him whose resources are annihilated with the termination of his life, or rather of that part of his life in which he is capable of labour; and lastly, inequality of instruction.

It will therefore behove us to shew, that these three kinds of real inequality must continually diminish; but without becoming absolutely extinct, since they have natural and necessary causes, which it would be absurd as well as dangerous to think of destroying; nor can we attempt even to destroy entirely their effects, without opening at the same time more fruitful sources of inequality, and giving to the rights of man a more direct and more fatal blow.

It is easy to prove that fortunes naturally tend to equality, and that their extreme disproportion either could not exist, or would quickly cease, if positive law had not introduced factitious means of amassing and perpetuating them; if an entire freedom of commerce and industry were brought forward to supersede the advantages which prohibitory laws and fiscal rights necessarily give to the rich over the poor; if duties upon every sort of transfer and convention, if prohibitions to certain kinds, and the tedious and expensive formalities prescribed to other kinds; if the uncertainty and expence attending their execution had not palsied the efforts of the poor, and swallowed up their little accumulations; if political institutions had not laid certain prolific sources of opulence open to a few, and shut them against the many; if avarice, and the other prejudices incident to an advanced age, did not preside over marriages; in fine, if the simplicity of our manners and the widsom of our institutions were calculated to prevent riches from operating as the means of gratifying vanity or ambition, at the same time that an ill-judged austerity, by forbidding us to render them a means of costly pleasures, should not force us to preserve the wealth that had once been accumulated.

Let us compare, in the enlightened nations of Europe, the actual population with the extent of territory; let us observe, amidst the spectacle of their culture and their industry, the way in which labour and the means of subsistance are distributed, and we shall see that it will be impossible to maintain these means in the same extent, and of consequence to maintain the same mass of population, if any considerable number of individuals cease to have, as now, nothing but their industry, and the pittance necessary to set it at work, or to render its profit equal to the supplying their own wants and those of their family. But neither this industry, nor the scanty reserve we have mentioned, can be perpetuated, except so long as the life and health of each head of a family is perpetuated. Their little fortune therefore is at best an annuity, but in reality with features of precariousness that an annuity wants: and from hence results a most important difference between this class of society and the class of men whose resources consist either of a landed income, or the interest of a capital, which depends little upon personal industry, and is therefore not subject to similar risks.

There exists then a necessary cause of inequality, of dependence, and even of penury, which menaces without ceasing the most numerous and active class of our societies.

This inequality, however, may be in great measure destroyed, by setting chance against chance, in securing to him who attains old age a support, arising from his savings, but augmented by those of other persons, who, making a similar addition to a common stock, may happen to die before they shall have occasion to recur to it; in procuring, by a like regulation, an equal resource for women who may lose their husbands, or children who may lose their father; lastly, in preparing for those youths, who arrive at an age to be capable of working for themselves, and of giving birth to a new family, the benefit of a capital sufficient to employ their industry, and increased at the expence of those whom premature death may cut off before they arrive at that period. To the application of mathematics to the probabilities of life and the interest of money, are we indebted for the hint of these means, already employed with some degree of success, though they have not been carried to such extent, or employed in such variety of forms, as would render them truly beneficial, not merely to a few families, but to the whole mass of society, which would thereby be relieved from that periodical ruin observable in a number of families, the ever-flowing source of corruption and depravity.

These establishments, which may be formed in the name of the social power, and become one of its greatest benefits, might also be the result of individual associations, which may be instituted without danger, when the principles by which the establishments ought to be organised, shall have become more popular, and the errors, by which a great number of such associations have been destroyed, shall cease to be an object of apprehension.

We may enumerate other means of securing the equality in question, either by preventing credit from continuing to be a privilege exclusively attached to large fortunes, without at the same time placing it upon a less solid foundation; or by rendering the progress of industry and the activity of commerce more independent of the existence of great capitalists: and for these resources also we shall be indebted to the science of calculation.

The equality of instruction we can hope to attain, and with which we ought to be satisfied, is that which excludes every species of dependence, whether forced or voluntary. We may exhibit, in the actual state of human knowledge, the easy means by which this end may be attained even for those who can devote to study but a few years of infancy, and, in subsequent life, only some occasional hours of leisure. We might shew, that by a happy choice of the subjects to be taught, and of the mode of inculcating them, the entire mass of a people may be instructed in every thing necessary for the purposes of domestic economy; for the transaction of their affairs; for the free developement of their industry and their faculties; for the knowledge, exercise and protection of their rights; for a sense of their duties, and the power of discharging them; for the capacity of judging both their own actions, and the actions of others, by their own understanding; for the acquisition of all the delicate or dignified sentiments that are an honour to humanity; for freeing themselves from a blind confidence in those to whom they may entrust the care of their interests, and the security of their rights; for chusing and watching over them, so as no longer to be the dupes of those popular errors that torment and way-lay the life of man with superstitious fears and chimerical hopes; for defending themselves against prejudices by the sole energy of reason; in fine, for escaping from the delusions of imposture, which would spread snares for their fortune, their health, their freedom of opinion and of conscience, under the pretext of enriching, of healing, and of saving them.

The inhabitants of the same country being then no longer distinguished among themselves by the alternate use of a refined or a vulgar language; being equally governed by their own understandings; being no more confined to the mechanical knowledge of the processes of the arts, and the mere routine of a profession; no more dependent in the most trifling affairs, and for the slightest information, upon men of skill, who, by a necessary ascendancy, controul and govern, a real equality must be the result; since the difference of talents and information can no longer place a barrier between men whose sentiments, ideas, and phraseology are capable of being mutually understood, of whom the one part may desire to be instructed, but cannot need to be guided by the other; of whom the one part may delegate to the other the office of a rational government, but cannot be forced to regard them with blind and unlimited confidence.

Then it is that this superiority will become an advantage even for those who do not partake of it, since it will exist not as their enemy, but as their friend. The natural difference of faculties between men whose understandings have not been cultivated, produces, even among savages, empirics and dupes, the one skilled in delusion, the others easy to be deceived: the same difference will doubtless exist among a people where instruction shall be truly general; but it will be here between men of exalted understandings and men of sound minds, who can admire the radiance of knowledge, without suffering themselves to be dazzled by it; between talents and genius on the one hand, and on the other the good sense that knows how to appreciate and enjoy them: and should this difference be even greater in the latter case, comparing the force and extent of the faculties only, still would the effects of it not be the less imperceptible in the relations of men with each other, in whatever is interesting to their independence or their happiness.

The different causes of equality we have enumerated do not act distinctly and apart; they unite, they incorporate, they support one another; and from their combined influence results an action proportionably forcible, sure, and constant. If instruction become more equal, industry thence acquires greater equality, and from industry the effect is communicated to fortunes; and equality of fortunes necessarily contributes to that of instruction, while equality of nations, like that established between individuals, have also a mutual operation upon each other.

In fine, instruction, properly directed, corrects the natural inequality of the faculties, instead of strengthening it, in like manner as good laws remedy the natural inequality of the means of subsistence; or as, in societies whose institutions shall have effected this equality, liberty, though subjected to a regular government, will be more extensive, more complete, than in the independence of savage life. Then has the social art accomplished its end, that of securing and extending for all the enjoyment of the common rights which impartial nature has bequeathed to all.

The advantages that must result from the state of improvement, of which I have proved we may almost entertain the certain hope, can have no limit but the absolute perfection of the human species, since, in proportion as different kinds of equality shall be established as to the various means of providing for our wants, as to a more universal instruction, and a more entire liberty, the more real will be this equality, and the nearer will it approach towards embracing every thing truly important to the happiness of mankind.

It is then by examining the progression and the laws of this perfection, that we can alone arrive at the knowledge of the extent or boundary of our hopes.

It has never yet been supposed, that all the facts of nature, and all the means of acquiring precision in the computation and analysis of those facts, and all the connections of objects with each other, and all the possible combinations of ideas, can be exhausted by the human mind. The mere relations of magnitude, the combinations, quantity and extent of this idea alone, form already a system too immense for the mind of man ever to grasp the whole of it; a portion, more vast than that which he may have penetrated, will always remain unknown to him. It has, however, been imagined, that, as man can know a part only of the objects which the nature of his intelligence permits him to investigate, he must at length reach the point at which, the number and complication of those he already knows having absorbed all his powers, farther progress will become absolutely impossible.

But, in proportion as facts are multiplied, man learns to class them, and reduce them to more general facts, at the same time that the instruments and methods for observing them, and registering them with exactness, acquire a new precision: in proportion as relations more multifarious between a greater number of objects are discovered, man continues to reduce them to relations of a wider denomination, to express them with greater simplicity, and to present them in a way which may enable a given strength of mind, with a given quantity of attention, to take in a greater number than before: in proportion as the understanding embraces more complicated combinations, a simple mode of announcing these combinations renders them more easy to be treated. Hence it follows that truths, the discovery of which was accompanied with the most laborious efforts, and which at first could not be comprehended but by men of the severest attention, will after a time be unfolded and proved in methods that are not above the efforts of an ordinary capacity. And thus should the methods that led to new combinations be exhausted, should their applications to questions, still unresolved, demand exertions greater than the time or the powers of the learned can bestow, more general methods, means more simple would soon come to their aid, and open a farther career to genius. The energy, the real extent of the human intellect may remain the same; but the instruments which it can employ will be multiplied and improved; but the language which fixes and determines the ideas will acquire more precision and compass; and it will not be here, as in the science of mechanics, where, to increase the force, we must diminish the velocity; on the contrary the methods by which genius will arrive at the discovery of new truths, augment at once both the force and the rapidity of its operations.

In a word, these changes being themselves the necessary consequences of additional progress in the knowledge of truths of detail, and the cause which produces a demand for new resources, producing at the same time the means of supplying them, it follows that the actual mass of truths appertaining to the sciences of observation, calculation and experiment, may be perpetually augmented, and that without supposing the faculties of man to possess a force and activity, and a scope of action greater than before.

By applying these general reflections to the different sciences, we might exhibit, respecting each, examples of this progressive improvement, which would remove all possibility of doubt as to the certainty of the further improvement that may be expected. We might indicate particularly in those which prejudice considers as nearest to being exhausted, the marks of an almost certain and early advance. We might illustrate the extent, the precision, the unity which must be added to the system comprehending all human knowledge, by a more general and philosophical application of the science of calculation to the individual branches of which that system is composed. We might shew how favourable to our hopes a more universal instruction would prove, by which a greater number of individuals would acquire the elementary knowledge that might inspire them with a taste for a particular kind of study; and how much these hopes would be further heightened if this application to study were to be rendered still more extensive by a more general ease of circumstances. At present, in the most enlightened countries, scarcely do one in fifty of those whom nature has blessed with talents receive the necessary instruction for the developement of them: how different would be the proportion in the case we are supposing? and, of consequence, how different the number of men destined to extend the horizon of the sciences?

We might shew how much this equality of instruction, joined to the national equality we have supposed to take place, would accelerate those sciences, the advancement of which depends upon observations repeated in a greater number of instances, and extending over a larger portion of territory; how much benefit would be derived therefrom to mineralogy, botany, zoology, and the doctrine of meteors; in short, how infinite the difference between the feeble means hitherto enjoyed by these sciences, and which yet have led to useful and important truths, and the magnitude of those which man would then have it in his power to employ.

Lastly, we might prove that, from the advantage of being cultivated by a greater number of persons, even the progress of those sciences, in which discoveries are the fruit of individual meditation, would, also, be considerably advanced by means of minuter improvements, not requiring the strength of intellect, necessary for inventions, but that present themselves to the reflection of the least profound understandings.

If we pass to the progress of the arts, those arts particularly the theory of which depends on these very same sciences, we shall find that it can have no inferior limits; that their processes are susceptible of the same improvement, the same simplifications, as the scientific methods; that instruments, machines, looms, will add every day to the capabilities and skill of man—will augment at once the excellence and precision of his works, while they will diminish the time and labour necessary for executing them; and that then will disappear the obstacles that still oppose themselves to the progress in question, accidents which will be foreseen and prevented; and, lastly, the unhealthiness at present attendant upon certain operations, habits and climates.

A smaller portion of ground will then be made to produce a portion of provisions of higher value or greater utility; a greater quantity of enjoyment will be procured at a smaller expence of consumption; the same manufactured or artificial commodity will be produced at a smaller expence of raw materials, or will be stronger and more durable; every soil will be appropriated to productions which will satisfy a greater number of wants with the least labour, and taken in the smallest quantities. Thus the means of health and frugality will be encreased, together with the instruments in the arts of production, of curing commodities and manufacturing their produce, without demanding the sacrifice of one enjoyment by the consumer.

Thus, not only the same species of ground will nourish a greater number of individuals, but each individual, with a less quantity of labour, will labour more successfully, and be surrounded with greater conveniences.

It may, however, be demanded, whether, amidst this improvement in industry and happiness, where the wants and faculties of men will continually become better proportioned, each successive generation possess more various stores, and of consequence in each generation the number of individuals be greatly increased; it may, I say, be demanded, whether these principles of improvement and increase may not, by their continual operation, ultimately lead to degeneracy and destruction? Whether the number of inhabitants in the universe at length exceeding the means of existence, there will not result a continual decay of happiness and population, and a progress towards barbarism, or at least a sort of oscillation between good and evil? Will not this oscillation, in societies arrived at this epoch, be a perennial source of periodical calamity and distress? In a word, do not these considerations point out the limit at which all farther improvement will become impossible, and consequently the perfectibility of man arrive at a period which in the immensity of ages it may attain, but which it can never pass?

There is, doubtless, no individual that does not perceive how very remote from us will be this period: but must it one day arrive? It is equally impossible to pronounce on either side respecting an event, which can only be realized at an epoch when the human species will necessarily have acquired a degree of knowledge, of which our short-sighted understandings can scarcely form an idea. And who shall presume to foretel to what perfection the art of converting the elements of life into substances fitted for our use, may, in a progression of ages, be brought?

But supposing the affirmative, supposing it actually to take place, there would result from it nothing alarming, either to the happiness of the human race, or its indefinite perfectibility; if we consider, that prior to this period the progress of reason will have walked hand in hand with that of the sciences; that the absurd prejudices of superstition will have ceased to infuse into morality a harshness that corrupts and degrades, instead of purifying and exalting it; that men will then know, that the duties they may be under relative to propagation will consist not in the question of giving *existence* to a greater number of beings, but *happiness*; will have for their object, the general welfare of the human species; of the society in which they live; of the family to which they are attached; and not the puerile idea of encumbering the earth with useless and wretched mortals. Accordingly, there might then be a limit to the possible mass of provision, and of consequence to the greatest possible population, without that premature destruction, so contrary to nature and to social prosperity, of a portion of the beings who may have received life, being the result of those limits.

As the discovery, or rather the accurate solution of the first principles of metaphysics, morals, and politics, is still recent and as it has been preceded by the knowledge of a considerable number of truths of detail, the prejudice, that they have thereby arrived at their highest point of improvement, becomes easily established in the mind; and men suppose that nothing remains to be done, because there are no longer any gross errors to destroy, or fundamental truths to establish.

But it requires little penetration to perceive how imperfect is still the developement of the intellectual and moral faculties of man; how much farther the sphere of his duties, including therein the influence of his actions upon the welfare of his fellow-creatures and of the society to which he belongs, may be extended by a more fixed, a more profound and more accurate observation of that influence; how many questions still remain to be solved, how many social ties to be examined, before we can ascertain the precise catalogue of the individual rights of man, as well as of the rights which the social state confers upon the whole community with regard to each member. Have we even ascertained with any precision the limits of these rights, whether as they exist between different societies, or in any single society, over its members, in cases of division and hostility; or, in fine, the rights of individuals, their spontaneous unions in the case of a primitive formation, or their separations when separation becomes necessary?

If we pass on to the theory which ought to direct the application of these principles, and serve as the basis of the social art, do we not see the necessity of acquiring an exactness of which first truths, from their general nature, are not susceptible? Are we so far advanced as to consider justice, or a proved and acknowledged utility, and not vague, uncertain, and arbitrary views of pretended political advantages, as the foundation of all institutions of law? Among the variety, almost infinite, of possible systems, in which the general principles of equality and natural rights should be respected, have we yet fixed upon the precise rules of ascertaining with certainty those which best secure the preservation of these rights, which afford the freest scope for their exercise and enjoyment, which promote most effectually the peace and welfare of individuals, and the strength, repose, and prosperity of nations?

The application of the arithmetic of combinations and probabilities to these sciences, promises an improvement by so much the more considerable, as it is the only means of giving to their results an almost mathematical precision, and of appreciating their degree of certainty or probability. The facts upon which these results are built may, indeed, without calculation, and by a glance only, lead to some general truths; teach us whether the effects produced by such a cause have been favourable or the reverse: but if these facts have neither been counted nor estimated; if these effects have not been the object of an exact admeasurement, we cannot judge of the quantity of good or evil they contain: if the good or evil nearly balance each other, nay, if the difference be not considerable, we cannot pronounce with certainty to which side the balance inclines. Without the application of this arithmetic, it would be almost impossible to chuse, with sound reason, between two combinations proposing to themselves the same end, when their advantages are not distinguishable by any considerable difference. In fine, without this alliance, these sciences would remain for ever gross and narrow, for want of instruments of sufficient polish to lay hold of the subtility of truth—for want of machines sufficiently accurate to sound the bottom of the well where it conceals its wealth.

Meanwhile this application, notwithstanding the happy efforts of certain geometers, is still, if I may so speak, in its first rudiments; and to the following generations must it open a source of intelligence inexhaustible as calculation itself, or as the combinations, analogies, and facts that may be brought within the sphere of its operations.

There is another species of progress, appertaining to the sciences in question, equally important; I mean, the improvement of their language, at present so vague and so obscure. To this improvement must they owe the advantage of becoming popular, even in their first elements. Genius can triumph over these inaccuracies, as over other obstacles; it can recognise the features of truth, in spite of the mask that conceals or disfigures them. But how is the man who can devote but a few leisure moments to instruction to do this? how is he to acquire and retain the most simple truths, if they be disguised by an inaccurate language? The fewer ideas he is able to collect and combine, the more requisite it is that they be just and precise. He has no fund of truths stored up in his mind, by which to guard himself against error; nor is his understanding so strengthened and refined by long exercise, that he can catch those feeble rays of light which escape under the obscure and ambiguous dress of an imperfect and vicious phraseology.

It will be impossible for men to become enlightened upon the nature and developement of their moral sentiments, upon the principles of morality, upon the motives for conforming their conduct to those principles, and upon their interests, whether relative to their individual or social capacity, without making, at the same time, an advancement in moral practice, not less real than that of the science itself. Is not a mistaken interest the most frequent cause of actions contrary to the general welfare? Is not the impetuosity of our passions the continual result, either of habits to which we addict ourselves from a false calculation, or of ignorance of the means by which to resist their first impulse, to divert, govern, and direct their action?

Is not the practice of reflecting upon our conduct; of trying it by the touchstone of reason and conscience; of exercising those humane sentiments which blend our happiness with that of others, the necessary consequence of the well-directed study of morality, and of a greater equality in the conditions of the social compact? Will not that consciousness of his own dignity, appertaining to the man who is free, that system of education built upon a more profound knowledge of our moral constitution, render common to almost every man those principles of a strict and unsullied justice, those habitual propensities of an active and enlightened benevolence, of a delicate and generous sensibility, of which nature has planted the seeds in our hearts, and which wait only for the genial influence of knowledge and liberty to expand and to fructify? In like manner as the mathematical and physical sciences tend to improve the arts that are employed for our most simple wants, so is it not equally in the necessary order of nature that the moral and political sciences should exercise a similar influence upon the motives that direct our sentiments and our actions?

What is the object of the improvement of laws and public institutions, consequent upon the progress of these sciences, but to reconcile, to approximate, to blend and unite into one mass the common interest of each individual with the common interest of all? What is the end of the social art, but to destroy the opposition between these two apparently jarring sentiments? And will not the constitution and laws of that country best accord with the intentions of reason and nature where the practice of virtue shall be least difficult, and the temptations to deviate from her paths least numerous and least powerful.

What vicious habit can be mentioned, what practice contrary to good faith, what crime even, the origin and first cause of which may not be traced in the legislation, institutions, and prejudices of the country in which we observe such habit, such practice, or such crime to be committed?

In short, does not the well-being, the prosperity, resulting from the progress that will be made by the useful arts, in consequence of their being founded upon a sound theory, resulting, also, from an improved legislation, built upon the truths of the political sciences, naturally dispose men to humanity, to benevolence, and to justice? Do not all the observations, in fine, which we proposed to develope in this work prove, that the moral goodness of man, the necessary consequence of his organization, is, like all his other faculties, susceptible of an indefinite improvement? and that nature has connected, by a chain which cannot be broken, truth, happiness, and virtue?

Among those causes of human improvement that are of most importance to the general welfare, must be included, the total annihilation of the prejudices which have established between the sexes an inequality of rights, fatal even to the party which it favours. In vain might we search for motives by which to justify this principle, in difference of physical organization, of intellect, or of moral sensibility. It had at first no other origin but abuse of strength, and all the attempts which have since been made to support it are idle sophisms.

And here we may observe, how much the abolition of the usages authorized by this prejudice, and of the laws which it has dictated, would tend to augment the happiness of families; to render common the virtues of domestic life, the fountain-head of all the others; to favour instruction, and, especially, to make it truly general, either because it would be extended to both sexes with greater equality, or because it cannot become general, even to men, without the concurrence of the mothers of families. Would not this homage, so long in paying, to the divinities of equity and good sense, put an end to a too fertile principle of injustice, cruelty, and crime, by superseding the opposition hitherto maintained between that natural propensity, which is, of all others, the most imperious, and the most difficult to subdue, and the interests of man, or the duties of society? Would it not produce, what has hitherto been a mere chimera, national manners of a nature mild and pure, formed, not by imperious privations, by hypocritical appearances, by reserves imposed by the fear of shame or religious terrors, but by habits freely contracted, inspired by nature and avowed by reason?

The people being more enlightened, and having resumed the right of disposing for themselves of their blood and their treasure, will learn by degrees to regard war as the most dreadful of all calamities, the most terrible of all crimes. The first wars that will be superseded, will be those into which the usurpers of sovereignty have hitherto drawn their subjects for the maintenance of rights pretendedly hereditary.

Nations will know, that they cannot become conquerors without losing their freedom; that perpetual confederations are the only means of maintaining their independance; that their object should be security, and not power. By degrees commercial prejudices will die away; a false mercantile interest will lose the terrible power of imbuing the earth with blood, and of ruining nations under the idea of enriching them. As the people of different countries will at last be drawn into closer intimacy, by the principles of politics and morality, as each, for its own advantage, will invite foreigners to an equal participation of the benefits which it may have derived either from nature or its own industry, all the causes which produce, envenom, and perpetuate national animosities, will one by one disappear, and will no more furnish to warlike insanity either fuel or pretext.

Institutions, better combined than those projects of perpetual peace which have occupied the leisure and consoled the heart of certain philosophers, will accelerate the progress of this fraternity of nations; and wars, like assassinations, will be ranked in the number of those daring atrocities, humiliating and loathsome to nature; and which fix upon the country or the age whose annals are stained with them, an indelible opprobrium.

In speaking of the fine arts in Greece, in Italy, and in France, we have observed, that it is necessary to distinguish, in their productions, what really belongs to the progress of the art, and what is due only to the talent of the artist. And here let us enquire what progress may still be expected, whether, in consequence of the advancement of philosophy and the sciences, or from an additional store of more judicious and profound observations relative to the object, the effects and the means of these arts themselves; or, lastly, from the removal of the prejudices that have contracted their sphere, and that still retain them in the shackles of authority, from which the sciences and philosophy have at length freed themselves. Let us ask, whether, as has frequently been supposed, these means may be considered as exhausted? or, if not exhausted, whether, because the most sublime and pathetic beauties have been seized; the most happy subjects treated; the most simple and striking combinations employed; the most prominent and general characters exhibited; the most energetic passions, their true expressions and genuine features delineated; the most commanding truths, the most brilliant images displayed; that, therefore, the arts are condemned to an eternal and monotonous imitation of their first models?

We shall perceive that this opinion is merely a prejudice, derived from the habit which exists among men of letters and artists of appreciating the merits of men, instead of giving themselves up to the enjoyment to be received from their works. The second-hand pleasure which arises from comparing the productions of different ages and countries, and from contemplating the energy and success of the efforts of genius, will perhaps be lost; but, in the mean time, the pleasure arising from the productions considered in themselves, and flowing from their absolute perfection, need not be less lively, though the improvement of the author may less excite our astonishment. In proportion as excellent productions shall multiply, every successive generation of men will direct its attention to those which are most perfect, and the rest will insensibly fall into oblivion; while the more simple and palpable traits, which were seized upon by those who first entered the field of invention, will not the less exist for our posterity, though they shall be found only in the latest productions.

The progress of the sciences secures the progress of the art of instruction, which again accelerates in its turn that of the sciences; and this reciprocal influence, the action of which is incessantly increased, must be ranked in the number of the most prolific and powerful causes of the improvement of the human race. At present, a young man, upon finishing his studies and quitting our schools, may know more of the principles of mathematics than Newton acquired by profound study, or discovered by the force of his genius, and may exercise the instrument of calculation with a readiness which at that period was unknown. The same observation, with certain restrictions, may be applied to all the sciences. In proportion as each shall advance, the means of compressing, within a small circle, the proofs of a greater number of truths, and of facilitating their comprehension, will equally advance. Thus, notwithstanding future degrees of progress, not only will men of equal genius find themselves, at the same period of life, upon a level with the actual state of science, but, respecting every generation, what may be acquired in a given space of time, by the same strength of intellect and the same degree of attention, will necessarily increase, and the elementary part of each science, that part which every man may attain, becoming more and more extended, will include, in a manner more complete, the knowledge necessary for the direction of every man in the common occurences of life, and for the free and independant exercise of his reason.

In the political sciences there is a description of truths, which, particularly in free countries (that is, in all countries in certain generations), can only be useful when generally known and avowed. Thus, the influence of these sciences upon the freedom and prosperity of nations, must, in some sort, be measured by the number of those truths that, in consequence of elementary instruction, shall pervade the general mind: and thus, as the growing progress of this elementary instruction is connected with the necessary progress of the sciences, we may expect a melioration in the doctrines of the human race which may be regarded as indefinite, since it can have no other limits than those of the two species of progress on which it depends.

We have still two other means of general application to consider, and which must influence at once both the improvement of the art of instruction and that of the sciences. One is a more extensive and more perfect adoption of what may be called technical methods; the other, the institution of an universal language.

By technical methods I understand, the art of uniting a great number of objects in an arranged and systematic order, by which we may be enabled to perceive at a glance their bearings and connections, seize in an instant their combinations, and form from them the more readily new combinations.

Let us develope the principles, let us examine the utility of this art, as yet in its infancy, and we shall find that, when improved and perfected, we might derive from it, either the advantage of possessing within the narrow compass of a picture, what it would be often difficult for volumes to explain to us so readily and so well; or the means, still more valuable, of presenting isolated facts in a disposition and view best calculated to give us their general results. We shall perceive how, by means of a small number of these pictures or tables, the use of which may be easily learned, men who have not been able to appropriate such useful details and elementary knowledge as may apply to the purposes of common life, may turn to them at the shortest notice; and how elementary knowledge itself, in all those sciences where this knowledge is founded either upon a regular code of truths or a series of observations and experiments, may hereby be facilitated.

An universal language is that which expresses by signs, either the direct objects, or those well-defined collections constituted of simple and general ideas, which are to be found or may be introduced equally in the understandings of all mankind; or, lastly, the general relations of these ideas, the operations of the human mind, the operations peculiar to any science, and the mode of process in the arts. Thus, such persons as shall have become masters of these signs, the method of combining and the rules for constructing them, will understand what is written in this language, and will read it with similar facility in the language of their own country, whatever it may happen to be.

It is apparent, that this language might be employed to explain either the theory of a science or the rules of an art; to give an account of a new experiment or a new observation, the acquisition of a scientific truth, the invention of a method, or the discovery of a process; and that, like algebra, when obliged to make use of new signs, those already known would afford the means of ascertaining their value.

A language like this has not the inconvenience of a scientific idiom, different from the vernacular tongue. We have before observed that the use of such an idiom necessarily divides societies into two extremely unequal classes; the one composed of men, understanding the language, and, therefore, in possession of the key to the sciences; the other of those who, incapable of learning it, find themselves reduced almost to an absolute impossibility of acquiring knowledge. On the contrary, the universal language we are supposing, might be learned, like the language of algebra, with the science itself; the sign might be known at the same instant with the object, the idea, or the operation which it expresses. He who, having attained the elements of a science, should wish to prosecute farther his enquiries, would find in books, not only truths that he could understand, by means of those signs, of which he already knows the value, but the explanation of the new signs of which he has need in order to ascend to higher truths.

It might be shown that the formation of such a language, if confined to the expressing of simple and precise propositions, like those which form the system of a science, or the practice of an art, would be the reverse of chimerical; that its execution, even at present, would be extremely practicable as to a great number of objects; and that the chief obstacle that would stand in the way of extending it to others, would be the humiliating necessity of acknowledging how few precise ideas, and accurately defined notions, understood exactly in the same sense by every mind, we really possess.

It might be shown that this language, improving every day, acquiring incessantly greater extent, would be the means of giving to every object that comes within the reach of human intelligence, a rigour, and precision, that would facilitate the knowledge of truth, and render error almost impossible. Then would the march of every science be as infallible as that of the mathematics, and the propositions of every system acquire, as far as nature will admit, geometrical demonstration and certainty.

All the causes which contribute to the improvement of the human species, all the means we have enumerated that insure its progress, must, from their very nature, exercise an influence always active, and acquire an extent for ever increasing. The proofs of this have been exhibited, and from their developement in the work itself they will derive additional force: accordingly we may already conclude, that the perfectibility of man is indefinite. Meanwhile we have hitherto considered him as possessing only the same natural faculties, as endowed with the same organization. How much greater would be the certainty, how much wider the compass of our hopes, could we prove that these natural faculties themselves, that this very organization, are also susceptible of melioration? And this is the last question we shall examine.

The organic perfectibility or deterioration of the classes of the vegetable, or species of the animal kingdom, may be regarded as one of the general laws of nature.

This law extends itself to the human race; and it cannot be doubted that the progress of the sanative art, that the use of more wholesome food and more comfortable habitations, that a mode of life which shall develope the physical powers by exercise, without at the same time impairing them by excess; in fine, that the destruction of the two most active causes of deterioration, penury and wretchedness on the one hand, and enormous wealth on the other, must necessarily tend to prolong the common duration of man's existence, and secure him a more constant health and a more robust constitution. It is manifest that the improvement of the practice of medicine, become more efficacious in consequence of the progress of reason and the social order, must in the end put a period to transmissible or contagious disorders, as well to those general maladies resulting from climate, aliments, and the nature of certain occupations. Nor would it be difficult to prove that this hope might be extended to almost every other malady, of which it is probable we shall hereafter discover the most remote causes. Would it even be absurd to suppose this quality of melioration in the human species as susceptible of an indefinite advancement; to suppose that a period must one day arrive when death will be nothing more than the effect either of extraordinary accidents, or of the slow and gradual decay of the vital powers; and that the duration of the middle space, of the interval between the birth of man and this decay, will itself have no assignable limit? Certainly man will not become immortal; but may not the distance between the moment in which he draws his first breath, and the common term when, in the course of nature, without malady, without accident, he finds it impossible any longer to exist, be necessarily protracted? As we are now speaking of a progress that is capable of being represented with precision, by numerical quantities or by lines, we shall embrace the opportunity of explaining the two meanings that may be affixed to the word *indefinite*.

In reality, this middle term of life, which in proportion as men advance upon the ocean of futurity, we have supposed incessantly to increase, may receive additions either in conformity to a law by which, though approaching continually an illimitable extent, it could never possibly arrive at it; or a law by which, in the immensity of ages, it may acquire a greater extent than any determinate quantity whatever that may be assigned as its limit. In the latter case, this duration of life is indefinite in the strictest sense of the word, since there exist no bounds on this side of which it must necessarily stop. And in the former, it is equally indefinite to us; if we cannot fix the term, it may for ever approach, but can never surpass; particularly if, knowing only that it can never stop, we are ignorant in which of the two senses the term indefinite is applicable to it: and this is precisely the state of the knowledge we have as yet acquired relative to the perfectibility of the species.

Thus, in the instance we are considering, we are bound to believe that the mean duration of human life will for ever increase, unless its increase be prevented by the physical revolutions of the system: but we cannot tell what is the bound which the duration of human life can never exceed; we cannot even tell, whether there be any circumstance in the laws of nature which has determined and laid down its limit.

But may not our physical faculties, the force, the sagacity, the acuteness of the senses, be numbered among the qualities, the individual improvement of which it will be practicable to transmit? An attention to the different breeds of domestic animals must lead us to adopt the affirmative of this question, and a direct observation of the human species itself will be found to strengthen the opinion.

Lastly, may we not include in the same circle the intellectual and moral faculties? May not our parents, who transmit to us the advantages or defects of their conformation, and from whom we receive our features and shape, as well as our propensities to certain physical affections, transmit to us also that part of organization upon which intellect, strength of understanding, energy of soul or moral sensibility depend? Is it not probable that education, by improving these qualities, will at the same time have an influence upon, will modify and improve this organization itself? Anology, an investigation of the human faculties, and even some facts, appear to authorise these conjectures, and thereby to enlarge the boundary of our hopes.

Such are the questions with which we shall terminate the last division of our work. And how admirably calculated is this view of the human race, emancipated from its chains, released alike from the dominion of chance, as well as from that of the enemies of its progress, and advancing with a firm and indeviate step in the paths of truth, to console the philosopher lamenting the errors, the flagrant acts of injustice, the crimes with which the earth is still polluted? It is the contemplation of this prospect that rewards him for all his efforts to assist the progress of reason and the establishment of liberty. He dares to regard these efforts as a part of the eternal chain of the destiny of mankind; and in this persuasion he finds the true delight of virtue, the pleasure of having performed a durable service, which no vicissitude will ever destroy in a fatal operation calculated to restore the reign of prejudice and slavery. This sentiment is the asylum into which he retires, and to which the memory of his persecutors cannot follow him: he unites himself in imagination with man restored to his rights, delivered from oppression, and proceeding with rapid strides in the path of happiness: he forgets his own misfortunes while his thoughts are thus employed; he lives no longer to adversity, calumny and malice, but becomes the associate of these wiser and more fortunate beings whose enviable condition he so earnestly contributed to produce.

DONATIEN ALPHONSE FRANÇOIS,
COMTE (called Marquis) DE SADE
(1740–1814)

A Bedroom Discourse[*]

After education at a Jesuit school in Paris, the Marquis de Sade saw service
as a cavalry officer and took part in the war against Prussia. His marriage
in 1763 was only an incident in a lurid career punctuated by trials for
murder and sexual offenses, condemnations to death, dramatic escapes
from prison, and at length incarceration in Vincennes and the Bastille,
where he diverted himself by writing plays and novels. In 1789 he was
transferred to a Charenton lunatic asylum, from which he was discharged
in the following year. For a period, the already notorious Marquis cast
his lot with the revolutionists, as a soldier and official of the Section des
Piques. His political moderantism, rather than his sexual extremism,
brought him into conflict with the authorities, however. He was jailed
once again, and regained his liberty only after Thermidor. His skirmishes
with the law came to an end in 1803, when he was recommitted to
Charenton as incurably mad. At Charenton, in a former convent of the
nuns of Picpus, De Sade produced plays of his own invention, drawing the
casts from among his fellow-inmates. And there he died, perhaps having
encountered a utopian of a different stripe, Henri Saint-Simon, who was
briefly immured in the same establishment. To De Sade's brief years of
freedom belongs the work excerpted here, *Philosophy in the Bedroom*. In a
pamphlet introduced into its dialogues, the republican and atheist De
Sade ruthlessly dissected the political and personal morality of his day and
called for a new order of peace and permissiveness. The pamphlet later
attracted the interest of the Saint-Simonians, who republished it in 1848.

---

*From Donatien Alphonse François, Marquis de Sade, *La Philosophie dans le boudoir* (1795), in
*Marquis de Sade, An Essay by Simone de Beauvoir, with selections from his writings chosen by Paul
Dinnage* (New York and London: Grove Press and Calder and Boyars, 1953), pp. 122–57.
Copyright © 1953, Grove Press and Calder and Boyars.

Imaginary portrait of the Marquis de Sade, contemporary print. (From Dante Serra, *L'Avventurosa vita del Marchese de Sade*, Milan: Ceschina, 1950, by courtesy of the publisher.)

The Manifesto

Frenchmen! You are too enlightened not to feel that a new government will necessitate a new way of living; it is impossible for the citizen of a free state to behave as the slave of a despotic monarch; these differences in interests, duties, and relationships in themselves determine an entirely different fashion of behavior in society; a mass of minor faults and social transgressions deemed essential under the rule of kings, who had to be more and more demanding as they needed the restraints that would make them lofty and unapproachable to their subjects—all these will become meaningless. Other crimes, known by the names of regicide and sacrilege, under a government that knows neither kings nor religions, must equally wither away in a republican state. In granting freedom of belief and freedom of the press, realize, Citizens, that at one remove from that you must accord freedom of action; that, excepting those things that bear directly against the government, there remain an uncounted number of crimes no longer punishable, for in reality there are very few actions that are criminal in a society based on freedom and equality, and if we scrupulously judge and examine matters, there is nothing truly criminal but what the law itself forbids. For Nature teaches us both vice and virtue in our constitution, or, in yet more philosophical terms, by reason of Nature's need for both vice and virtue, her promptings would become a true guide to the precise determinations of what is good or bad. In order the better to develop my ideas upon such an essential subject, let us classify the various actions of man's life which up to now have been named criminal, and we will then measure them against the true duties of a republican.

First, those which his conscience and his credulity impose on him towards the Supreme Being;

Second, those which he must fulfill towards his fellow men;

Third, and finally, those which relate only to himself.

The assurance we should feel that no god has ever had a hand in our existence and that we are here because it could not be otherwise, inevitable creatures of Nature like plants and animals—this assurance without doubt quite demolishes, as one can see, the first group of duties, those which we falsely believe we have towards divinity; and with them disappear all the religious transgressions, all those known under the vague and intangible names of *impiety, sacrilege, blasphemy, atheism,* etc.: the transgressions, in fact, which Athens punished so unjustly in Alcibiades, and France in the unfortunate Labarre. If there is one thing in the world grotesque beyond others, it is to see men, with only their own circumscribed ideas of their god and what this god demands, wish nevertheless to determine the nature of what pleases or angers this ridiculous phantom of their imagination. I would not stop at allowing all the sects an equal liberty; I should like a man to be free to ridicule and scoff at anything; I should like men gathered in this temple or the other and invoking the eternal, each in his own fashion, to look like comedians in a theater whom anyone is free to go and laugh at. If you do not look at religions in this light, they will regain the seriousness that makes them seem of consequence; soon they will start to defend their views, and then it will not be a question of disputing religions but of fighting for them;[1] equality, destroyed by the preference or protection accorded to one religion, will soon vanish from the government, and out of *theocracy* reborn will spring *aristocracy.*

I cannot say this too often: no more gods, Frenchmen, no more gods, unless you wish their mournful rule to plunge you once more into all the horrors of despotism! Only you, by ridiculing them, can destroy them; all the dangers they bring with them will revive at once if you allow them scope and importance. Do not dash down their idols in anger; crush them in play, and prejudice will die out of itself.

This suffices, I hope, to prove that no law should be passed against religious crimes—for he who offends against a myth offends no one—and that it is the utmost frivolity to punish those who outrage or despise a sect which has no apparent superiority over any other; that would perforce mean taking sides and would at once influence the balance of equality, which is the prime law of your new government.

Let us pass to the second class of the duties of man, those which connect him with his fellows; this class is the most extensive of all.

Christian morality, far too vague on the subject of man's relation to his fellows, proposes axioms so full of sophistry that we cannot admit them; for if one wishes to erect principles one must take care not to base them on

---

1. Every people claims to have the best religion and bases it upon an infinity of proofs which are not only at odds with each other but almost entirely contradictory. In our present profound ignorance of what might please God (supposing that there is one), the wise course is either to protect all equally or forbid all equally; now, forbid them is assuredly the wisest, since we have the moral certainty that all are farces equally indifferent to a god who does not exist.

sophistries. This absurd morality tells us to love our neighbor as ourselves. Nothing indeed could be more sublime, if only falsity did not often have the appearance of beauty. There is no question of loving one's neighbor as oneself, for that is against all the laws of Nature, and Nature should be the sole guide of our life; it is only a question of loving our fellow men as brothers, as friends given to us by Nature and with whom we will be able to live far better in a republican state, when distances between us are abolished and ties made closer.

Let humanity, fraternity, benevolence so prescribe our mutual duties, and let each one individually fulfill them with the amount of energy with which Nature has endowed him, without blaming and above all without punishing the phlegmatic or the melancholy who do not feel the same delight as others in these tender bonds; for, let us agree, it would be a palpable absurdity to wish to prescribe universal laws; it would be like the ludicrous procedure of a general who dressed all his soldiers in uniforms of the same size; it is a fearful injustice to expect men of different temperament to bow to the same laws; what suits one man does not suit all.

I agree that one could not make as many laws as there are men; but the laws could be so mild, so few, that all men, whatever their character, might easily obey them. Again, I would insist that these few laws be of a kind that could easily adapt themselves to different characters; and their administrator should be prepared to strike more or less severely according to the individual in question. It has been proved that such and such a virtue is impossible to certain men just as such and such a medicine cannot agree with a certain constitution. Therefore, what a consummation of injustice would it be to use the law to punish a man incapable of obeying that law! Would it not be an iniquity equal to forcing a blind man to distinguish colors?

From these first principles develops the necessity for making benevolent laws, and above all for abolishing forever the death penalty, for a law that strikes at a man's life is impracticable, unjust, inadmissible. It is not—as I shall state—that there are not numberless cases when, without outraging Nature (and that is what I shall prove), men are given entire liberty by this common mother to attempt the life of other men, but that it is not possible for the law to have the same privilege, for cold-blooded law by itself cannot be subject to the passions that legitimize in man the cruel action of murder; man receives sensations from Nature that may make that action pardonable, while the law, on the contrary, always in opposition to Nature and receiving nothing from her, cannot be permitted the same licence; not having the same motives, it cannot have the same rights. These are knowing and subtle distinctions that escape many people, for there are few people who reflect;

but they will be accepted by the thinking men to whom they are addressed, and they will, I hope, influence the new code that is being prepared for us.

The second reason for which the death penalty should be abolished is that it has never restrained crime, for crime is committed every day at the very foot of the scaffold.

This penalty must be abolished, in a word, because there can be no worse logic than to execute one man for having killed another, since the obvious result of this procedure is that two men are now dead instead of one, and only rascals and imbeciles are familiar with such arithmetic.

In sum, there are only four major crimes against our fellows: *calumny, theft,* offences caused by *uncleanness* which have a harmful effect on others, and *murder.*

Are all these actions, which are considered capital offences under a monarchal government, equally serious in a republican state? That is what we shall examine by the torch of reason, for it is by this light alone that we can conduct our enquiry. Let no one tax me with being a dangerous innovator; let no one say that there is a danger in awakening remorse in the souls of criminals, as these writings may do, that the leniency of my moral system will increase the criminals' leanings to crime; I formally testify that I have none of these perverse opinions; I am revealing the ideas I have held since I attained the age of reason, ideas opposed by the infamous despotism of tyrants for centuries; so much the worse for those who could be corrupted by these noble thoughts, who can only grasp evil from philosophic ideas and would be corrupted by anything. Perhaps they would be poisoned even by reading Seneca or Charon! It is not to them that I speak; I speak to those who are capable of understanding me, and they will be able to read me without danger.

I confess with complete frankness that I have never believed calumny to be an evil, especially under a government like our own, where all men are more united, more approachable, and therefore have more need to know each other well. Two things may result: either the calumny falls upon a man who is in fact wicked, or it falls on a virtuous man. You will agree that in the first case it makes very little difference whether evil is spoken of a man already known to do wrong; perhaps the falsely imputed crime will bring to light the true ones and make his villainy known.

If, let us suppose, there is an unhealthy climate at Hanover, but which would only expose me to an attack of fever, should I bear a grudge against a man who told me, to prevent me from going, that I should die on arriving there? Undoubtedly not; for by frightening me with a great danger he has saved me from a small one.

Should the calumny fall, on the contrary, on a virtuous man, let him have no fear; let him reveal himself frankly, and all the venom of the calumniator will recoil upon himself. For such men, calumny is only a purifying test from which their virtue emerges even brighter. The sum of virtue in the republic can even profit by this; for this virtuous and sensitive man, annoyed at the injustice he has experienced, will attempt to live better still; he will wish to overcome this attack from which he had thought himself safe, and his good deeds will acquire an extra degree of effort. Thus, in the first case, the calumniator will have brought about good results by exaggerating the vices of the dangerous man; in the second, he will produce even better results by forcing virtue to dedicate itself entirely to us.

Now, I ask you in what respect the calumniator can seem to you dangerous, especially in a society where it is essential to expose the vicious and increase the efforts of the virtuous? Let us take care then to establish no penalties for calumniation; rather, let us consider it as a searchlight or as an incentive, and as useful as either. The legislator, whose ideas must be as lofty as his task, should never study the effect of a crime which strikes only at individuals; he must study its effect on the mass of people, and when he thus observes the results of calumniation I defy him to discover anything punishable; on the contrary, he would be a truly just and sincere man if he were to favor and reward it.

Theft is the second of the moral offences which we propose to scrutinize.

If we scan antiquity, we find that theft was permitted and rewarded in all the Greek republics; Sparta and Lacedaemon openly favored it; other peoples regarded it as a wartime virtue; certainly it maintains courage, strength, skill, all the virtues, in fact, which are useful to a republican government and thus to our government. I might venture to ask without prejudice whether theft, which tends to redistribute wealth, is really a great evil in a society whose whole aim is equality? No, undoubtedly not; for as it encourages equality on the one hand, on the other it makes people more watchful over their property. There was once a nation which punished, not the thief, but him who was robbed, in order to teach him to guard his property. This brings us to more detailed considerations.

Far be it from me to attack or overthrow the oath on the respect of property which the nation has just taken; but may I be allowed a few words on the injustice of this oath? What is the spirit of a vow made by all the individuals of a nation? Is it not to maintain a complete equality among the citizens, to place them all equally under the law protecting all property? Now, I ask whether a law which commands the man possessing nothing to respect the man who has everything is indeed just? What are the essentials of the social contract? Does it not consist in giving up a small amount of freedom and property in order to preserve both of them?

These principles underlie all laws; they motivate the punishment of those who abuse their liberty; they authorize taxes. When a citizen is asked to pay taxes, he does not complain because he knows that what he gives is used to preserve what remains with him; but, once again, why should the man with nothing associate himself with a pact that protects only the man who has everything? If you are committing a just act in respecting, by your agreement, the properties of the rich, are you not committing an injustice in forcing the man who respects it, and yet has nothing, to submit to your agreement? What interest can he have in your agreement? And why do you expect him to make a promise that benefits only the man who differs so much from him by reason of his riches? There certainly could be nothing more unjust; an agreement should have the same effect for all the parties who subscribe to it; a man who has no interest in maintaining it cannot really be bound by it, for then it is no longer the pact of a free people; it becomes the law of the strong against the weak, who would then be in constant revolt against it. This then is what has taken place in the agreement on the respect of property which the nation has just passed; it is the rich man who binds the poor man to it; it is the rich man who gains from the promise made so unwillingly by the poor man, which he sees as a promise extorted from him in his good faith, and under which he agrees to do something that could never in fact be done to him.

Now that you are convinced, as you must be, of this barbarous inequality, do not aggravate the injustice of it by punishing the poor man for daring to rob the rich: your unfair agreement gives him a stronger right than ever. By forcing him to perjure himself through this meaningless agreement, you legitimize all the crimes which his perjury will bring about; thus it is not for you to punish what you yourself have caused. I will say no more to make you realize the horrible cruelty of punishing thieves. Imitate the wise law of the nation I mentioned; punish the man negligent enough to let himself be robbed, but inflict no penalty on the robber; reflect that it was your agreement that authorized him to do this, and that in giving in to it he is only following the first and most sacred impulse of Nature, that of preserving one's own existence at the expense of others.

The crimes which we now come to examine, in this second class of man's duties to his fellows, consist of the actions performed by libertinism, the most noteworthy of which are *prostitution, incest, rape* and *sodomy*. We should have no doubt that everything which goes under the name of moral crime, that is to say all the actions of the types we have just mentioned, are quite indifferent to a government whose sole duty is to maintain by one means or another a state of affairs that guarantees its existence—that is the only morality of a republican government.

Now, since this is always opposed by the tyrants who surround the country, one could scarcely imagine reasonably that its means of defending this state could be *moral means*: for it can only defend itself by war, and nothing is less moral than war.

Now, I should like to ask how it could be proved that in a state that is obliged to be *immoral*, the individuals should be *moral*? I go further; I say it is better that they should not be. The legislators of ancient Greece fully realized the important necessity of corrupting the limbs of the state so that their *moral dissolution* influenced the vital parts of the body and resulted in insurrection, which is indispensable to a society that is as perfectly happy as is a republican society, a condition which is bound to excite the hatred and jealousy of surrounding states. Insurrection, these wise legislators believed, is certainly not a *moral* state; and yet it must be the permanent state of a republic; it would therefore be as absurd as it would be dangerous to demand that men who had to maintain a perpetual *immoral* disturbance of the machinery of state should themselves be very *moral* beings, for the moral state is one of peace and tranquillity, while the *immoral* state is one of perpetual movement, equivalent to the necessary state of insurrection into which the republican must guide his government.

Let us go into more detail now, and begin by analyzing modesty, that pusillanimous impulse that is hostile to all impure affections. If it were Nature's intention that man should be modest, she certainly would not have had him born naked; an infinite number of peoples, less degraded by civilization than we, go naked and feel no shame at it; there is no doubt that the custom of clothing oneself is simply caused by the inclemency of the climate, and by the coquetry of women; women felt that they would soon lose the effects of desire if they anticipated it; ... thus modesty, far from being a virtue, was no more than one of the first effects of corruption, than one of the first means of female coquetry.

Lycurgus and Solon, who well understood that the results of immodesty held the citizen in the *immoral* state essential to the laws of republican government, required young girls to show themselves nude in the theaters.[2] Rome

2. It has been said that the intention of these legislators, in dulling the passion that men experience for a nude woman, was to render more active that which men experience now and then for their own sex. These sages required to be shown that which they wished to breed disgust for, and they hid that which they believed inspired the softest desires; in any case, did they work for any other end than that we have just described? They sensed, one realizes, the need for immorality in republican mores.

imitated this example: they danced nude in the fete of Flora; the majority of pagan rites were celebrated thus; nudity even passed for virtue with some peoples. Be that as it may, lewd propensities arise from immodesty; and the results of these propensities make up the so-called crimes that we are analyzing, and of them the first result is prostitution.

Now that we are freed of all that pack of religious errors that formerly held us captive, and now that we are closer to Nature by reason of having demolished a quantity of prejudices, be assured that if there be a crime, it is rather to resist the desires that Nature has inspired in us (as well as to combat them); and, persuaded that desire was a result of these propensities, [be assured] that, rather than extinguish this passion in us, it is better to arrange the means for satisfying it in peace. We must then attempt to establish order here and to guarantee the necessary security to the citizen with a need to approach the objects of his desire, free to vent on these objects all those passions prescribed in him, without ever being restrained by anything; because there is no passion in man that needs so total an extension of liberty as this. Various health establishments, vast and suitably furnished, and secure in all points, will be erected in the city; there, all sexes, all ages, all creatures possible will be offered to the caprices of the libertines who wish pleasure; and the most complete subordination will be the rule for the individuals offered; the lightest refusal will be punished immediately and arbitrarily by him who has met with it. I must explain this further—the regulation of republican mores; I have promised the same logic in everything, and I will keep my word.

If, as I have just said, there is no passion that so needs every possible extension of liberty as this one, there is also none that is so tyrannical; in this, man loves to command, to be obeyed, to surround himself with slaves constrained to satisfy him; now whenever you deny a man a secret means of expelling the deposit of tyranny that Nature has put into his heart, he will turn and vent it upon his surroundings; he will agitate against the government. If you wish to avoid this danger, allow a free scope to these tyrannical desires, which will torment a man in spite of himself; then, content at having wielded his petty sovereignty among the harem of Oriental servants and wives offered him by your money and organization, he will issue forth satisfied and with no desire to disturb a government that secures so willingly for him every object of his lusts; but should you, on the other hand, take different action and impose upon these objects of public lusts the ridiculous restraints formerly invented by ministerial tyranny and the lubricity of our

Sardanapalus:[3] then each man will quickly become embittered against your government, jealous of the despotism that he sees you alone exercising, and will throw off the yoke with which you burden him and, tired of your fashion of ruling, will change it as he has just done.

Notice how the Greek legislators, thoroughly imbued with these ideas, treated debauchery in Lacedaemon and Athens; they intoxicated the citizen with it, far from forbidding it; no form of lechery was denied him; and Socrates, called by the oracle the wisest philosopher on earth, passed from the arms of Aspasia to those of Alcibiades and was not any less the glory of Greece. I will go further, and however opposed my ideas may seem to our present customs—since my object is to prove that we must hasten to change these customs if we wish to preserve our chosen government—I will try to convince you that prostitution for so-called decent women is no more dangerous than it is for men, and that we should not only involve them in the orgies in the brothels I would establish, but should even build some for them where their whims and the needs of their temperament, so differently passionate from ours, could be satisfied in the same way with all sexes.

By what right do you claim, first, that women should be exempted from the blind submission to men's whims that Nature ordains for them; and second, by what right do you claim to enslave them to continence, which is foreign to their nature and absolutely unnecessary to their honor?

I will treat these two questions separately.

It is certain that in a state of Nature women were born vulvovaginal, enjoying, that is to say, the advantages of other female animals, and like them belonging without exception to all males; such, doubtless, were the first laws of Nature and the only rules of the first societies made by men. *Self-seeking, egoism,* and *love* degraded these first simple and natural ideas; men believed they were adding to their wealth by taking a wife and her family inheritance; that is how the first two emotions I have mentioned came into being; yet more often men carried off their women and grew attached to them; that is how the other motive was born; and with it in every case went injustice.

Never can an act of possession be carried out upon a free being; it is as unjust to possess a woman exclusively as to possess slaves; all men are born free, all are equal in law; let us never lose sight of these principles; for this reason the right can never be given to one sex to take possession of the other;

3. It is known that the infamous and rascally Sartine furnished a means of lust to Louis XV by having La Dubarry read to him three times a week the intimate details, embellished by himself, of all that happened in the low quarters of Paris. That particular libertinism of the French Nero cost the state three millions!

and never can one of the sexes or classes have an arbitrary right over the other. In the pure state of Nature's laws, a woman cannot even allege in refusal of one who desires her that she loves another, for this becomes a reason for exclusion; and no man can be excluded from the enjoyment of a woman when it becomes clear that she belongs to all men. The act of possession can only be exercised upon a piece of furniture or an animal; it can never be used upon a human being of our own kind; and any tie you may imagine which can bind a woman to a man is as unjust as it is fantastic.

If, then, it appears beyond contradiction that Nature has given us the right to carry out our wishes upon all women indifferently, it appears equally that we have the right to force her to submit to our wishes, not in exclusivity, for then I would contradict myself, but momentarily.[4] It is beyond question that we have the right to establish laws which will force woman to yield to the ardors of him who desires her; violence itself being one of the results of this right, we can legally employ it. Has not Nature proved to us that we have this right, by allotting us the strength necessary to force them to our desires?

In vain may women protest modesty or attachment to other men in their defence; these chimerical reasons count for nothing; we have already seen that modesty is an artificial and despicable emotion. Neither has love, which might be called *madness of the soul,* any right to justify their fidelity: it satisfies only two individuals, the beloved and the lover, and cannot therefore increase the happiness of others; but women were given to us for the general happiness, not for an egotistical and privileged enjoyment. All men, then, have an equal right to the enjoyment of all women; and there is no man, according to Nature's laws, who can institute a unique and personal claim to any woman. The law which will oblige them to prostitute themselves in the brothels I have spoken of, which will force them if they evade it, is therefore the most equitable of laws and one against which no legitimate excuse can be urged.

A man who wishes to enjoy any woman or girl may thus, if you pass just laws, summon her to appear in one of the houses I have described; and there, safeguarded by the matrons of this temple of Venus, she will be offered in complete meekness and submission to satisfy all the caprices he wishes to indulge with her, however strange and irregular they may be, for there is

---

4. Let no one say at this point that I am contradicting myself, and that having established above that we have no right to bind a woman to ourselves, I now destroy this principle by saying that we have the right to force her; I repeat that it is not a question of property but of enjoyment; I have no right to the ownership of the fountain that lies in my path, but I certainly have the right to make use of it; I have the right to enjoy the limpid water offered up to my thirst; in the same way I have no actual claim to the possession of such and such a woman, but I have an incontestable one to the enjoyment of her; and I have the right to force her to this enjoyment if she refuses me for any motive whatsoever.

none that is not inspired by Nature, none that she can refuse. It would only remain then to fix the age; but I claim that that cannot be done without hampering the freedom of whoever desires a girl of such and such an age.

Whoever has the right to eat the fruit off a tree may assuredly pluck it either ripe or green according to his taste. But it will be objected that at this age the interference of a man will have a decisively bad effect on the health of the child. That consideration is meaningless: once you have accorded me the right to enjoyment, this right is independent of the effects of the enjoyment; from that moment on, it makes no difference whether the act of enjoyment is beneficial or harmful to the object submitting to it. Have I not already proved that it would be legal to force a woman, and that as soon as she kindles a desire to enjoy her, she must submit to being enjoyed without any egotistical considerations?

It is the same with her health. The moment that the enjoyment of him who desires and has the right to take possession is spoiled or weakened by such considerations, the question of age must be forgotten; for we are not concerned with the sensations of the object condemned by Nature and the law to assuage momentarily another's desires; we are only concerned in this analysis with what pleases the one who desires. We shall redress the balance.

Yes, it shall be redressed, it undoubtedly must be; these women that we have served so cruelly must certainly be recompensed; and this is going to form the reply to the second question I asked.

If we admit, as we have just done, that all women should submit to our desires, surely we should also allow them fully to satisfy their own; our laws should in this respect look favorably upon their ardent natures; and it is absurd that we have assigned both their honor and their virtue to the unnatural strength they must use to resist the inclinations with which they have been far more profusely endowed than we. This social injustice is even more glaring since we agree both to weaken them by our seduction and then to punish them when they yield to all our efforts to make them fall. The whole absurdity of our morals, it seems to me, is contained in that atrocious injustice, and the revelation of that alone should be enough to make us realize the absolute necessity of changing it for a purer morality.

I claim that women, who have far more violent desires than we for the pleasures of lust, should be able to express them as much as they wish, free from the bonds of marriage, from all the false prejudices of modesty, completely returned to the state of Nature. I want the law to permit them to enjoy as many men as they like; I want the enjoyment of both sexes and all parts of their bodies to be allowed to them as to men; and under the ruling that they suffer themselves to be enjoyed by whoever wants them, they must also be allowed the freedom to enjoy whoever they think is capable of satisfying them.

What, I ask you, are the dangers of such license? Children without a father? What does this matter in a republic, where citizens should have no mother but their country, where all infants are born children of their country! How much greater will be their love for their country when they have known no other mother, when they know they must look to their country for everything! Do not imagine you can make good republicans by isolating children in their families when they should belong only to the republic. By giving their affection to a few individuals instead of to all their fellow men, they inevitably adopt the often dangerous prejudices of these individuals; their ideas and opinions isolate them, characterize them, and all the virtues of a citizen escape them completely. They give their whole heart to those who brought them into the world and have no affection left for the country that teaches them to live, to understand themselves, and make their name—as though these latter benefits were not more important that the former! If it is to our great disadvantage to let infants imbibe the interests of the family and not the very different ones of the mother country, then it is indeed to our advantage to separate them from the family; and this would happen naturally under the conditions I have outlined; for by completely destroying the bonds of marriage, the fruit of pleasure in women would be children forbidden any knowledge of their fathers and thus prevented from belonging to a family, instead of being, as they should, children of their country alone.

We will, then, have brothels destined for the concupiscence of women; and like those for men, they will be under the protection of the government; there, all the individuals of either sex that they might desire will be supplied, and the more they frequent these houses the more they will be respected. Nothing is so barbarous and ridiculous as the fact that we have identified woman's virtue and honor with the resistance she employs against the desires she has received from Nature and which burn continually in those who have the barbarity to condemn her for submitting to them. From the most tender age,[5] therefore, a young girl who is free from a father's care, having no need to save herself for marriage—completely abolished by the wise laws I advocate, free from the prejudice that has enslaved her sex, will be able to surrender herself to all that her temperament commands, in places devoted to this

---

5. Babylonian females did not wait till the age of seven to bring their first fruits to the temple of Venus. The first stirring of desire that a girl feels is the moment that Nature means her to prostitute herself, and with no other consideration in mind, she should obey Nature's voice; she outrages her laws if she resists them.

subject; there she will be received with respect, satisfied in profusion, and on her return to society she can speak as publicly of the pleasure she has tasted as today she speaks of a ball or an excursion. Fair sex, you will be free; you will enjoy, as men do, all the pleasures that are your duty to Nature; you will stop at nothing. Must one half of humanity chain the diviner half? Oh, break the chains, Nature commands it; know no other curb but your preferences, no other laws but your desires, no other morality but Nature's; no longer languish beneath those savage prejudices that wither your charms, fetter the divine impulses of your hearts;[6] you are as free as we are, and the career of Venus' battles is open to you as to us; no longer fear absurd reproaches; pedantry and superstition are overthrown; we will never again see you blush at your charming excesses; crowned with myrtle and roses, our esteem for you will be the greater as you give these excesses yet wider scope.

Our foregoing analysis obviously makes it unnecessary to discuss adultery; let us glance at it, nevertheless, however meaningless it becomes after the laws I have established. How ridiculous it was to consider it a crime under our former institutions! If there was one thing in the world particularly absurd it was the eternal duration of the marriage bond; one had surely only to observe or experience the weight of these chains to cease to consider any alleviating action a crime; and Nature, as we have remarked, having endowed women with a more passionate temperament and greater sensibility than the other sex, the marriage bond was undoubtedly more stifling for them.

Ardent women, on fire with the flames of love, recompense yourselves now without fear; realize that there cannot be any harm in following Nature's impulses, that she did not create you for one man but for the delight of all. Let nothing restrain you. Imitate the Greek republicans; their legislators never dreamed of making adultery a crime, and they nearly all authorized women's excesses. Thomas More in his Utopia proves that it is advantageous to a woman to give herself up to debauchery, and this great man's ideas were not always mere fantasy.[7]

Among the Tartars, the more a woman prostituted herself the more she was honored; she showed the marks of her immodesty openly on her neck; and a woman with none of these decorations was considered worthless. In

6. Women do not realize how much their sensualities embellish them. Compare two women of about the same age and beauty, one of whom lives in celibacy and the other in libertinism; you will see how the latter takes the prize for brilliance and bloom; any transgression against Nature is more aging than an excess of pleasures; and everyone knows that confinements make a woman more beautiful.

7. He also suggested that betrothed couples should see each other naked before marrying. How many marriages would not take place if this law were enforced! It will be admitted that otherwise it is a case of what we call buying a pig in a poke.

Pegu, wives and daughters are lent by the family to passing travelers; they are hired out at so much a day like horses or carriages! Volumes could be written to prove that sexual indulgence was never considered criminal among any of the wiser nations. Every philosopher realizes that we have only the Christian impostors to thank for making it a crime. The priests had a good reason for forbidding us indulgence; this command, by keeping the knowledge and absolution of these secret sins for them alone, gave them unbelievable power over women and opened the way to a life of unlimited lust. We know how they profited by it and how they would still if they had not irretrievably lost their credit.

Is incest more dangerous? Undoubtedly not; it extends the family ties and consequently makes the citizen's love of his country more active; it is commanded us by Nature's first laws; we feel the necessity of it; and it makes the enjoyment of objects that belong to us seem yet more delicious. The earliest institutions favored incest; it is found in primitive societies; it has been consecrated by all religions, and favored by all laws. If we survey the whole world we see that incest has been established everywhere. The Negroes of the Pepper Coast and the Gaboon pimp for their wives to their own children; the eldest son of Judah had to marry his father's wife; the peoples of Chile sleep with sisters or daughters indifferently and marry mother and daughter at the same time. To put it briefly, I dare affirm that incest should be the rule under any government based on fraternity. How could reasonable men go to the absurd lengths of thinking that the enjoyment of mother, sister, or daughter could ever be a crime? I ask you, is it not abominably prejudiced to make a man a criminal if he enhances his appreciation of the object closest to him by ties of Nature! It is like saying that we are forbidden to love too much just those individuals whom Nature teaches us to love the most, and that the more she inclines us towards an object, the more she also bids us keep our distance. These contradictions are absurd; only races debased by superstition could believe in them or adopt them. Since the communal state of women that I propose would necessarily involve incest, there is little more to say about this supposed crime that is so obviously a fallacy; and we will pass to rape, which seems at first sight to be the most clearly injurious of all forms of libertinism because of its apparent outrage. It is nevertheless certain that rape, so rare and hard to prove, does less harm than robbery, for the latter appropriates the property, while the former only spoils it. And how could you answer a violator if he objected that in fact he had done but slight harm, since he had only made a certain alteration in an object which would soon have been made in any case through marriage or desire?

But sodomy, then, this so-called crime which brought the wrath of heaven upon the cities given over to it, is this not a monstrous perversion that cannot be too severely punished? It is undoubtedly painful for us to have to reproach our ancestors with the legal murders which they permitted for this cause. Is it possible to be so uncivilized as to condemn an unfortunate individual to death because he has different tastes from ours? It makes one shudder to realize that our legislators were still at that point less than forty years ago. Have no fear, Citizens; such absurdities will not happen again; the wisdom of your legislators will see to that. Now that we are enlightened on this subject of the weakness of certain men, we realize today that such a weakness cannot be criminal, and that Nature could not attach enough importance to the fluid in our loins to be angry over which channel we choose to direct it into.

What is the only crime that can exist here? It is assuredly not in placing oneself in one particular place or another, unless one tries to maintain that the different parts of the body are not really all exactly the same and that some are pure and some filthy; but since it is impossible to put forward such absurdities, the only so-called crime in this case must be the actual loss of semen. Now I ask you, is it likely that that semen is so precious in Nature's eyes that in releasing it one commits a crime? Would she permit this release every day if that were so? Does she not authorize it by permitting the semen to escape during dreams or during the enjoyment of a pregnant woman? Is it conceivable that Nature would enable us to commit a crime that outraged her? Could she consent to men destroying her pleasures and so becoming stronger than she? We fall into an endless gulf of absurdities if we thus abandon the light of reason in our arguments. Let us rest assured, therefore, that it is as natural to have a woman in one way as in another, that it is absolutely indifferent whether we enjoy a boy or a girl, and that once it is agreed that no other desires can exist in us but those received from Nature, Nature herself is too wise and too logical to implant in us anything that could offend her.

The taste for sodomy is the result of our constitution, which we do not foster in vain. Children show this preference from a tender age and never swerve from it. Sometimes it is the fruit of satiety; but even then, is it not still a part of Nature? From every point of view, it is Nature's handiwork, and all that she inspires must be viewed with respect. If it could be proved, by taking an exact census, that this taste is infinitely more widespread than the other, that its pleasures are far keener, and that for this reason its supporters are far more numerous than its enemies, might it not be possible to conclude that this vice, far from outraging Nature, accords with her purposes, and that she is far less concerned with reproduction than we foolishly believe. If we take the whole world into consideration, how many peoples do we see who despise women! Some of them will have nothing to do with women except to get a child to succeed them. In a republic the custom of men living side by side always makes this vice more frequent, but it is not dangerous. Would the legislators of Greece have introduced it into their republic if they had thought so? Far from it, they thought it necessary in a fighting nation. Plutarch tells us with enthusiasm of the battalion of the *lovers and the beloved:* they alone continued to defend the liberty of Greece. This vice reigned in a society of brothers in arms; it strengthened it. The greatest men have been interested in it. The whole of America, when it was discovered, was peopled with men with these inclinations. Among the Illinois in Louisiana, men dressed as women prostituted themselves like courtesans. The Negroes of Bengela openly had relations with men; in Algeria, nearly all the seraglios today are wholly populated by young boys. In Thebes, the love of boys was not only tolerated but recommended; the Cheronean philosopher advised it to sweeten the love of young men.

We know to what extent it held sway in Rome; there were public places where young boys prostituted themselves in the disguise of women, and girls in the dress of boys. Martial, Catullus, Tibullus, Horace, and Virgil wrote to men in the terms used to a mistress; and we read in Plutarch[8] that women should have no part in the love of men. The Amasians on the island of Crete used to carry off young boys with unusual ceremonies. When someone was attracted by a boy, the parents were informed of the day the seducer intended to take him away; the youth put up some resistance if he did not like his lover; otherwise he went off with him, and the seducer sent him back to his family as soon as he had had enough; for with this passion as with the love of women, to have enough is to have too much.

Strabo tells us that on the same island the seraglios contained only boys; they were publicly prostituted.

Is another authority needed to prove how useful this vice is in a republic? Listen to Jerome the Peripatetic: the love of boys, he says, spread throughout Greece, for it gave us courage and strength and helped to expel the tyrants. Pacts were formed among the lovers, and they would rather be tortured than reveal their accomplices; thus patriotism sacrificed everything for the good of the state; it was certain that these bonds strengthened the republic; women were inveighed against, and it became a weakness characteristic of

8. *Moralia*, treatise on love.

tyrants to attach oneself to such creatures. Homosexuality was always the vice of warlike nations. Caesar tells us that the Gauls were very much given to it. The wars which a republic had to undertake encouraged this vice by separating the sexes; and when it was realized that this result was so useful to the state, religion soon blessed it. It is known that the Romans consecrated the love of Jupiter and Ganymede. Sextus Empiricus assures us that this inclination was enforced among the Persians. Finally the women, jealous and despised, offered their husbands the same service that boys gave them; some tried this and returned to their former habits, finding the illusion impossible to sustain.

The Turks, greatly given to this perversion which is blessed in the Koran, assert nevertheless that a very young virgin can take the place of a boy; and their females seldom become women without having passed this ordeal. Sixtus V and Sanchez permitted this license; the latter even undertook to prove that it was advantageous to propagation and that a child conceived after this preliminary was infinitely the better for it. The women made amends among themselves. This diversion certainly has no more drawbacks than the other, for the result is only a refusal to propagate, and the power of those who have the taste for reproduction is too strong to be destroyed by its adversaries. The Greeks even supported this perversion of women for reasons of state. It had the result that women were satisfied with each other, and since their communications with men were less frequent, they meddled less in the affairs of the republic. Lucian tells us what progress was made by this license, and it is not without interest that we observe it in Sappho.

In a word, there is no danger at all in any of these manias; should they go even further, to the caresses of monsters and animals, which we notice in the history of all nations, there would not be the slightest danger in any of these whims; for corrupt habits, often very useful to a government, cannot injure it in any way; and we must expect enough wisdom and prudence from our legislators to be sure that they will issue no law repressing these peculiarities, which are an inextricable part of the individual constitution and could no more be laid to the guilt of the owner than a congenital deformity.

There remains only murder to be examined under the second group of crimes against our fellow men, and then we will pass to man's obligations to himself. Of all man's offenses against his fellow man, murder is without contradiction the cruelest, for it deprives him of the one gift he has received from Nature, the only one whose loss is irreparable. Nevertheless several questions arise at this point, apart from the wrong which murder does to its victim.

1. Considering Nature's laws only, is it really criminal?
2. Is it criminal in relation to the laws of politics?
3. Is it harmful to society?
4. How should it be considered in a republican state?
5. Finally, should murder be punished by murder?

We will examine each of these questions separately; the object is important enough to allow us to linger; our ideas will perhaps be found somewhat strong, but what matter? Have we not gained the right to say all we wish? Let us reveal great truths to men; they expect them from us; error must be dissipated, its blindfold must fall beside that of kings. Is murder a crime in Nature's eyes? Such is the first question.

We are doubtless now going to humiliate man's pride by reducing him to the stature of all the other productions of Nature; but the philosopher does not pander to trivial human vanities; ardent in the pursuit of truth, he extricates it from the crass prejudices of self-love, grasps it, develops it, and bravely shows it to the astonished world.

What is man, and what difference is there between him and the other plants, the other animals of the earth? None, certainly. Fortuitously situated, like them, on this earth, he is born like them, propagates, grows, withers like them; like them he reaches old age, and like them falls into nothingness after the span assigned to each species by Nature according to its physical characteristics. If these similarities are such that the scrutinizing eye of the philosopher can perceive no difference, then there is just as much harm in killing an animal as a man, or just as little, and the difference arises solely from the prejudices of our vanity; unfortunately nothing is more absurd than the prejudices of vanity. But let us take the question further. You cannot disagree that it is the same to kill a man or an animal; but is not the destruction of any living creature wrong, as the Pythagoreans believed and as some dwellers on the banks of the Ganges still believe? Before replying let us remind the reader that we are only examining the question in relation to Nature; we will consider it later with regard to men.

Now I ask you how valuable can creatures be to Nature that cost her neither trouble nor care? The workman only values his handiwork because of the work he put into it, because of the time spent in creating it. Does man cost Nature anything? And if he does cost her something, is it more than a monkey or an elephant? I will go further; what are the regenerative materials of Nature? What are newborn creatures created from? Do not the three elements of which they are made come originally from the destruction of other bodies? If every individual were eternal, would it not become impossible for

Nature to create new ones? If eternal life is impossible for living things, their destruction is one of Nature's laws.

If this destruction is so necessary to Nature that it is impossible for her to do without it, and if she cannot create without drawing on the mass of dead matter prepared for her by death, then the idea of annihilation which we associate with death becomes meaningless; there will be no simple annihilation; what we call the end of a living creature will no longer be the actual end but a mere transmutation of matter, which is accepted by all modern thinkers as one of the first laws. Death, according to these irrefutable principles, is only a change of form, an imperceptible transition from one existence to another, which is what Pythagoras called metempsychosis.

Once these truths are admitted, can one possibly maintain that destruction is a crime? Do you dare to say, for the sake of preserving your absurd prejudices, that transmutation is the same as destruction? Certainly not, for you would have to prove that matter underwent a moment of inaction, a time of quiescence. This you will never discover. Small animals come into being the moment a large animal breathes its last, and the life of these tiny creatures is only a necessary and inevitable result of the temporary sleep of the greater. Can you venture to say at this time that one is more pleasing to Nature than the other? You would have to prove an impossibility—that a long or square shape is more pleasing or useful to Nature than an oblong or triangular one; you would have to prove that even in view of Nature's sublime plans, a sluggard who grows fat in idleness and inaction is more useful to Nature than the horse, whose service is so essential, or the ox, whose body is so precious that every part of it can be used; you would have to prove that the venomous serpent is more necessary than the faithful dog.

Now, since all these propositions are untenable, we must agree to admit the impossibility of destroying any of Nature's works; that given the assurance that the only thing we are doing in allowing ourselves to destroy is to make a change in the forms of things, but without extinguishing life, then it is beyond human power to prove that there is any crime in the so-called destruction of a creature, of any age, sex, or species you can imagine. To follow the train of consequences yet further, and linking one event to another, we see that the action of altering the forms of Nature is beneficial to her, since it produces the material for her reconstructions which would be impossible for her if nothing were destroyed.

Well, let her do it herself! you will be told. Certainly let her do it, but it is at her inspiration that man gives way to murder; it is Nature that prompts him, and the man who destroys his fellow is to Nature what a plague or famine is, sent by her hand in the same way, for she uses all possible means to obtain the raw material of destruction so essential to her work. Let us vouchsafe for a moment to illumine our minds with the holy light of philosophy; what other voice but Nature's suggests to us the personal hatreds, vengeances, wars, in fact all the eternal motives for murder? Then if she prompts them, it is because she needs them. How, in that case, can we imagine that we are guilty towards her, when we are only following her wishes?

This is already more than sufficient to convince any enlightened reader that murder could never be an offense against Nature.

Is it a political crime? Let us frankly admit that it is, on the contrary, one of the greatest powers in politics. Was it not through murders that Rome became mistress of the world? Is it not by means of murders that France has freed herself today? It is useless to say that we are now speaking of murders caused by war and not of atrocities committed by the seditious and rebellious; the former was worthy of public execration and need only be remembered to excite general horror and indignation. What human science most needs to be maintained by massacre? Only one that sets out to deceive itself, which aims at the aggrandizement of one nation at the expense of another. Are wars, the sole fruit of this uncivilized policy, anything but the means of fostering, defending, and supporting it? And what is war but the science of destruction? What a strange lack of insight we show by publicly teaching the art of killing, rewarding the most successful, and then punishing whoever is revenged on his enemy in a personal matter. Is it not time to change such barbarous errors?

Is murder, then, a crime against society? Who could seriously imagine so! What does it matter to a populous society whether there is one member more or less in its midst? Are its laws, morals, or customs thereby weakened? Can the death of an individual ever have any influence on the mass of people? And after the losses of a great battle—or I may as well say after the extinction of half the population, of the whole of it, if you like—would the few beings left alive experience the slightest material alteration? Alas, no; nor would the whole of Nature experience any alteration; and the stupid pride of mankind, that believes that everything was created for itself, would be astonished to realize that after the total destruction of the human race nothing in Nature was changed nor the stars slowed down in their courses. But let us proceed.

How should murder be viewed in a martial republican state?

It would undoubtedly be thoroughly dangerous either to look unfavorably on this action or to punish it. The pride of the republican demands a certain amount of ferocity: if he becomes soft and loses his power, he will soon be subjugated. A strange idea becomes apparent at this point; but since it is true as well as daring, I will voice it. A nation that starts as a republic can only maintain itself by the virtues, for to arrive at the greater, one must start with the lesser; but a nation that is already old and corrupt, and bravely throws off the yoke of monarchist government to adopt the republican rule, can only maintain itself by crimes; for it is already criminal; and to pass from crime to virtue, from a violent state to a quiet one, would be to fall into an inertia which would quickly result in ruin. What would become of a tree transplanted from fertile ground to a dry sandy soil? All intellectual ideas are so subordinated to physical nature that a comparison with growing things will always provide a moral guide.

Savages, the most independent of men and the nearest to Nature, every day indulge in murder with impunity. In Sparta and Lacedaemon they hunted slaves as we hunt partridges. The freest peoples are those who look on this with most favor. In Mindanao, the boy who wishes to commit a murder is elevated to the ranks of the brave, and he is decorated with a turban; among the Caraguos, seven men must be killed before obtaining this headdress; the natives of Borneo believe that those they put to death will have to serve them when they are dead themselves; even the pious Spaniards made a vow to Saint James of Galicia to kill twelve American natives a day; in the kingdom of Tangut, a strong and vigorous young man is chosen and permitted on certain days of the year to kill everyone he meets! Was there ever a race more sympathetic to murder than the Jews? It appears in all forms on every page of their history.

The emperor and mandarins of China occasionally take measures to make the people revolt, so that they can have an excuse for effecting a dreadful slaughter. Should this meek and effeminate nation free itself from the yoke of its tyrants, it will slaughter them in turn, with better cause, and murder, once again found necessary and adopted, will only have changed its victims; it was first the enjoyment of one side and it will become the pastime of the other.

An infinite number of nations tolerate public assassination; it is openly allowed in Genoa, Venice, Naples, and the whole of Albania; at Kachao, on the San Domingo River, assassins dressed in a well-known and recognized uniform, will butcher according to orders, before your very eyes, whatever individual you name. The Indians take opium to spur themselves on to murder, then rush into the streets and massacre everyone they meet; English travelers have observed this mania in Batavia.

What other nation has ever been both as great and as cruel as the Romans, and what other nation has kept its splendor and freedom for so long? The gladiatorial shows sustained their courage: they became warlike through the custom of making a game of killing. Twelve or fifteen hundred victims filled the circus arena every day; and there the women, more cruel than the men, dared to demand that the dying men fall gracefully and strike an attitude even in the throes of death. The Romans went from this to the pleasures of watching dwarfs slaughter each other; and when the Christian cult infected the earth and persuaded men that killing was an evil, the Romans were at once enslaved by tyrants, and the heroes of the world soon became its playthings.

All over the world, in fact, it has been rightly believed that the murderer, that is to say, the man who stifles his sensibility to the point of killing his fellow man and defying public or private vengeance, must be very brave and therefore very valuable to a warlike or republican society. If we glance at nations who are fiercer still and do not stop at sacrificing children, often their own, we see that these actions are universally adopted, sometimes even embodied in the laws. Many savage tribes kill their children as soon as they are born. On the banks of the Orinoco River, mothers used to sacrifice female children as soon as they had brought them into the world, for they were convinced their daughters were only born to be unhappy, destined to be married in a region where women were scarcely tolerated. In Trapobania and the kingdom of Sopit, all deformed children were killed by their own parents.

The women of Madagascar exposed all children born on certain days of the week to the attacks of wild animals. In the Greek republics all newborn children were carefully examined, and if they were not found to be formed well enough to defend their republic some day, they were immediately destroyed; it was not considered necessary to erect lavishly endowed institutions[9] to preserve this vile scum of human nature. Up until the removal of the seat of empire, all Romans who did not want to bring up their children threw them into the sewer. The legislators of the ancient world did not scruple to condemn infants to death, and none of their codes put any check on the rights which a father considered he held over his family. Aristotle advised abortion; and these republicans of the old days, filled with enthusiasm and ardor for their country, did not know the individual sympathy found in modern nations: they loved their children less, but they loved their country more. In every town in China an incredible number of abandoned children are found in the streets

---

9. It is hoped that the nation will do away with this expense, the most unnecessary one of all; any individual born without the necessary qualities to serve the republic later on has no right to life; and the best thing to do is to take it from him as soon as he receives it.

every day; a cart collects them at dawn, and they are thrown into a ditch; often the midwives themselves rid the mothers of them by immediately suffocating their offspring in tubs of boiling water or by throwing them into a stream.

At Peking they are put into little rush baskets and left on the canals; these canals are scoured every day, and the famous traveler Duhalde estimates the number picked up each day at more then thirty thousand. It cannot be denied that it would be very necessary and extremely useful to put a limit to the population in a republican state; from an opposite point of view, the population should be encouraged in a monarchy; there the tyrants, rich only in proportion to the number of their slaves, certainly need more men; but an overabundant population, make no mistake about it, is a real evil in a republican state; nevertheless there is no need to slaughter in order to reduce it, as some of our modern decemvirs would; it is only a question of not allowing it to spread beyond the bounds that well-being prescribes. Take care not to multiply a population where every man is a king; and realize that revolutions are always the natural result of too large a population.

If, for the glory of the state, you give your soldiers the right to destroy men, then for the preservation of this same state, give each individual an equal right to destroy, wherever he can without outraging Nature, children that he cannot bring up, or who will bring no support to the country; allow him also to rid himself at his own risk of all the enemies who might injure him; for the result of all these actions, meaningless in themselves, will be to keep the population in check, and never numerous enough to overthrow your government. Let monarchists say that a state is only great according to the size of its population: the state will always be poor if its population exceeds its means of supporting life, and it will always flourish if it is kept within limits and can trade its superfluous goods. Do you not prune a tree when it has too many branches? Do you not clip the branches to preserve the trunk? Any system that departs from these principles is an extravagance and a source of abuses that will soon lead to the total overthrow of the structure we have erected with so much labor; but it is not the full-grown man we should destroy in order to decrease the population. It is unfair to cut short the life of a fully formed individual; but it is not so, I maintain, to prevent a creature who is certain to have no use in life from growing up. The human race should be thinned out from the cradle; the being that you realize can never be useful to society is the one whose life should be cut short at the breast; these are the only reasonable ways of diminishing a population whose increase would, as I have proved, become a most dangerous abuse.

Now let us resume our argument.

Should murder be punished by murder? Certainly not. Let us impose no punishment on the murderer but the risk he incurs from the vengeance of the friends or relatives of the murdered man. *I give you my pardon,* said Louis XV to Charolais, who had killed a man for amusement, *but I also give it to the man who kills you.* The whole foundation of the law against murderers is contained in that sublime saying.[10]

To sum up, murder is a horror, but often a necessary horror and never a criminal one, and it must be tolerated in a republican state. I have shown that the whole universe gives us examples of this; but must it be considered an action punishable by death?

Those who can solve the following problem will have answered the question:

Is crime a crime or not?

If it is not, why make laws to punish it?

If it is, by what barbarous and idiotic illogicality do you punish it by a similar crime?

It now remains to discuss man's duties towards himself. Since the philosopher only adopts such duties inasmuch as they minister to his pleasure or self-preservation, it is useless to recommend their adoption or to impose penalties if they are not observed.

The only crime of this type that a man could commit would be suicide. I shall not amuse myself here by pointing out the imbecility of people who make that action into a crime; I shall send anyone with doubts on the matter to Rousseau's famous letter. Almost all the governments of the ancient world authorized suicide on political or religious grounds. The Athenians disclosed to the Areopagus their reasons for killing themselves; then they stabbed themselves. All the Greek republics tolerated suicide; it was a part of the scheme of the ancient legislators; people killed themselves in public and made a formal ceremony of death.

The republic of Rome encouraged suicide; the famous sacrifices for the motherland were simply suicides. When Rome was taken by the Gauls, the most illustrious senators vowed themselves to death; by adopting the same

---

10. The Salic law punished murder only by a fine; and since the guilty man could easily find a means of avoiding it, Childebert, King of Austrasia, decreed in a ruling made at Cologne a punishment of death, not against murderers, but against anyone who evaded a fine imposed on a murderer. The Ripuarian law also imposed only a fine for this action, graded according to the individual who had been killed. It was very expensive for a priest: a leaden tunic was made to fit the assassin, and he had to pay in gold an equivalent of the weight of the tunic, otherwise he and his family became slaves of the Church.

attitude we shall acquire the same virtues. A soldier killed himself, during the campaign of '92, for sheer grief at not being able to follow his comrades at Jemappes. If we are constantly measured against these proud republicans, we shall soon surpass their virtues: the government makes the man. The agelong habit of despotism has sapped our courage completely; our ways have become depraved; but we are being born again; soon it will be seen what sublime actions the French genius and character are capable of when they are free; let us maintain at the cost of our fortunes and our lives, that liberty that has already cost us so many victims, let us not regret one of them if we reach our goal: they gave themselves to it voluntarily; let us not allow that blood to have been spilt in vain; but let us unite . . . unite, or we will lose the fruit of all our labors; let us now try to make fine laws after the victories we have won; our first legislators, still enslaved to the despot we have laid low, have given us laws worthy of the tyrant whom they still flatter: let us re-fashion their work and remember that we are working for republicans now; let our laws be as mild as the people they govern.

In disclosing here, as I have done, the nullity, the indifference of an infinite number of actions that our ancestors, misled by a false religion, believed to be criminal, I am reducing our task to a very simple one. Let us make few laws, but good ones—it is not a question of multiplying restraints but of making those we do employ quite indestructible—let the laws that we promulgate have no other object than the peace and happiness of the citizen and the glory of the republic; but after expelling the enemy from your soil, Frenchmen, I hope that your ardor to propagate your ideas will not take you any further; you can take them to the ends of the earth only by fire and sword. Before carrying out such resolutions, think of the failure of the crusades. When the enemy is on the other side of the Rhine, then, believe me, you must protect your frontiers and stay at home; reorganize your commerce, put energy into manufacturing, and find markets for your goods; let your arts flourish once again; encourage agriculture, which is necessary to a government such as yours and which should provide enough for everyone without the help of anyone else; leave the thrones of Europe to crumble away by themselves; your example and prosperity will soon overthrow them without the need for you to interfere.

Unassailable in your domestic policy, and a model among nations for your police and your wise laws, there will be no government that does not strive to imitate you, none that will not be honored by alliance with you; but if, for the useless honor of spreading your principles abroad, you abandon the study of your own prosperity, then despotism will wake again from its half-sleep, internal dissensions will rend you apart, you will exhaust your finances and your soldiers, and all that only to go back to kissing the chains that will be laid on you again by tyrants during your absence; all that you want can be done without leaving your homes: let other nations see that you are happy, and they will hasten to happiness by the trail that you have blazed for them.

FRANÇOIS NOËL (CAIUS GRACCHUS) BABEUF
(1760–1797)

A Society of Equals*

Babeuf came to Paris from Picardy, where he had been variously employed as a
domestic servant and a surveyor who assisted landlords in maintaining their
feudal rights. In 1789, with an abrupt volte-face, he drew up an article
for the cahier of the electors of Roye demanding the abolition of feudal
privilege. He made his debut as a publicist in a brochure proposing
fiscal reform to the government (1790), he dabbled in politics as a member
of the General Council of the Somme, and he was involved, perhaps
innocently, in national land scandals. After Thermidor, though he hailed
the end of the Terror, he violently attacked the government for failure
to deal with inflation and the widespread misery it entrained. His song
"Dying of hunger, dying of cold" was chanted in the cafés of Paris, while
his journals called for the end of private property and the institution of
absolute communist egalitarianism. In 1796, with his confederates Darthé
and Buonarroti, he formed the "Conspiracy of the Equals" to overthrow
the Directorate. The plot was discovered, and Babeuf was arrested and
executed after an attempt at suicide. The "Manifesto of the Equals" was
among the papers seized when he was apprehended. Its actual drafting is
thought to be the work of Pierre-Sylvain Maréchal (1750–1803), a lawyer
and litterateur who had been imprisoned under the old regime for his
writings. Though not approved as the official declaration of the movement,
the "Manifesto of the Equals" is the most forthright and dramatic
statement of its aims. The "Analysis of Babeuf's Doctrine," also reprinted
here, was probably written by Babeuf himself.

*From Philippe Buonarroti, *History of Babeuf's Conspiracy for Equality*, trans. Bronterre O'Brien
(London: H. Hetherington, 1836), pp. 314–26.

Babeuf, engraving by François Bonneville.

Manifesto of the Equals

"REAL EQUALITY—THE LAST END OF THE SOCIAL ART."—CONDORCET, *Picture of the Human Mind.*

PEOPLE OF FRANCE!—During fifteen ages you have lived slaves, and consequently unhappy. During six years you breathe with difficulty in the expectation of independence, of prosperity, and of equality.

EQUALITY!—first vow of nature, first want of man, and chief bond of all legitimate association! People of France! you have not been more favoured than the other nations which vegetate on this ill-fated globe! Always and everywhere does the unfortunate human species, delivered over to cannibals more or less artful, serve for a plaything to all ambitions—for pasture to all tyrannies. Always and everywhere have men been fooled by fine words; never and nowhere have they obtained the *thing* with the word. From time immemorial we have been hypocritically told—*men are equal;* and from time immemorial does the most degrading and monstrous inequality insolently oppress the human race. Ever since the first existence of civil societies has the finest apanage of man been uncontradictedly *acknowledged;* but never, up to this moment, has it been once *realized.* Equality has never been other than a beautiful and barren fiction of law. Even now, when it is claimed with a stronger voice, we are answered, "Be silent, miserables!—absolute equality is but a chimæra; be content with conditional equality; you are all equal before the law. Rabble! what more do you want?" What more do we want? Legislators, governors, rich proprietors—listen in your turn.

We are all equal, are we not? This principle remains uncontested, because, without being self-convicted of folly, one cannot seriously say that it is night when it is day.

Well! we pretend henceforward to live and die equal, as we are born so. We desire real equality or death; behold what we want. And we shall have this real equality, no matter at what price. Woe to them who will interpose themselves between it and us! Woe to him who will offer resistance to so determined a resolve!

The French Revolution is but the forerunner of another revolution far more grand, far more solemn, and which will be the last. The people has marched over dead bodies against the kings and priests coalesced against it; it will do the same against the new tyrants—against the new political Tartuffes who have usurped the places of the old.

"What do we want," you ask, "more than equality of rights?" We want that equality not merely written in the "Declaration of the Rights of Man and of the Citizens;" we want it in the midst of us—under the roofs of our houses. We consent to everything for it—to become as *pliable wax, in order to have its characters engraven upon us.* Perish, if needs be, all the arts, provided real equality abides with us!

Legislators and governors, who are as destitute of genius as of honesty—you rich proprietors, without bowels of pity—in vain do you essay to neutralize our holy enterprize, by saying, "They are only re-producing the old Agrarian law, so often demanded already before them."

Calumniators! be silent in your turn; and in the silence of confusion hearken to our pretensions, dictated by nature herself, and based upon eternal justice. The Agrarian law, or partition of lands, was only the instantaneous wish of certain soldiers without principles—of certain small tribes, moved by instinct rather than by reason. We aim at something more sublime, and more equitable; we look to *common property,* or the *community of goods!* No more individual property in lands. *The earth belongs to no one.* We claim—we demand —we *will* the communal enjoyment of the fruits of the earth; *the fruits belong to all.*

We declare that we can no longer suffer that the great majority of men shall labour and sweat to serve and pamper the extreme minority. Long enough, and too long, have less than a million of individuals disposed of what belongs to more than twenty millions of men like themselves—of men in every respect their equals. Let there be at length an end to this enormous scandal, which posterity will scarcely credit. Away for ever with the revolting distinctions of rich and poor, of great and little, of masters and servants, of *governors* and *governed.*

Let there be no longer any other differences in mankind than those of age and sex. Since all have the same wants, and the same faculties, let all have accordingly the same education—the same nourishment. They are content with one sun, and the same air for all; why should not the like portion, and the same quality of food, suffice for each according to his wants?

But already do the enemies of an order of things, the most natural that can be imagined, declaim against us,—"Disorganizers, and seditionists," they exclaim, "you want but massacres and plunder."

PEOPLE OF FRANCE!—We will not waste our time to answer them; but we will tell you,—"the holy enterprise we are organizing has no other object in view than to put an end to civil dissensions and to public disorder. Never was a more vast design conceived and put in execution. At distant intervals in the history of the world it has been talked of by some men of genius—by a few philosophers—but they spoke it with a low and trembling voice. Not one of them has had the courage to speak the entire truth.

The moment for great measures has arrived. Evil is at its height; it has reached its *maximum,* and covers the face of the earth. Chaos, under the name of politics, has too long reigned over it. Let everything revert to order, and resume its proper place. At the voice of equality, let the elements of justice and felicity be organized. The moment is come to found the REPUBLIC OF EQUALS—that grand asylum open to all human kind. The days of general restitution are come. Weeping families, come and seat yourselves at the common table provided by nature for all her children.

PEOPLE OF FRANCE!—The purest of all earthly glories has been reserved for you—yes, 'tis you who are first destined to present the world with this touching spectacle.

Old habits, old prejudices, will again seek to oppose obstacles to the establishment of the REPUBLIC OF EQUALS. The organization of real equality— the only one which satisfies all wants, without making victims, without costing sacrifices—will not, perhaps, at first please everybody. The egotist, the ambitious, will yell with rage. Those who possess unjustly, will raise the cry of injustice. Exclusive enjoyments, solitary pleasures, personal ease and privileges, will cause poignant regrets to some few individuals who are dead or callous to the pangs of others. The lovers of absolute power, the vile instruments of arbitrary authority, will feel it hard that their haughty chiefs should bend to the level of equality. Their short-sightedness will, with difficulty, penetrate into the future of public happiness, however near; but what can avail a few thousand malcontents against such a mass of human beings, all happy, and astonished at having been so long in quest of a felicity which they had within hands' reach. On the day that follows this real revolution, they will say to one another in amazement—"What—universal happiness depended on so little! We had but to will it. Ah, why had we not willed it sooner? Was it then necessary to have it told to us so often? Yes, no doubt, a single man on the earth, more rich, more powerful, than his fellow men, than his equals, destroys the equilibrium, and crime and misfortune come on the world.

PEOPLE OF FRANCE!—By what sign then ought you henceforward to recognise the excellence of a constitution? . . . That which altogether reposes on actual, absolute equality, is the only one that can be suitable to you, and satisfy all your desires.

The aristocratic charters of 1791 and 1795 riveted your chains, instead of breaking them. That of 1793 was a great practical step towards real equality; never before was equality so nearly approached; but that Constitution did not yet touch the end, nor was it fully competent to attain general happiness, of which, however, it has solemnly consecrated the great principle.

PEOPLE OF FRANCE!—Open your eyes and hearts to the fulness of felicity; recognize and proclaim with us the

REPUBLIC OF EQUALS!

———————◆———————

Analysis of the Doctrine of Babeuf

PROSCRIBED BY THE EXECUTIVE DIRECTORY FOR HAVING TOLD THE TRUTH!

ARTICLE I

Nature has given to each individual an equal right to the enjoyment of all the goods of life.

PROOFS, DRAWN FROM THE DISCUSSION TO WHICH THIS PIECE GAVE RISE

1. Previously to their first coming together, or forming societies, all men were equally masters of the productions which nature spread with profusion around them.

2. Finding themselves together upon an uncultivated land, what could have established amongst them the inequality of this right? Is it their natural difference? But they have all the same organs and the same wants. Is it the dependence of some upon others? But no one was sufficiently strong to make

servants of the rest, who might disperse on the slightest occasion for discontent; and the advantage of mutual succours, and of co-operative benevolence, rendered it necessary for all to respect in others, the rights with which they felt themselves invested by nature. Is it the ferocity of their hearts? But compassion is the immediate consequence of their organization, and ferocity springs only from the exasperation of the passions. Is it an inborn penchant for humiliation and servitude? But the sight of distinctions is even for the most savage beings a painful sensation—a source of jealousy and hatred.

3. If families have been the first models of societies, they are also the most striking proofs of the right we speak of. Equality in families is the pledge of tenderness on the part of parents—of union and happiness on that of the children. Is that equality broken? Forthwith anger and jealousy introduce disorder and violence. Everything—even the fondness of parents—inspires the children with a hatred of partialities, which the parents themselves cannot apply without risking the introduction of dangerous passions into the family.

4. The most strict equality must have been consecrated by the first conventions; for what could have induced persons, hitherto the enemies of all distinction, to consent to privations and inferiority?

5. The forgetfulness of this equality has introduced amongst mankind—
   False ideas of happiness;
   Perversion of the passions;
   Deterioration and decay of the species;
   Violences, troubles, wars;
   The tyranny of some, and the oppression of others;
   Institutions, civil, political, and religious, which, by consecrating injustice, end with dissolving societies, after having for a long time distracted and torn them to pieces.

The sight of distinctions, of pomp, and of pleasures enjoyed only by a few, was, and ever will be, an inexhaustible source of torments and uneasiness to the mass. It is given to only a few philosophers to preserve themselves from corruption, and moderation is a blessing which the vulgar can no longer appreciate, when once their thoughts have been weaned from it. Do certain citizens create to themselves new factitious wants, and introduce into their enjoyments refinements unknown to the multitude? Simplicity is no longer loved, happiness ceases to consist in an active life and tranquil soul, distinctions and pleasures become the supreme of goods, nobody is content with his station, and all seek in vain for that happiness, the entrance of which into society is debarred by inequality.

The more distinctions we obtain, the more we desire, the more we excite jealousy and covetousness; thence that insatiable and criminal thirst for gold and power; thence those sanguinary wars caused by the spirit of conquest, and by the jealousy of commerce, which leave miserable humanity scarcely a moment of repose.

In the midst of this subversion of ideas, sloth and vexations destroy a part of the species, enervate another part, and prepare for society generations incapable of defending it. From the love of distinctions arise the precautions taken to preserve them, in despite of the envy and discontent they engender; these precautions are, barbarous laws, exclusive forms of government, religious fables, servile morality; in a word, tyranny on the one hand, oppression on the other. However, the voice of nature cannot be entirely stifled; at times she makes her ungrateful children turn pale, she avenges by occasional outbreaks the tears of humanity, and if she rarely succeeds in re-establishing its rights, she ends always by overthrowing the societies which have neglected her laws.

If equality of goods be a consequence of that of our organs and wants—if public and private calamities—if the ruin of societies—are inevitable effects of all criminal attempts against it, this equality is, therefore, a *natural right*.

ARTICLE II

The end of society is to defend this equality, often assailed by the strong and wicked in the state of nature; and to augment, by the co-operation of all, the common enjoyments of all.

PROOFS

1. By *Society* is here understood, association regulated by conventions; and by *State of Nature*, that of casual and imperfect society in which men necessarily lived before they submitted to laws.

Without examining here, whether criminal attempts against equality, of the nature mentioned in this article, could have had place in the state of nature, it is evident that if the inconveniences of that state determined men to establish laws, they must have been only such as arose from the violation of equality. At all events, the preservation of equality is the end of association, because, by equality alone can men living together be rendered happy.

2. By uniting their strength, men assuredly desired to procure to themselves the greatest number of enjoyments of which they had the idea, and by the least possible trouble.

Now, the abundance of necessary things ensures these enjoyments, and is itself ensured by the labour of those associated together, which is the least possible for each, only when it is fairly distributed amongst all.

ARTICLE III

Nature has imposed on each person the obligation to work; nobody could, without crime, evade his share of the common labour.

PROOFS

Labour is for each a precept of nature.

1. Because man, isolated in the deserts, could not, without some kind of labour, procure himself subsistence.

2. Because the activity which moderate labour occasions, is for man a source of health and amusement.

This obligation could not be weakened by society, either for all or for each of its members.

1. Because the preservation of society depends upon it.

2. Because the labour of each is the least possible only when all participate of it.

ARTICLE IV

Labour and enjoyments ought to be common.

EXPLANATION

That is to say, all ought to bear an equal portion of labour, and derive from it an equal quantity of enjoyments.

The justice of this principle follows from the proofs of the preceding Articles I. and III. But what do we understand by community of labour? Is it meant that all the citizens should be engaged in the same occupations? No; but it is meant that the different branches of labour should be distributed in such manner as to leave no able-bodied person idle or unemployed; it is meant that the increased number of workers should, at the same time that it diminished individual toil, guarantee abundance for the whole; it is meant, that in return for his labour each person shall receive from society the means of providing for his natural wants, and for the small number of factitious wants which all may satisfy.

But it may be objected—What will become of those productions of industry, which are the fruits of time and genius? Is it not to be feared that, being no longer better recompensed than other descriptions of work, they will be altogether extinguished to the injury of society? Sophism! It is to the love of glory, not to the thirst for riches, that we have been at all times indebted for the efforts of genius. Every day do millions of poor soldiers devote themselves to death for the honour of serving the caprices of a cruel master; and shall we doubt of the prodigies that might be operated on the human heart by the sentiment of happiness, the love of equality and country, and by the noble incentives of a wise policy? Besides, should we have the same longings for the display of the arts, and for the tinsel of luxury, if we had the happiness to live under the laws of equality?

ARTICLE V

There is oppression wherever one part of society is exhausted by labour, and in want of everything, whilst the other part wallows in abundance, without doing any work at all.

PROOFS

1. *Inequality and oppression are synonymous;* if to oppress an individual consist in violating a general law to his detriment, those whom inequality *overcharges with toil* are oppressed, because inequality violates the natural law, to which it is absurd to oppose human laws.

2. To oppress signifies either to restrain the faculties of a person, or to unjustly augment his burdens; that is precisely what inequality does, by diminishing the enjoyments of him whose duties it aggravates.

ARTICLE VI

Nobody could, without crime, exclusively appropriate to himself the goods of the earth or of industry.

EXPLANATION AND PROOFS

If we demonstrate that inequality has no other cause than this exclusive appropriation, we shall have demonstrated the crime of those who introduced the distinction of *mine* and *thine* (*meum* and *tuum*).

From the moment lands were divided arose the exclusive right of property. Then each person became absolute master of all he could derive from the fields which had devolved to him, and from whatever industry he could exercise. It is probable that men, devoted to the arts of first necessity, were at the same time excluded from all territorial possession, which they had not time to cultivate. Thus one portion of the people remained masters of the things necessary to existence, whilst the rest had only a right to such salaries, or wages, as the former chose to pay them. Nevertheless, this change did not involve a very sensible one in the distribution of enjoyments, so long as the number of those receiving wages did not exceed that of the possessors of the soil. But as soon as natural accidents, acting conjointly with the economy or address of some, with the prodigality or incapacity of others, had concentrated the territorial properties in a small number of families, the men of wages became vastly more numerous than the proprietors, and, as a natural consequence, were utterly at their mercy. The possessors, proud of their opulence, soon reduced the labourers to a life of privations.

From this revolution date the sinister effects of inequality, developed in the first Article. Thenceforward we have seen the idle man fatten, by a revolting system of injustice, on the sweat of the laborious man, who sinks under the weight of fatigues and privations. We have seen the rich man take possession of the State, and, like a master, dictate tyrannical laws to the poor man, exasperated by want, degraded by ignorance, and deceived by religion.

Miseries and slavery are consequences of inequality, which is itself the result of property. Property is, therefore, the greatest scourge of society; it is a veritable public crime.

We shall be told, I know, that property is a right anterior to society, which has been instituted to protect it. But how could the idea of such a right have been formed, before conventions had guaranteed to the proprietor the fruits of his labour? How could society have owed its origin to an institution the most subversive of all social sentiment?

Lastly, let it not be said that it is just that the laborious and economical man should be recompensed by opulence, and that the idle man should be punished by misery. No doubt, it is equitable that the active man, having discharged what he owes his country, should receive in return what she can afford to give him, without destroying herself; it is equitable that his conduct be rewarded by public gratitude; but he cannot thereby acquire the right to poison his country, more than a soldier can acquire, by his valour, that of reducing her to slavery.

There are, doubtless, many sad fellows, who ought to impute to their own vices the poverty they are reduced to; but it would be to outrage experience and reason to range all the unhappy poor in this class, which comprises so small a portion of them. What multitudes of labourers and artisans live unpitied and uncared for, upon bread and water, in order that an infamous libertine may squander in peace the accumulations of an inhuman father, and that a *millionaire* master-manufacturer may export fabrics and trinkets at low prices to countries, which, in return, supply our lazy and voluptuous Sybarites with the perfumes of Arabia, and the birds of *Phase*. Would even the bad members of the working classes be what they are, were it not for the vices and follies in which they are involved by our social institutions, which punish in them the effects of passions, whose developments they provoke?

ARTICLE VII

In a veritable society there ought to be neither rich nor poor.

ARTICLE VIII

The rich, who are not willing to renounce their superfluities in favour of the indigent, are the enemies of the people.

ARTICLE IX

No one can, by accumulating to himself all the means, deprive another of the instruction necessary for his happiness. Instruction ought to be common to all.

PROOFS

1. This accumulation deprives the men of labour, of even the possibility of acquiring the knowledge necessary to every good citizen.

2. Although the people have no need of very great instruction, they require a certain portion to save them from being the prey of professional craft, and of pretenders to learning and science. The people, above all, require to know their rights and duties.

ARTICLE X

The end of the French Revolution is to destroy inequality, and to re-establish general prosperity.

PROOFS

Where is the honest man who could wish to deliver his fellow-citizens to the convulsions and evils of a political revolution, which had no other object than to render them more miserable, or to place them in a condition which should necessarily entail their total ruin? To skilfully lay hold of the proper moment for reform is not the least task of an able and virtuous politician.

ARTICLE XI

The Revolution is not terminated, because the rich absorb all valuable productions, and command exclusively; whilst the poor toil like real slaves, pine in misery, and count for nothing in the State.

ARTICLE XII

The Constitution of 1793 is the veritable law of Frenchmen, because the people has solemnly accepted it; because the Convention had not the right to change it; because to succeed in superseding it, the Convention has caused the people to be shot for demanding its execution; because it has hunted and massacred the deputies, who performed their duty in defending it; because a system of terrorism against the people, and the influence of emigrants, have presided over the fabrication and pretended acceptation of the Constitution of 1795, which, nevertheless, had not a quarter of the number of suffrages in its favour that the Constitution of 1793 has obtained; because the Constitution of 1793 has consecrated the inalienable right of every citizen to consent to the laws, to exercise political rights, to meet in assembly, to propose what he deems useful, to receive instruction, and not to die of hunger; rights which the counter-revolutionary Act of 1795 has openly and completely violated.

ARTICLE XIII

Every citizen is bound to re-establish and defend, in the Constitution of 1793, the will and happiness of the people.

ARTICLE XIV

All the powers emanating from the pretended Constitution of 1795 are illegal and counter-revolutionary.

ARTICLE XV

Those who have used violence against the Constitution of 1793 are guilty of high treason against the nation.

CLAUDE-HENRI DE SAINT-SIMON

(1760–1825)

A Golden Age for
Posterity

Saint-Simon was a paradox—a nobleman who denounced the "do-nothing classes" and became the exponent of an industrial society based on the development of capacities and dedicated to increased production. Though a prisoner for a time during the French Revolution, he acquired immense wealth through land speculation. His fortune was spent lavishly entertaining savants, on whom he at first pinned his hopes for the progress of humanity. Fallen on evil days of poverty and madness and ignored by the official scientists of the Napoleonic establishment, he rallied to become a publicist for the bankers and entrepreneurs under the Restoration. Their support, however, was withdrawn after a trial that followed the almost simultaneous publication of his "Parable" (here reprinted) and the assassination of the Duc de Berry, whose sudden demise it envisioned. Though Saint-Simon was acquitted of any complicity in the crime, his writings were branded as dangerous and he became persona non grata to the respectable bourgeois. In his last years, Saint-Simon recast his doctrines as a religion, "the new Christianity," and attracted to his side a group of brilliant young disciples, who later founded the Saint-Simonian school.

Saint-Simon, lithograph by Gottfried Engelmann, 1825. (Photo Viollet.)

The Rule of the Scientists*

I am no longer young, I have observed and reflected actively throughout my life, and your happiness has been the aim of all my labours. I have conceived a plan which I think may be useful to you, and I propose to put it before you.

Open a subscription in honour of Newton's memory; let every one, whatever his position may be, subscribe what he wishes.

Let each subscriber nominate three mathematicians, three physicists, three chemists, three physiologists, three authors, three painters, three musicians: the subscriptions to be renewed annually as well as the nominations, though every one should be left free to nominate the same persons indefinitely.

The amount of the subscriptions should be divided between the three mathematicians, the three physicists, etc., who have obtained the most votes.

Invite the President of the Royal Society of London to receive the subscriptions for this year. In subsequent years let the person who has made the largest subscription be given this honourable duty.

Make it a condition for those who are nominated that they should take no posts, honours, or money from any particular group among you, but leave each of them completely free to use his abilities as he wishes.

Men of genius will then enjoy a reward worthy of themselves, and of you. This reward will put them in the only position which will enable them to give you all the service of which they are capable. It will become the ambition of the most active minds, and will turn them away from pursuits which may disturb your tranquillity.

Finally, by this means, you will be giving leaders to those who work for the progress of your enlightenment, you will endow these leaders with great prestige, and you will place large funds at their disposal. . . . I have presented this plan directly to humanity, because it concerns humanity as a whole: but I have not entertained the absurd hope of seeing it suddenly put into effect. I have always thought that success depended on the degree of activity that persons of great influence over humanity would choose to exert on this

*From Henri de Saint-Simon, *Letters from an Inhabitant of Geneva to his Contemporaries* (1803), in *Henri Comte de Saint-Simon, Selected Writings*, edited and translated with an introduction by F. M. H. Markham (Oxford: Basil Blackwell, 1952), pp. 1–6, 8–11.

occasion. The best way to obtain their support is to throw as much light on the subject as possible. For this purpose I address my remarks to different sections of humanity, in which I distinguish three classes. The first, to which you and I have the honour to belong, marches beneath the banner of human progress: it consists of the scientists, the artists, and of all men of liberal ideas. On the banner of the second class is inscribed 'No innovation.' All the property-owners who do not qualify for the first class belong to the second. The third class, which rallies to the word 'equality,' comprises the rest of humanity.

To the first class I say as follows. Everybody to whom I have spoken of the plan which I present to humanity has, in the end, approved it after a brief discussion. They have all said that they wished it success, but have also betrayed their fear that it would altogether fail. In view of the unanimity of their opinions, it seems to me likely that I shall find all men, or the majority of them, similarly disposed. If this forecast is correct, the force of inertia will be the only obstacle to my purpose.

You, the scientists and artists, and those of you also who devote something of your energies and means to promoting enlightenment, are the section of humanity who possess the greatest intellectual force, and are best fitted to grasp a new idea. You are the most directly interested in the success of the subscription; it is for you to overcome the force of inertia. Let the mathematicians, who are in the vanguard, begin!

Scientists and artists, examine with the eye of genius the present condition of the human mind. You will perceive that the sceptre of public opinion is in your hands; seize it, therefore, boldly. You have the power to bring happiness to yourselves and to your contemporaries; to preserve posterity from the evils we have suffered and are suffering still. Therefore subscribe, all of you.

To the property-owners of the second class I shall then address this argument:

Gentlemen,

In comparison with the have-nots you are few in number. How is it, then, that they are willing to obey you? It is because your superior enlightenment enables you to combine your forces, which normally gives you the advantage in the struggle which, in the nature of things, always and inevitably exists between you and them.

Once this principle is admitted, it is clearly to your interest to win over to your side the have-nots who, by their important discoveries, have shewn the superiority of their intelligence. It is equally clear that, as your class is collectively interested in contributing, each of its members should do so.

Gentlemen, I have lived much in the company of scientists and artists; I have observed them intimately, and I can assure you that these people will compel you, in the end, to sacrifice your pride and money to place their leaders in the highest position of esteem, and to provide them with the necessary means for the conclusive exploitation of their ideas. I should be guilty of exaggeration if I gave you the impression that such an intention is precisely formulated in the minds of the scientists and artists. No, gentlemen, I can even say that such an intention is quite vague; but I am convinced, from long observation, that it is real and that it influences all their ideas. Until, gentlemen, you adopt the course I propose, you will be exposed, each in his own country, to misfortunes of the kind recently suffered in France by those of your class who happened to be established there. To be convinced of the truth of what I have said, you have only to reflect on the course of events in France since 1789.

The first popular movement there was secretly stirred up by the scientists and artists. As soon as the insurrection acquired some respectability by its success, they declared themselves openly as its leaders. The resistance they encountered in directing the insurrection towards their objective, namely the destruction of all institutions which wounded their self-esteem, provoked them to exalt more and more the ambition of the ignorant, and to break the bonds of subordination which contained the wild passions of the have-nots. They succeeded in their aims; all the institutions they originally intended to overturn were inevitably laid in ruins. In short, they won the battle and you lost it. The victory was costly to the victors: but you who were conquered suffered still more. Some scientists and artists, victims of the insubordination of their army, were massacred by their own troops. From an ethical point of view, they have all had to endure the reproaches which you have cast upon them, with an appearance of justification, that they were responsible for the atrocities committed against you and the disorders of every sort which, under the barbarous impulse of ignorance, were committed by their followers. Once the evil had reached its height, the remedy became possible. You offered no further resistance; the scientists and artists, enlightened by experience and acknowledging your superiority in enlightenment to the have-nots,[1] desired to see you resume such power as was necessary to restore regularity

---

1. I ask the reader to reflect on this observation: the haves govern the have-nots, not because they own property; they own property and govern because, collectively, they are superior in enlightenment to the have-nots.

of function to the organization of society. The have-nots had been bearing almost the whole burden of the famine to which their extravagant measures had given rise. They were curbed. The people of France, though induced by the force of events to desire passionately the restoration of order, could only be reorganized as a society by a man of genius. Bonaparte understood this task and has succeeded. One of the suggestions which I have put before you is that you lost the battle. If you still have doubts on this matter, compare the degree of prestige and wealth which the scientists and artists possess to-day in France, with that which they enjoyed before 1789.

Avoid, gentlemen, a quarrel with these men, for you will be beaten in any war which you give them an opportunity of fighting against you. You will suffer more than they will in a struggle, and peace will leave you at a disadvantage. Allow yourselves the merit of doing with a good grace what the scientists, artists and men of liberal ideas, allied with the have-nots, will sooner or later compel you to do. Every one of you subscribe: it is the only way of preventing the evils with which I see you threatened.

Since this question has been raised, let us have the courage, before passing on, to take a glance at the political situation of the most enlightened part of the world.

In Europe the functioning of governments is not, at this moment, troubled by any open opposition from the governed. But in view of the state of opinion in England, in Germany, in Italy, it is easy to predict that this calm will not last long if the necessary precautions are not taken in time: for, gentlemen, I must not conceal from you the fact that the crisis in which the human mind is involved is common to all enlightened peoples, and that the symptoms which appeared in France during the frightful explosion which occurred there are at this moment perceptible, to the intelligent observer, among the English and even among the Germans.

Gentlemen, by adopting the plan which I propose, you will reduce the crises which these peoples are fated to undergo (and no power on earth can prevent them) to simple changes in their governments and finances, and you will avert from them this general upheaval experienced by the people of France; an upheaval in which all the existing relations between the members of a nation become precarious, and anarchy, the greatest of all scourges, rages unchecked, until the misery in which it plunges the nation afflicted by it arouses a desire for the restoration of order even in the most ignorant of its members.

I should appear, gentlemen, to doubt your intelligence if I added further arguments to convince you that it is to your interest to adopt the measure I propose, on account of the evils which it enables you to avoid.

It gives me pleasure now to present this plan from another aspect which will flatter your self-esteem. Consider yourselves as the 'governors' of the progress of the human mind. You can play the part; for if, by this subscription, you give to men of genius esteem and ease, one of the conditions attaching to the subscription, which debars those who are selected from a post in any government, will safeguard you, and the rest of humanity, from the disadvantages of placing in their hands direct political power.

Experience has shewn that new, powerful and sound ideas on which discoveries are based, contain, at the moment of their conception, an admixture of false ideas. Despite this, the inventor, if he had a free hand, would often demand that they should be put into practice. This is one particular disadvantage: there is another of a general nature to which I shall draw your attention. Whenever a discovery, to be put into practice, requires a different outlook and habits from those prevailing when it appears, it is a treasure which can be enjoyed by the generation which has witnessed its birth, only through a feeling of affection for the future generation which is destined to profit by it.

I conclude this short discourse which I have ventured to address to you, by saying: gentlemen, if you remain in the second class, it is by your own wish, for you have the capacity to rise into the first class.

I turn now to the third class:
My friends,

In England there are plenty of scientists. The educated classes in England have more respect for scientists than for kings; everybody in England knows how to read, write, and add. Well, my friends, in that country the workers in the towns and even in the country eat meat every day.

In Russia, if a scientist displeases the emperor, they cut off his nose and ears and send him to Siberia. In Russia, the peasants are as ignorant as their horses. Well, my friends, the Russian peasants are badly fed, badly clothed, and are soundly beaten with sticks.

Up to the present, the rich have had little occupation except to order you about. Force them to enlighten themselves and educate you. They make your hands work for them; make their heads work for you. Do them the service of lifting from them the burden of boredom. They pay you with money, pay them with respect: it's precious coin, respect. Luckily the poorest possess some of it; spend wisely what you have, and your lot will quickly improve. . . .

It is a fact established by a long series of observations that every man experiences to a stronger or lesser degree the desire to dominate every other man.[2] It is obvious that every man who is not in a state of isolation is in an active and passive state of domination in his relations with other men, and I urge you to employ the small degree of domination you can exercise over the rich. But before I go further, I must discuss with you a matter which is a source of great dismay to you. You argue: 'We are ten, twenty, a hundred times more numerous than the property-owners, and yet they exercise over us domination much greater than we have over them.' I understand, my friends, your frustration, but remember that the property-owners, though inferior in numbers, are more enlightened than ourselves, and that, in the general interest, domination should be proportionate to enlightenment. Consider what happened in France when your comrades achieved domination: they produced a famine.

Let us return to the plan which I propose. If you adopt it and maintain it, you will place permanently in the hands of the twenty-one most enlightened men the two great weapons of domination—prestige and wealth. The consequence will be, for many reasons, rapid progress in the sciences. It is a fact that, with every advance in the sciences, discovery becomes easier; so that those who, like yourselves, can only devote little time to your education, will be able to learn more, and, as you become educated, you will diminish the domination gained by the rich. You will soon see, my friends, excellent results. But I cannot spend more time on matters which are comparatively remote consequences of a course of action on which you have not yet embarked. Let us talk of what is immediately in view. You give your respect, that is to say, you voluntarily concede a degree of domination to men who perform services which you consider useful to you. The mistake which you make, in common with the whole of humanity, is in not distinguishing clearly enough between the immediate and more lasting benefits, between those of local and more general interest, between those which benefit a part of humanity at the expense of the rest, and those which promote the happiness of the whole of humanity. In short, you have not yet realized that there is but one interest common to the whole of humanity, the progress of the sciences.

If the mayor of your village obtains for you an advantage over your neighbours, you are pleased with him, you respect him. The inhabitants of the towns shew the same desire to be superior to neighbouring towns; the

2. There are two routes by which a man may reach a position of superiority: one of them combines the individual and the general interest. My aim is to improve this way, and scatter thorns on the other.

provinces are rivals, and between nations there are struggles, called wars, for their particular interests.[3]

What part of the efforts of these fractions of the human race has a direct influence on the general interest? It is small, indeed; which is not surprising, considering that humanity has not yet taken steps collectively to reward those who do successful work in the general interest. To gather up and unite all these forces acting in different, and often contrary, directions; to direct them as far as possible to the single purpose of improving the lot of humanity —I do not think a better means can be found than the one I propose.

For the moment I have said enough of the scientists; let us speak of the artists.

On Sundays eloquence has charms for you: you take pleasure in reading a well-written book, in looking at beautiful pictures and statues, or in listening to music which holds your attention. A great deal of work is required to speak or write in a way which will amuse you, to create a picture or statue which pleases you, or to compose music which interests you. Is it not just, my friends, that you should reward the artists who fill your leisure hours with pleasures which develop your intelligence, by evoking the most delicate and subtle sensations?

My friends, let all of you subscribe, however little; you are so many that the total sum will be considerable. Moreover, the esteem which will accrue to those who are nominated, will give them an immeasurable force. You will see how the rich will strive to attain distinction in the sciences and arts, when this career leads to the highest positions of esteem. If you achieve nothing more from it than to distract them from quarrels caused by idleness, quarrels merely to decide how many of you shall be under their orders, quarrels which always involve yourselves, and in which you are the dupes, that will be a considerable gain.

If you are convinced by my plan, there will be one difficulty for you, that of selection. I will explain the way in which I should make my choice. I would

3. Moralists contradict themselves when they condemn egoism in the individual and approve patriotism. Patriotism is nothing but national egoism; and this egoism causes nations to commit against each other the same injustices as individual egoism.

Opinions are still divided on the question of egoism. Although discussion has hotly continued on this subject since the beginning of the world, the solution of the problem lies in opening up a path, which is the same for the individual and for the common interest. Egoism is essential to the security of organisms: every effort to combine the interests of individuals is a step in the right direction, but every argument of the moralists which goes beyond the conciliation of interests, and tries to destroy egoism, is an error which is easily recognizable. Moralists often mistake words for things. The first generations of humanity were those in which there was the greatest individual egoism, because individuals did not combine their interests.

ask all the mathematicians I know, who, in their opinion, are the three best mathematicians, and I would nominate the three who had the most votes of those whom I had consulted. I would do the same in the case of the physicists, etc.

Having divided humanity into three groups, and having put before each of them the reasons which should convince them, I shall now address my contemporaries as a whole, to put before them my reflections on the French Revolution.

The suppression of the privileges of birth required an effort which had ended by breaking up the old organization, and it was not in itself an obstacle to a re-organization of society. But the appeal which had been made to all members of society to fulfil frequently the functions of legislation, was unsuccessful. Apart from the fearful atrocities to which this application of the principle of equality led through the inevitable results of putting power in the hands of the ignorant, it ended by producing a form of government which was absolutely impracticable. The rulers, given salaries in order to include the have-nots, were so increased in number that the work of the governed was barely sufficient to support them. This was a result which was absolutely contrary to the most constant desire of the have-nots, which was to pay as few taxes as possible.

Here is an idea which seems to me sound. The elementary needs of life are the most imperative. The have-nots can only satisfy them inadequately. A physiologist can see clearly that their most constant desire must be to reduce taxation, or to increase wages, which comes to the same thing. I believe that all classes of society would benefit from an organization on these lines: the spiritual power in the hands of the scientists, the temporal power in the hands of the property-owners; the power to nominate those who should perform the functions of the leaders of humanity, in the hands of all; the reward of the rulers, esteem.

European Community*

After a violent convulsion Europe fears fresh disasters, and feels the need for a long repose; the sovereigns of all the European nations are assembled to give her peace. All of them seem to desire peace, all are famed for their wisdom, yet they will not reach their goal. I have asked myself why all the efforts of the statesmen are powerless against the evils which afflict Europe, and I have perceived that there is no salvation for Europe except through a general reorganization. I have thought out a plan of reorganization: the explanation of this plan is the subject of this work.

First, I shall establish the principles on which the organization of Europe should rest; then I shall apply these principles, and finally I shall point out how existing circumstances make it possible for a start to be made in carrying out this plan. Thus the first part will necessarily be somewhat abstract, the second less than the first, the third even less, since the discussion in this part will be solely on events which are taking place before our eyes, in which we are all actors or spectators.

A congress is now assembled at Vienna. What will it do? What can it do? That is what I wish to examine. The aim of this congress is to re-establish peace between the powers of Europe, by adjusting the claims of each and conciliating the interests of all. Can one hope that this aim will be achieved? I do not think so, and my reasons for so predicting are as follows. None of the members of the congress will have the function of considering questions from a general point of view; none of them will be even authorized to do so. Each of them, delegate of a king or a people, dependent and holding his rights, powers, mission as such, will come prepared to present the particular policy of the power which he represents, and to shew that this plan coincides with the interest of all. On all sides, the particular interest will be put forward as a matter of common interest. Austria will try to argue that it is important for the repose of Europe that she should have a preponderance in Italy, that she should keep Galicia and the Illyrian provinces, that her supremacy in the whole of Germany should be restored: Sweden will demonstrate, map in hand, that it is a law of nature that Norway should be her dependency; France will demand the Rhine and the Alps as natural frontiers; England will claim that she is, by nature, responsible for policing the seas, and will insist that the

*From Henri de Saint-Simon, *The Reorganization of the European Community* (1814), in *Henri Comte de Saint-Simon, Selected Writings*, edited and translated with an introduction by F. M. H. Markham (Oxford: Basil Blackwell, 1952), pp. 33–6, 50–1, 66–8.

despotism which she exercises there should be regarded as the unalterable basis of the political system.

These claims, presented with confidence, perhaps in good faith, in the guise of means to ensure the peace of Europe, and sustained with all the skill of the Talleyrands, Metternichs, and Castlereaghs, will not, however, convince anybody. Each proposition will be rejected because nobody, apart from the mover, will see in it the common interest since he cannot see in it his own interest. They will part on bad terms, blaming on each other the lack of success of the assembly; no agreement, no compromise, no peace. Sectional leagues, rival alliances of interests, will throw Europe back into this melancholy state of war from which vain efforts have been made to rescue her.

That is what the outcome will shew even more clearly; that is what neither good-will, nor wisdom, nor the desire for peace will be able to avoid. Assemble congress after congress, multiply treaties, conventions, compromises, everything you do will lead only to war; you will not abolish it, the most you can do is to shift the scene of it.

Yet the failure of these methods does not enlighten anybody on their weakness. In politics there is a routine which nobody dares to shake off, although experience clamours to us to change our methods. We blame the force of the evil rather than the weakness of the remedy; and we continue to kill each other without knowing when the carnage will finish, without hope of seeing it end. Europe is in a restless state—everybody knows it and says it—but what is this state? How did it arise? Has it always been so? Can it be stopped? These questions are still unanswered.

It is the same with political as with social relations; their stability is assured by similar means. With a union of peoples as with a union of individuals, common institutions and an organization are required. Without these everything is decided by force. To seek peace in Europe by means of treaties and congresses is to seek the maintenance of a society by conventions and agreements. In both cases a compelling force is required which will unite wills, concert movement, make interests common and undertakings firm.

It is the fashion to show a disdainful contempt for the centuries called the Middle Ages. We see in them only a time of stupid barbarism, gross ignorance, repellent superstitions, and we do not notice the fact that it is the only time when the political system of Europe had a real foundation and a common organization. I do not deny that the Popes may have been greedy for power, quarrelsome, despotic, more concerned with satisfying their ambition than curbing that of the kings; that the clergy may have joined in the quarrels of princes, and kept the people brutish in order to tyrannize over them with greater impunity. These evils, melancholy results of an age of ignorance, did not extinguish what was beneficial in this institution. As long as it remained there were few wars in Europe and these wars were of little importance.[1] Hardly had the revolution brought about by Luther caused the collapse of the political power of the church than Charles V conceived this idea of universal dominion, which was attempted after him by Philip II, Louis XIV, Napoleon and the English people; and there broke forth the religious wars, ending in the Thirty Years' War, the longest of all wars!

Despite so many striking examples, prejudice has been so strong that the greatest minds have been unable to combat it. Everybody dates the political system of Europe from the sixteenth century only; everybody regards the treaty of Westphalia as the real basis of this system.

Yet it is sufficient to examine what has happened since this time to realize that the balance of powers is a completely false conception; since peace is its aim, and it has produced nothing but wars, and what wars!

Only two men have seen the evil and come near to the remedy: they were Henry IV and the Abbé St. Pierre. The one died before he could realize his plan, which was forgotten after him; the other was treated as a visionary because he had promised more than he could perform.

Certainly the idea of linking all the European peoples by means of a political organization is by no means a dream, since for six centuries such an order of things existed, and for six centuries wars were fewer and less terrible.

This is all that the plan of the Abbé de St. Pierre amounts to, stripped of those grandiose trappings which have made it ridiculous. It was by means of a federal government common to all the nations of Europe, that he hoped to establish his impracticable 'perpetual peace'. This plan, chimerical in its results, imperfect and defective as it was, is, however, the most powerful conception which has been produced since the fifteenth century. Good results are only reached after long trials and many unsuccessful attempts, and the man who first conceives a good idea is rarely able to give it the finality and precision which it acquires with time.

The Abbé de St. Pierre's book has been little read and is hardly known except for the title, and its general reputation as the dream of a man of good will.

* * *

Men may fail for a long time to realize their own advantage, but the time comes when they are enlightened and act accordingly. The French have

1. The Crusades, the political aim of which was to discourage the Saracens from the conquest of Europe, were wars of the confederation as a whole against the enemies of its liberty.

adopted the English constitution, and all the peoples of Europe will adopt it gradually, as they become sufficiently enlightened to appreciate its advantages. Now the time when all the European peoples are governed by national parliaments will unquestionably be the time when a common parliament can be established without difficulties. The reasons for this proposition are so evident that it seems to me pointless to enumerate them.

But this time is still far off, and frightful wars and repeated revolutions will afflict Europe in the meantime. What is to be done to avert these new evils, the melancholy results of the disorganization in which Europe still remains? We must use our intelligence, and find means of abolishing the causes of these evils, with less delay.

I return to what I have already said. The establishment of the European parliament will be brought about without difficulty as soon as all the peoples of Europe live under a parliamentary régime. It follows that the European parliament can begin to take shape as soon as that part of the European population governed by a representative régime is superior in force to that which remains subject to arbitrary government.

Now this state of affairs is precisely what exists at present: the English and the French are unquestionably superior in power to the rest of Europe, and the English and the French have a parliamentary form of government. It is therefore possible to begin at once on the reorganization of Europe. Let the English and the French join together and establish a common parliament: let the principal aim of this association be to grow by attracting to it other peoples; consequently, let the Anglo-French government encourage among all the other nations the supporters of a representative constitution; let them back them with all their power, in order that parliaments can be established of the peoples subject to absolute monarchies, and let every nation, as soon as it has adopted the representative form of government, join the association and nominate representatives of her own to the common parliament. Thus the organization of Europe will be achieved gradually without wars, catastrophes, or political revolutions.

The composition of the Anglo-French parliament should be the same as that which I have suggested for the great European parliament. The French will have only a third of the representatives: that is to say, England should provide two deputies and France one for each million men who are literate.

This condition is important for two reasons; firstly, because the French are still inexperienced in parliamentary politics and need to be under the guidance of the English, who are trained and experienced; secondly, because in agreeing to the establishment of this body England would be making in some ways a sacrifice, whereas France can gain from it nothing but advantage.

It is to the interest of France and England to unite in a political association. The union of France and England can lead to the re-organization of Europe. This union, hitherto impracticable, is now possible because France and England have the same political principles and the same form of government. But is the mere possibility sufficient to bring about a reform? Certainly not; it still needs the will to do it.

England and France are each threatened with a great political upheaval and neither can by itself find means to avert it. Both will inevitably trip up if they do not mutually support each other. By a strange and fortunate coincidence, the only resource which they have against an inevitable revolution is this union which will increase the prosperity of both and put an end to the misfortunes of Europe. . . .

I have tried in this work to prove that the establishment of a political system in conformity with the present state of enlightenment, and the creation of a common power possessing force enough to repress the ambitions of peoples and kings, is the only means of producing a stable and peaceful order in Europe. In this respect the actual plan of organization which I have suggested is of secondary importance; if it were refuted, if it were found to be essentially faulty, I would still have done what I set out to do, provided some other plan were adopted.

From another point of view, the plan I have suggested is the most important part of my work. For a long time it has been agreed that the present political system is decayed to its very foundations, and that another system must be set up.

Yet in spite of the fact that this view is widespread, and that men's minds, wearied by revolutions and wars, are prepared to grasp at any means to recover order and repose, nobody has risen above the old routine. They have continued to act on the old principles, as if it was impossible to have any better ones; they have rung the changes on the old system in a thousand different ways, but nothing new has been thought of. The plan of organization which I have put forward is the first which is new and comprehensive.

Doubtless it would have been desirable that the plan of re-organization of the European community should have been thought out by one of the more powerful sovereigns, or at least by a statesman experienced in affairs and renowned for his political talent. Such a plan, backed by great power, or a great reputation, would have converted men's minds more quickly. The feebleness of human intelligence did not allow matters to follow this course. Was it possible for those who are engaged in the day-to-day conduct of affairs, and forced inevitably to reason according to the principles of the old system, which they maintain for lack of a better one, to pursue simultaneously two different courses? With their attention fixed on the old system and the old devices, could they conceive and keep before their eyes a new system and new methods?

With great effort and labour I have reached the standpoint of the common interest of the European peoples. This standpoint is the only one from which it is possible to perceive both the evils which threaten us, and the means of averting them. If those who are in charge of affairs can reach the same level as I have done, they will all be able to see what I have seen. The divisions of public opinion arise from the fact that each man has too narrow a view, and does not dare to free himself from this standpoint from which he persists in judging affairs.

For clear-thinking men there is only one method of reasoning, only one way of seeing things, if they are looking at them from the same point of view. If men who have the same nobility of sentiment, uprightness of judgment, desire for the public welfare, loyalty to the King, yet have such different opinions, it is because each has his own point of view which he will not abandon.

Let them rise above it, and put themselves in the position to which I have tried to elevate men's minds, and all these different opinions will merge into one.

Thus by a happy transformation, beneficial to the State, we shall see all the finest characters, the most enlightened minds, the Montesquious and the Raynouards, the d'Ambrais and the Lanjuinais, and all the others separated by their opinions but united by their feelings, aiming at the same goal and co-operating for the same purpose. There will come a time, without doubt, when all the peoples of Europe will feel that questions of common interest must be dealt with before coming down to national interests; then evils will begin to lessen, troubles abate, wars die out. That is the ultimate direction in which we are steadily progressing; it is there that the progress of the human mind will carry us. But which is more worthy of man's prudence—to hasten towards it, or to let ourselves be dragged there?

Poetic imagination has put the Golden Age in the cradle of the human race, amid the ignorance and brutishness of primitive times; it is rather the Iron Age which should be put there. The Golden Age of the human race is not behind us but before us; it lies in the perfection of the social order. Our

ancestors never saw it; our children will one day arrive there; it is for us to
clear the way.

———◆———

A Parable*

Suppose that France suddenly lost fifty of her best physicists, chemists,
physiologists, mathematicians, poets, painters, sculptors, musicians, writers;
fifty of her best mechanical engineers, civil and military engineers, artillery
experts, architects, doctors, surgeons, apothecaries, seamen, clockmakers;
fifty of her best bankers, two hundred of her best business men, two hundred
of her best farmers, fifty of her best ironmasters, arms manufacturers, tanners,
dyers, miners, cloth-makers, cotton manufacturers, silk-makers, linen-makers,
manufacturers of hardware, of pottery and china, of crystal and glass, ship
chandlers, carriers, printers, engravers, goldsmiths, and other metal-workers;
her fifty best masons, carpenters, joiners, farriers, locksmiths, cutlers, smelters,
and a hundred other persons of various unspecified occupations, eminent in
the sciences, fine arts, and professions; making in all the three thousand leading
scientists, artists, and artisans of France.[1]

These men are the Frenchmen who are the most essential producers, those
who make the most important products, those who direct the enterprises
most useful to the nation, those who contribute to its achievements in the
sciences, fine arts and professions. They are in the most real sense the flower
of French society; they are, above all Frenchmen, the most useful to their
country, contribute most to its glory, increasing its civilization and prosperity.
The nation would become a lifeless corpse as soon as it lost them. It would
immediately fall into a position of inferiority compared with the nations which
it now rivals, and would continue to be inferior until this loss had been
replaced, until it had grown another head. It would require at least a generation
for France to repair this misfortune; for men who are distinguished in work of

*From Henri de Saint-Simon, *The Organizer* (1819), in *Henri Comte de Saint-Simon, Selected
Writings*, edited and translated with an introduction by F. M. H. Markham (Oxford:
Basil Blackwell, 1952), pp. 72–5.

1. Artisan usually means an ordinary workman. To avoid cirumlocution, I mean by this
expression all those who are concerned with material production, viz., farmers, manufacturers,
merchants, bankers, and all the clerks and workmen employed by them.

positive ability are exceptions, and nature is not prodigal of exceptions, particularly in this species.

Let us pass on to another assumption. Suppose that France preserves all the men of genius that she possesses in the sciences, fine arts and professions, but has the misfortune to lose in the same day Monsieur the King's brother, Monseigneur le duc d'Angoulême, Monseigneur le duc de Berry, Monseigneur le duc d'Orléans, Monseigneur le duc de Bourbon, Madame la duchesse d'Angoulême, Madame la duchesse de Berry, Madame la duchesse d'Orléans, Madame la duchesse de Bourbon, and Mademoiselle de Condé. Suppose that France loses at the same time all the great officers of the royal household, all the ministers (with or without portfolio), all the councillors of state, all the chief magistrates, marshals, cardinals, archbishops, bishops, vicars-general, and canons, all the prefects and sub-prefects, all the civil servants, and judges, and, in addition, ten thousand of the richest proprietors who live in the style of nobles.

This mischance would certainly distress the French, because they are kind-hearted, and could not see with indifference the sudden disappearance of such a large number of their compatriots. But this loss of thirty-thousand individuals, considered to be the most important in the State, would only grieve them for purely sentimental reasons and would result in no political evil for the State.

In the first place, it would be very easy to fill the vacancies which would be made available. There are plenty of Frenchmen who could fill the function of the King's brother as well as can Monsieur; plenty who could take the place of a Prince as appropriately as Monseigneur le duc d'Angoulême, or Monseigneur le duc d'Orléans, or Monseigneur le duc de Bourbon. There are plenty of Frenchwomen who would be as good princesses as Madame la duchesse d'Angoulême, or Madame la duchesse de Berry, or Mesdames d'Orléans, de Bourbon, and de Condé.

The ante-chambers of the palace are full of courtiers ready to take the place of the great household officials. The army has plenty of soldiers who would be as good leaders as our present Marshals. How many clerks there are who are as good as our ministers? How many administrators who are capable of managing the affairs of the departments better than the existing prefects and sub-prefects? How many barristers who are as good lawyers as our judges? How many vicars as expert as our cardinals, archbishops, bishops, vicars-general, and canons? As for the ten thousand aristocratic landowners, their heirs could need no apprenticeship to do the honours of their drawing-rooms as well as they.

The prosperity of France can only exist through the effects of the progress of the sciences, fine arts and professions. The Princes, the great household officials, the Bishops, Marshals of France, prefects and idle landowners contribute nothing directly to the progress of the sciences, fine arts and professions. Far from contributing they only hinder, since they strive to prolong the supremacy existing to this day of conjectural ideas over positive science. They inevitably harm the prosperity of the nation by depriving, as they do, the scientists, artists, and artisans of the high esteem to which they are properly entitled. They are harmful because they expend their wealth in a way which is of no direct use to the sciences, fine arts, and professions: they are harmful because they are a charge on the national taxation, to the amount of three or four hundred millions under the heading of appointments, pensions, gifts, compensations, for the upkeep of their activities which are useless to the nation.

These suppositions underline the most important fact of present politics: they provide a point of view from which we can see this fact in a flash in all its extent; they show clearly, though indirectly, that our social organization is seriously defective: that men still allow themselves to be governed by violence and ruse, and that the human race (politically speaking) is still sunk in immorality.

The scientists, artists, and artisans, the only men whose work is of positive utility to society, and cost it practically nothing, are kept down by the princes and other rulers who are simply more or less incapable bureaucrats. Those who control honours and other national awards owe, in general, the supremacy they enjoy, to the accident of birth, to flattery, intrigue and other dubious methods.

Those who control public affairs share between them every year one half of the taxes, and they do not even use a third of what they do not pocket personally in a way which benefits the citizen.

These suppositions show that society is a world which is upside down.

The nation holds as a fundamental principle that the poor should be generous to the rich, and that therefore the poorer classes should daily deprive themselves of necessities in order to increase the superfluous luxury of the rich.

The most guilty men, the robbers on a grand scale, who oppress the mass of the citizens, and extract from them three or four hundred millions a year, are given the responsibility of punishing minor offences against society.

Ignorance, superstition, idleness and costly dissipation are the privilege of the leaders of society, and men of ability, hard-working and thrifty, are employed only as inferiors and instruments.

To sum up, in every sphere men of greater ability are subject to the control of men who are incapable. From the point of view of morality, the most immoral men have the responsibility of leading the citizens towards virtue; from the point of view of distributive justice, the most guilty men are appointed to punish minor delinquents.

On Social Organization*

The mechanism of social organization was inevitably very complicated so long as the majority of individuals remained in a state of ignorance and improvidence which rendered them incapable of administering their own affairs. In this state of incomplete intellectual development they were swayed by brutal passions which urged them to revolt and every kind of anarchy.

In such a situation, which was the necessary prelude to a better social order, it was necessary for the minority to be organized on military lines, to obtain a monopoly of legislation, and so to keep all power to itself, in order to hold the majority in tutelage and subject the nation to strong discipline. Thus the main energies of the community have till now been directed to maintaining itself as a community, and any efforts directed to improving the moral and physical welfare of the nation have necessarily been regarded as secondary.

To-day this state of affairs can and should be completely altered. The main effort should be directed to the improvement of our moral and physical welfare; only a small amount of force is now required to maintain public order, since the majority have become used to work (which eliminates disorder) and now consists of men who have recently proved that they are capable of administering property, whether in land or money.

As the minority no longer has need of force to keep the proletarian class in subordination, the course which it should adopt is as follows:

(1) A policy by which the proletariat will have the strongest interest in maintaining public order.

*From Henri de Saint-Simon, *On Social Organization* (1825), in *Henri Comte de Saint-Simon, Selected Writings*, edited and translated with an introduction by F. M. H. Markham (Oxford: Basil Blackwell, 1952), pp. 76–80.

(2) A policy which aims at making the inheritance of landed property as easy as possible.

(3) A policy which aims at giving the highest political importance to the workers.

Such a policy is quite simple and obvious, if one takes the trouble to judge the situation by one's own intelligence, and to shake off the yoke enforced on our minds by the political principles of our ancestors—principles which were sound and useful in their own day, but are no longer applicable to present circumstances. The mass of the population is now composed of men (apart from exceptions which occur more or less equally in every class) who are capable of administering property whether in land or in money, and therefore we can and must work directly for the improvement of the moral and physical welfare of the community.

The most direct method of improving the moral and physical welfare of the majority of the population is to give priority in State expenditure to ensuring work for all fit men, to secure their physical existence; spreading throughout the proletarian class a knowledge of positive science; ensuring for this class forms of recreation and interests which will develop their intelligence.

We must add to this the measures necessary to ensure that the national wealth is administered by men most fitted for it, and most concerned in its administration, that is to say the most important industrialists.

Thus the community, by means of these fundamental arrangements, will be organized in a way which will completely satisfy reasonable men of every class.[1]

1. Men are not as bad as they think they are: they are more severe on themselves than they deserve. It is true that theoretically they appear to be strongly inclined to despotism, but, in actual fact, they prefer equality.

If an Englishman obtains a post in India, he goes there with enthusiasm, and in his imagination pictures the delights that despotism will procure for him. He can, if he likes, keep a harem; he will be surrounded by hundreds of servants—some to keep off the flies which might irritate him, others always ready to carry him in a palanquin. The whole population will crawl before him; he will have the power to order a beating for any Indian who does not obey his wishes with enough zeal or intelligence.

Well, this Englishman who in India wallows in the delights of despotism, hastens to return to England, as soon as he has made his fortune, to enjoy again the advantages of equality. The moment he arrives in harbour in Great Britain he finds himself rudely hustled by the people, and yet that does not make him wish to return to the place where everybody makes way for him.

We see Russians of vast wealth leaving their country to live in western Europe, while western Europeans only go to Russia to make their fortune, and hasten to bring back to their own homes the wealth they have acquired there.

There are good reasons why rich men prefer to live in countries where equality between the members of the community is most far advanced, since these countries are at the same time those where they can most easily and fully satisfy their wants.

There will no longer be a fear of insurrection, and consequently no longer a need to maintain large standing armies to suppress it; no longer a need to spend enormous sums on a police force; no longer a fear of foreign danger, for a body of thirty millions of men who are a contented community would easily repel attack, even if the whole human race combined against them.

We might add that neither princes nor peoples would be so mad as to attack a nation of thirty millions who displayed no aggressive intentions against their neighbours, and were united internally by mutual interests.

Furthermore, there would no longer be a need for a system of police-spying in a community in which the vast majority had an interest in maintaining the established order.

The men who brought about the Revolution, the men who directed it, and the men who, since 1789 and up to the present day, have guided the nation, have committed a great political mistake. They have all sought to improve the governmental machine, whereas they should have subordinated it and put administration in the first place.

They should have begun by asking a question the solution of which is simple and obvious. They should have asked who, in the present state of morals and enlightenment, are the men most fitted to manage the affairs of the nation. They would have been forced to recognize the fact that the scientists, artists and industrialists, and the heads of industrial concerns are the men who possess the most eminent, varied, and most positively useful ability, for the guidance of men's minds at the present time. They would have recognized the fact that the work of the scientists, artists, and industrialists

---

In any French town of some importance, a man with money can, at any hour and without previous notice, eat well at a moderate price. In Russia only the great nobles can obtain good food.

If a traveller has a breakdown of his carriage anywhere in England, he can either have his carriage repaired or buy on the spot a carriage as good as the other. In Russia, a traveller whose carriage breaks down on a main road between big towns, is forced to finish his journey in a peasant's cart.

Thus, in fact, the richest and most powerful men have an interest in the growth of equality, since the means of satisfying their wants increases in the same proportion as the levelling of the individuals composing the community.

It is commonly assumed that those who profit by an abuse are strongly attached to it. This is an error; what they are determined on is not to let themselves be deprived of advantages which pass into the hands of others. It was the nobles who in France initiated the suppression of the privileges which they enjoyed, and they regretted this sacrifice only when they saw, first, all the former commoners behave towards them like members of a privileged order, and then a new aristocracy growing up in which the former nobles were only admitted as inferiors.

In conclusion to this note, let me say what perhaps should have been stated first, that the improvement of the lot of the masses secures the welfare of men of every class, and that, to improve the lot of the masses, it is necessary not merely to transfer privilege, but to abolish it. It is necessary not merely to let abuses change hands, but to eliminate them.

is that which, in discovery and application, contributes most to national prosperity.

They would have reached the conclusion that the scientists, artists and leaders of industrial enterprises are the men who should be entrusted with administrative power, that is to say, with the responsibility for managing the national interests; and that the functions of government should be limited to maintaining public order.[2]

The reformers of 1789 should have said to themselves as follows.

The kings of England have given a good example to monarchy by agreeing to give no order without the approval and signature of a minister. The magnanimity of the kings of France demands that they shew still greater generosity to their people, and that they should agree to make no decision affecting the general interests of the nation without the approval of the men most fitted to judge their decisions—that is to say, without the approval of the scientists and the most eminent artists, without the approval of the most important industrialists.

The community has often been compared to a pyramid. I admit that the

2. I propose to explain briefly how the imposition of government on top of administration produces harmful effects at the present day, when the mass of the nation consists of men who no longer require to be closely supervised, since they have shewn themselves capable of administering all kinds of property. To-day the proletarian class can only become dangerous to public order, if the administrators of the national interests are so inept or selfish as to let them become unemployed.

It is easy to convince oneself, and others, that one has the capacity to govern, because the ability or lack of ability to govern can only be proved by experience. Any man can imagine and persuade others that he would govern well, so long as he has not governed already.

It is not the same in the case of mathematics, physics, chemistry, physiology, mechanics, poetry, painting, sculpture, architecture, farming, manufacture, commerce, and banking.

It is easy for any man to judge whether he possesses great ability in the sciences or arts; it is easy to verify whether he has attained great importance in a branch of industry. In any case, errors of this sort would not be serious, since his neighbours would soon open his eyes, if they were blinded by vanity.

It follows from what I have said that the ambition of scientists, artists and industrialists, to participate in the administration of national interests, is not dangerous to the community. It is advantageous rather, since they can only succeed in their ambition through solid achievements; while the ambition which aims at a place in the government is harmful to the community, because the most incapable men may be consumed by such an ambition and, in order to satisfy it, strive to overthrow the whole social order.

One of the important effects of this ambition, which inflamed almost all Frenchmen when the government of the unfortunate Louis XVI was overturned, is very extraordinary. It was with the aim of being governed less, and less expensively, that the nation embarked on revolution. Up to the present it has achieved as a result more government, and more expensive government, than it had before the Revolution.

The industrialists produce much more than before the Revolution, but a great part of the increased production is used to pay useless military staffs, and a mass of clerks who employ their time for the most part in reading newspapers and sharpening pens—a result which satisfies neither the needs nor the feelings of the producers.

nation should be composed as a pyramid; I am profoundly convinced that the national pyramid should be crowned by the monarchy, but I assert that from the base of the pyramid to its summit the layers should be composed of more and more precious materials. If we consider the present pyramid, it appears that the base is made of granite, that up to a certain height the layers are composed of valuable materials, but that the upper part, supporting a magnificent diamond, is composed of nothing but plaster and gilt.

The base of the present national pyramid consists of workers in their routine occupations; the first layers above this base are the leaders of industrial enterprises, the scientists who improve the methods of manufacture and widen their application, the artists who give the stamp of good taste to all their products. The upper layers, which I assert to be composed of nothing but plaster, which is easily recognizable despite the gilding, are the courtiers, the mass of nobles whether of ancient or recent creation, the idle rich, the governing class from the prime minister to the humblest clerk. The monarchy is the magnificent diamond which crowns the pyramid.

The Loving
and Productive Society

The devotees who were the solace of Saint-Simon's declining years founded their movement immediately upon his death (1825)—he had said to them "The pear is ripe, pluck it!"—and gave it the character of a new religion. The society they envisaged was to be a fusion of science, industry, and art, animated with the spirit of universal love. The Saint-Simonians held public lectures in which they preached, among other reforms, the emancipation of women and the rehabilitation of the flesh; they affected extravagant dress and conduct; and they established at Ménilmontant near Paris their own community, which dissension and schism finally dissolved. Some of the "family" were prosecuted and imprisoned for immorality; others set out for the East in search of the Female Messiah. For a time their influence extended throughout Europe and even penetrated the Western hemisphere. In France, they numbered among their adherents men who under the Second Empire became prominent bankers, industrialists, and engineers. The expositions of their doctrine, given when the movement was in its prime, were largely a collective work, though one or another disciple was usually designated orator and spokesman.

Saint-Simonian missionaries: Barrault, Chevalier, Duveyrier, contemporary drawing. (From Richard K. P. Pankhurst, *The Saint-Simonians, Mill and Carlyle*, London: Sidgwick and Jackson [1957], by courtesy of the author.)

On Moral Education[*]

Gentlemen:

We have made it our task to make you understand the importance of moral education and to make you realize that it should be the object of a social plan and of a political function. We have shown how in this respect its progress is linked to the general emancipation of mankind. And finally we have proved that present day opinions which reject all systematization of this type of education necessarily lead to man's loss of dignity. We must yet explain our views on the nature, scope, and method of moral education.

The word "education" usually calls to mind the upbringing of children. Since this first epoch of life is, indeed, a preparation for the following ones, ideas on education relate to it particularly. Education, however, and especially that type of education with which we are dealing, is not limited to childhood. It should accompany man throughout the course of his life. If one considers that man's action is indeed determined at each stage of his life by desire and influenced by his sympathies, one recognizes how important it is to extend social foresight to all that is able to awaken and to develop within him sympathies in conformity with the goal that society has set for itself. And if man is susceptible all his life to benefiting from moral instruction, society ought to make sure that he never lacks this instruction.

Nothing can take the place of education during youth. Once thrown into active life, man no longer has the moral flexibility necessary for the assimilation of the culture he lacks, although he has twice as much need for it. Since his desires must be translated into action, the result is that when they are not directed toward the good, that is to say toward social progress, but are left alone, they lead to evil, namely egoism. Thus, lack of education must almost always be understood as education for evil, and someone whose early education has been neglected not only has to learn but also to unlearn. Only a very small number of privileged persons exist who, sustained and animated by the thought that they have a mission to fulfill, can triumph over an inferior early education.

[*]From *The Doctrine of Saint-Simon: An Exposition, First Year, 1828-1829,* trans. Georg G. Iggers (Boston: Beacon Press, 1958), pp. 149–59.

It is true that history presents examples of entire generations somehow suddenly transported from one moral sphere to another. But first of all, these changes are never as abrupt as they seem at first sight. When we look closer, we shall always find that they have been in the making for a long time prior to the moment when they suddenly manifested themselves. It will then be seen that they appeared at first only in the most general order of feelings, ideas, and interests, and that it was only much later and by stages that they succeeded in invading the sphere of deeds and thoughts and secondary affections. Thus we also see that generations which supposedly were suddenly converted were for a long time unable to bring about completely the state of society for which the newly professed principles called. The peoples that were subject to the Roman Empire for several centuries had been prepared by the works of the philosophers to receive the word of the apostles, but nevertheless they remained more pagan than Christian for several centuries after the preaching of the Gospels, which they recognized as law. There was no truly Christian society until the guardians of the new doctrine could take hold of a man at birth, free him from the attitudes and customs of the old social order, and inculcate in him attitudes, ideas, and customs in conformity with the new social order.

The education of youth is doubtless the most important but it is not sufficient. If these impressions are not reinforced and renewed in later active life, they soon pass into a state of vague memories. Before long they are entirely wiped out by numerous considerations about one's individual position, which absorb a person's whole attention and monopolize his whole activity. More-over, if the person should reflect on the moral precepts he was taught, he may conclude that he understands neither their suitability, purpose, nor utility, and he may consider them to be in conflict with the things which impress him and which he considers necessary. In order that early educational impressions retain their influence, they must constantly be reproduced. In other words, moral education must be extended through the individual's entire life.

The more civilization has progressed, the more moral education has increased in vision and extended the duration of its impact on the individual's life.

In antiquity each citizen—the numerous class of the slaves is, of course, not included under this heading—called upon to discuss the interests of the community in the forum and to take part in the enterprises undertaken in the public interest found himself in a position high enough to perceive the relationship between his personal acts and the general interests. But this awareness did not dispense with the early education that revealed to him the society of which he was a member. Without any doubt, the precepts of this education could have remained firmly impressed upon his mind even without the help of a special institution established for that purpose. And yet, look at the pomp of the Olympic games, the mysteries, the religious ceremonies, the numerous class of priests, sybils, and augurers. Everywhere a living instruction in the destiny of society awakened devotion and enthusiasm.

This situation has changed. Peoples are no longer confined to the interior of a city and no longer have room in a public place where the common interests can be debated by all. The division of labor, one of the essential conditions of the progress of civilization, which restricted individuals to increasingly more limited circles, also increasingly removed them from the direct consideration of general interests, and this at the time when these interests were becoming more difficult to grasp because of increasingly complicated social relations. As the division of labor became more extensive, it was necessary to put more emphasis on intensive and orderly moral education in order to realize the advantages which specialized education brought. In this way alone could man regain the general outlook which he had lost through the specialization of labor.

Moreover, more care has to be taken to see to it that the impressions of early education are preserved and incessantly strengthened during the individual's life by outward, direct, and systematic action.

But if the division of work immediately resulted in narrowing the sphere of individual occupation, it also permitted privileged organizations to devote themselves more exclusively to the contemplation of general facts, and, through their action upon other men, to return with large dividends the same advantages to society which can be attributed to the confusion of all types of work in the hands of each.

We shall now examine which faculty makes man receptive to moral education and which faculty should dominate among those who are called upon to direct this education.

The philosophers, when comparing modern and ancient times, do not hesitate to ascribe superiority to the former and generally see it in the ever growing predominance of reason over feeling. They consider feeling as an attribute of mankind's childhood and reason as that of manhood. This opinion might perhaps have a semblance of accuracy if it were limited to explaining the progress made through the progressively felt separation of these two manifestations of human activity, which is to say through the direct application of each of them to the order of work with which each is particularly connected. This opinion would be accurate if its object were to point out disadvantages resulting from the confusion which, as we have said above, existed at the beginning of societies between poetry and science. But if, on the other hand, one perceives the decline of feeling in this useful division of labor, mankind is unduly mutilated. It suffices to hear the daily defense of reason and the violent attacks against feeling to be assured that such is the general opinion in our days. With what affected scorn they ridicule all that comes from that sublime source, love! How naively they imagine that an idea or an enterprise can be totally disproven or discredited by merely labelling it as "pure feeling"! Inspiration, which is to say genius, it seems, is the evil principle of our nature, and all our efforts must attempt to rid us of this formidable enemy. And this procedure, unfortunately, usually succeeds.

This opinion is doubtless not always expressed so frankly, but it is at the basis of all the systems which claim to be part of mankind's progress. When seeing us take up the defense of feeling against reason, one may be wrongly led to believe that we intend to apologize for spirtualism at the expense of materialism. These two opinions, when confronted, fight each other with the same weapon—reason. Neither of them knows what love is. Both analyze, divide, and break spirit or matter into their smallest form or tiniest molecule. Both reduce to dust the field they cross. Both carry death everywhere; neither of them shall have life.

Let us come back to reason's claim of superiority over feeling. Evidently this opinion must necessarily exert a great influence on the way the subject with which we are dealing is understood. From this point of view, indeed, the special, if not exclusive purpose of education appears to be the cultivation of man's rational or scientific faculty. It aims at enabling each individual to acquire for himself, by proof, the dogmas of social science, and to act only after having maturely calculated the consequences of an act for himself as well as for society as a whole. It is held that everyone would then be sheltered from the surprises and illusions of his sentiments and mainly from the influence of men who have the power to move him. And the belief that such a pitiful result is being achieved is a general source of gratification.

We need not now characterize those two great manners of being and of existence, reason and feeling, or describe the different forms in which the world and man appear to man himself and according to which he proceeds in his investigations in a rational or a sentimental way. This interesting analysis will always concern us. We shall be satisfied for the moment to expound dogmatically those ideas of the doctrine, which are particularly bound up with this problem.

The rational faculty does not become perfect in the development of mankind at the expense of the faculty of feeling. Both develop in equal proportion. If the rational faculty seems to dominate today, this shows only that there exists among us as little association and as little union as is possible among men joined in society. It should be easy to realize this situation fully if the characteristics we have assigned to the critical epochs are recalled.

Man lives and is sociable through feeling. Feeling binds us to the world and to man and to all which surrounds us. When this bond is broken, when the world and man seem to reject us, when the affection attracting us toward them is weakened and annihilated, life ceases for us. Without those sympathies that unite man with his fellow-men and that make him suffer their sorrows, enjoy their joys, and live their lives, it would be impossible to see in societies anything but aggregations of individuals without bonds, having no motive for their actions but the impulses of egoism.

Feeling makes man inquire about his destiny, and feeling first reveals the answer to him. Then doubtless science has an important role to fulfill. It is called upon to verify these inspirations, revelations, and divinations of feeling, and to furnish man with the insights to make him move rapidly and securely toward the goal discovered for him. But it is again feeling which, by making him desire and love this goal, can alone give him the will and the necessary strength to attain it.

Despite this great role which, contrary to general opinion, we assign to feeling, we are most assuredly far from wanting to curb or deprecate the efforts by which the present generation attempts to advance on the road of reason. If one wants to go back to our first sessions, one will recall that far from considering our century as having passed the limits of rational growth, we think rather that it has remained within limits. In this respect our age still has immense progress to make and in spite of its claims, it shows itself to be very much inferior to several centuries that precede it if its numerous elements are considered. If one returns to what we have said about the positive method, its value, the way it is to be used, and the use we ourselves have made of it in the study of the great phenomena of mankind's collective life, one will be convinced that we attach no slight importance to rational procedures, and we do not show ourselves to be less rigorous in applying them than those men whose work is regarded today as the most positivistic— namely as the product of the purest rationalism.

But this should give us at least a right to repeat that man's total moral existence is not confined to the rational faculty, that he has other means of knowing than the positive method, and other sources of faith and conviction than scientific demonstrations; for as we have already said, all science presupposes axioms.

The general scholars—and from the point of view of our doctrine, we mean the trustees of the science of mankind, namely social physiology—these scholars can doubtless deduce the future from observation of the past and point out, with the aid of indications given them by the new conception and with the help of the method which it teaches them to use, at what stage the series of already achieved deeds will end. One can also easily recognize their ability to determine through continued investigation of secondary facts or through logical reasoning the social combination best adapted to the goal revealed to them by sympathy, consequently, also, their ability to describe the individual's obligations in terms of this proper place in the social hierarchy. But this place can only be assigned by love, which is to say by the men who are most strongly animated by the desire of improving the fate of mankind. And moreover, although one may attribute this ability to science, is there any reason to conclude that science ought to preside over moral education? However little one may reflect about this, one will realize science's powerlessness in fulfilling such a mission. This mission is beyond it.

And indeed, for the precepts of science to contain an obligation to act, one must suppose that through demonstrations these precepts become the work and the creation of those who hold them. But such a demonstration would demand a perfect acquaintance with social science on the part of everyone. Yet supposing that all men were able to acquire it, they would still have to dedicate to this end all the time intended for special education which they need in order to fulfill their functions within society satisfactorily. This is evidently impossible.

The results of social science can be presented to almost all men only in a dogmatic form. Only the small number of those who devote their whole life to its study can prove these problems to themselves. These men are also the only ones of whom one may suppose that they will under all circumstances be guided by the precepts of science. But this is clearly only a supposition. Indeed, scientific demonstration can well justify the logical suitability of such and such an act but is insufficient to establish it. To do so, it would be necessary for scientific demonstrations to make us love these acts, and that is not the role of science. A demonstration does not contain within itself any necessary reason for action. Science, as we have just said, can indicate the means to be used in attaining a certain goal. But why one goal rather than another? Why not remain stationary? Why not even retrogress? Feeling, that is, strong sympathy for the discovered goal, alone can cut through this difficulty.

For the individual willing to restrict himself to a prescribed circle, it is not enough that the goal of the society and the means of attaining it are known to him. It is necessary that this goal and these means are objects of love and desire for him. The scholars can doubtless verify them and say what must be loved if one is not to go contrary to the march of civilization as indicated by the interlinking of historic facts. But they are unable to produce the feelings the need for which they recognize.

This mission belongs to another class of men, to those whom nature has particularly endowed with a capacity for sympathy. We most certainly do not claim that the men who are to be given the responsibility of leading society should remain strangers to science, but science takes on a new character in their hands. It is imbued with the life and sanction which only those men can give it who relate science to the destiny of mankind.

To convince ourselves of the preceding, we need only investigate what men and what means have always determined social volition and action and from what source the individual has always derived the satisfaction that follows the fulfillment of one's duties. One will find that the direction of society has at all times and in all places belonged to the men who have spoken to the heart; that the constructions of reason and syllogisms have always been only secondary and indirect means; and finally, that society has never been directly stirred onward except by the various expressions of feeling.

These expressions of feeling, called "cult" in organic epochs or "fine arts" in critical epochs, always result in arousing the desire for conformity with the goal that society sets itself in proving the actions necessary for progress. In this respect no difference is found between one state of society and another, organic or critical, except in the nature of the feelings that the cult or the fine arts are called upon to develop and the duties which they demand. In all these respects, the Middle Ages show themselves superior to the earlier times. Here we should speak of a means of education and of moral discipline peculiar to that epoch which we mentioned in the preceding session. We mean confession, which in recent times has been the object of unanimous censure. It has been viewed only as a means of seduction and espionage, as a practice put to use by the clergy to support ambitions and satisfy individual passions. This judgment was a logical consequence of the condemnation of Catholic doctrine in its entirety.

Since this doctrine has come to be considered a fraud, used as a sanction for a despotism for the profit of the few, evidently all that could have contributed to strengthening and propagating it, particularly confession, which is so effective in achieving this result, should have been rejected with mistrust and disgust. But if, from another point of view, Catholicism, that is Christianity as a social institution, is considered to have been at the time of its greatest power the moral doctrine best adapted to society's needs, it will be recognized that the institutions intended to make these needs penetrate men's minds were most eminently useful and moral as long as the doctrine itself remained in harmony with the needs of mankind. It was only when this harmony ceased that confession, except for the exaggerations that accompany every reaction, deserved the reproaches directed against it today. But at the time when the doctrine was at its peak and confession was one of its principal means of action, confession ought to be viewed only as a form of consultation by which less moral and less enlightened men came to look for insight and strength, which they lacked, from those superior to them in intelligence and morality. It was also a means employed by the latter to awaken and sustain the social and individual sympathies which they were to develop and direct. And if one reflects about the virtue of rehabilitation inherent in confession, one cannot help recognizing in it a moral power and an educational means of the highest order. While the sermon and the catechism, which were addressed to all, could only deal with general cases and were calculated for the intelligence and feelings of the average person, confession served as a commentary, made decisions in the many individual cases, and thus adapted the doctrine to each person's intelligence and sensitivity. No procedure so powerful in continuing and sustaining the first impressions of education was used by the ancients.

We have said that moral education was to teach through feeling, and that the guidance of this education should belong to the men with the greatest capacity for feeling. We may affirm that this is the first condition of any association; for no society exists where there is not a desired goal and where the collected individuals are not led, guided, and incited onward by those men who most ardently strive to attain the goal. This condition will be realized in the future as it was everywhere in the past. This does not mean that the same practices, and the same forms should be perpetuated, or that the catechism and the cult, which formerly passionately stirred the hearts of the faithful, should be kept. Nor should the form of consultation and rehabilitation known under the name *confession* remain the same. We merely wish to say that analogous but more perfect means should be put to use in the future to prolong the education of man during the entire course of his life.

The Emancipation of Women*

... I come to participate in the glorious task proposed by our Father Enfantin for the devotion, aspiration, and love of all his sons. I hasten to make my voice heard, too, in so sacred a cause; to show you all the grief and confusion, all the tyranny and fraud that the present condition of women breeds in this society; to make you understand how nobility, loyalty, purity, and happiness will reappear in all the relationships of the two sexes, as soon as the marriage law established by Christ and his successors has been modified to eliminate whatever is contrary to human nature, and is replaced by a new law based at once on the social equality of men and women and on the rehabilitation of the needs and pleasures of the flesh.

I am aware that in accomplishing this task we will see our goals misconstrued and our intentions falsified. . . . I am reminded of how the Christians, having disseminated their first message of peace and love in the world, became the fearless denouncers of pagan society, the denouncers of its vices, of its *virtues*, of its very *gods*. I am sensible of the horrible clamor that then arose on every side. And I am reminded, too, that in response to that wild shrieking, the courage of the Christians mounted to the very heights of heroism. That is why, when we come to shake the foundations of Christian society, when we come with the same message to attack both its vices and its virtues . . . when, I say, we come to condemn in Christian society the little that remains of its morality and its God, I expect that a terrible outcry will surge up around us as well. I am prepared. Our voices need to be reinforced by a strong accompaniment. But after all, we are here to give women the strength and freedom they need to press directly for their own emancipation and for the amelioration of the lot of the working classes; why, then, should we lack a sacred faith in our cause, and why, as we await the defilement that threatens us, should our brows not be crowned with an ennobling shamelessness? . . .

The fundamental principle of Christian morality, insofar as it regulates the relationships between the sexes, is *exclusive love*. Christian marriage law establishes an indissoluble and eternal union of the espoused. According to Christianity rigorously understood and practiced, a male or female virgin— virginal both in mind and body—must find straightway, without prior experience, that man or woman among all mankind who will be able to make him happy for the remainder of his life.

*From Abel Transon, *Affranchissement des femmes, prédication du 1er janvier, 1832* (Paris, 1832), pp. 1–10; translated by the editors.

I deny emphatically all that is absolute in these principles and in this morality. I deny, in other words, that the *exclusive love* of one man for one woman lasting their whole lives is a law or even a *universal* tendency of mankind. I deny that this precept conforms and is applicable to the nature of *all* men and *all* women without *exception*.

I ask all men of good faith, I ask all women who have felt deep compassion for the sufferings of their sex, I ask of everyone: If we were confronted by Christianity in all its vigor and original purity, would it not be sufficient to fight and overthrow it simply to recall here that Christianity proclaimed *celibacy* as the state most exalted and most agreeable to God? There is no dispute here between Protestants and Catholics. For all Christian priests, of whatever persuasion, is not the life of Jesus the most perfect model that humanity can take for itself? Now, according to the Christian faith, Jesus, born of a virgin, himself lived as a virgin. I say, then, that to fight and overthrow the principle of Christian love we would need merely to declare that a religion which saw in celibacy the state most favorable to salvation and the one closest to perfection was too ignorant of human nature to have been capable of giving marriage a solid and stable base.

But our task is even easier than I supposed! We have, thank God, no great opponent to combat and vanquish, and it would be all wrong to view the work we are accomplishing in the moral sphere as in any way analogous to that which the revolutionaries of the last three centuries undertook in politics and religion. If we are the first who dare to proclaim the powerlessness of Christian morality to assure the happiness of mankind, is that the same as saying we would plunge humanity into an *orgy* and we would precipitate a reign of *anarchy and moral terror*? How can one seriously believe that the social and religious order could have been toppled with impunity, without the moral law having first been seriously undermined in the hearts of men? Because today all of us have less audacity than our fathers, do you suppose that the examples they set us have been totally expunged from our customs? Because that glittering nobility has disappeared which, in its arrogant disdain for the rest of the nation, paraded its vices as well as its virtues in broad daylight, does one believe that after the gay and delightful life the *good* King led, after the weaknesses of the *great* King, after the incestuous obscenities of the Regent, after the endless orgies of that *well-loved* King who, without regard for courtly privilege, went chasing the daughters of the people into the very houses of debauchery, in order to prostitute his royal person with them in the face of a dumbfounded Europe—after so many and such resplendent models, I say, can one believe that anybody in the world is still presumptuous enough to think that he can precipitate a moral dissolution? I repeat, the critical work, the work of blind demolition, has already been done, and has advanced as far in the moral order as in the political and the religious. Our avowed position in regard to all three is the same and our role identical.

With regard to *Religion*, for a long time the upper classes condoned the brazen impudence of Voltairean philosophy, but in the end they perceived that religion was good at least for the masses. They understood that in a society where the laboring classes, deprived of education and social standing, work from day to day beset by hunger and poverty, it was very good, very useful, very convenient indeed that they should believe in a religion which teaches mankind to suffer with resignation. And seeing this, they combined forces to restore the Christian religion in France. Therefore we have come to say to the upper classes: "The Christian religion must disappear to make room for a greater and more beautiful religion. Christian religious sentiment, the sentiment of resignation to evil, has been exhausted. To defend it still is to lie before God and humanity. The time has come for all men to feel united, linked in a common destiny, a destiny of earthly progress, a destiny of joy, of riches, and of happiness."

In *Politics*, the bourgeoisie, having long marched in the vanguard of the liberal movement, having fervently proclaimed social equality as long as it saw itself unequal with those above it, now feels overwhelmed with terror for the consequences of the very principles it had professed. Indeed, it was the bourgeoisie that gave the first blows to the social order, the bourgeoisie that was the first to clamor for the abolition of privileges. But now, having disavowed the hereditary principle of monarchy, having ended the hereditary peerage, having in its improvident joy torn up one by one the old stones supporting the edifice, now the bourgeoisie in consternation uncovers the last stone, and on that final base it contemplates with trepidation the words: "*Privilege of birth, inheritance of property.*" Ah! The bourgeoisie now halts its work of destruction. It cries plaintively that it is no more a matter of ministry or dynasty, that henceforth the life of the whole society is at issue. And the bourgeoisie is for rallying to some program of political restoration, or quasi-restoration, already believing itself menaced—so much can fear muddle the wisest heads—by another barbarian invasion. That is why we have come to say to the bourgeoisie: "Your hesitation is justified and your fears excusable, inasmuch as you still do not know the foundation upon which the social structure of the future shall be erected. But do not expect to save society by extending to the masses political rights that are of little concern to them, or even by procuring work for them. If society is to be saved, the people must finally cease to be your hired-hands; they must become your associates. Since the memory of the barbarians has come to trouble your repose, you may as well recall that the Empire could not save itself by granting the barbarians *Roman citizenship* which, once they had planted their victorious standard atop the Capitol, they hardly coveted. Recall further that the Empire could no more be saved through procuring work for the barbarians by taking them in its hire. Rather, civilization escaped total shipwreck only by the appearance of a new truth, by the preaching of the Gospel which, becoming a pledge of alliance between victors and vanquished, permitted a new order to rise from the debris of the old."

In religion as in politics, if we condemn what the past has bequeathed us, it is to herald and initiate something better for the future. So too with *Morality*.

Attempts have also been made, and not without reason, to stem the progressive dissolution of manners effected by the previous century. Yes, in *Morality*, too, the bourgeoisie has attempted a quasi-restoration. In truth, men have not actually gone back to adopting the moral precepts of the Gospel for regulating their own conduct—to chastity, to constancy, to fidelity. But they continue to invoke them in passing judgment on women. As with the noblemen of the old regime, all the sons of our bourgeoisie glory in their sexual conquests and boast of their amorous escapades. But for the sake of honor and the maintenance of public morality, they find it very useful to brand with infamy the poor girl who was unable to resist seduction. Not one of them would want for anything to take a wife before having himself enjoyed a broad experience of life, but when they dream of settling down from their wanton liberty into marriage, they are at least as scrupulous about the past conduct of the bride-to-be as about the size of her dowry. Ah! That is why we preach the emancipation of women. That is why, in view of the sacred mission to which all women can henceforth dedicate their lives, I solemnly proclaim free, free to give their love and their bodies, all women who have been betrayed or sold, bought or taken. And do not tell me that I am still ignorant of the code of modesty and propriety, since women are not yet our equals. Do not tell me I am lacking in morals and that I have no right here to make a case against yours. For I tell you from the bottom of my heart: I have received from the head of the Saint-Simonian doctrine—and all of us have it—a morality with respect to women that is superior to the morality of all men who have preceded us. No one before us was so permeated with a belief in the social equality of men and women, and thus no one could so deeply appreciate and respect in women simple human dignity. Men animated by such sentiments will never behave as masters toward women. With all their might they will condemn, castigate with a righteous anathema, anything even vaguely resembling seduction or violence. Nor will they ever accept slavish love from any woman, love that cannot be shown and proudly revealed in the full light of day.

In truth, we cannot pretend to regulate definitively the relationships between the sexes as long as the aspirations of women are not united with ours. Christian law places women under the tutelage of men, and that is the real reason why Christ was able to propound his moral law without the concurrence of women. But we who summon woman to equality, we would be lying to God and to ourselves if we pretended to establish a comprehensive and definitive moral system before the position of women had been improved to the point where they could speak without fear and could accept the moral law freely and willingly.

Our entire aim at this moment, then, is to give women a sense of their strength and their dignity, so that they can make all their sufferings and desires known without shame. Jesus brought women a first degree of emancipation, feeling himself moved by a tender compassion for those who had sinned against the ancient law of oppression, and he challenged the world to throw the first stone. We will do something a little bit greater. As we have come to *achieve* the emancipation of women, we will give every woman the power to speak, that she may herself hurl a challenge not only at her persecutors but at those who judge her. Oh! When women have the strength to speak, especially the daughters of the lower classes, those whom poverty places in service to the bourgeois, to the landholder, the magistrate, then will we come to understand the morality of these men who are without pity for women, who give them tasks beyond their strength. And then also we shall know what a price has been exacted from humanity by this public morality, so jealously guarded by the laws, when prostitutes tell us how they were betrayed, when they name those who seduced and deserted them.

Yes, the prostitutes! And why should I fear to speak of them before you? Ah! Ladies, prostitutes are also women. Alas! I am in error: those who will never become cherished wives and honored mothers, they are not women! They are only girls. But after all, they are the girls of the people. Oh! Who took stock in some brochure published six months ago against the *so-called disciples of Saint-Simon*? Who hoped to crush us by delivering to the world in apocalyptic style a prophecy that we would plunge into the deepest mire in our search for the common flesh of the gutters? Is this flesh not the flesh of the people? Oh! The people! The poor people! It is sometimes said that they are exempt from direct taxation. In fact, they have no farmers, tenants, lands, or houses on which taxes could be levied. The masses exempt from direct taxation! And is it not on their sons you count for replacing yours on the field of battle? O last degree of shame and misery, is it not upon the daughters of the people, on the *prostitution* of its daughters, that you often depend to protect the honor of your own daughters and wives from a too-pressing danger? The masses exempt from direct taxation! But they contribute their blood, their flesh, their lives, where you contribute only your money.

Come then, let the woman step forth who has the power to speak! Whether she imprisoned her life in Christian chastity, or whether she rolled her freedom in the mud, for her emancipated voice, gentlemen, I will enforce silence.

CHARLES FOURIER
(1772–1837)

The System of
Passionate Attraction

During the French Revolution, Fourier lost the fortune he had inherited from his father, a rich Besançon cloth merchant, and was reduced to earning a livelihood as a minor clerk in a business house. In this post and in the dreary pensions where he lodged, he conceived a bitter hatred for the frauds, monotony, and vices of his society. He dreamed of a new system that would exalt the passions. "Civilization," a pejorative term in his writings, would be replaced by the "Combined Order." Its unit, the phalanstery, would be composed of all possible psychological types, assigned tasks attractive to their diverse temperaments. Though Fourier believed in communal organization, he did not advocate abolition of private property or of distinctions based upon wealth; but he conjured up images of sensuous pleasures abundantly produced for all classes of society. Fourier's doctrines inspired the establishment of numerous experimental communities, including Brook Farm near Boston, Massachusetts (1841). In his last years, the irascible Fourier spent much of his energy in bitter attacks on the disciples of Robert Owen and on the Saint-Simonians, on the ground that they sought the transformation of human nature, instead of its expansion and glorification.

Fourier, lithograph. (From *Fourier*, *Pages choisies*, Paris: Editions Sirey, 1932, by courtesy of the publisher.)

Development of the Senses*

It is scarcely credible that after 3000 years of studies, men have not yet thought of classifying the senses. At present even our five senses are cited pell-mell; no distinction of rank is admitted between them. Nevertheless no equality exists between the senses: Taste and Touch play a superior part. Taste is evidently the first in rank among the sensual passions; you can exist though deprived of the active use of each of the four other senses, but you cannot live without eating, without the active exercise of the sense of taste. It is consequently the first as to the uses of necessity; perhaps it is so too in regard to pleasures; for it is the first and the last enjoyment of man, it is almost the only resource of children and old men in matters of pleasure. Taste is therefore the chief of the five material passions, although others may procure pleasure superior to those of taste.

Long details are not required to prove that the sense of *Touch-rut*[1] holds the second rank among the five. It has, like Taste, the faculty of procuring active pleasures, whereas two other very valuable senses, Sight and Hearing, only yield passive pleasures, and are of a subaltern rank. Sight itself, although of inestimable value, is excluded from voluptuous sensations; it has very direct and positive sufferings; it has only pleasures indirect and subordinate to thought. It is an effect that must be explained to habituate the reader to recognize a gradation amongst the senses, as among the other passions, which are not equal to one another. Our eye finds a passive well-being in certain sights, like that of verdure, which has affinities with man's vision. Yet it does not procure him pleasure that is active, or backed by nervous sensation, as happens sometimes when you eat excellent viands. Our eye, as relates to pleasure, enjoys therefore negatively, like the foot which is incommoded on a rugged ground, and free from constraint on an even ground.

In the second case, there is only absence of uneasiness for the foot, but no real pleasure; in short, in every impression which affects vision, it is the thought alone which enjoys,—the eye is only passive in the agreeable sensations that sight procures us.

*From Charles Fourier, *The Passions of the Human Soul*, trans. the Reverend John Reynell Morell (London: Hippolyte Bailliere, 1851), I, pp. 29–36, 41–52.

1. I.e., erotic touch (ed. note).

The same thing happens with the ear, which gives pleasure without experiencing any itself. The most harmonious music cannot excite any tickling in the ear; harsh sounds draw the tympanum, true sounds delight us, but without any physical enjoyment for the tympanum. It is still thought which is the arbiter of this pleasure; and in proof of it, we see that in concerts and operas any distraction makes us lose the enjoyment of the sounds; an idea may absorb us suddenly, and cause us to forget the piece which the performers are singing; the ear becomes insensible to it the moment that it is not supported by thought and attention. Frequently at the opera a man whose head is full of something, is angry with himself for having lost, by distraction, a certain passage that he wished, and even expectantly longed to hear. He only perceives this inadvertency in the middle or at the end of the passage. It is a proof that the ear, by itself and without the aid of thought, is unfit to enjoy the sounds that are most flattering to it.

It is not thus with Smell. A tuberose that were placed under our nose, would make itself felt, and would stimulate, in spite of distractions, because Smell is a sense of active irritability, though very inferior in importance to Touch and Taste.

We may deduce from these considerations the classification of the senses into two actives, two passives, and one mixed; namely:—

Two active senses,—Taste and Touch.

One mixed sense,—Smell.

Two passive senses,—Sight and Hearing.

I class Smell as a mixed or neutral sense because it participates in both the others; it enjoys actively, but without notable influence. It is like a subordinate guide destined to serve Taste: it serves also vision and the other senses in certain researches. Finally, in all respects it occupies a middle rank between the active and the passive senses, of which it participates equally.

Here we have a distinction in the senses, indifferent at the first glance, and yet very essential. How comes it, that an age all infatuated about analytical methods, thus despises elementary analyses in the study of the passions. It is by similar blunders that the calculus of passional attraction has been entirely missed. Science ever fails, by trying on the first start to rise to the clouds, before keeping its eyes fixed upon the humble region of common sense, in which are found the primordial notions of every science.

The two active senses, Taste and Touch, exert a colossal influence in material concerns, as well by necessity as by refinement. The two passive senses, Hearing and Vision, and the neuter sense, Smell, have only a feeble empire in comparison with the two actives, which are really kings of the social world: for the furies of ambition, the inclination of the populace for insurrection, for atrocities, only spring from the want of satisfying these two senses. The people would by no means perpetrate crime to slake the three other senses,—to procure pictures, perfumes, or concerts. These three sorts of pleasures would not be able to move the mob, which on the contrary, is entirely devoted to the impulsions of the two active senses,—Taste and Touch. The mob requires to be fed and clothed. Everything is sacrificed, with the people, to these two senses, which are very powerful again in the opulent class, not in the light of necessity, but as a goad to gluttony, effeminacy, and lubricity.

These influences may appear vicious to us in the existing order of things; we must wait till we know what have been God's motives in giving so much influence to two sensual passions. We can only be initiated into this mystery by studying the mechanism of the passional series, in which the pleasures of the senses are accordant with propriety and virtue, and become the springs of general equilibrium.

The enormous and tyrannical influence of these two senses ought to make us suspect an affinity of functions between them. For instance, we see that *Touch-rut* is very intimately married to the affective passion called sentimental love, which is the cardinal hyperminor. We ought to conjecture that Taste may have a similar connection with the cardinal hypermajor, called honorism (ambition in the subversive vocabulary). There was an interesting enigma to be explained, touching this connection of good cheer and honor: the secret of it will be seen in the treatise on Gastrosophic Cabal. It is so extraordinary a subject that I cannot give an abridged notion of it. I shall only venture a word of prelude upon this great problem.

The human species being subject to the abuse of the five senses in the social limbo, or civilized, barbarian, patriarchal, and savage states of society, the philosophers have, for this reason, devoted the sensual pleasures to contempt. Yet it ought to appear very ridiculous to us, that two senses, which so imperiously direct human and animate beings, should be reputed contemptible. How great would be the inconsistency of God were He to vilify the two principal springs which He employs to direct beings!

The moralists, to support their attacks against gormandism, pretend that it assimilates us to the beasts, which are the slaves of their belly, according to Sallust,—*prona et ventri obedientia.* This subjection of animals and of men to the sense of Taste is a sign of the eminent rank which that sense ought to hold in the balanced or harmonic movement. It is already balanced in beasts, since they do not abuse it. When men shall have reached the first degree of wisdom, good cheer will have nothing ignoble in their eyes, and will be able to rise to the rank of the first sensual spring, the most honorable spring of the five, and the one which ought to occupy the highest rank, since hunger is the most stimulating of the five sensual appetites. It is the one respecting which the human body cannot deliberate. The more its present excesses may have dishonored the sense of taste, the more lustre will this sense acquire when it shall have attained to equilibrium, and shall become the germ of all the agricultural and chemical studies, etc. Gormandism once raised to this character, will be the magnetic needle of health and of wisdom; it will be a title to honor as a path of science; it will only lead man to work to satisfy the senses of others, at the same time that he is satisfying his own, and securing health to all. It will constitute the science named Gastrosophy, which will place good cheer in strict alliance with honor and the love of glory.

Gormandism being the most frequent of all our enjoyments, the first and the last pleasure of man, it ought to be the chief agent of wisdom in future harmony, where all concurs to satisfy the collective passions by the development of the individual passions. A clever gastrosopher, expert in the three functions of Gastroculture and Gastrohygiene, will be revered as an oracle of supreme wisdom;—and the most clever gastrosophers will be in their lifetime promoted to Saintship, of which they will have the rank and the title. A major saintship and a minor saintship are admitted in harmony. The first is founded on the combined development of the two passions abused amongst us, ambition and good cheer.—We only value in the present day the *gastronomer,* who understands good living; in harmony he will be required to be gastroculturist, or experienced in the laws of agriculture, and the culinary preparations that a dish may require. He will require, moreover, to be gastrohygienist, knowing the suitableness of a dish with the different temperaments, which will be classed into 810. The gastrosopher will therefore be a very eminent *savant,* in whom gormandism must be allied to all the springs of scientific honor. Thus will be formed the alliance of the two passions, Taste and Ambition; thus the sense of Taste, one of the two rectors, will be united to the hypermajor cardinal affective, called Honorism, Honor; just as the other rector sense, Touch-rut, is united to the hyperminor cardinal, called Sentimental Love; and the two rector senses will be in marriage with the two rector affectives, Honor and Love, which, in this order of things, will only be able to develop themselves in perfect balance, free from all excess, balance being an inalienable property of the passional series.

Without this alliance, God would therefore have condemned to disgrace the principal spring of the movement, which is the sense of Taste: it is surprizing that men have not rather presumed the brilliant use which is in store for this sense.

For the rest, the civilizee mechanism is so remote from all kind of passional equilibrium, that it would have foundered on all the problems of this description. It has made men able to believe foolishly in the infamy of the chief one amongst the springs that make us move. Hence it comes that gormandism is dishonored in opinion; it deserves this affront in an order of things in which it has produced a Vitellius; but when the passional balance shall exist, gormandism will hold a rank so eminent, that it will be encouraged even amongst those children who are sufficiently inclined to it. It will no longer be a vice in them, when it will become a stimulant to labor and study, without ever leading to any excess. Consequently all children will be excited in harmony to systematic gormandism (I do not mean gluttony), and a harmonian child will be as early as the age of nine years a cleverer gastronome than the Apicius's of our capitals, who, with all their pretended delicacy, could not on eating a dish of poultry, point out the errors committed in its education, nor rise to the rank of gastroculturists, still less to that of gastrohygienists.

We shall often be obliged to establish a distinction between the passions, which is that of major mode and minor mode. The major comprises the strong and free (shades), the minor comprises the slight shades that are compatible with suppleness of character. Hence it comes that the passions of women are commonly of minor shade, with some exceptions, and those of men of major shade, with some exceptions; but in either mode they are in all cases the same passions, always the twelve radicals.

Confining ourselves to the five sensual passions, which are the object of this chapter, the reader perceives that many inequalities and differences exist between them; amongst others that of simple, comprising vision and hearing; that of mixed or neuter, which is smell; and that of compound, which applies to Taste and Touch-rut.

A new omission of our analysts. They have committed the same inadvertence in the difference of the simple and compound as in that of the active and passive.

The two senses of Taste and Touch are compound. You find two very distinct pleasures in Taste, which can be enjoyed separately. These are eating and drinking. You find in the same manner in material love, or love considered as a sensual effect, two distinct pleasures which can be separated; they are copulation and kissing. Besides this material ambiguity, they are moreover subject to a spiritual ambiguity, invisible in the sense of Taste, but very evident in the sense of Touch, which unites two actions, two affections, the material or rutting, and the animic or celadony; an affective *penchant,* which is very distinct from the sensual *penchant.* This bi-composition is not found in the three other senses, which are of the simple order; it is one of the advantages which constitute the eminent superiority of Taste and Touch-rut. On these two senses reposes a great mystery of social equilibrium; I mean the balance of the directing passions.

I designate by the name of rector passions a quadrille of two sensitives and two affectives, married in the following order:—

Minor—Gormandism and Honor.

Major—Lubricity and Celadony.

Bless me! they will say, what connection is there between Gormandism and Honor? I have given farther back the outline of an answer on this subject. It is necessary, before solving the problem, to wait till I have depicted *social honor* in the mechanism of the series, and have dissipated the prejudices of the civilizees, of whom some place honor in precedence of ceremony, the contempt of labor, the exercise of tilting; others no less ridiculous, notwithstanding their title of sages, make honor to consist in stifling the passions, and robbing oneself of the most valuable possessions.

We shall have to dissipate these prejudices, in order to make known true honor, in its harmonic or social acceptation, according to which no conduct is honorable but that which serves at once the collective and the individual interest. Amongst us the man is thought praiseworthy who sacrifices his personal interest to the good of the mass; he acts honorably, no doubt; he develops honor in a diverging or negative sense; the positive or converging development must favor both the collective and the individual passions. It is only under this condition that honor becomes harmonic. For the rest, the above specified condition of honor adapted to the collective and individual necessities, will thin out of the ranks of men of honor that crowd of *civilizees* who plume themselves upon their idleness, and style themselves very proper people, *gens comme il faut,* because they do nothing, and produce nothing; so that if all the world were as it should be, *comme il faut,* conformably to *civilizee* honor, the human race would die of hunger the following year. Harmony will not suffer these absurdities of *comme-il-faut* idleness; it will only reckon that honorable which will concur in producing, in enriching the mass; true it is that its industrial functions will be sufficiently attractive to catch even the class called proper people, *comme il faut,* and to make it acknowledge that in civilization it was very improper, *comme il ne faut pas.*

We are at present engaged only about corporeal or sensual studies. Before inquiring about the perfection to which the senses may attain, and about the immensity of the means of nature on this head, we must previously become convinced of their material and artificial imperfection. This is what I am about to treat of.

If luxury is internal by means of the physical faculties, and external by means of riches, the same is the case with poverty. It is internal and external with each of the five senses.

1st. Internal poverties, or deficiency of faculties.

Internal poverty is composed of the faculties in which our senses are wanting, and which they will acquire in the future. Thus the want of co-nocturnal vision, like that of the lion or cat, is an internal poverty of the fourth degree to us. The absence of the telescope was, for the Romans, an internal poverty of a mixed degree, between the sixth and seventh.

This said possession of the telescope is an internal luxury for us, since it gives a great extension of faculties to one of our senses. But this luxury is still only simple internal, inasmuch as the glasses of our telescopes are of a subversive material, which has not the compound properties that will accrue to glasses manufactured of substances that will be yielded by the harmonic creations.

Our senses, besides the want of faculties which constitute internal negative poverty, are subject to a host of maladies which cause internal positive poverty. To confine our remarks to sight, how many infirmities may attack it from the natural ones, such as myopia, down to those that are accidental, like cataract. These maladies, considering their present frequency, become poverty relatively to the future order of things, which will prevent all these disasters, or will reduce them to the minimum. Then Egypt and Lapland, at present so dangerous from ophthalmia and blindness, will be regions as favorable to the health of the eye as can be now the healthiest provinces; and immediately on passing into harmony, the internal positive or internal negative poverties will cease at once.

The greater number of the positive internal poverties are accidental, such as the hydrophobic, psoric, syphilitic, pestilential poisons; and so many besides, which a good administration might extirpate or prevent in every part of the globe, even before the foundation of harmony. All these poisons no longer exist even in the sixth society, called guaranteeism. When we consider that civilization, far from having extirpated them, has recently hatched three new plagues, the yellow fever, the typhus, and the new cholera-morbus of Bengal, which is a contagious disease, we may judge of the excess of internal poverty that afflicts the limbic societies, and of the impudence of the jugglers who trumpet perfectibility.

Harmony is a social system, so admirably suited to the sanitary wants, that scarce a hundredth part of our civilizee infirmities will be seen in it. The harmonians, one out of twelve of whom will reach the age of 144 years, will be, in the course of this long career, so little subject to diseases, that many phalanxes of about 1500 persons of all ages will be heard to boast at times of not having a single invalid, except in the two ages of transition, babes and patriarchs, who cannot escape some infirmities. I also except the accidental cripples, a fall and the fracture of a limb not being a vice of diet or of insalubrity. But, putting these three sorts of inevitable accidents out of sight, you will often see, in the whole body of the fourteen amphichoirs, number 2 to 15, the entire phalanx in full health; and it is then that the doctors will gain most, for each phalansterian pays them in proportion to the general health.

It proceeds in the same way as those who, in civilization, subscribe to a doctor, say £25 per annum. It is for the interest of a doctor that such a subscriber should enjoy a long life and sound health. The physician has thus so much more profit and so much less trouble. Each phalanstery enters into treaty in the same way with the groups of physicians and surgeons. But Civilization, which styles itself perfectibilized, acts in the contrary fashion, since it makes all the doctors and lawyers interested in there being many law-suits and sick: hence we ought not to be surprized that they wish for an abundance of patients and plantiffs; or that, on the other hand, those of harmony should everywhere agree in preventing maladies and disputes.

The state of general health will not, however, amount to internal luxury; it will be nothing more than the absence of internal poverty, which comprises diseases avoidable by a wise regimen. As to internal luxury, it will be requisite in order to possess it, that each sense should enjoy all its potential faculties in a scale analogous to those of vision.

These advantages can only be accorded to the generations of several [quarters] of harmony. The co-nocturnal vision will not be acquired with the first generation. It will take a number of [successive] quarters to give by degrees to the human race the forces necessary to develop in it these useful properties, and it will only be at the ninth [quarter] that men will begin to possess them in complete gamut. Some of them will be deferred to the sixteenth.

As to the state of general healthiness, of which I spoke above, it will only begin to be complete for the first generation of harmony. The present one, which is the product of civilizee and barbarian education, has not been able to acquire, in the existing social order, half the strength that the children born and bred in harmony will enjoy. This is a parallel which can be made as early as the fourth year, when the effects of harmonian education will already be apparent; it will make itself slightly felt in the civilizee children of a tender age, who will already participate in the benefit of the natural institution, the system of which will be shewn farther on. As to the adults, who will pass from the existing order to harmony, they will gain by it, in matters relating to health, the absence of accidental diseases, such as the plague, etc., which will be extirpated by a general quarantine; next the rapid diminution of the essential diseases, fever, gout, rheumatism, etc., which will be almost entirely prevented by the property of passional and sensual equilibrium inherent in harmony.

2ndly. External poverties or want of riches.

Independently of the numerous chances of internal poverty that I have just passed in review, we have a vast series of *external poverties* in our present privations. It is seasonable to observe some of their details in each sense, in order to confound the pretensions of our chanters of perfectibility.

External poverty comprises all the avoidable privations and inconveniences, such as want of carriages, or clumsy carriages. These privations are very immense, even in the case of kings. Let us judge of them by an examination of some sensual injuries.

First, HEARING. A king, like any other man, is exposed to hear rude brogues that he doth not understand, disagreeable sounds around his palace, cries in the streets of his capital, voices out of tune, which he will find at every step in France; this nation, that has neither ear nor measure, being the most savagely determined to hum tunes.

If this king wants to pass through the country, to enjoy the charm of simple nature, he will hear the croaking of some thousands of frogs and toads, which neither spare the ears of kings nor of shepherds. The king will suffer even more than the shepherd by all these shocking noises of the country and of the town. And what will it be, in case he takes a journey in countries whose language he does not understand? He will be like every one else, in a state of blockade *relatively to hearing*, since he will not be able to make use of the most precious faculty of hearing. It is in vain that he will pay interpreters; to be obliged to have recourse to interpreters is to lose all the pleasures of conversation.

The difference of tongues, the shame of civilized societies, is the most distressing of the disasters experienced by the sense of hearing. Habit makes us almost indifferent about this hindrance, very real though little observed.

A host of *lesions* of hearing are met with. I have observed that often a workman hammering, or a learner of the clarinet, suffices to desolate a whole district, particularly people who like to sleep in the morning. I refer the reader for details of these nuisances to an English author, who has filled three volumes with a collection of these civilizee bores and sensual kill-joys, from the cackling of geese down to that of discordant singers, far more detestable.

Our philosophers have inoculated us with a sort of fatalism respecting these sensual *lesions*, from which we suffer every instant. They have fashioned us to consider these miseries as necessary, and to habituate ourselves to them as apathetically as Turks do to the plague. It is necessary to be convinced of their extent to appreciate the benefit of harmony, which is about to deliver us from them. Every man could, like the English author, fill volumes with these material misfortunes, a few of which only I shall point out in each sense, by way of definition of the five external poverties.

Secondly, SIGHT. It will be maintained again that the poverties on this head are relative, imaginary. Yet it is quite certain that a man transported from the verdant banks of the Saône to the arid regions of Provence, where you see nothing but naked rocks, print-steps of the ravages of the elements;— that such a man, I say, has his sight continually offended, unless he is a vandal, incapable of distinguishing between a graceful and a hideous landscape. It is a real pain for every man of good sense; he suffers positively by the sight of a frightful landscape, and relatively by the memory of the beautiful scenes, and the cultivated and woody mountains that he enjoyed in other places. The same thing happens to him who, coming from the clean and well-built villages of Flanders and Brisgau, perceives the disgusting structures of the French peasants, the villages of Picardy, of Bresse, of Champagne, their miserable mud huts, their dirty wooden barracks, heaped together as if space were wanting in the fields. When he visits the inside of these hovels, he will find them as dirty and miserable within as they are ugly without; he will quickly change the name of *belle France* into that of *sale*, dirty France, a name truly deserved by the far greater number of its provinces; for you scarcely ever find there cleanliness and elegance in the buildings, except in those like Flanders, which have formerly belonged to another power.

Amongst all these nuisances that affect vision, none is more frequent than the sight of the people and of the peasantry, especially in the lands of dirt, such as Spain and France. The sight of rags saddens us as effectually as that of the fogs of Holland, on arriving from the fine climate of Tuscany. Now in what country can you avoid seeing a populace in rags?

Again, the sight of ill-cultivated lands, of puny animals and plants, becomes a *lesion* relatively to sight for a man who reflects on the improvements of which agriculture is susceptible. This visual disgrace will become more sensible when men shall have pictures of harmony; when they shall know that instead of mud huts, in which two or three hundred Picard families are piled up, we ought to see a vast and regular edifice, which even without ornament would be beautiful by the general effect and unity of the component parts, by the choice of situation, the judicious distribution of the stables, workshops, water-conduits, reservoirs, etc. Thus, although the ugliness and poverty of the civilizee towns and countries even now wound our eyes in all directions, the evil will become much more intolerable when men shall know the beautiful order that would reign in harmony, and even in the sixth period (guaranteeism), still little removed from civilization.

Thirdly, SMELL. Fetid odors and stinks are so general a nuisance in civilization, especially in the tenements of the poor, that some nations, like the Germans, have invented a plan of remedying it by one absorbent stink, which is tobacco smoke, grown rancid by the heat of stoves, and concealing the bad smells which are fused into a single one. This is replacing numerous infections by another, which at all events is not unhealthy.

France is more intrepid on this head, and the workmen of its great factories, Lyons, Rouen, pass their lives with great apathy in stinking garrets, where they are huddled together by scores, and where prevail perpetually putrid smells, which spread abroad, infect the stairs, the court and the narrow alleys. Many of these streets preserve a mouldy and close smell, whilst the philosophers cry out about the perfectibility of the sensations of perceptions. They have never passed through these sickening streets in which the French populace dwell; and where the din of the trades, of the hammers, quarrels and beggars, the sight of the hanging rags, of the dirty dwellings and unpalatable labors of the poor, the stifling smell of the drains in which they swarm, so painfully affect the sight, hearing and smell, and so well belie the boasts of the perfection of the sensations of perception that our ideologists find in their *belle France!*

Would they not deserve—these babblers of perfectibility—that they should be condemned to dwell in the little country towns, in their dirty streets answering the purpose of privies, where reigns, ever since the creation of the world, an antique crust of foecal matter, kept up every day by the "vases of ordure," which these provincial bumpkins insolently throw upon the heads of passengers with the cry, "*Passarés n'a degun.*"[2] What would the ideologists

---

2. A stranger knows not what the word '*passarés*' means. He thinks that they are calling an individual bearing that name. Moreover, the people of Provence are not so nice about it, and throw without caring on whom the article may alight. All is justified by that one word '*passarés.*' They have many other perfidies on this score,—such as furnishing their window-sills

and perfectibilizers of Paris think, if they saw, like dom Japhet, their face and clothes suddenly covered with this commodity? Thus bathed and perfumed, they would understand, by the sensations of perception, that if they have raised their belle France to perfectibility, it is not at least in what relates to smell, as ill-used as sight and hearing in *la belle* France!

Instead of this system of perpetual infection, we shall have to describe an order of general perfume. Independently of the salubrity of the air and of that of the buildings, the luxury of smell will be pushed so far as to give to the high roads the accidental perfume of plants, and to give to the street-gallery (warmed and ventilated communication on the first story) the perfume of the unitary aromas, which have, like the orange blossom, the double property of salubrity and olfactory charm.

Well! but what will the districts do, bordering on the Pontine marshes, the marshes of Egypt, Polesia, Guyana, Louisiana, and others? Let us wait till we hear how the harmonians work, and what is the power of the work carried on by passional series and attractive armies. When the reader shall have studied this theory, it will be seen that the impossibilities which arrest feeble civilization, such as the drying up of the Pontine marshes, will be only child's play for the industrial armies of harmony.

Fourth, Taste. We are so new in all relating to the sense of taste and to the perfection of good living, that my criticism would not be understood if I confined myself to the surface of the debate. I defer it to the section that treats of gastrosophy, a science of which some sybarites have given a caricature in their gastronomical pretensions. Let us remark only that civilization deteriorates incessantly in good living, owing to the progress of the spirit of trade, which alters the nature of all eatables, applies all the discoveries of modern chemistry to falsify and poison aliments, to multiply cheats, such as beet-root sugar, and poisons like chicory coffee, wine of Kinarodon, and mercantile tricks of all kinds.

The perfectibilizers will proceed to reply that the class of respectable people lives very well, and does not eat beet-root sugar. That is false; the rich people, even while paying well, are gulled at every step. I have not frequented the great, yet I have happened to be sometimes at their board, and I have perceived that they are still more deceived than the middle class.

---

with their unclean vases; so that an ideologist, lodging on the second floor, and placing himself, in the morning at the window to enjoy the charms of sweet nature, and reflect on the perfectibility of the sensations, would perceive the steam mounting to his nose; then, looking about him to the window below and crying out, "Where the deuce does this stink come from?" he will have the perfections of sensations of perfectibility of beautiful Provence.

For a shop-keeper who wishes to give a dinner, looks twice at all that he buys, and sees with his own eyes; a prince is obliged to delegate his business to a house steward, who wishes to gain and divide with the tradesmen; hence it comes that the great have commonly very indifferent things at their table, especially in the article of wines, which they give out as good on the word of the tradesman, or the steward, and no guest will go and tell the Amphitryo that his wine is not good. However, even were it true that respectable people live very well, have on their table nothing but dishes of excellent quality, that would at most only prove that civilizee philosophy only labors for respectable people, who are infinitely few in number, and that it simply ends in multiplying the relative privations of the multitude. Men ought to value so much the more a new science that teaches how to augment the pleasures of the rich man, at the same time that it increases those of the poor; this is what the reader will learn in the treatise on the passional series, and on their kitchen, distributed like all their labors by graduated and contrasted shades even for the poor.

Fifth, Y Simple Touch. To give a measurement of our imperfection in this sense, I refer to the section where I shall treat of the street-gallery, by means of which you can, in harmony, attend to all your occupations, pass through all the workshops, the stables, the public saloons, the assemblies of pleasure, without being affected either by heat or cold, or any inclemency. The reader will judge, by this single arrangement of Harmony, how far the great are from procuring the pleasures of touch, even those of which the enjoyment is possible to the civilizees, and does not depend on an organic regeneration of which I shall speak in the following chapters,—Potential Luxury.

If we consider that, in the regions which style themselves perfectibilized, like France, the people have not the means of warming and clothing themselves, we may say that they are in the sense of Touch in an equal degree as in the sense of Taste, reduced to live on nettles and other filth in years of distress.

Let us not lose sight of the fact that the position applies to the rich as well as to the poor. I shall prove that the opulent class doth not reach, in any of the senses, a fourth part of the pleasures that Harmony must procure for it. The single annoyance of travelling would suffice to prove this assertion. A king, notwithstanding the most costly preparations, cannot, on a journey into the *interior of his kingdom*, find a fourth part of the pleasure that a private individual will find over the whole earth in Harmony. What shall we say, then, when the king leaves his states to travel in a barbarous country; and what must happen with a man of the middle classes who travels in a semi-

barbarous country like Spain, which has not even inns, and in those perfectibilized countries like France, where vermin swarm by myriads in the inn-beds
of Provence and Languedoc?

Fifth, Λ is TOUCH-RUT, or *ambiguous touch*. I shall speak elsewhere of this
subdivision of the fifth sense. Let us conclude about the imperfection of
external luxury in civilization.

You must call to mind here the distinction that I have made in the
development of the senses,—the difference of harmonic and of subversive
development.

I have named *harmonic development* the gradation of pleasures that our
senses will obtain when a material regeneration of the race shall have raised
the senses to the accords of all internal degrees, of which I shall give an idea
in the following chapters.

I call *brute* or *mean development,* the dose of pleasure which the present state
of the senses can admit.

I call *subversive development* the scale of privations, which, in the present
system, extend more or less to the various classes, and reduce the lot of the
multitude so far beneath that of kings and sybarites, who yet only attain to
the brute or mean development.

You may judge by this analysis or rather this view of external luxury, of
the sad condition of the civilizees, of whom the immense majority is reduced
to run through the scale of privations, and of whom a very small number,
which is named the class of sybarites, only arrives at the mean degree in
external luxury, and at the brute degree, in internal luxury, which can only be
enjoyed after the sensual regeneration of which I shall treat in the following
chapters.

I have proved that civilization only develops the five luxuries for the purpose of creating five scales of poverty, each terminated by a shadow of
happiness that is only reserved for the rich, and which serves to drive to
despair the immense mass of the unhappy, whose relative privations increase
in proportion to the progress of luxury. It would be impossible for the
council of devils to organize the sensual persecution of the human race more
scientifically than it is in this perfectibilized civilization, in which the unhappy
have not even the double stay of fatalism and brutality that supports the
barbarians, and in which refined executioners communicate enlightenment
and the reasoning power to the people without giving it the means of
enrichment. So that the people only becomes enlightened to be more apt to
judge of the extent of its miseries,—only that it may see positive suffering
increased by relative suffering.

*Arts, Sciences, and Spectacles in the Combined Order**

To appreciate the heights of splendor attained by the Arts and Sciences in the Combined Order, you must first understand what enormous rewards have been decreed for artists and scientists.

Every Phalanstery draws up annually by majority vote a list of the inventions or compositions which have appeared in the preceding twelve months and which have come to its notice. Each of these items is judged by the competent Series—a tragedy, by the Series on literature and poetry, and so with all the new creations.

If the work is considered worthy of remuneration, they decide the sum to be awarded the author; for example, 20 sous to Racine for his tragedy *Phèdre*.

After setting up the table of awards, each Phalanstery sends it to an office which polls the votes of the canton and makes up a provincial list. This is passed on to a regional office which operates in the same way with the provincial lists. And in this fashion, the count reaches the Ministry in Constantinople by echelons. There the final count is taken, and announcement is made of the authors who have been acclaimed by vote of the majority of Phalansteries in the world. The author is awarded the average of the sums voted by that majority. If a million Phalansteries voted 10 sous, a million 20 sous, and a million 30 sous, the award would be 20 sous per Phalanstery.

Let us suppose that the poll gave one Tours pound to Racine for the tragedy *Phèdre*; and three pounds to Franklin for the invention of the lightning-rod. The Ministry would then send drafts on the Congress of his region to each of the two winners: to Racine, the sum of three million pounds, to Franklin, nine million pounds. Each of the three million Phalansteries of the globe is assessed for its portion of the total sum.

In addition, Franklin and Racine receive the triumphal decoration, are declared citizens of the world, and everywhere they go enjoy in all the Phalansteries the same prerogatives as Magnates of the canton.

These awards, which are an insignificant charge on the individual Phalanstery, amount to vast sums for the authors, the more so since they can be won repeatedly. It can happen that Racine and Franklin will win a like sum the following year, covering themselves with glory in some other effort that obtains the majority vote of the world.

*From Charles Fourier, *Théorie des Quatre Mouvements et des Destinées Générales* (1808); translated by the editors from the 2nd edition (Paris: Bureaux de la Phalange, 1841), pp. 226–36.

The smallest works, provided they are accorded some distinction by public opinion, are still worth enormous sums to the authors; for if the world decrees that Haydn should have 1 sou for such and such a symphony, Lebrun, 2 sous for such and such an ode, Haydn will get 150,000 pounds, and Lebrun 300,000 pounds for works on which they will have spent perhaps only one month. They could earn that figure several times in a single year.

As for works such as statues, which cannot be passed around for global judgment, there exist other means of having the whole world reward their creators. Thus in the Combined Order he who possesses superior talent in any field is assured an immense fortune, and the artist or scientist has no need of any patronage or solicitation; on the contrary, any patronage will serve only to humiliate the patron and his protégé.

For instance, let me suppose that Pradon, through soliciting votes, succeeds in lining up for his *Phèdre* some twenty neighboring cantons where he has friends through whom he managed to get the piece played; I will go further and say that these cantons were weak enough to award Pradon a prize. What good will it do him to have the vote of twenty Phalansteries out of three million? And how disgraced these twenty Phalansteries will be when the census of votes is published by the Ministry in Constantinople. Anyone who scrutinizes the list will see that an unknown *Phèdre*, composed by a Mr. Pradon, found rooters in twenty cantons of the globe which are such and such, all cronies and neighbors of the aforesaid Pradon. You can imagine how, at such an announcement, both the author and the twenty cantons, his would-be protectors, are covered with shame before the whole world. But what would really happen, in spite of all Pradon's intrigues? The twenty cantons he would have solicited would not want to expose themselves to such an insult, nor associate their vote with a piece so mediocre; and far from being able to hope for fifteen hundred thousand or half the votes of the world, the piece is not even countenanced twenty leagues away, in cantons where Pradon no longer has special friends.

Thus in the Combined Order all intrigue or patronage serves only to confound a bad author without benefiting him, while a man of talent quickly reaches the apex of glory and fortune without the assistance of intrigue or patronage. There is only one means of success, and that is to captivate the majority of the world's Phalansteries. The exceptions will be very rare indeed. If some lofty personage, such as a relative of the Emperor of Unity, takes it into his head to write a bad play, or some bad verse, the status of the author would make the piece famous, and it could be that the world would be indulgent enough to give it an award; but personages worthy of such partiality in the eyes of the whole world will be exceedingly few in number, and the little favoritism that might be shown to them will not put any obstacle in the path of the men of real talent, who today can hardly ever succeed, because they have not the means of developing their skills, nor sufficient recompense, nor the intriguer's art, without which one gets nowhere in Civilization.

After this digression on rewards in the Combined Order, let us see how they will exert their influence on spectacles, for instance. I have said that there will be ways for the whole world to compensate local scientists and artists even when their talents cannot be universally judged. A famous surgeon or singer cannot place his skills before all eyes, unlike a poet or engraver whose work is distributed far and wide; but they too will be recompensed, with sums which will quickly mount to several millions for those possessing exceptional merit. Whence it follows that every poor man will have no greater concern than the development of whatever budding talent his offspring might have; the minute it becomes evident that the child has some chance of distinguishing himself in the arts or sciences, the father will be drunk with joy. He will be congratulated on all sides, and people will keep telling him: "Your child will be a famous man of letters, a famous actor; he will win the triumphal decoration, he will earn *millions*"; and it is well known how such predictions tickle the ears of poor parents, nay even rich ones.

Who then will have the most enthusiasm for education? The poor and their children. Now, as the conduct of the theatre involves every kind of scientific and artistic discipline—even mechanics, which has great utility on the stage—poor people will be especially eager to see their children trained and educated in the Phalanstery theatre, under the aegis of the rich, who in all countries have a penchant for patronizing the theatre. Thus all children from their earliest years will become accustomed to playing on the dramatic or lyric stage, to taking part in programs of elocution, singing, dancing, music; rich or poor, all of them will appear there, because the Phalanstery in effect becomes an amateur theatrical company performing for itself and its neighbors. And so a canton with a population of 1000 will have at least 800 actors or musicians to put on shows for holidays, since every child will have been trained in the theatre and will have spontaneously participated in some one of its operations. In the Combined Order, a youngster of four would not dare to seek admission to the Neophytes' chorus and to the parade if he were not already proficient in dance steps and stage business.

The chapter entitled *Study of Passionate Attraction* made it clear that nature's chance distribution in a group of 800 people would yield all the temperaments required for carrying out the functions of society surpassingly well. Consequently, a canton of about 1000 persons necessarily finds in its midst great actors of all types, if from childhood the natural propensities of each person have been developed and cultivated. This is what happens in the Combined Order. The child is emancipated from the tyranny of institutions and prejudices; he moves naturally toward those occupations for which nature has destined him, and he advances solely through competition. The only stratagem used to develop first-rate actors is to take them en masse to neighboring cantons to witness the performances given by their rivals and to make them enter the lists against them.

There is no reason to worry: "Who pays the bill for an opera house?" Only one need be constructed, and three millions are slowly but surely raised for it. If the cantons are in constant competition, they will not rest until they have equaled their neighbors; and to erect an amusement hall, have not all of them Series of masons, carpenters, mechanics, painters, etc.; besides all sorts of products to pay for the purchase of building materials?

If each Phalanstery has at least seven to eight hundred actors, musicians, and dancers out of a population of about 1000, it can by itself put on all the spectacles which are enjoyed in an enormous capital like Paris or London. The result is that in the humblest canton of the Alps or Pyrenees there will be opera like that of Paris; I could even say better, for in the pursuit of the arts and the refinement of taste, education in the state of Civilization cannot produce the wonders that natural education will effect.

If the actors of neighboring cantons join forces on holidays, what brilliant spectacles will be put on by the stars assembled from several Phalansteries! On such occasions one will enjoy a gathering of talent such as a dozen capitals like Paris might provide! Now, since the poorest man can attend these performances, in this respect he will have pleasures far superior to that of civilized Potentates.

Fortune shines on them indeed, if one can imagine a procession of itinerant actors, as one often sees in the Combined Order, forming a great caravan of knights errant, who seek adventure, playing whatever role suits their fancy. Today will witness the arrival of the *Rose Troops* from Persia, whose skills are *dramatic and lyric*; several days later there will be a visit from the *Lilac Troops* of Japan, whose speciality is *poetic and literary*; and throughout the year the succession of these caravans will bring festivities and delights to every lover of the arts or sciences. Troops of every sort will come through; they will receive into their ranks only those persons, of both sexes, who will be a credit to the troop.

I see in my mind's eye the Rose Troops from Persia reaching the suburbs of Paris; they are composed of three hundred male and female knights errant, all selected from Persians of the greatest distinction in the dramatic and lyric arts. The Troops announce a stop at the St. Cloud Phalanstery; they arrive with great pomp, displaying countless flags acquired on their expeditions and inscribed with the *exploits of the Rose Troops of Persia.*

On arrival at St. Cloud, they are received by the *permanent knightly company,* consisting of wealthy patrons of theatre and music who form a corporation to support and entertain their favorite Troops.

Since the Rose Troops are picked from the élite of Persia, every man or woman selected was a *Molé* or a *Contat* in his own Phalanstery. All of them are the top singers, dancers, and musicians of Persia, and they give performances of surpassing excellence. In turn, the region assembles for them an array of its foremost talents.

Meanwhile the *Hydrangea Troops of Mexico* appear on the scene, come to try their skill with the *Rose Troops of Persia,* and the two match their talents on the stage of Saint-Cloud Phalanstery, Neuilly, Marly, and so on. If the Rose Troops are decidedly better, the district will award them a flag to be displayed with their other trophies. On it will be the legend: "Defeat of the Hydrangea Troops of Mexico at St. Cloud Phalanstery."

In the course of their travels, Troops of the same kind will encounter one another coming and going, and engage in trials of strength that will delight the countryside where these contests take place. The members of the Troops will not make their way in herds like our regiments, but will disperse. If the Rose Troops have announced as their next stop the Phalanstery of the Loiret near Orleans, they will already have found at St. Cloud deputies of the Phalansteries along the Orleans road; these delegations are composed of the most winsome men and women, whose mission it is to beguile and entice the Rose knights and ladies. They will be lured into cantons remote from the main road.

Each Phalanstery will contend for the honor of being their host for a day, and each knight, male or female, will find in the Phalanstery which has invited him the same enthusiastic reception accorded to the whole Troop at St. Cloud. The headquarters staff will independently take the main road and on the appointed day the whole group will reassemble at Orleans to make a solemn entry into the Phalanstery of the Loiret, there to exhibit its prowess once again. Thus will the road companies travel as caravans of knights errant, everywhere leading the gay life, and living off the whole world without themselves incurring the least expense, since they will be supported by the permanent knightly companies in whatever places they visit.

It is now apparent that as far as spectacles are concerned, the poorest man will enjoy gratis a hundred times as many as the richest Sovereigns today; for he will often see a contest of thousands of famous actors, singers, dancers, and musicians; today one of them would be enough to make the court and the whole city go into raptures, while they are inaccessible to any of the rural districts, and even cities of a hundred thousand inhabitants cannot support a proper theatre. How shabby, how pitifully feeble are the pleasures of Civilization, compared to those which the most inconsiderable canton in the world will enjoy in the Combined Order!

Epilogue on Social Chaos[*]

Inventors of dubious social sciences, why do you sham at working for the good of the Human Race? Do you think that six hundred million Barbarians and Savages are outside the human race? And yet they suffer. Eh! What have you done for them? Nothing. Your systems can be applied only to Civilization, where they show empiricism as soon as they are put to the test. But since you would possess the art of making us happy, do you think you will be carrying out God's plan when you try to limit that happiness to the Civilized peoples, who occupy only the tiniest part of the Globe? For God the whole human Race is only one family, and all its members have a right to His beneficence; it is His will that the entire race of men be happy, or that happiness should be enjoyed by none.

To further the design of God, you ought to be in quest of a Social Order which can be instituted in the entire World, and not just among a few nations. The vastly greater numbers of Barbarians and Savages should serve notice on you that you can civilize them only by Attraction and not by Constraint. Eh! Did you think to win them over by parading before them those institutions of yours that are sustained with the gibbet and the bayonet? Institutions loathed even by your own people, who in every country would rise up forthwith if they were not restrained by the dread of punishment!

[*]From Charles Fourier, *Théorie des Quatre Mouvements et des Destinées Générales* (1808); translated by the editors from the 2nd edition (Paris: Bureaux de la Phalange, 1841), pp. 409–21.

Far from succeeding in civilizing and uniting the Human Race, your theories will be treated with profound contempt by the Barbarians, and your institutions will provoke the irony of the Savages; their worst imprecation against an enemy is to wish him our fate and to say to him: "May you be reduced to tilling the soil!" Words that should be regarded as a curse uttered by Nature herself. Yes, civilized Industry has been repudiated by Nature, since it is abhorrent to free peoples who would embrace it in a moment if it were in harmony with the passions of Man.

Thus God has not allowed such industry to make progress nor has He permitted an extension to the entire Globe of a culture so thankless to those who bear its burden. He has cooped it up in several places, in China, India, and Europe, where the needy swarm like ants, reserves for establishing the combined Order, which in its initial stages will thereby have available masses of farmers; these poor wretches will be scoured from the congested areas where they now live, and the Emperor of Unity will resettle them in appropriate places to further the orderly development of the Globe.

But you would strive in vain to expand civilized Industry and spread over the whole world an incoherent system of work; God (for various reasons which I cannot explain here) would never have endured the extension to all arable land of an Order contrary to His designs, and He had taken measures to repress it in every instance, either through civil wars or through Barbarian invasions.

If Industry has made some progress in Europe, has it not lost in Asia vast regions? If Civilization founded in America some puny colonies, already threatened with decline by the revolt of the Negroes, has it not lost at the gateways of Europe the most extensive empires—Egypt, Greece, Asia Minor, Carthage, Chaldea, and part of the Near East? Industry has been smothered in great and glorious regions, like Bactria, where it had made a beginning; the empire of Samarkand, once celebrated throughout the East, and the whole territory stretching from the Oxus to the outfall of the Indus have suffered political retrogression, and their inhabitants have once again formed themselves into marauding bands. The vast empire of Hindustan is moving swiftly to its ruin under English tyranny; it is creating an aversion to civilized existence and encouraging assimilation with the Mahrattas, whose hordes are already a powerful Tartar nucleus in the center of Mongolia. With time they can take up a position in the chain of the Gates and rally to their standard the peoples of Malabar and Coromandel, weaning them away from Industry with their forays.

These Hordes encroach daily on the civilized states of Asia, and overflow more and more their natural barrier, the chain of the Imaüs, which extends from Bukarie to China. At our very portals, the Hordes are pressing on every point in Turkey; another fifty years of persecution, of Ottoman anarchy, will see this whole fine Empire reduced to nomadic or Tartar existence, which will spread at an alarming rate to every place under Turkish rule. Other once-flourishing Empires like Pegu and Siam have sunk back into utter debility and degradation, and their cultures, like those of Turkey, seem to have hardly more than a century to last; if the present disorder of the Globe should be prolonged, Asia, vast Asia, on all sides will tend to abandon Industry. Even China, that niggardly and absurd colossus, China is in a state of perceptible decline; the recent accounts of Van-Braam have opened our eyes wide on its pretensions to splendor. The tone of society has been on the downgrade since the intermingling with the Tartars; barbarian hordes occupy in China immense territories, and, in that Empire so much extolled for its industry, one finds four leagues from Peking fine lands practically unknown and wasted, while in the Southern provinces priests vainly exhort the people to till the soil; they let vast regions lie fallow, and more and more run off to join the Horde. The Horde is a volcano always ready to engulf Civilization; it is a chronic distemper, which, hardly suppressed, erupts again, which reappears as soon as one leaves off treating it for a moment. In short, that universal tendency of workers to relapse into barbarism leads back all political thinking to one problem: *How to find a new Social Order which would guarantee to the humblest worker enough well being so that he would have a constant and passionate devotion to his work instead of yearning for the indolence and brigandage to which he aspires today.*

As long as you have not resolved this problem, Nature will continually launch attacks against you; you will build Empires to serve only as playthings for Nature, who will amuse herself by destroying them in Revolutions; you are but a load on her shoulders, a prey to her vengeance; your marvels of science always end in poverty and upheavals; your heroes, your law-makers build only on sand; all the vision of a FREDERICK cannot prevent his feeble successors from allowing the rape of his sword at his very tomb. Civilization begets the heroes of today only to humiliate those of the past; thus it disparages those to whom it owes all its splendor. What a cause for anxiety to the Great Men who in their turn will have puny successors! Will they not inevitably feel more anguish at the Revolutions to come than joy at their present triumphs? How can they not abhor that perfidious Civilization which only awaits their demise to undermine and subvert their work? Yes, the Civilized Order is staggering more and more; the volcano activated in 1789 by philosophy is only in its first eruption; others will follow as soon as a weak regime provides a favorable soil for agitators. The war of Poor against Rich was such a blessed success that adventurers in every country are impatient to renew it. In vain are ways sought to prevent it; Nature makes sport of our wisdom and our caution; it will manage to generate Revolutions from the very measures we take to insure tranquillity, and if Civilization is prolonged only a half-century, how many children will beg at the portals of the mansions now inhabited by their fathers! I would not dare to evoke such a frightful prospect, if I could not furnish the key to guide Politics through the labyrinth of the passions and deliver the World from Civilization, become more revolutionary and more odious than ever.

Civilized Nations! While the Barbarians who lack your intelligence know how to maintain their Societies and their Institutions for thousands of years, why are yours annihilated so promptly, often in the same century which gave them birth? One forever hears you deplore the frailty of your works and the cruelty of Nature which so swiftly demolishes your wonderful structures. Cease blaming time and chance for these catastrophes; they are the consequence of the ineptness of your social systems, which fail to guarantee the needy the means of work and subsistence. It is to lead you to confess your error that Nature brandishes the sword over your Empires and finds pleasure in their ruins.

Let me echo for a moment your political elegies. What has become of those monuments that were the pride of civilization? Thebes and Babylon, Athens and Carthage are transformed into ash-heaps. What a prognosis for Paris and London, and for those modern Empires whose mercantile frenzies are already a burden to reason and nature. Sick of our societies, it overthrows them each in its turn, it makes banter about our virtues or our crimes without distinction; the laws reputed to be oracles of wisdom and the ephemeral codes of the agitators alike lead us to political shipwreck.

As a crowning insult, we have seen the rough-hewn laws of China and India defy the scythe of time for 4000 years, while the prodigies of Civilized Philosophy have passed like shadows. Our sciences, after so many efforts to build Empires, seem to have worked only to provide sport for vandalism, which periodically comes to life to destroy in short order the work of centuries.

A few monuments have survived, but only to the shame of Statecraft. Rome and Byzantium, once Capitals of the greatest Empire, have become metropolises to mock at; at the Capitol, the temples of the Caesars have been invaded by the gods of obscure Judea; on the Bosphorus, the basilicas of Christianity are sullied by the gods of ignorance. Here Jesus rises on the pedestal of Jupiter, there Mahomet sets himself up on the altar of Jesus. Rome and Byzantium, Nature preserved you to consign you to the scorn of the

Nations you had enchained; you have become two arenas for political mas-
querades, two Pandora's boxes from which vandalism and pestilence have
spread through the East, superstition and its madness through the West!
Through your abasement Nature insults the great Empire which she
destroyed; you are both mummies preserved to adorn her triumphal chariot
and to give to modern Capitals a foretaste of the destiny which awaits the
monuments and works of Civilization.

It would seem that Nature amuses herself by raising this hateful Society
for the pleasure of laying it low, to prove, through its downfall for the
hundredth time, the absurdity of the sciences which direct it. A replica of the
culprit Sisyphus, who climbs up a steep rock and falls back at the point of
reaching its summit, Civilization seems condemned to climb toward the ideal
form of being and to fall back at the very moment when it perceives an end
to its ills. The most prudently thought-out reforms end only in spilling a sea
of blood. Yet the centuries slip by, and the Peoples groan with pain, as they
wait for new Revolutions to plunge into the void our tottering Empires,
destined to destroy one another so long as they place their trust in Philosophy,
in a science hostile to a system of Politics based on unity, a science which is
but a masque for intrigue and serves only to stir up periodically the ferments
of revolution.

To the disgrace of our intelligence, each day sees multiply the seeds of
disorganization which threaten our frail Societies. Yesterday, scholastic
disputes about equality overthrew the thrones, altars, and property laws:
Europe was marching to Barbarism; tomorrow Nature will invent other
weapons to use against us, and Civilization, put to new trials, will succumb
once more. It seems to flirt with death in every century: it was in the last
throes when the Turks besieged Vienna, it would have been lost if the Turks
had adopted European tactics. In our day, it has been on the very brink of
ruin: the wars of the Revolution might have led to the invasion and dismem-
berment of France; after that Austria and Russia would have divided Europe;
and when they fell out afterward, Russia (which has resources unknown to
itself and the world) would have been able to crush Austria and Civilization.
It is the fate of this criminal Society to shine for several centuries in order to
burn itself out the faster, to be reborn only to collapse once again. If the
Civilized Order could assure human happiness, God would have concerned
Himself with its preservation; He would have taken measures to establish it
firmly. Why then does He permit your Societies to last a few minutes and then
to be buried under the debris of Revolutions? That is a question to perplex
your wise men, who formulate social theories based on their own whims, while

God, less arrogant than these philosophers, by no means regulates the laws of the universe according to His will alone, but in all His works acts in harmony with the eternal arbiter of justice, with Mathematics whose truths are independent of Him and whose laws He nevertheless follows rigorously.

Cease your astonishment, then, if your Societies destroy one another, and do not look for anything stable under laws emanating from man alone, under sciences inimical to the divine spirit, which is trying to establish Unity on earth as in the heavens. A world deprived of a unitary Head, of a central Government, resembles, does it not, a universe without a God to direct it, where stars would gravitate without any fixed order and would forever be colliding with one another? Thus do the several nations present to the Wise One the spectacle of an arena full of wild beasts intent on tearing one another to pieces, on mutual extermination.

When the downfall of your Societies, one after the other, moved you to pity, you did not understand that they had set themselves against the Divine Intent; now that His Plans have been unveiled before you, are you not at once disillusioned about the excellence of Civilization? Do you not realize that it has abused human patience, that a new Social Order is required to lead us to happiness; that it is necessary to rally to God's design to find a Social Order which applies to the whole earth and not only to the corner inhabited by Civilized peoples; that it is, finally, necessary to STUDY THE SOCIAL VICES OF THE HUMAN RACE AND NOT THOSE OF CIVILIZATION, WHICH IS ONLY A PORTION OF THE HUMAN RACE?

Let us establish on this foundation the thesis of the political infirmity of the globe.

Three Societies share the Earth: Civilization, Barbary, and Savagery. One of the three is necessarily better than the others. Now, the two imperfect ones, which do not rise to the level of or identify themselves with the best, are afflicted with that torpor which Montesquieu conjectured, with some reason, had struck the Human Race.

As for the third Society that is imagined to be the best, and that does not know how or is unable to persuade the other two to imitate its example, it is obviously inadequate to achieve the good of the Human Race, since it allows the greater part of mankind to languish in a state inferior to its own.

Consequently, two of the three current Societies are paralyzed, and the third is politically impotent. And now decide which of the three Societies is responsible for the spread of a disease which visibly affects the Social Mechanism of the whole Globe.

In discussing this thesis, you will readily recognize that the two paralyzed Societies are Savagery and Barbarism, which make not the least effort to better their condition, and which are obstinately stagnant in their ways good or bad. As to Civilization, it is afflicted with political impotence, for it is in a constant state of agitation as it attempts innovations every day to deliver itself from its malaise.

Humans who pass from savage inertia to barbarous and civilized industry have then passed from apathy to active pain, for the Savage does not lament his fate or look to change it, while the Civilized man is endlessly uneasy and corroded with desires, even amid riches.

> He burns with a fever that has no remedy,
> Less rich with what he owns
> Than poor with what he has not.

Apostles of error, Moralists and Statesmen! After proving yourselves blind so often, will you still pretend to enlighten the Human Race? The Nations will reply: "If your Sciences inspired by Wisdom have served only to perpetuate Poverty and Discord, we would rather have Sciences inspired by Folly, as long as they can still the Furies and relieve the wretchedness of the peoples."

Oh, far from that Happiness that you promised, you knew only how to depress Man below the condition of animals. If an animal sometimes lacks the necessities of life, he at least does not have to worry about providing for his needs before he feels them. The lion, well-clad, well-armed, takes his nourishment where he finds it, without concerning himself over the welfare of his family or the next day's hazards. How much better is his lot than that of the poor, ashamed to beg, who are crowded like ants in your cities, than that of the wretched workers who, unemployed, harassed by creditors and bailiffs, after all their mortification end up as mendicants, and display their sores, their nakedness, and their starving children throughout your cities, which resound with their doleful laments. There, philosophers, are the bitter fruits of your Sciences: Poverty, eternal Poverty! And yet you pretend to have perfected Reason, when you knew only how to lead us from one abyss to another. Yesterday you reproached Bigotry for the Saint-Bartholomew massacre; today, the prisons of September are cast in your teeth; yesterday it was the Crusades that depopulated Europe, today Equality mows down three million young men, and tomorrow some other cmhiera will bathe the civilized Empires in blood. Treacherous scientists, to what abject condition have you reduced societal Man, and how shrewd were the Governments that you most flattered to be leery of your help! You were always an object of fear even to those Sovereigns whom you counted among your disciples. Sparta thrust you from her bosom, and Cato wanted you to be expelled from Rome. Once again, in our day, Frederick used to say that if he wished to punish one of his provinces, he would give it to the *Philosophes* to be governed, and Napoleon eliminated the section of political and moral science from the temple where the *useful* Sciences sit. Eh! Are you not even more suspect to yourselves? Do you not admit that in dealing with the Passions you are like children who play with fireworks in the midst of gunpowder kegs? The French Revolution is here to seal that truth and cover your Sciences with ineradicable opprobrium.

You had a presentiment that these fatuous Sciences would be annihilated the moment doubt could touch them; thus you concerted to stifle the voices of a few men who tried to be sincere, such as Hobbes and J.-J. Rousseau, who perceived in Civilization a violation of Nature's designs, a methodical development of all the vices. You suppressed these flashes of intelligence, so that your arrant boasts about perfectibility would be heeded.

The scene is changing, and Truth, which you feigned to seek, will appear to confound you. It remains for you, as for the dying gladiator, to fall with honor. Prepare yourself the hecatomb which you owe to Truth; seize the torch, throw on the pyres the rubbish of your philosophical libraries.

ETIENNE CABET

(1788–1856)

Work and Play in Icaria*

Cabet was a teacher and lawyer from Dijon who entered public life during the Revolution of 1830. In its early years, he served the July Monarchy as attorney-general in Corsica, but was discharged when he criticized the government's failure to institute social reforms. Subsequently he sat in the Chamber as a deputy from the Côte-d'Or, was condemned for articles published in his journal *Le Populaire,* and in 1834 fled to England, where he was drawn into the orbit of Robert Owen. Shortly after an amnesty permitted his return to France, Cabet published the *Journey to Icaria* (1840), a novel written largely under Fourierist influence. This stilted account of the bounties of collectivism won enthusiastic converts, and in 1848, 1500 of them set sail to found a real Icaria in the New World. The group was beset by sickness and insolvency and had to disband. Cabet died in St. Louis, despondent over the failure of his experiment.

*From Etienne Cabet, *Voyage en Icarie* (2nd edition; Paris: J. Mallet, 1842), pp. 39–55; translated by the editors.

The last Icarians, photographed at New Icaria (Corning, Iowa), September 5, 1887. (From J. Prudhommeaux, *Icarie et son fondateur, Etienne Cabet*, Paris: E. Cornély, 1907.)

Short History of Icaria

. . . And Corilla began the history of Icaria.

"I will not trouble you with the tale of how Icaria, like almost all other countries, was conquered and laid waste by wicked conquerors, then long oppressed and tyrannized by wicked kings and wicked aristocrats who pauperized the workers and made their poor wives wretched indeed: it is the sad lot of humanity all over the world.

"Thus, for centuries, there was nothing but frightful clashes between the *rich* and the *poor*, revolutions, and horrible massacres.

"About sixty years ago—I do not recall the year (1772, put in Valmor)—the old tyrant Corug was overthrown and put to death, his young son was exiled, and the beautiful *Cloramide* was elevated to the throne.

"At first the young queen was popular because of her gentleness and benevolence. But the hapless creature allowed herself to be dominated by her prime minister, the wicked *Lixdox*, and his tyranny provoked a final revolution (June 13, 1782, the grandfather interpolated), after two days of dreadful fighting and appalling bloodshed.

"What a blessing that the dictator elected by the people, the good and brave *Icar*, proved to be the best of men! It is to him, to our noble forebears who were his comrades, that we owe the happiness we enjoy today. They organized the Republic and the Community, for which they had risked their lives and toiled prodigiously, to secure the happiness of their wives and children.

"Judge for yourself, then, William, how much love we feel for our good Icar and our good grandpa, one of his most intimate friends, a benefactor and liberator of his country."

At these words the old man, who until that point seemed to take pleasure in his grand-daughter's story, reproved her gently for this minor offense to his modesty; but Corilla threw herself on his neck, and her grandfather kissed her tenderly.

"It is Icar who inspired us to action," he cried, his eyes dewy and shining; "his alone is the honor and the glory! Let us sing, my children, sing to Icar and the fatherland!"

And we all sang their hymn of gratitude to Icar and their patriotic anthem.

When I returned to my own place in a fever over everything I had just learned and seen, my brain kept whirling as I tried to fathom or guess all the things that still puzzled me.

Nor could I stop thinking of the ease, the eloquence, the grace with which Valmor, Dinaros, and especially Corilla expressed themselves; and I would have liked to banish the night, in order to hasten the hour appointed for the excursion to which that charming girl had invited me.

I had had so much trouble falling asleep that I was still slumbering when Eugene entered my bedroom raving like a madman and told me that the night before by a curious coincidence he too had learned about Icar and Icaria.

"What a man, or rather what a God was this Icar!" he exclaimed; "what a people! what a country! lucky Icarians! Ah! why didn't fate give us an Icar after our July Revolution! What glorious days! As glorious as the two days of the Icarians! Oh people of Paris! How splendid you were, how great, heroic, noble, magnanimous! What a new road of glory and happiness was opening for my fatherland! Why could it not be? Ill-starred France, France that I flee, that I scorn, that I hate . . . oh no, that I adore more than ever!"

And he paced up and down as if he had been alone; his eyes were filled with tears; and his agitation, which had at first seemed funny to me, in the end moved me profoundly.

When his emotion had subsided, he read me a letter he had written to his brother; it seemed to me so interesting and informative that I asked him to let me copy it; and Valmor's family, to whom I read it, listened to it with so much pleasure that they voiced a wish to know its author and allowed me to present Eugene.

Here is the letter:

MODEL CITY

"Tear up your city plans, my poor Camille, and yet rejoice, for I am sending, to replace them, the plan of a *model city* which you have long wanted. I feel the keenest regret that you are not here to share my wonderment and delight.

"First of all, imagine in Paris or London the most magnificent *reward* offered for the plan of a *model city*, a great open *competition*, and a big *committee* of painters, sculptors, scholars, travelers, who gather the plans or descriptions of all known cities, sift the opinions and ideas of the whole population including foreigners, discuss all the advantages and disadvantages of existing cities and proposals submitted, and choose among thousands the most perfect *blueprint*. Envision a city more beautiful than any which have preceded it; you will then begin to have a notion of Icara, especially if you bear in mind that all its citizens are equal, that it is the republic which is in command and that the rule invariably and constantly followed in all matters is: *first the necessary, then the useful, and last the pleasing.*

"Now, where shall I start? That's a problem for me! All right, I will follow the rule that I have just mentioned and begin with the necessary and the useful.

"I will pass over the measures taken to promote good *health,* to assure the free circulation of pure *air,* to decontaminate it if required. Within the city there are no cemeteries, no noxious products manufactured, no hospitals: all these establishments are on the outskirts, in open places, near swift-flowing streams or in the country.

"I could never tell you how resourceful they are in devising methods to keep the streets *clean.* That the side-walks are swept and washed every morning and are always perfectly clean goes without saying: but in addition, the streets are so paved or constructed that the water constantly drains out of them into *subterranean canals.*

"If *mud* forms, it is collected in one place by ingenious and handy equipment and washed down into the same canals by water from the fountains; but every conceivable means is employed to minimize the accumulation of mud and *dust* in the first place.

"Examine the construction of the streets! Each has eight *tracks* of iron or stone to accommodate four coaches, two going in one direction and two in the other. The wheels never jump the tracks and the horses do not stray from the middle ground. These four areas are paved with stone or pebbles, all the other strips with brick. The wheels stir up neither mud nor dust, the horses practically none, the engines on railroad-streets none at all.

"Note too that the big workshops and warehouses are situated along the canal streets and railroad streets; that the wagons, which incidentally are never overloaded, move only on these streets; that streets with tracks are reserved for omnibuses; and that half the streets do not even admit omnibuses or wagons but only carts pulled by big dogs for making daily deliveries to families residing there.

"Then, no sort of trash is ever thrown from the houses or shops into the street; never are straw, hay, or manure dumped there because all the stables and their provisioners are on the outskirts; all the wagons and conveyances shut so tightly that none of their contents can spill out of them, and all unloading is done with machines so that nothing dirties the sidewalk and the gutter.

"In each street, *fountains* supply the water for cleaning, laying the dust, and refreshing the air.

"Thus everything is arranged, as you see, so that the streets are naturally clean, not misused, and easy to tidy up.

"The law—you will be inclined to laugh but this will give way to admiration—the law has decreed that the pedestrian must be *safe*, that there are never to be any accidents caused by vehicles, horses or other animals, or anything else. Reflect, and you will soon realize nothing is impossible for a government that *wants* the good of its citizens.

"First, frisky *saddle horses* are not allowed inside the city; riding is permitted only outside it, and the stables are located at the city limits.

"As for stage coach-, bus-, and draft-horses, apart from all sorts of precautions to keep them from running away, they can never leave their tracks or mount the sidewalks, and their *drivers* are obliged to lead them on foot as they near pedestrian cross-walks; these *intersections* furthermore are surrounded by every sort of necessary precaution: they are usually indicated by columns extending across the street and forming a sort of gateway for vehicles, and by a kind of intermediary platform where the pedestrian can halt until he ascertains that it is safe to proceed. Needless to say, these cross-walks are almost as clean as the sidewalks. In some streets, the passage is even underground like the *tunnel* in London, while in some others it is a *bridge* beneath which vehicles move.

"There is another simple precaution which eliminates many accidents, but which is not taken seriously in our cities because nothing is done to teach it to people and encourage them to observe it: everywhere vehicles and pedestrians keep to the right of the road.

"You understand also that *drivers* of vehicles, all of them workers for the Republic and not in anyone's private employ, have no interest in exposing themselves to accidents and are on the contrary eager to avoid them.

"You realize further that since the whole population is in the workshops or at home until three o'clock, and the transport vehicles circulate only when the omnibuses do not run and when pedestrians are few, and the wheels never jump the tracks, accidents and collisions are pretty much eliminated.

"As to other animals, one never sees droves of *oxen* and flocks of *sheep* like those which encumber and disgrace the streets of London, causing a thousand accidents, creating anxiety and often spreading terror and death, while people become habituated to the idea of slaughter. For here the *slaughter-houses* and the *butcher shops* are outside the city; the beasts never come into it, one never sees *blood* or *animal carcasses*; and great numbers of butchers do not become calloused to human butchery through constantly steeping their knives and hands in the blood of other kinds of victims.

"I shall not abandon the subject of the animals without speaking of the *dogs*. The Republic feeds, shelters, and employs a great number of dogs remarkable for their size and strength to convey many goods with still less danger than if horses were used. These dogs, well fed, always bridled and muzzled or led on a leash, can never go *mad*, or bite, or frighten anyone, or create the kind of scene which, in our cities, destroys in a moment all the worth of years of training.

"Everything is so well figured out that no chimney, flower-pot, nor any object whatsoever can be flung down by a storm or thrown from a casement.

"Pedestrians are protected even against the caprices of the weather; for all the streets are equipped with *side-walks*, and all these side-walks are covered with glass panes to keep out the rain without excluding the light, and with awnings to combat the heat. One even finds some streets entirely covered, especially those connecting the great warehouses, and all the cross-walks are likewise covered.

"They have pushed these measures to the extent of constructing, at different points on each side of the street, covered platforms where the omnibuses stop, so that one can board or alight without fear of rain or mud.

"You see, dear friend, that one can go all over the city of Icara, in a carriage when one is in a hurry, through the gardens when the weather is fine, and under the porticoes when it is bad, without ever requiring a parasol or an umbrella and with perfect confidence; while thousands of accidents and disasters, which each year overwhelm the people of Paris and London, point a finger at the shameful impotence or barbarous indifference of their governments.

"You are right if you think that the city is perfectly *illuminated*, as well as Paris and London, even much better, because the source of light is not absorbed by the shops, since there are none, or by the factories, since nobody works at night. Illumination is then concentrated on the streets and public monuments; and not only is the *gas* odorless because means have been found to purify it, but the illumination combines to the highest degree the pleasing and the useful, through the elegant and varied forms of the street lamps and the thousand shapes and colors which they give the light. I have seen fine illumination in London in some streets on certain holidays; but in Icara the illumination is always magnificent, and sometimes it creates a veritable fairy-land.

"You would see here neither *cabarets,* nor roadhouses, nor *cafés,* nor smoking joints, nor the stock-exchange, nor gaming or lottery houses, nor establishments for shameful or culpable pleasures, nor barracks and guard-rooms, nor gendarmes and stool-pigeons, just as there are no prostitutes or pickpockets, no drunkards or mendicants; but instead you would find everywhere PRIVIES, as elegant as they are clean and convenient, some for women, others for men, where modesty may enter for a moment without fear for itself or for public decency.

"You would never again be offended by the sight of all those *cartoons,* drawings, scrawls which defile the walls of our cities even as they make one avert one's eyes with shame; for the children are trained not to spoil or dirty anything, and to blush at whatever might be indecent or knavish.

"You would not even have the pleasure or annoyance of seeing so many *signs* and *posters* above the doors of the houses, nor so many notices and *advertisements* which usually disfigure buildings: instead you would see beautiful *inscriptions* on the monuments, workshops, and public depots, just as you would see all the useful hand-bills, attractively printed on papers of many colors, and posted by the Republic's placarders on special bulletin boards, in such a way that the notices themselves are ornamental.

"You would see no more those rich and pretty *shops* of every sort that one finds in Paris and London in all the houses on commercial streets. But what are the finest of these shops, the richest of these stores and bazaars, the most extensive of these markets or fairs, compared with the *factories,* shops, *stores* of Icara! Imagine that all the goldsmith and jewelry *workshops* and *stores* of Paris or London, for example, were merged into one or two of each; imagine the same for all branches of industry and commerce; and tell me if the stores for jewelry, watches, flowers, feathers, piece goods, fashions, instruments, fruits, and so on, would not inevitably cast into the shade all the shops in the rest of the world; tell me whether you would not feel as much and perhaps more pleasure in visiting them than in touring our museums and artistic monuments. Ah well, such are the shops and stores of Icara!

"And all of them are purposely spread through the city to enhance its beauty and serve the maximum convenience of the inhabitants, and to make them even more decorative, they are built to resemble on the outside monuments where simplicity and the marks of industry are the dominant notes.

"I have just mentioned utilitarian *monuments*: I need hardly say that all the monuments and *useful* institutions that exist elsewhere are, with all the more reason, found here—the schools, hostels, temples, courts, places of popular assembly, even arenas, circuses, theaters, museums of all sorts, and all the establishments whose agreeableness makes them more or less essential.

"No aristocratic *mansions*, likewise no private *carriages*; but no *prisons* or *almshouses*! No royal or ministerial palaces; but the schools, hostels, popular assemblies are as impressive as palaces, or, if you like, all the palaces are dedicated to public purposes!

"I would never finish, my dear brother, if I were to enumerate all the useful things contained in Icara: but I have said enough, perhaps too much, although I am sure that in your love for me you will relish all these details; and now I will pass to the *pleasing,* where you will once more find *variety* the constant companion of *uniformity.*

"Let us look then at the externals of the houses, the streets, and the monuments.

"I have already told you that all the *houses* in a street are similar, but that all the streets are different, and all the attractive houses of foreign lands are represented.

"Your eye would never be offended here by the sight of those *hovels, dumps,* and *street-corner hangouts* that elsewhere crowd the most magnificent palaces, nor by the view of those *rags and tatters* that are the neighbors of aristocratic luxury.

"Your gaze would no longer alight on those dismal railings that surround the moats of London houses, and combine with the sooty bricks to give them the appearance of a vast prison.

"The *chimneys,* so hideous in many other countries, are here an ornament or are at least inconspicuous, while iron *balustrades* give a charming aspect to the tops of the houses.

"The sidewalks or gracefully-columned *porticoes* which border every street, already magnificent, will be something enchanting when, as is planned, all the colonnades are bedecked with foliage and flowers.

"Shall I undertake to describe to you the *fountains,* the *squares,* the *promenades,* the *columns,* the *public monuments,* the colossal *gates* of the city, and its magnificent *avenues*? No, my friend: my vocabulary would be inadequate to depict my admiration, and besides I would have to write you volumes. I will bring you all the plans, and will limit myself here to giving you only a general idea.

"Ah, how sorry I am that I cannot visit them again with my brother! You would see that each fountain, square, monument, is unique, and that all the varieties of architectural style are here exemplified. You would think yourself in Rome, Greece, Egypt, India, everywhere; and never would you be infuriated, as we have been in London at St. Paul's, by the shops which deprive you of a birdseye view of the whole magnificent monument.

"Nowhere would you see more *paintings, sculpture, statues* than here in the monuments, on the squares, along the promenades, and in the public gardens; for, while elsewhere these works of art are hidden in the palaces of kings and rich men, while in London the museums, shut on Sundays, are never open to the People, who cannot leave their work to visit them during the week, here all the curios exist only for the People and are displayed only in the spots frequented by them.

"And since it is the Republic under whose auspices the painters and sculptors work, since the artists, fed, clad, lodged, and equipped by the Community, have no other motive but love of art and glory, and no other guide but the inspirations of genius, you can imagine the results.

"Nothing useless and especially nothing harmful, but everything directed toward the goal of utility! Nothing favoring despotism and Aristocracy, fanaticism and superstition, but everything favoring the People and their benefactors, liberty and its martyrs, or opposing the old tyrants and their minions.

"Never those paintings of *nudes* or voluptuous scenes which are publicly shown to cater to the tastes of influential libertines, all the while that hypocrites pay endless lip service to decency and chastity. Such pictures no husband would want his wife and the mother of his children to behold.

"Never more those works which betray only ignorance or lack of skill, works that elsewhere poverty sells for a pittance to buy bread, and that corrupt public taste while they dishonor the arts; for here nothing is passed by the Republic without examination; and as in Sparta weak or deformed children were destroyed at birth, here they mercilessly thrust into oblivion whatever productions are unworthy of the radiance of the God of the arts.

"I am stopping, dear Camille, although I had much to tell you about the garden-streets, the river and canals, the quays and bridges, and the monuments which have just been started or planned.

"But what will you say when I add that all the cities of Icaria, though much smaller, are built on the same plan, except for the omission of the large national institutions.

"And so I hear you exclaim with me: Lucky Icarians! Unlucky Frenchmen!"

The more I moved about the city after that, the more accurate did Eugene's description appear to me.

When I had made a copy of the letter, the two of us set out to visit one of the Republic's *bakeries*.

We went through five or six enormous buildings set up in parallel rows, one for *flour*, another for *dough*, a third for the *ovens*, a fourth for *fuel*, and a fifth for piling up the *bread*, whence vehicles distribute it to consumers everywhere.

The flour and fuel are carried along the canal and then transferred to storage bins by mechanical means. Big funnels dump the flour into the kneading machines, while other funnels pour in water as needed. Very ingenious indeed are the machines that knead the dough, cut it, and carry it to the ovens, as other machines bring up the fuel; meanwhile still others carry away the finished bread and deposit it in the last building.

Eugene could not stop marveling at how this system eased the burdens of the workers and what tremendous economies it effected.

All the time I joined in his admiration, I kept thinking of the excursion in prospect, and at five o'clock I promptly betook myself to Valmor's.

They were ready to leave, and at my arrival practically the whole family set off. Valmor gave his arm to one of his cousins; and the lovely Corilla took mine with a warm friendliness so engaging that I would have lost my head had I been less fortified against these charms.

We passed along garden streets, many of them full of young girls, or children, or men who were watering or planting.

The more I saw those gardens, the more delightful did they seem to me; the lawns, a thousand kinds of roses and other flowers, the shrubs in bloom, the walls covered with jasmine, vines, lilacs of Judaea, honeysuckle, in short, greenery dotted with a thousand colors, the perfume in the air, the picture of workers and children—it was altogether an enchanting sight.

But the *promenade* seemed to me more enchanting still: sandy walks, straight or winding; immense lawns; bushes of all sorts; magnificent trees; little thickets and flowery arbors everywhere; at each step handsome benches painted green; grottoes or artificial hillocks where birds crowded; waterfalls, rivulets, cascades, fountains, spouts; charming bridges; statues and little monuments; everything that the lively imagination of the cleverest draftsman could dream up is there, even birds and all sorts of aquatic and terrestrial animals.

And what adorns this promenade still more than all the fascinations of art and nature are the number of large families thronging it—fathers, mothers, children usually walk there together. Thousands of youths and maidens of every age, all neatly and attractively clad, run, skip, dance, and play at a thousand games, always in groups and under the eyes of their parents. Only joy and pleasure are evident; only laughing, happy shouts, songs, and music are heard.

"It seems," said I to Corilla, "that your compatriots have a passion for *music.*"—"Yes," she answered, "and it is good Icar who instilled this taste in us, like the taste for foliage, flowers, and fruits. Since his day, education has made these passions universal among us. Everybody acquires a general knowledge of things pertaining to vegetation and farming. All the children, without exception, learn vocal music and know how to sing; each one learns to play an instrument. Thus you will hear music and singing always and everywhere, at home as well as at public meetings, in temples and workshops as well as at public spectacles and along the promenades. We will come upon bands of musicians of every sort, sitting in attractive salons designed expressly for them, besides many concerts played, instead of by musicians, by mechanical means which so expertly imitate them that you would be fooled.

"A trumpet gives nearly all signals; at the sound of the horn, our thousands of public vehicles take off and are speeded on their way. Don't you find their flourishes charming?"

"Truly I do."—"And you will see what sort of music we have on our national holidays, with choirs of fifty- or a hundred-thousand voices."

At that point we reached the bridle path, and we saw passing by hundreds of little cavalcades composed of men and women of all ages, handsomely clad, though altogether differently from our horsemen and horsewomen of London and Paris. As I was amazed at the grace of the women and the beauty of the horses—proud for the men, tractable for the women, very small and engaging for the children—Corilla said to me: "Don't be surprised; for since the Republic decided to give us the pleasures of horseback riding, it has devoted special care to the breeding and training of horses, and has even imported the best strains from foreign lands. For the same reason, horsemanship is part of childhood instruction, and you would not find today a single Icarian who is not a good rider."

"But," I said, "how do you provide enough saddle horses for everyone?" "This is how it is done," she answered: "The Republic has only a thousand saddle horses for each communal city and sixty thousand for Icara; but these horses are shared among all the citizens, so that each family can enjoy them once in ten days."

"And all these horses belong to the Republic?"

"Certainly, and they are lodged in its stables and cared for by its workers."

We chatted about all sorts of things, holidays, theaters, dancing, pleasures, the manners and customs of the country. She even talked to me about the public assemblies and the press, and always with so much poise and grace that I did not realize night was falling while I enjoyed my education at the hands of so charming a teacher.

FOOD

On the day of rest, the Icarian Sunday or rather the tenth day of the Icarian week, Valmor, who had given me two days advance notice, called for Eugene and me early in the morning to take us to the country.

I will later recount all the means devised and put into operation by the Republic to encourage these excursions and picnics. From spring to autumn, the Icarians go in for them with great enthusiasm.

We all set out, some on foot, others on nice donkeys, mules or horses, still others in omnibuses, and we journeyed to a fountain of great repute, situated two leagues from Icara on the slope of a delightful hillock overlooking the city.

The road itself presented an almost indescribable spectacle: it was thronged with carriages, horses, donkeys, mules, dogs, hikers, and provisions, all of them heading for the same spot. Nor could I depict the ravishing beauty of the view, of the lawns, thickets, and fountain on which art and nature had lavished all their riches, nor the delightful scenes of hundreds of groups picnicking, singing, laughing, skipping, running, dancing, and playing at a thousand games.

At her grandfather's behest, Corilla gave us a brief description of twenty or thirty country walks where the people of Icaria ordinarily spent holidays and rest days. She explained to us that all these charming spots, which are at present the joy of the whole people, were formerly the exclusive preserve of a few lords and were contained within the walls and moats of their castles and parks.

Interesting as was Corilla's talk, which she invested with so much charm besides, Valmor engaged me still more when he expounded the system adopted by the Republic for *feeding* its citizens.

I would have reported here the substance of his discourse, if I had not found the system perfectly detailed in another of Eugene's letters to his brother; the letter, which I shall quote here, will then take the place of my own account. And in order to get to it sooner, I shall content myself with saying that our return from the country was no less lively, no less gay, than our departure and sojourn there, and that my soul expanded with the happiness which I saw all about me.

EUGENE'S LETTER TO HIS BROTHER

"Oh dear Camille, how broken-hearted I am when I think of France and when I see the happiness which the people of Icaria enjoy! Judge of it yourself when you hear about the agencies they have set up to handle FOOD and *clothing*.

"In our unhappy land, everything that has to do with this prime need of man, and indeed all his other needs, is left to chance and marked by monstrous abuses. Here, on the contrary, everything is regulated by the most enlightened policy and the most generous solicitude.

"First of all, dear brother, bear in mind that there is absolutely nothing regarding nourishment that is not regulated by *law*. The law allows or prohibits any and all foodstuffs.

"A *committee* of scientists, national in character, assisted by all the citizens, has drawn up a *list* of all known foodstuffs, indicating the good and the bad, with the good and bad points of each.

"More than that, they have divided the good ones into the necessary, the useful, and the pleasing, and have published the list in several volumes, with a copy for each family.

"Still more, they have described the best way to prepare each food, and every family also has this *Cook book*.

"The Republic sees to it that the approved foodstuffs are produced by the farmers and workers and distributed to the families; and as no one has access to foods other than these, you see that no one can eat foods other than those which have passed muster.

"The Republic directs the production first of necessities, then useful foods, then pleasing ones, and as much of all of them as possible.

"It divides them equally among all the citizens so that everyone gets the same quantity of any food in ample supply, and everyone gets in his turn by year or day such foods as are insufficient for the whole population.

"Everybody then enjoys an equal share of all foodstuffs whatever, from what we call the plainest to the fanciest; and the whole population of Icaria is as well and better fed than the wealthy of other lands.

"You see then, my poor friend, that the government here operates entirely differently from our monarchy; while royalty makes such a fuss over a good king who wants every peasant to have a *chicken in the pot* on Sunday, the Republic here quietly gives everyone everyday what elsewhere adorns only the tables of Aristocrats and Kings!

"Not only does the Republic take care of raising all the cattle, poultry, and fish that are needed, not only does it supervise the cultivation and distribution of all the fresh vegetables and fruits which are consumed, but it uses every means to process and distribute stocks of dried foods, conserves, and so on.

"That is not all: the committee that I mentioned a few moments ago has discussed and informed the people about the number of *meals*, their hour, duration, the number, kind, and sequence of dishes, endlessly varying them not only according to the season and month, but even the day, so that in a given week every dinner is different.

"At six in the morning, before beginning their tasks, all workers, that is all citizens, eat together in their workshops a simple pre-breakfast (which Parisian workers call a "drop" or "morning snack"), prepared and served by the workshop cook.

"At nine, they breakfast in the shop, while their wives and children eat at home.

"At two, all the residents on a street eat in common in their *republican restaurant* a dinner prepared by one of the Republic's chefs.

"And in the evening, between nine and ten, each family in its own dwelling takes a meal prepared by the woman of the house.

"At all these repasts, the first toast is drunk to the *glory of the good Icar, benefactor of workers*, BENEFACTOR OF FAMILIES, BENEFACTOR OF CITIZENS.

"Supper consists chiefly of fruit, pastry, and sweets.

"But the sumptuousness of the common dinner, served in lofty and elegantly decorated rooms holding one to two thousand persons, defies the imagination. Our finest Parisian restaurants and cafés are nought in my eyes compared to the restaurants of the Republic. Perhaps you will be incredulous when I tell you that apart from the abundance and delicacy of the dishes, apart from the flower pieces and other kinds of decorations, delightful music beguiles the ears and the scent of delicious perfumes fills the air.

"And so when young people marry, they do not have to eat up their doweries in a bad wedding feast and bankrupt ahead of time their unborn children; the dinners which a husband can eat in his wife's restaurant and a wife can eat in her husband's, and the two families together at either of them, take the place of the most splendid meals in other countries.

"And yet you can understand that these common repasts are vastly more economical than private ones and this adds to their enjoyment.

"You can understand also that the community of meals among workers and neighbors has other great advantages, notably promoting fraternity among the masses and greatly simplifying household tasks for the women.

"And since the Republic is concerned only for the happiness of its children, you will not be surprised either to learn that it carries its tender indulgence to the point of giving them on Sundays the means of eating all their meals with their families at home, of dining there with their own friends, even of going to the country for the day. And with that end in view it has all the restaurants prepare cold plates which are taken home, and it places at their disposal other means of transport when they want to taste the pleasures of the *country*.

"Truly, brother, I am not lying when I assure you that this land is a paradise which rejoices the soul as well as the senses; and yet I go mad here. . . . I . . . a Frenchman who adores his country; sometimes I suffer for it all the torments of Tantalus!

"Ah well, courage and hope! And while we wait, let us study!"

AUGUSTE COMTE
(1798–1857)

The Religion of
Humanity*

Auguste Comte, founder of sociology, had a rigorous scientific education at
the École Polytechnique in Paris, followed by a "philosophical apprenticeship" as secretary to Henri Saint-Simon in 1818–23. Personal and intellectual differences brought the relationship to a turbulent end, and Comte
on his own developed a positivist theory of progress based on the evolution
of the sciences and their ordering in a hierarchy. After the death in 1846
of Clothilde de Vaux, the great love of his life, Comte's doctrines were
invested with a new emotionality. He began to look for the reform and
unification of society through a Religion of Humanity, in which Clothilde
was apotheosized as the Virgin-Mother. Oppressed by an unhappy
marriage, bouts of madness, poverty, and isolation, Comte nevertheless
produced two mammoth works, on the Positive Philosophy (1831–42)
and on the Positive Polity (1851–54), and attracted influential disciples
in both hemispheres.

*From Auguste Comte, *System of Positive Polity or Treatise on Sociology, Instituting the Religion of
Humanity* (London: Longmans Green, 1875–77), II, pp. 122–8, 276, 286–93; trans. Frederic
Harrison from the *Système de politique positive* (Paris, II, 1852).

Auguste Comte, lithograph by Tony Toullion.

The Expansion of Sympathy

Let us, as a method of examination, suppose an imaginary case, in which human nature should be free to develop its emotional and intellectual force, without being compelled to make use of the powers of action. The actual preponderance of the latter order of cerebral functions is solely due to our material necessities. We can therefore conceive all necessity temporarily removed, where the situation was very favourable to supplying them, without supposing man to be free from the wants of his vegetative nature. It would be enough that the solid aliment was procured with as little effort as is the material of our liquid, or gaseous sustenance. In climates where the other physical wants are not great, certain instances of peculiar fertility closely approach the case supposed. It exists still more distinctly amongst the privileged classes; where an artificial situation frees them almost entirely from anxiety respecting these lower wants of our nature. Such would be, in the Final System, the natural condition of every one during the age of education. In this period, Humanity would undertake entirely to provide for its future servants, in order to promote their moral and mental training without obstacle. These two exceptional cases, the former a rare but permanent type, the latter common though destined to disappear, serve to show that the hypothesis in question has sufficient abstract reality to admit of special analysis; and without such a study, the social tendencies of feeling and intelligence would remain indistinct. Besides its utility in theory, the treatment of a hypothetical case will have considerable practical purpose, if it serves to exhibit the moral type proper for such situations. When poetry is regenerated, and has succeeded in duly idealising for all a natural existence free from all material necessities, it will furnish us with the true model of human conduct, the type towards which all, even the least prepared to attain it, ought constantly to tend. It will suffice here to use the hypothesis proposed simply for the purpose of ascertaining the true influence possessed by the active powers over human life; and we shall infer what this is, in tracing the modifications that the original and abstract type will undergo, under the pressure of material necessities.

In the case assumed, the great Problem of human Life would be spontaneously solved, by the natural predilection, which would be felt for the unselfish system of existence. Although the personal instincts greatly predominate in the constitution of the brain, the paramount place they hold is chiefly due to the constant stimulus of physical wants. Were this removed, they would be easily restrained by forces arising from the varied contact of society. The natural course of human relations would dispose us all to cultivate the only instincts, which admit of a perfectly universal and almost boundless expansion. We should then find out that characteristic quality of the sympathetic feelings, that a great and continuous exercise of them would make up for their natural inferiority of force. The peculiar charm which they possess would soon place them above the selfish feelings, which, although more largely developed in the organ, would be neutralised by their habitual inertia. We can even conceive that, on the biological principles of inheritance, a few generations would succeed in modifying the cerebral organisation itself in a society so constituted, the volume of the organs of feeling becoming augmented or diminished by continual exercise or disuse.

We may now consider what would become of our intellectual life. We can see at once that practical speculations would be little cultivated, since they are chiefly due to our corporal wants. With this, true scientific training would lose its chief purpose, which is to direct industrial activity. The speculative instincts, which impel us to seek for the explanation of phenomena, are naturally much too weak to produce really sustained efforts. In a situation, where the environment gave them no strong practical impulse, either personal or social, they would soon weary of futile exertion, and would do little more than sketch out a few easy conceptions from the simplest analogies in nature. The human intelligence would then be free to follow its natural bent for artistic invention, a pursuit far more congenial to its nature than scientific, or even constructive labour. The work of conception would be made distinctly subordinate to that of expression, the natural preponderance of which shows itself in so many ways, and results from its relation to man's social spirit. Practically the main result of this apparent inversion of our actual condition would be to make the feelings the great object of the use of language, which now is devoted chiefly to express the thoughts called out by the external necessities around us, as these need to be modified by our collective activity. Every strong emotion awakens in us a desire to express it; and all experience shows us, how the very expressing it reacts on the feeling. This reaction of expression is felt, even where the existence is one of solitude; but it is much increased when language is carried out to its real purpose, that of interchange of ideas. Now this gratification belongs chiefly to the instincts of sympathy, for no others can be adequately communicated, or shared by expression. It is owing to this fortunate concurrence of qualities that Art really predominates both over Science and Industry, ever tending as it does to overcome the obstacles suggested by reason, in the hard necessities of the external world. In the most miserable forms of existence, man exhibits unmistakably this tendency, the moment that he is relieved from the pressure of material want. When the claims of nature have been satisfied, the degraded savage, the poor infant, and even the unhappy prisoner, like all sociable beings, turn their whole efforts to the direct expression of their better emotions. The gratification which this expression produces increases with the sphere of the sympathies engaged. Where these accumulated sympathies are successive in time, they augment the pleasure more even than where they are coexistent together. Hence the incomparable charm inspired by the great poems of antiquity, the undoubted beauty of which is inseparably connected in our minds with the continued admiration they have awakened in so many successive generations.

To complete the hypothesis, we have to consider the form of activity in the case supposed. As our practical existence relates chiefly to our material wants, we can conceive how, in such a society, its intensity and even its character would be essentially modified. But the activity of man would not be utterly extinguished by a condition, which is not found to affect so completely the many animals, that our providence artificially protects from these necessities. According to the first law of animal life, the active region of the brain, still more than the speculative region, tends continually to a direct exercise, quite apart from any external object. The only consequence is that its exercise becomes artistic, instead of being technical, without ceasing to be subordinate to the impulse of the affections. These do not, it is true, originate actions, properly so called, but merely manifestations; yet the same movements are needed for expression as for action. In a word, actions become games, which are not mere preparations for active life, but simple modes of exercise and expansion. This transformation would become particularly obvious in the case of the activity of the social body; which, being no longer absorbed by material undertakings, would give itself up to festivals, whereby to express and develop the common affections of the society. The artistic character would predominate in practical, as well as in speculative, life. We thus feel how much better Art is adapted to our nature than Science, or even Industry; for it has a more direct and purer relation to the emotions, which animate our lives. We should then have no Industry, save that of perfecting our special modes of Expression; and our only Science would be the *"Gay Science,"* so artlessly preferred to any other in the knightly times of old.

An individual existence such as this would be attended by a similar collective existence, whether domestic or political; and it would be one, in which the instincts of Sympathy would gain an easy ascendancy. This would be marked by a more complete development of the family, and a less complete activity of the social life. The latter, indeed, is mainly stimulated to its intensity by the ever increasing need of the cooperation, requisite to meet our external necessities. But the immediate charm of the emotions of Sympathy becomes ever deeper, as the sphere of their action becomes more close. The highest of the benevolent instincts, simple Benevolence, though it be the least energetic of all, would still continue to inspire us directly with universal affection. At the same time, for want of any real common activity, it would be ordinarily engaged in communicating the domestic emotions; and these would find no antagonism springing up to mar their free expansion. In a word, social life, having no decided practical end, would, like personal life, assume a character essentially esthetic. But this artistic character of life would become more pure and more fixed, and would thus supply us with enjoyment, hard for us even to imagine, and which by its unfailing sweetness would unite profoundly in one the various families able to share in it duly. The influence exercised of old amongst the different Greek tribes by the national Festivals, apart from any active bond of union, may serve to give us but a feeble notion of what these associations will grow to be.

In the condition we have supposed, classification of rank, based on personal merit, would at once supplant that which arises from material superiority, which is a mere consequence of our physical necessities. Again the natural order which sets moral, above physical, and even intellectual, excellence would be better recognised, and less disputed. Government there would be far more spiritual than temporal. We may even assume, that the active and speculative sex would place itself in voluntary subordination to the affectionate sex, so soon as the excellence of woman had been abundantly manifested by a situation, where women had the freest scope for developing their nature. The sweet reign of woman over life would be established all the easier, from the fact, that it would be confirmed by intellectual preeminence. For the chief intellectual efforts of such a race would be in the direction of Art; thus it would harmonise more often with those emotions, which women most value, and express most happily.

The successive phases, which such a society would assume, would exhibit a considerable modification of the law of the three states. In particular, the intermediate stage would disappear almost entirely. It would be impossible to dispense with the simplest phase, that of Fetichism; nay, this would be ever found in a purer form, and would continue longer, for there would be no material activity to interrupt the natural preponderance of Feeling. Still, I have no doubt whatever that the final result, in Positivism, would be made in such a world more rapid and more easy. There is nothing inconsistent in this, if we reflect, that Theologism is properly, only a long transition, first Polytheistic then Monotheistic, from Fetichism to Positivism. I have already remarked, that such an intermediate state is especially required by social conditions, which, in the case supposed, would cease to be influential. Under the intellectual aspect alone, which would then be most important, Positivism could, as I have shown, succeed Fetichism directly, where the population was suitably prepared for a systematic modification. Now this would be the same, in that spontaneous evolution, which I have assumed for the case supposed. The simple belief, that Matter possesses a Will, would be prolonged by a situation, which did not stimulate the scientific spirit. On the other hand it would favour the passage to the notion of natural Laws, without that of Gods and Entities being seriously interposed. Although the intelligence would have lost the stimulus of those practical necessities, which have so greatly seconded the rise of the Positive spirit, its exercise alone would lead the mind ultimately to separate the Activity, natural to matter, from Vitality properly so called. And at bottom there is no difference in theory but this between Fetichism and Positivism, which would thus directly succeed to it. In the temporal sphere the reasoning would coincide with that for the spiritual sphere; for although the Industrial life would not be very much developed, the Military existence, which precedes it, would lose all its intense and permanent stimulus, in the absence of any material want. As there would thus be no habitual conflict of importance to disturb the free expansion of the sympathies, they would soon extend from the Family to Humanity, without being long arrested by Patriotism, the chief sphere of Theologism. This earlier development of the highest feeling would favour the similar concentration of the intellect, and directly tend to its cultivation.

The hypothesis assumed brings us therefore to the general conclusion, that the continued suppression of our material necessities would result in a more simple and more perfect type of humanity, and render its development more free and speedy. There is thus both a theoretical and a practical utility in this fiction; inasmuch as it brings out the essential quality of every animal nature, the constant subordination of the Activity and the Intelligence to Feeling. We may thus correct many dangerous illusions and many erroneous tendencies, which lead us so often to mistake the means for the end.

Before closing the inquiry into the case assumed, it must be pointed out that it is necessarily an ideal one; it can be supported only by theory, and cannot be tested in practice. The two actual cases, which were at first alluded to as the nearest approach to our hypothesis, are yet too distinct, to enable us to estimate the conditions by themselves. For both the rich and the young are only relieved from the chief physical necessities by the special protection of society; which itself is paramount over them, and which with its imperious wants reacts greatly on their exceptional case. At the same time we must not forget, how completely this sociological fiction accords with the conceptions of the poets as to the natural rise of civilisation. In fact, the Fetichist populations, where the conditions of life are very favourable, necessarily furnish the best concrete approximation of this abstract type. Still, the constant modification imposed on such a type even there, from practical necessities, makes it a very imperfect and occasional mode of verification; one which may assist the theoretic study, but can in no way supersede it.

The Subjective Life, expanded and regulated by Positivism, will best realise this fundamental type of Humanity; for the conditions essential to it would be obtained, so soon as the physical world passes away of itself, and the moral world is brought out into full freedom.

* * *

The Positive Organization of Social Existence

For every living being, we need to introduce, between the kindred ideas of organisation and of life, an intermediate term, one at present vaguely conceived, and for which we must reserve the special name of *existence*. It may be applied to all real substances, in order to express their proper and continuous form of active energy. In Biology, it corresponds with the fixed side of every system of vital phenomena: the *life* of every being consisting of the series of modifications to which its *existence* is subject. This general distinction becomes more and more marked, as we reach organisms of greater complexity and more easily modified. Its chief use is in Sociology, where it has held its ground under an indirect form, ever since Aristotle founded the theory of Order, without any notion of laws of Progress, which were left for modern thought. Whilst science regarded human societies as immovable, the term *life* could not be properly applied to them, for it implies a series of changes always terminating in death. The word is only in place, when the idea of constant Progress is established. The general term, *existence*, was therefore more apt to express the essential active side of the Great Organism.

*   *   *

It would be wrong to attribute any essential novelty to the sacred Formula of Positivists, which sums up human existence individual and collective and each of its modes: *The Principle, Love; the Basis, Order; the End, Progress.* This programme is new only in the systematic form given to it. But its substance may be seen in the oldest germs of it, for its roots lie deep in the unchangeable nature of man. Thus the middle term, or Order, made its appearance as a principle in the ancient Theocracies, embracing in itself, without extinguishing, the other two. As to the first term, I have already remarked that the continuous influence of the benevolent affections long preceded the theoretic explanation which they have now received. Before they had any sanction from the teaching of Religion, their existence was fully recognised by all the minds emancipated from the system of official belief, and certainly by the poets of antiquity. We might even say the same thing as to the last term of the formula, Progress; although it was long a fixed dogma that the order of human life was immutable. As to home life, we have the continual search after moral Progress held up to us as the noble end of Humanity in the most ancient monuments of human wisdom, the admirable books of the Hebrew Theocracy. As to public life, a sense of the same high aim is at once manifest, as soon as any true collective activity has been formed under the inspiration of the military system, with its universal thought of growing Empire. In this way, we may say that the formula adopted in its explicit form by the adult stage of Humanity may be found in its implicit form associated with the infancy and the youth of Humanity, and investing both with a new meaning.

In the same way we may trace the normal institution of the Priesthood, late as its actual establishment has been, showing itself in the most ancient attempts to give system to human life. It fulfils a purpose ever present in social needs, and springs from the necessities of our nature. Each of its essential conditions was spontaneously recognised in early times; it is the organisation of them all into a system which is now for the first time achieved. The most crucial of all the requirements of a true Priesthood, the sincere and habitual renunciation of Power and even of Wealth, was always unconsciously preferred either by the great types of the priestly character, or by the general instinct, as being necessary for the intellect no less than for the heart. Catholicism in the Middle Age, even when the course of events drove it to sacrifice this fundamental duty from the very fact that its own fine attempt to found a Spiritual Power was premature, saw in the possession of Wealth and Power a certain cause of inward degradation. Again, when the Priesthood under a temporary but unavoidable necessity, as the next volume of this work will show, imposed the rule of celibacy on itself, it felt even more forcibly how contrary to the natural law was this violation of principle; for the domestic affections are at once the source and the guarantee of true social feeling. The wisdom of the Theocracies which had been popularised by ancient Poetry, had made this estimate of the Family familiar to men's minds.

Lastly, the very constitution of the Spiritual Power, not only in itself but in its two social allies, will show us how the characteristics of the final system, as set forth in the General View, were at all times spontaneously active. In spite of the state of civil subjection in which Women were placed by the ancients, the natural affinity of the affectionate sex for the contemplative order of men, and their common opposition to the ascendancy of material force, gave a continual and valuable aid to the Priesthood. Long before the Middle Age, which first gave woman her just position, the Theocracies of Egypt, of Chaldæa, and of India, as afterwards those of Peru and Mexico, availed themselves largely of this domestic help for the due fulfilment of their social functions. The same thing is true of the powerful help of the People, who have attained their full social position even later than Women. From the earliest ages of Theocracy, the natural decomposition of material force into the concentrated force of Wealth and the dispersed force of Numbers supplied the Priesthood with an aid similar to that of the modern proletariat, only less developed. The military system could not prevent an influence of the same kind; for we see of old the soldiers rising against their officers, under the instigation of the Priests; often, it must be said, not without just cause.

On every ground, therefore, we ought to avoid the metaphysical tendency to look only at the appearance in regular form of the different human institutions, instead of at their earliest spontaneous germ; for these are as ancient as civilisation itself. The rule of Positive thought on the other hand will direct the new priesthood to represent every organisation as founded upon a long period of previous existence in an empirical form. In its essence the true form of any Spiritual Power must always be radically the same. Its duty is to change the will without compelling actions. It is very late that it succeeds in obtaining systematic shape, and can disengage itself sufficiently from the mysticism and the fictions under which its social purpose lies concealed. In our time it is more direct and more complete, and its character therefore may be more easily understood. But having thus grasped its spirit in the instance which is best adapted to display it rightly, we may properly use this type as an instrument to guide us in the positive study of all preceding ages. There is a reason also upon the moral ground which enhances the value of this logical expedient; for the Positivist priesthood are bound by a generous sense of fellowship towards all their predecessors under Theological and even under Fetichist systems. The Religion, which most strongly brings out the idea and the feeling of human Continuity, will naturally incline its ministers ever to regard themselves as the heirs of the various Priesthoods of old. But for this habitual attitude of mind and of heart, they would be powerless in the present day, even to picture forth the Great Being as coextensive with man's planet; since its different regions present still types of religion which recall those of the various social ages.

Such are the reasons which induce me to make free use of the full-grown type of Humanity as an instrument for the abstract study of its Social Existence organised by the Priesthood. In my General View, I have described in outline the natural Order of man; and I shall now apply it to the service of my Statical study; since in abstract Statics we must disregard all considerations of time and of manner belonging to concrete realisation. At the same time, this normal order will be treated only in its essential features: those which concern the mere end of *preservation*, apart from the question of *development*, except only so far as this is the necessary object of existence.

In this organisation of social Existence by the Priesthood, the leading principle rests on the two positive conceptions: of Human Order individual or collective, on the one hand; and of the Universal Order of nature controlling it, on the other. This was the foundation of every truly religious doctrine under the incoherent fictions natural to the societies of the long infancy of man. Even before civilisation had existed long enough to call out a real need for any organisation, every Family and every City from its origin felt the pressure of two insurmountable forces, the one artificial, the other natural. On every side Man was forced to recognise the continual influence over him of the external order of Nature; and beside this, each generation experiences the irresistible pressure upon its life of the whole of the preceding generations. The influence of the Past indeed is commonly perceived even sooner than the influence of Nature. A doctrine which aims at affecting human wills is bound to offer an explanation of this twofold Necessity; so that each adherent it acquires may learn therein his own relations to the Whole, which he unconsciously contributes to form or to maintain. A religion which does not do this, and to do it involves a simultaneous study of the World and of Man, will never receive that free acceptance which is indispensable for its effect over society.

But when this task is fulfilled, as far as the civilisation then current permits, a Priesthood necessarily obtains a Spiritual authority; and this becomes the natural base of its threefold function, as we described it in the preceding chapter. What it has then to do, is only to arrange and teach this fundamental doctrine, whereby it acquires its hold over society, so long as its conduct is worthy of its great mission. Such an intellectual vantage ground enables a true Priesthood, even when represented by a single capable head, within its own province to overcome the most powerful material force, whether of riches or of numbers. In fact it will thus call out, as I shall presently show, those moral and mental influences which the preceding chapter showed to be necessary to form and maintain these material forces.

This principle shows us, that for the religious organisation of every human society, there are two conditions requisite, which must be properly combined in durable union. In the first place the Priesthood must sufficiently comprehend the laws both of Material Order and Social Order; and consequently of the Vital Order which forms the link between them. On the other hand, it must gain the requisite acceptance of this synthetic conception; so as to satisfy the universal craving for instruction and direction, which forms its influence upon society. This implies that it should present a Philosophy, higher than the untutored suggestions of general opinion; and secondly, a system of general Education to infuse the views of the Priesthood into the public mind. Thus every Priesthood, after forming the best theory it can of the universal Order of Nature, is brought face to face with the standing problem of Social Order; which, apart from its greater difficulty and its superior importance, is directly concerned with the chief sacerdotal function. So long as this sphere of Social Order remains to it, it still retains, though with serious loss, a real influence over society; even when it has given up, one by one, its other intellectual claims. In the Middle Age we saw Catholicism in this position. But when any Priesthood abandons the social and proper field of its labours, it speedily loses its credit in the State, and next its power within the Home; for it is proved at length to be incompetent to fulfil its proper offices: to *counsel*, to *consecrate*, and to *control*; and thereby to *classify*, and finally to *judge*. Thus the final blow was inevitably given to Theology, retrograde as it had been since the end of the Middle Age, when the establishment of my system of Sociology cut from under it its old title to teach Morality and direct Society, a title which my great predecessor, Descartes, was willing that it should retain. Neither in the Family nor in the City can men choose freely as guides of their conduct in actual life priests who are without any sort of knowledge of the laws which regulate the facts of human existence. Public confidence, the only real basis of a Spiritual Power, will naturally be accorded to any Priesthood which can show that it has this knowledge of social laws; always provided that its own moral position is equal to its claims. Hence we shall soon see the inevitable triumph of Positivism over Catholicism throughout the West and all its associated communities.

This, the Positive organisation of Social Existence, based on the fundamental theory of the Order of Nature, may be first regarded from the point of view of human society as a whole, and may then be illustrated by special explanation of the main elements of that society.

Each City, in its entirety, presents us with a continuous cooperation of three kinds of social function, answering to the three elements of man's cerebral system. The same are perceptible also in the Families which form the units of each City; only in domestic existence, these functions are represented not by classes, but by individuals. In the City they are more marked and more easily analysed, as soon as the classes are sufficiently separated; and they may be traced by sound philosophy in very early societies. The theory of Social Existence is thus the same as that of the last chapter as to the Structure of the Social Organism, that is to say, the coordinate action of three natural Powers: special organs, personal or collective, of the Intellect, the Feeling, and the Activity. In the smallest cities capable of separate existence, we find these three classes: the Priests who guide our speculations, the Women who inspire our highest affections, and the practical Leaders who direct our activity, be it in war or in industry. Here the Priesthood comes in the first rank, because it is a question of political, not of domestic existence; with an ultimate view to social organisation, which is always an intellectual function. But, as shown in my General View, such is not the ultimate order which the Positive Religion assigns to these three classes; for then the Heart must be publicly recognised as superior to the Intelligence, according to the principles of man's unity. When I explain in the fourth volume this, the true order of rank, I hope that all will see the social necessity for placing the moral providence of Humanity, the special part of Women, above the intellectual providence, the allotted function of the Priesthood. Both take precedence, according to cerebral order, of the material providence of the temporal Chiefs; though the latter takes precedence in the corporal order, the sole direct link between the order of Man and the order of the World. Thus the noble ideal of our pious and chivalrous ancestors in the Middle Age finds its support in philosophy, in spite of the sophistical attacks of modern criticism.

But this first general view of Social Existence requires as a supplement a further step. The three Providences of human society, moral, intellectual, and material, present, by virtue of the very peculiarity of their natures, some serious inconveniences; and these would disturb the general harmony, unless something arose to temper them all. Thus women are ever ready to exaggerate the influence of Feeling; undervaluing that of Reason, and even that of Activity. In like manner the contemplative class, whose task it is to insist everywhere on generality of ideas, has a tendency to over-estimate Theoretic conditions, to the neglect of Practical necessities and the wants of the Affections. The danger is increased when the separation between the Priesthood and the Government is effected, essential though this separation be to the true influence of a Spiritual Power. It would be unnecessary to insist on similar abuses even more common in the Practical authority, since it is these which mainly require a special Priesthood to restrain them. Thus each of the providences which direct this world, whilst duly fulfilling its own function, has a tendency to overlook the other two kinds of human wants.

It is true that the three mutually counterbalance each other, and do something to restrain their respective defects. But this would not be enough to prevent or to subdue violent conflicts between them, were it not that the Social Existence of itself called out a new order of providence, in direct connection with each of the three principal ones, and well fitted to preserve the harmony that should reign between them all. This is found in the mass of the People; for they are united to the affectionate sex by domestic ties, to the Priesthood through the medium of the education and advice which it gives them, and to the practical leaders through common action and the protection afforded them. So long as national action remained in the warlike stage, the consequent slavery of the material workmen limited the people, properly so-called, to the body of free citizens. Yet even then this fourth social providence already began its proper task by leading the other three from too engrossing attention to their special parts. The name which modern civilisation seems inclined to adopt to designate this last element of the City, is drawn indeed from the language of antiquity. But the complete abolition of personal slavery was evidently needed that the Proletariat, the element in question, should become really free to play its part. The fourth volume treating of the final order of Humanity will show the great part sustained by this general Providence, which is so well adapted to remedy the defects inherent in the three special Providences. The third volume will trace the history in the past of the rise of the industrial proletariat, and thus explain the features of its normal condition.

We have thus obtained by analysis the four elements always present in civil existence. But this division strictly holds good only for the society of coexisting families: that is to say, for the Present, united by mere objective Solidarity. Now this is in no way a sufficient or ultimate analysis of human association, the grand feature of which it does not take into account. Societies in the other animal races exhibit, at any rate in a rudimentary form, similar characteristics, in every case ending in cooperation between the members. The special mark of the societies of man is that they alone possess the faculty of cooperation between generations; and this is a power which cannot long be possessed by more than one of the races upon earth. The great principle of Aristotle in its full comprehensiveness always implies a combination continuous in time, as well as a combination effective in space. Thus understood, this luminous conception may really serve as the single basis of Social Statics, and explain Existence no less than Organisation. Positivism gives this principle systematic completeness; and in obedience to it places objective Solidarity second to subjective Continuity. It is the latter which it takes as the dominant character of the human City.

PIERRE-JOSEPH PROUDHON
(1809–1865)

Anarchism and Order

Proudhon was a cooper's son who quit school to earn his living as a compositor and proof-reader. Assisted in further study by a stipend from the Besançon Academy, he created a sensation with his *What is Property?* (1840), where he defined property as theft. In opposition to the communists, he believed that a just, free, egalitarian, and peaceful society could be organized around free credit and equitable exchange without the intervention of state power. As a deputy to the National Assembly during the Revolution of 1848, he tried unsuccessfully to initiate a "people's bank." For Proudhon, anarchism and order were thoroughly compatible. His ardent espousal of radical economic reforms in the journals he edited led to his imprisonment in 1849. After his release he lived rather circumspectly, until a work expressing his distrust of government and religious institutions (1858) brought him under the suspicion of Napoleon III's police. To escape prosecution he fled to Brussels, returning in ill health some years later to die at Passy. His writings had a lasting influence on the French syndicalist movement.

Proudhon and his children, painted by Gustave Courbet in 1865–67 from earlier sketches. (Paris, Petit Palais.)

What is Property?*

If I were asked to answer the following question: *What is slavery?* and I should answer in one word, *It is murder*, my meaning would be understood at once. No extended argument would be required to show that the power to take from a man his thought, his will, his personality, is a power of life and death; and that to enslave a man is to kill him. Why, then, to this other question: *What is property?* may I not likewise answer, *It is robbery*, without the certainty of being misunderstood; the second proposition being no other than a transformation of the first?

I undertake to discuss the vital principle of our government and our institutions, property: I am in my right. I may be mistaken in the conclusion which shall result from my investigations: I am in my right. I think best to place the last thought of my book first: still am I in my right.

Such an author teaches that property is a civil right, born of occupation and sanctioned by law; another maintains that it is a natural right, originating in labor,—and both of these doctrines, totally opposed as they may seem, are encouraged and applauded. I contend that neither labor, nor occupation, nor law, can create property; that it is an effect without a cause: am I censurable?

But murmurs arise!

Property is robbery! That is the war-cry of '93! That is the signal of revolutions!

Reader, calm yourself: I am no agent of discord, no firebrand of sedition. I anticipate history by a few days; I disclose a truth whose development we may try in vain to arrest; I write the preamble of our future constitution. This proposition which seems to you blasphemous—*property is robbery*— would, if our prejudices allowed us to consider it, be recognized as the light-ning-rod to shield us from the coming thunderbolt; but too many interests stand in the way! . . . Alas! philosophy will not change the course of events: destiny will fulfill itself regardless of prophecy. Besides, must not justice be done and our education be finished?

*From Pierre-Joseph Proudhon, *What is Property?*, trans. Benjamin R. Tucker from *Qu'est-ce que la propriété* (New York: Humboldt Publishing Company, 189–), pp. 11–13, 259–62.

Property is robbery! . . . What a revolution in human ideas! *Proprietor* and *robber* have been at all times expressions as contradictory as the beings whom they designate are hostile; all languages have perpetuated this opposition. On what authority, then, do you venture to attack universal consent, and give the lie to the human race? Who are you, that you should question the judgment of the nations and the ages?

Of what consequence to you, reader, is my obscure individuality? I live, like you, in a century in which reason submits only to fact and to evidence. My name, like yours, is TRUTHSEEKER.[1] My mission is written in these words of the law: *Speak without hatred and without fear; tell that which thou knowest!* The work of our race is to build the temple of science, and this science includes man and Nature. Now, truth reveals itself to all; to-day to Newton and Pascal, to-morrow to the herdsman in the valley and the journeyman in the shop. Each one contributes his stone to the edifice; and, his task accomplished, disappears. Eternity precedes us, eternity follows us: between two infinites, of what account is one poor mortal that the century should inquire about him?

Disregard then, reader, my title and my character, and attend only to my arguments. It is in accordance with universal consent that I undertake to correct universal error; from the *opinion* of the human race I appeal to its *faith.* Have the courage to follow me; and, if your will is untrammelled, if your conscience is free, if your mind can unite two propositions and deduce a third therefrom, my ideas will inevitably become yours. In beginning by giving you my last word, it was my purpose to warn you, not to defy you; for I am certain that, if you read me, you will be compelled to assent. The things of which I am to speak are so simple and clear that you will be astonished at not having perceived them before, and you will say: "I have neglected to think." Others offer you the spectacle of genius wresting Nature's secrets from her, and unfolding before you her sublime messages; you will find here only a series of experiments upon *justice* and *right,* a sort of verification of the weights and measures of your conscience. The operations shall be conducted under your very eyes; and you shall weigh the result.

*　　*　　*

I ought not to conceal the fact that property and communism have been considered always the only possible forms of society. This deplorable error has been the life of property. The disadvantages of communism are so obvious that its critics never have needed to employ much eloquence to thoroughly disgust men with it. The irreparability of the injustice which it

---

1. In Greek, σκεπτικός, examiner; a philosopher whose business is to seek the truth.

causes, the violence which it does to attractions and repulsions, the yoke of iron which it fastens upon the will, the moral torture to which it subjects the conscience, the debilitating effect which it has upon society; and, to sum it all up, the pious and stupid uniformity which it enforces upon the free, active, reasoning, unsubmissive personality of man, have shocked common sense, and condemned communism by an irrevocable decree.

The authorities and examples cited in its favor disprove it. The communistic republic of Plato involved slavery; that of Lycurgus employed Helots, whose duty it was to produce for their masters, thus enabling the latter to devote themselves exclusively to athletic sports and to war. Even J. J. Rousseau—confounding communism and equality—has said somewhere that, without slavery, he did not think equality of conditions possible. The communities of the early Church did not last the first century out, and soon degenerated into monasteries. In those of the Jesuits of Paraguay, the condition of the blacks is said by all travellers to be as miserable as that of slaves; and it is a fact that the good Fathers were obliged to surround themselves with ditches and walls to prevent their new converts from escaping. The followers of Babeuf—guided by a lofty horror of property rather than by any definite belief—were ruined by exaggeration of their principles; the St. Simonians, lumping communism and inequality, passed away like a masquerade. The greatest danger to which society is exposed to-day is that of another shipwreck on this rock.

Singularly enough, systematic communism—the deliberate negation of property—is conceived under the direct influence of the proprietary prejudice; and property is the basis of all communistic theories.

The members of a community, it is true, have no private property; but the community is proprietor, and proprietor not only of the goods, but of the persons and wills. In consequence of this principle of absolute property, labor, which should be only a condition imposed upon man by Nature, becomes in all communities a human commandment, and therefore odious. Passive obedience, irreconcilable with a reflecting will, is strictly enforced. Fidelity to regulations, which are always defective, however wise they may be thought, allows of no complaint. Life, talent, and all the human faculties are the property of the State, which has the right to use them as it pleases for the common good. Private associations are sternly prohibited, in spite of the likes and dislikes of different natures, because to tolerate them would be to introduce small communities within the large one, and consequently private property; the strong work for the weak, although this ought to be left to benevolence, and not enforced, advised, or enjoined; the industrious work for the lazy, although this is unjust; the clever work for the foolish, although this is absurd; and, finally, man—casting aside his personality, his spontaneity, his genius, and his affections—humbly annihilates himself at the feet of the majestic and inflexible Commune!

Communism is inequality, but not as property is. Property is the exploitation of the weak by the strong. Communism is the exploitation of the strong by the weak. In property, inequality of conditions is the result of force, under whatever name it be disguised: physical and mental force; force of events, chance, *fortune;* force of accumulated property, etc. In communism, inequality springs from placing mediocrity on a level with excellence. This damaging equation is repellent to the conscience, and causes merit to complain; for, although it may be the duty of the strong to aid the weak, they prefer to do it out of generosity,—they never will endure a comparison. Give them equal opportunities of labor, and equal wages, but never allow their jealousy to be awakened by mutual suspicion of unfaithfulness in the performance of the common task.

Communism is oppression and slavery. Man is very willing to obey the law of duty, serve his country, and oblige his friends; but he wishes to labor when he pleases, where he pleases, and as much as he pleases. He wishes to dispose of his own time, to be governed only by necessity, to choose his friendships, his recreation, and his discipline; to act from judgment, not by command; to sacrifice himself through selfishness, not through servile obligation. Communism is essentially opposed to the free exercise of our faculties, to our noblest desires, to our deepest feelings. Any plan which could be devised for reconciling it with the demands of the individual reason and will would end only in changing the thing while preserving the name. Now, if we are honest truth-seekers, we shall avoid disputes about words.

Thus, communism violates the sovereignty of the conscience, and equality: the first, by restricting spontaneity of mind and heart, and freedom of thought and action; the second, by placing labor and laziness, skill and stupidity, and even vice and virtue on an equality in point of comfort. For the rest, if property is impossible on account of the desire to accumulate, communism would soon become so through the desire to shirk.

Society without Authority[*]

GIVEN:

Man, *The Family*, SOCIETY.

An individual, sexual and social being, endowed with reason, love and conscience, capable of learning by experience, of perfecting himself by reflection, and of earning his living by work.

The problem is to so organize the powers of this being, that he may remain always at peace with himself, and may extract from Nature, which is given to him, the largest possible amount of well-being.

We know how previous generations have solved it.

They borrowed from the Family, the second component part of Humanity, the principle which is proper to it alone, AUTHORITY, and by the arbitrary use of this principle, they constructed an artificial system, varied according to periods and climates, which has been regarded as the natural order and necessary for humanity.

This system, which may be called the system of order by authority, was at first divided into spiritual and temporal authority.

After a short period in which it preponderated, and long centuries of struggle to maintain its supremacy, sacerdotalism seems at last to have given up its claim to temporal power: the Papacy, with all its soldiery, which the Jesuits and lay brothers of to-day would restore, has been cast out and set below matters of merely human interest.

For two years past the spiritual power has been in a way to again seize supremacy. It has formed a coalition with the secular power against the Revolution, and bargains with it upon a footing of equality. Both have ended by recognizing that their differences arose from a misunderstanding; that their aim, their principles, their methods, their dogmas, being absolutely identical, Government should be shared by them; or rather, that they should consider themselves the complements of each other, and should form by their union a one and indivisible Authority.

Such at least would have been the conclusion which Church and State would have perhaps reached, if the laws of the progress of Humanity rendered such reconciliations possible; if the Revolution had not already marked their last hour.

*From Pierre-Joseph Proudhon, *General Idea of the Revolution in the Nineteenth Century* (1851), trans. John Beverley Robinson (London: Freedom Press, 1923), pp. 240–7, 280–7, 289–92.

However that may be, it is desirable, in order to convince the mind, to set alongside each other the fundamental ideas of, on the one hand, the politico-religious system (Philosophy, which has for so long drawn a line between the spiritual and the temporal, should no longer recognize any distinction between them); on the other hand, the economic system.

Government then, that is to say, Church and State indivisibly united, has for its dogmas:

1. The original perversity of human nature;
2. The inevitable inequality of fortunes;
3. The permanency of quarrels and wars;
4. The irremediability of poverty.

Whence is deduced:

5. The necessity of government, of obedience, of resignation, and of faith.

These principles admitted, as they still are, almost universally, the forms of authority are already settled. They are:

a. The division of the people into classes or castes, subordinate to one another; graduated to form a pyramid, at the top of which appears, like the Divinity upon his altar, like the king upon his throne, AUTHORITY;

b. Administrative centralization;
c. Judicial hierarchy;
d. Police;
e. Worship.

Add to the above, in countries in which the democratic principle has become preponderant:

f. The separation of powers;

g. The intervention of the People in the Government, by vote for representatives;

h. The innumerable varieties of electoral systems, from the Convocation by Estates, which prevailed in the Middle Ages, down to universal and direct suffrage;

i. The duality of legislative chambers;

j. Voting upon laws, and consent to taxes by the representatives of the nation;

k. The rule of majorities.

Such is broadly the plan of construction of Power, independently of the modifications which each of its component party may receive; as, for example, the central Power, which may be in turn monarchical, aristocratic or democratic; which once furnished publicists with a ground for classification, according to superficial character.

It will be observed that the governmental system tends to become more and more complicated, without becoming on that account more efficient or more moral, and without offering any more guaranties to person or property. This complication springs first from legislation, which is always incomplete and insufficient; in the second place, from the multiplicity of functionaries; but most of all, from the compromise between the two antagonistic elements, the executive initiative and popular consent. It has been left for our epoch to establish unmistakeably that this bargaining, which the progress of centuries renders inevitable, is the surest index of corruption, of decadence and of the approaching dissolution of Authority.

What is the aim of this organization?

To maintain *order* in society, by consecrating and sanctifying obedience of the citizen to the State, subordination of the poor to the rich, of the common people to the upper class, of the worker to the idler, of the layman to the priest, of the business man to the soldier.

As far back as the memory of humanity extends, it is found to have been organized on the above system, which constitutes the political, ecclesiastical or governmental order. Every effort to give Power a more liberal appearance, more tolerant, more social, has invariably failed: such efforts have been even more fruitless when they tried to give the People a larger share in Government; as if the words, Sovereignty and People, which they endeavored to yoke together, were as naturally antagonistic as these other two words, Liberty and Despotism.

Humanity has had to live, and civilization to develop, for six thousand years, under this inexorable system, of which the first term is *Despair* and the last *Death*. What secret power has sustained it? What force has enabled it to survive? What principles, what ideas, renewed the blood that flowed forth under the poniard of authority, ecclesiastical and secular?

This mystery is now explained.

Beneath the governmental machinery, in the shadow of political institutions, out of the sight of statesmen and priests, society is producing its own organism, slowly and silently; and constructing a new order, the expression of its vitality and autonomy, and the denial of the old politics, as well as of the old religion.

This organization, which is as essential to society as it is incompatible with the present system, has the following principles:

1. The indefinite perfectibility of the individual and of the race;
2. The honorableness of work;
3. The equality of fortunes;

4. The identity of interests;

5. The end of antagonisms;

6. The universality of comfort;

7. The sovereignty of reason;

8. The absolute liberty of the man and of the citizen.

I mention below its principal forms of activity:

a. Division of labor, through which classification of the People by INDUSTRIES replaces classification by *caste;*

b. Collective power, the principle of WORKMEN'S ASSOCIATIONS, in place of *armies;*

c. Commerce, the concrete form of CONTRACT, which takes the place of *Law;*

d. Equality in exchange;

e. Competition;

f. Credit, which turns upon INTERESTS, as the governmental hierarchy turns upon *Obedience;*

g. The equilibrium of values and of properties.

The old system, standing on Authority and Faith, was essentially based upon *Divine Right.* The principle of the sovereignty of the People, introduced later, did not change its nature; and it is a mistake to-day, in the face of the conclusions of science, to maintain a distinction which does not touch underlying principles, between absolute monarchy and constitutional monarchy, or between the latter and the democratic republic. The sovereignty of the People has been, if I may say so, for a century past, but a skirmishing line for Liberty. It was either an error, or a clever scheme of our fathers to make the sovereign people in the image of the king-man: as the Revolution becomes better understood, this mythology vanishes, all traces of government disappear and follow the principle of government itself to dissolution.

The new system, based upon the spontaneous practice of industry, in accordance with individual and social reason, is the system of *Human Right.* Opposed to arbitrary command, essentially objective, it permits neither parties nor sects; it is complete in itself, and allows neither restriction nor separation.

There is no fusion possible between the political and economic systems, between the system of laws and the system of contracts; one or the other must be chosen. The ox, while it remain an ox, cannot be an eagle, nor can the bat be at the same time a snail. In the same way, while Society maintains in the slightest degree its political form, it cannot become organized according to economic law. How harmonize local initiative with the preponderance of a central authority, or universal suffrage with the hierarchy of officials; the principle that no one owes obedience to a law to which he has not himself consented, with the right of majorities?

If a writer who understood these contradictions should undertake to reconcile them, it would prove him, not a bold thinker, but a wretched charlatan.

This absolute incompatibility of the two systems, so often proved, still does not convince writers who, while admitting the dangers of authority, nevertheless hold to it, as the sole means of maintaining order, and see nothing beside it but empty desolation. Like the sick man in the comedy, who is told that the first thing he must do is to discharge his doctors, if he wants to get well, they persist in asking how can a man get along without a doctor, or a society without a government. They will make the government as republican, as benevolent, as equal as possible; they will set up all possible guaranties against it; they will belittle it, almost attack it, in support of the majesty of the citizens. They tell us: You are the government! You shall govern yourselves, without president, without representatives, without delegates. What have you then to complain about? But to live without government, to abolish all authority, absolutely and unreservedly, to set up pure *anarchy*, seems to them ridiculous and inconceivable, a plot against the Republic and against the nation. What will these people who talk of abolishing government put in place of it? they ask.

We have no trouble in answering.

It is industrial organization that we will put in place of government, as we have just shown.

In place of laws, we will put contracts.—No more laws voted by a majority, nor even unanimously; each citizen, each town, each industrial union, makes its own laws.

In place of political powers, we will put economic forces.

In place of the ancient classes of nobles, burghers, and peasants, or of business men and working men, we will put the general titles and special departments of industry: Agriculture, Manufacture, Commerce, etc.

In place of public force, we will put collective force.

In place of standing armies, we will put industrial associations.

In place of police, we will put identity of interests.

In place of political centralization, we will put economic centralization.

Do you see now how there can be order without functionaries, a profound and wholly intellectual unity?

You, who cannot conceive of unity without a whole apparatus of legislators, prosecutors, attorneys-general, custom house officers, policemen, you have never known what real unity is! What you call unity and centralization is nothing but perpetual chaos, serving as a basis for endless tyranny; it is the advancing of the chaotic condition of social forces as an argument for despotism—a despotism which is really the cause of the chaos.

Well, in our turn, let us ask, what need have we of government when we have made an agreement? Does not the National Bank, with its various branches, achieve centralization and unity? Does not the agreement among farm laborers for compensation, marketing, and reimbursement for farm properties create unity? From another point of view, do not the industrial associations for carrying on the large-scale industries bring about unity? And the constitution of value, that contract of contracts, as we have called it, is not that the most perfect and indissoluble unity?

And if we must show you an example in our own history in order to convince you, does not that fairest monument of the Convention, the system of weights and measures, form, for fifty years past, the cornerstone of that economic unity which is destined to replace political unity?

Never ask again then what we will put in place of government, nor what will become of society without government, for I assure you that in the future it will be easier to conceive of society without government, than of society with government.

Society, just now, is like the butterfly just out of the cocoon, which shakes its gilded wings in the sunlight before taking flight. Tell it to crawl back into the silken covering, to shun the flowers and to hide itself from the light!

But a revolution is not made with formulas. Prejudice must be attacked at the foundation, overthrown, hurled into dust, its injurious effects explained, its ridiculous and odious nature shown forth. Mankind believes only in its own tests, happy if these tests do not addle its brains and drain its blood. Let us try then by clear criticism to make the test of government so conclusive, that the absurdity of the institution will strike all minds, and Anarchy, dreaded as a scourge, will be accepted as a benefit. . . .

He that is guilty of one is guilty of all, says the Gospel. If the Revolution allows any portion of government to remain, it will soon return in its entirety. But how can we dispense with government in dealing with foreign affairs?

A nation is a collective being which continually deals with other collective beings like itself; which therefore must establish an organ, a representative, in short, a government, for its international relations. Here at least, then, is not the Revolution about to be false to its own principle; and to justify its lapse by quoting the stupid pretence that *the exception proves the rule?* That would be deplorable, and moreover is inadmissible. If the government is indispensable for diplomacy, it is as much so for war and for the navy; and, as all is comprised in power and society, we should soon see governmentalism reestablish itself in the police, then in the administration, then in the judiciary, and then where would the Revolution be?

This dwelling upon foreign politics is what best shows how weak is still the conception of the Revolution among us. It shows a prejudiced fidelity to the traditions of despotism, and a dangerous leaning toward counter-revolution in European democracy, unceasingly busy in maintaining the balance of power among the nations.

Let us try, in this as in other matters, to reconstruct our ideas, and to free ourselves from habit.

After the Revolution has been accomplished at home will it also be accomplished abroad?

Who can doubt it? The Revolution would be vain if it were not contagious: it would perish, even in France, if it failed to become universal. Everybody is convinced of that. The least enthusiastic spirits do not believe it necessary for revolutionary France to interfere among other nations by force of arms: it will be enough for her to support, by her example and her encouragement, any effort of the people of foreign nations to follow her example.

What then is the Revolution, completed abroad as well as at home?

Capitalistic and proprietary exploitation stopped everywhere, the wage system abolished, equal and just exchange guaranteed, value constituted, cheapness assured, the principle of protection changed, and the markets of the world opened to the producers of all nations; consequently the barriers struck down, the ancient law of nations replaced by commercial agreements; police, judiciary, administration, everywhere committed to the hands of the workers; the economic organization replacing the governmental and military system in the colonies as well as in the great cities; finally, the free and universal commingling of races under the law of contract only: that is the Revolution.

Is it possible that in this state of affairs, in which all interests, agricultural, financial and industrial, are identical and interwoven, in which the governmental protectorate has nothing to do, either at home or abroad, is it possible that the nations will continue to form distinct political bodies, that they will hold themselves separate, when their producers and consumers are mingled; that they will still maintain diplomacy, to settle claims, to determine prerogatives, to arrange differences, to exchange guaranties, to sign treaties, etc., without any object?

To ask such a question is to answer it. It needs no demonstration; only some explanations from the point of view of nationalities.

Let us recall the principle. The reason for the institution of government, as we have said, is the economic chaos. When the Revolution has regulated this chaos, and organized the industrial forces, there is no further pretext for political centralization; it is absorbed in industrial solidarity, a solidarity which is based upon general reason, and of which we may say, as Pascal said of the universe, that *its centre is everywhere, its circumference nowhere.*

When the institution of government has been abolished, and replaced by the economic organization, the problem of the universal Revolution is solved. The dream of Napoleon is realized, and the chimera of the Dean of St. Peter's becomes a necessity.

It is the governments who, pretending to establish order among men, arrange them forthwith in hostile camps, and as their only occupation is to produce servitude at home, their art lies in maintaining war abroad, war in fact or war in prospect.

The oppression of peoples and their mutual hatred are two correlative, inseparable facts, which reproduce each other, and which cannot come to an end except simultaneously, by the destruction of their common cause, government.

This is why nations will inevitably remain at war, as long as they remain under the rule of kings, tribunes, or dictators; as long as they obey a visible authority, established in their midst, from which emanate the laws which govern them: no Holy Alliance, Democratic Congress, Amphictyonic Council, nor Central European Committee can help the matter. Great bodies of men thus constituted are necessarily opposed in interests; as they cannot merge, they cannot recognize justice: by war or by diplomacy, not less deadly than war, they must quarrel and fight.

Nationality, aroused by the State, opposes an invincible resistance to economic unity: this explains why monarchy was never able to become universal. Universal monarchy is, in politics, what squaring the circle or perpetual motion are in mathematics, a contradiction. A nation can put up with a government as long as its economic forces are unorganized, and as long as the government is its own, the nationalism of the power causing an illusion as to the validity of the principle; the government maintains itself through an interminable succession of monarchies, aristocracies, and democracies. But if the Power is external, the nation feels it as an insult: revolt is in every heart, it cannot last.

What no monarchy, not even that of the Roman emperors, has been able to accomplish; what Christianity, that epitome of the ancient faiths, has been unable to produce, the universal Republic, the economic Revolution, will accomplish, cannot fail to accomplish.

It is indeed with political economy as with other sciences: it is inevitably the same throughout the world: it does not depend upon the fancies of men or nations: it yields to the caprice of none. There is not a Russian, English, Austrian, Tartar, or Hindoo political economy, any more than there is a Hungarian, German or American physics or geometry. Truth alone is equal everywhere: science is the unity of mankind.

If then science, and no longer religion or authority, is taken in every land as the rule of society, the sovereign arbiter of interests, government becoming void, all the legislation of the universe will be in harmony. There will no longer be nationality, no longer fatherland, in the political sense of the words: they will mean only places of birth. Man, of whatever race or color he may be, is an inhabitant of the universe; citizenship is everywhere an acquired right. As in a limited territory the municipality represents the Republic, and wields its authority, each nation on the globe represents humanity, and acts for it within the boundaries assigned by Nature. Harmony reigns, without diplomacy and without council, among the nations: nothing henceforward can disturb it.

What purpose could there be for entering into diplomatic relations among nations who had adopted the revolutionary programme:

No more governments,

No more conquests,

No more custom houses,

No more international police,

No more commercial privileges,

No more colonial exclusions,

No more control of one people by another, one State by another,

No more strategic lines,

No more fortresses?

Russia wants to establish herself at Constantinople, as she is established at Warsaw; that is to say, she wants to include the Bosphorus and the Caucasus in her sphere. In the first place, the Revolution will not permit it; and to make sure, it will begin by revolutionizing Poland, Turkey, and all that it can of Russian provinces, until it reaches St. Petersburg. That done, what becomes of the Russian relations at Constantinople and at Warsaw? They will be the same as at Berlin and Paris, relations of free and equal exchange. What becomes of Russia itself? It becomes an agglomeration of free and independent nationalities, united only by identity of language, resemblance of occupations, and territorial conditions. Under such conditions conquest is meaningless. If Constantinople belonged to Russia, once Russia was revolutionized Constantinople would belong to it neither more nor less than if it had never lost its sovereignty. The Eastern question from the North ceases to exist.

England wants to hold Egypt as she holds Malta, Corfu, Gibraltar, etc. The same answer from the Revolution. It notifies England to refrain from any attempt upon Egypt, to place a limit upon her encroachments and monopoly; and, to make sure, it invites her to evacuate the islands and fortresses whence she threatens the liberty of the nations and of the seas. It would be truly a strange misconception of the nature and scope of the Revolution to imagine that it would leave Australia and India the exclusive property of England, as well as the bastions with which she hems in the commerce of the continent. The mere presence of the English in Jersey and Guernsey is an insult to France; as their exploitation of Ireland and Portugal is an insult to Europe; as their possession of India and their commerce with China is an outrage upon humanity. Albion, like the rest of the world, must be revolutionized. If necessary to force her, there are people here who would not find it so hard a task. The Revolution completed at London, British privilege extirpated, burnt, thrown to the winds, what would the possession of Egypt mean to England? No more than that of Algiers is to us. All the world could enter, depart, trade at will, arrange for the working of the agricultural, mineral and industrial resources: the advantages would be the same for all nations. The local power would extend only to the cost of its police, which the colonists and natives would defray.

There are still among us *chauvinists* who maintain absolutely that France must recapture her *natural* frontiers. They ask too much or too little. France is everywhere that her language is spoken, her Revolution followed, her manners, her arts, her literature adopted, as well as her measures and her money. Counting thus, almost the whole of Belgium, and cantons of Neufchatel, Vaud, Geneva, Savoy, and a part of Piedmont belong to her; but she must lose Alsace, perhaps even a part of Provence, Gascony and Brittany, whose inhabitants do not speak French, and some of them have always been of the kings' and priests' party against the Revolution. But of what use are these repetitions? It was the mania for annexations which, under the Convention and the Directory, aroused the distrust of other nations against the Republic, and which, giving us a taste for Bonaparte, brought us to our finish at Waterloo. Revolutionize, I tell you. Your frontiers will always be long enough and French enough if they are revolutionary.

Will Germany be an Empire, a unitary Republic, or a Confederation? This famous problem of Germanic unity, which made so much noise some years ago, has no meaning in the face of the Revolution; which proves indeed that there has never been a Revolution. What are the States, in Germany as elsewhere? Tyrannies of different degrees of importance, based on the invariable pretexts, first, of protecting the nobility and upper class against the lower classes; second, of maintaining the independence of local sovereignty. Against these States the German democracy has always been powerless, and why? Because it moved in the sphere of political rights. Organize the economic forces of Germany, and immediately political circles, electorates, principalities, kingdoms, empires, all are effaced, even the Tariff League: German unity springs out of the abolition of its States. What the ancient Germany needs is not a confederation but a liquidation.

Understand once for all: the most characteristic, the most decisive result of the Revolution is, after having organized labor and property, to do away with political centralization, in a word, with the State, and as a consequence to put an end to diplomatic relations among nations, as soon as they subscribe to the revolutionary compact. Any return to the traditions of politics, any anxiety as to the balance of power in Europe, based on the pretext of nationality and of the independence of States, any proposition to form alliances, to recognize sovereignties, to restore provinces, to change frontiers, would betray, in the organs of the movement, the most complete failure to understand the needs of the age, scorn of social reform, and a predilection for counter-revolution.

The kings may sharpen their swords for their last campaign. The Revolution in the Nineteenth Century has for its supreme task, not so much the overthrow of their dynasties, as the destruction to the last root of their institution. Born as they are to war, educated for war, supported by war, domestic and foreign, of what use can they be in a society of labor and peace? Henceforth there can be no more purpose in war than in refusal to disarm. Universal brotherhood being established upon a sure foundation, there is nothing for the representatives of despotism to do but to take their leave. How is it that they do not see that this always increasing difficulty of existence, which they have experienced since Waterloo, arises, not as they have been made to think, from the Jacobin ideas, which since the fall of Napoleon have again begun to beset the middle classes, but from a subterranean working which has gone on throughout Europe, unknown to statesmen, and which, while developing beyond measure the latent forces of civilization, has made the organization of those forces a social necessity, an inevitable need of revolution?

As for those who, after the departure of kings, still dream of consulates, of presidencies, of dictatorships, of marshalships, of admiralties and of ambassa-dorships, they also will do well to retire. The Revolution, having no need for their services, can dispense with their talents. The people no longer want this coin of monarchy: they understand that, whatever phraseology is used, feudal system, governmental system, military system, parliamentary system, system of police, laws and tribunals, and system of exploitation, corruption, lying and poverty, are all synonymous. Finally they know that in doing away with rent and interest, the last remants of the old slavery, the Revolution, at one blow, does away with the sword of the executioner, the blade of justice, the club of the policeman, the gauge of the customs officer, the erasing knife of the bureaucrat, all those insignia of government which young Liberty grinds beneath her heel. . . .

Humanity, in the theologico-political sphere, wherein it has been tossed these six thousand years, is like a society which, instead of being placed on the outside of a solid planet, is shut up inside a hollow one, lighted and warmed by a stationary sun in the centre, and apparently in the zenith for the countries curving around it, like the subterranean world of Virgil. Who knows whether there is not such an arrangement in the infinite variety of worlds? The rings of Saturn are not less extraordinary.

Imagine such a world, wherein all positions are the inverse of our own. Distance would prevent the inhabitants from seeing the boundaries of their situation, while barbarism, war, and lack of means of communication would keep them within their respective limits. For a long time they would imagine that the space above, beyond the sun, was the abode of gods, and that the ground under their feet covered the home of the damned far away. What tales the imagination of their poets would hang upon this! What cosmogonies, what revelations their mystagogues would bring forth, founding upon them religion, morality, and laws.

Nevertheless the progress of civilization, even of conquest, would bring great disturbances to these infernal regions, voyages of circumnavigation would be made: the earth would be traversed in every direction, and mathe-matical and experimental certainty would be reached that this splendid universe, to which the imagination could assign no limits, was only a hollow globe, several thousand miles in diameter inside; wherein the inhabitants, regarding themselves as perpendiculars at every point of the surface toward the centre, must really stand head to head. These strange news must have created a terrible scandal among the doctors of the ancient religions. Doubtless some Galileo paid with his blood for the glory of having discovered that the world was round, and that there were anticephales.

But what occurred to redouble the anxiety was that, at the same time that ancient beliefs were falling away, it was noticed that the habitable space was not proportionate to the activity and fecundity of the race which was therein imprisoned; the world is too small for the humanity which works it; air is lacking, and after some generations, we shall die of hunger!

Then these men who at first had regarded their orb as infinite, and had sung its praises, now found themselves imprisoned like a nest of beetles in a clod of earth; and began to blaspheme God and Nature. They accused the Sovereign Creator of having deceived them; the despair and confusion was frightful. The bolder swore, with terrible imprecations, that they would not stay there. Threatening heaven with eye and fist, they began audaciously to bore into the ground, so well that one day the drill encountering only emptiness they concluded that the concave surface of their sphere corresponded to an external convex surface of an outer world, which they set about visiting.

From the point of view of our political and religious ideas, with which our intelligence is hemmed in as by an impenetrable sphere, we are in exactly the same position as these men, and we have reached the same result.

From the origin of societies, the spirit of man, confined and enveloped by the theologico-political system, shut up in a hermetically closed box, of which Government is the bottom and Religion the top, has taken the limits of this narrow horizon for the limits of a rational society. God and King, Church and State, twisted in every way, worked over to infinity, have been his Universe. For a long time he has known nothing, imagined nothing beyond. At last, the circle has been traversed; the excitement of the systems suggested by this has exhausted him; philosophy, history, political economy, have completed the triangulation of this inner world; the map of it has been drawn; and it is known that the supernatural scheme which humanity contemplates as its horizon, and its limit, is but itself; that, far as humanity may look into the depths of its consciousness, it sees but itself; that this God, source of all power, origin of all causality, of which humanity makes its sun, is a lamp in a cavern, and all these governments made in his image are but grains of sand that reflect the faint light.

These religions, these legislations, these empires, these Governments, this wisdom of State, this virtue of Pontiffs, all are but a dream and a lie, which all hang upon one another and converge toward a central point, which itself has no reality. If we want to get a more correct idea of things, we must burst this crust and get out of this inferno, in which man's reason will be lost, and he will become an idiot.

To-day we have become aware of this. The old world of thought, which for so many centuries has absorbed human speculation, is but one side of that given us to traverse. The drill of philosophy has pierced it here and there; soon we shall be free and clear of our embryonic shell. We are about to gaze on new skies, to see face to face and in its essence, the infinite, *Sicuti est facie ad faciem.*

When society has turned from within to without, all relations are over-turned. Yesterday we were walking with our heads downwards: to-day we hold them erect, without any interruption to our life. Without losing our personality, we change our existence. Such is the nineteenth century Revolution.

The fundamental, decisive idea of this Revolution is it not this: NO MORE AUTHORITY, neither in the Church, nor in the State, nor in land, nor in money?

No more Authority! That means something we have never seen, something we have never understood; the harmony of the interest of one with the interest of all; the identity of collective sovereignty and individual sovereignty.

No more Authority! That means debts paid, servitude abolished, mortgages lifted, rents reimbursed, the expense of workship, justice, and the State suppressed; free credit, equal exchange, free association, regulated value, education, work, property, domicile, low price, guaranteed: no more antagonism, no more war, no more centralization, no more governments, no more priests. Is not that Society emerged from its shell and walking upright?

No more Authority! That is to say further: free contract in place of arbitrary law; voluntary transactions in place of the control of the State; equitable and reciprocal justice in place of sovereign and distributive justice; rational instead of revealed morals; equilibrium of forces instead of equilibrium of powers; economic unity in place of political centralization. Once more, I ask, is not this what I may venture to call a complete reversal, a turn-over, a Revolution?

JOSEPH ERNEST RENAN
(1823–1890)

The Higher Organisms of
the Centuries to Come[*]

Renan was one of France's greatest scholars and orientalists, with interests
that ranged widely from philosophy, linguistics, and religion to archae-
ology and the natural sciences. He took the tonsure in 1843 and was
ordained the next year; but after some tergiversation, he definitively left
the Catholic Church. Renan became a librarian, writer, traveler to the
Orient, and Professor of Hebrew at the Collège de France (1862), though
he was suspended until 1870 because of his unorthodox reference to Jesus
as an "incomparable man." In his youth Renan flirted with socialism, he
was briefly attracted by the Saint-Simonians and their gospel of love, and
under the Empire he made some ineffectual forays into politics. The debacle
of 1870 led him to speculate over the cause of the French military defeat
and to write his *Intellectual and Moral Reform*, where the influence of
German philosophy upon his thought is evident. In the philosophical
fragment that follows, Renan voiced his anxieties about the future of
science and humanity. His elitist doctrine seems to presage Nietzsche's
concept of the superman.

*From Joseph Ernest Renan, *Philosophical Dialogues and Fragments* (1871), trans. Râs Bihârî
Mukharjî (London: Trübner, 1883), pp. 62–74.

Ernest Renan photographed in his study. (From the *Revue Encyclopédique*, November 1, 1892.)

Dialogue on the Elite of Reason

THEOCTISTES.—Do not . . . push me too far, or else I will propound to you a hypothesis that will make my nightmare-dream a possibility. I have never said that the future would prove cheerful. Who knows but that truth is of a sad nature? Power has been hitherto maintained over mankind only by the care which those possessed of it have taken to keep the barbarous masses placed in their hands as blind tools of their purposes. The positivist tyrants that we have been speaking of would hardly hesitate to maintain, in some lost district of Asia, a nucleus of Bashkirs or Kalmuks, obedient machines, unencumbered by moral scruples and prepared for every sort of cruelty. Please to notice, besides, that I am now supposing an immense advancement of the human consciousness, a realisation of the true and of the just, of which we have not yet seen any instance. I am supposing (and I believe I am right in this) this step in advance accomplished, not by the whole race, but by an aristocracy placed at the head of humanity, and which will be the depository of the reason of the mass. It is clear that the absolute reign of one portion of humanity over another is odious, if we suppose the governing body to be swayed only by personal egoism or by class egoism; but the aristocracy of which I dream would be the incarnation of reason; this would be a papacy of real infallibility. Power, in its hands, could not but be beneficial, and there would be no need to haggle with such an aristocracy for it. This would be legitimate power *par excellence,* since it would enforce true opinions on the ground of real terrors. The Church and Bráhmanism were based upon an error. No Bráhman ever blighted any one with his curse; he therefore founded a false doctrine on an unfounded fear. But the being possessed of science would set up unlimited terror in the service of truth. Terrors, however, would soon become superfluous. The inferior portion of humanity, on such a supposition, would soon be checkmated by evidence, and the very idea of revolt would disappear.

Truth will one day be power. That "knowledge is power," is the noblest word that was ever spoken. The ignorant will see the effects and will believe; theory will be verified by its applications. A theory which shall lead to the invention of terrible engines, overpowering and subjugating all, will establish its truth by irrefragable evidence. The forces of humanity will thus be concentrated in a very small number of hands, and become the property of a league capable of regulating the life of the planet, and of, by that threat, terrifying the whole world. On the day when a few persons favoured of reason shall really possess the means of destroying the planet, their supremacy will be established; these privileged persons will rule by means of absolute terror, because they shall have in their hands the life of all; we may almost say that they will be gods, and that the theological epoch dreamt of by the poet for primitive humanity will then be a reality. *Primus in orbe deos fecit timor.*

Thus we may imagine a time when power will actually establish the reign of reason without the need of having recourse to imposture, which is only the weapon of the weak, and a substitute for power. The worship of reason will then be a truth; for, whoever shall offer any resistance to it, that is to say, shall not recognise the reign of science, will have to atone for his offence on the spot. What childish folly it was to celebrate the Feast of Reason when its army was composed of an unintelligent people, with exceedingly little reason and no constancy, and armed with pikes and bad muskets! When reason shall be all-powerful, she will indeed be a veritable goddess. Then it will no longer be necessary to speak of authority; that word has now no meaning, except to denote a force of opinion that is ineffective: it is a pure trick of language. Then the power of reason will be effective in the highest degree, since all disregard of that power will be punished with instant death. Preventive measures will be useless. This will be the realisation of what was formerly fabled as the vengeance of the gods; but the reality will be far superior to the myth, inasmuch as the vengeance of the gods was slow, uncertain, imperfect, and as we now know, devoid of truth; while, on the other hand, the sanctions of scientific law will be infallible, instantaneous, and, like Nature herself, without appeal.

EUDOXES.—Among a thousand objections that I might make to your views, I shall mention but one. You suppose an immense improvement in science, and you are right, but you say nothing of the condition of the thinking subject. Now, the advance in science and power that you have just delineated far exceeds the capability of any brain whatever. There is a contradiction between the conquests of reason that you imagine, and the intellectual and physical capacities, which always remain very limited.

THEOCTISTES.—I have told you that the class of ideas with which I am now dealing, refers but imperfectly to the planet earth, and that such speculations must be understood to aim at what transcends humanity. No doubt the knowing and thinking subject will be always limited, but knowledge and power are unlimited, and, consequently, the thinking nature itself will be capable of being greatly improved without quitting the known domain of biology. A broad application of the discoveries of physiology and of the principle of selection might lead to the creation of a superior race, deriving its right to rule not only from its science, but from the very superiority of its blood, its brain, and its nerves. Thus there might be a race of gods, or *devas*, beings of ten times greater worth than we are, and capable of subsisting in artificial *media*. Nature produces nothing but what is capable of living under general conditions; but science may extend the limits of viability. As yet Nature has produced only what she could; spontaneous forces will not pass beyond the low-water mark which they have reached. It is for science to take up the work where Nature has left it. Botany artificially maintains certain vegetable products, which would disappear unless the hand of man continually sustained them. It is possible to conceive a time when the production of a *deva* might be estimated at a definite capital, representing costly apparatus, slow processes, elaborate selections, a complicated education, and the laborious preservation of such a being in antagonism to Nature. A manu-factory of Ases, an *Asgaard*, may be re-established in the heart of Asia; and, if myths like these are repugnant to any one, let him note carefully the method that ants and bees employ to determine the functions to which each individual is to be devoted; let him reflect, especially, on the means employed by botanists when they create their artificial rarities. It is always the nutrition, or rather the development, of one organ by the atrophy of another which is the secret of these anomalies. Call to mind the *Vedic* doctor whose name, according to Burnouf, signified "he whose semen has gone to his head." As double flowers are obtained by the hypertrophy, or the transformation of the organs of generation, as florescence and fructification exhaust the vital powers of the being that performs these functions, so also it is possible that means may be found one day of concentrating in the brain the entire power of the nervous system, and of transmuting all nerve-energy into brain-energy, by atrophying, if we may say so, the opposite pole. One of these functions is an enfeeblement of the other; what is given to the one is taken away from the other. It is unnecessary to say that we are not speaking of those shameful suppressions that produce only imperfect beings. We are speaking of an inner transfusion by means of which the forces that Nature has directed towards various operations might be employed for one and the same object.

We may imagine, then (no doubt, beyond the limits of our planet), the possibility of beings who might be almost as superior to man as man is to the lower animals; a time when science would supersede existing animals by higher organisms, just as we see that by chemistry whole series of natural products have been supplanted by far more perfect ones. As humanity issued from animality, so from humanity would issue divinity. There might exist beings who would employ man as he now employs the lower animals. Man hardly pauses at the thought that a single step, a movement of his, crushes myriads of animalcules. But, I repeat, intellectual superiority carries with it religious superiority; these future masters we must conceive of as incarnations of the good and the true; there would be joy in being subject to them.

The principle most strongly denied by the democratic school is the inequality of races and the legitimacy of the rights derived from superiority of race. Far from seeking to exalt the race, democracy tends to lower it; she would have no great men; and if there were a democrat present, and he heard us dwelling on the improved means of creating masters for other men he would be a little surprised. It is absurd and unjust, in fact, to impose upon men, by a sort of divine right, masters who are in no respect superior to them. The aristocracy of the present day in France is insignificant enough, since the titles of nobility, of which three-fourths are usurped, and of which the remaining fourth, with hardly ten exceptions, is derived from royal grants and not from conquest, no longer correspond, as at their institution, to a superiority of race. But this superiority of race might again become real; and then the fact of nobility would be as scientifically true, and as undeniable, as the pre-eminence of civilised man over the savage, or of man in general over the lower animals.

Thus we can imagine a time when all that formerly held sway in the form of prejudice and groundless opinion may hold sway as genuine and true: gods, heaven, hell, spiritual power, monarchy, nobility, legitimacy, superiority of race, supernatural powers, may all be revived by virtue of the existence of man and of reason. Should such a solution ever be in any measure realised on the face of the planet earth, it seems as though Germany would fulfil it.

EUDOXES.—Do you mean this as a eulogium or a criticism?

THEOCTISTES.—Take it whichever way you please. France always inclines to liberal and democratic solutions; that is her glory; the happiness of men and liberty is her ideal. If the final upshot of things is that individuals should enjoy in peace their little limited destiny (as it possibly may be, after all), liberal France will have been in the right; but she is not the country that will ever attain great harmony, or rather that great subordination of consciousness of which we speak. On the other hand, the government of the world by reason, should it ever come to pass, seems more suited to the genius of Germany, which shows little anxiety for the equality, or even the dignity, of individuals, and which aims before everything at increasing the intellectual powers of the race.

EUTHYPHRON.—You forget that in the age of the far-off avatars, Frenchmen, Sclavs, and Germans will have long ago ceased to exist, and that history will have altogether ceased to remember these mean provincial varieties.

THEOCTISTES.—My aim was merely to draft from existing humanity some outline of the great battles of the future.

EUDOXES.—But don't you think that the people, when they see their master growing up, will foresee the danger and be on their guard?

THEOCTISTES.—Assuredly. If the order of ideas that we are now tracing ever attain to any reality, there will arise persecutions against science, more particularly against physiology and chemistry, compared with which those of the Inquisition will seem mild. With a profound instinct the crowd of simple beings will detect their enemy. Science will again take refuge in hiding-places. A time may come when a work on chemistry will compromise its owner as much as a work on alchemy did in the Middle Ages. Probably the most dangerous moments in the life of a planet are those in which science begins at length to unmask its hopes. There may then arise fears and reactions destructive to the spirit. Thousands of humanities have perhaps foundered in this strait. But among them there will be one that will clear it; mind will triumph.

Necessity, moreover, is in this case the best of securities. Man cannot any longer do without science. In degraded epochs, as, for example, in the Middle Ages, medicine was the only stay of the rational spirit; because a patient desires at any cost to be cured, and no cure can be wrought without a measure of science. But at the present time, war, machinery, the industrial arts require science, so that even persons most opposed to the scientific spirit are obliged to learn Mathematics, Physics, and Chemistry. The supremacy of science is, on all hands, thrust even upon its enemies.

EUDOXES.—Your hypothesis of the oligarchical triumph of the spirit conducts you only to a gloomy picture of things. Why not allow that the advent of a superior humanity may prove a benefit to all, and that this very superiority may consist in the advantages being distributed less than they are in our sad world, all men being then assimilated and deified into a single glorious type? But I wait impatiently to hear what conception you have of the monarchical future of the universe. That will be more comforting, I hope. I feel the need of a Heavenly Father to deliver me from your hell.

THEOCTISTES.—St. Paul has admirably said: "That God may be all in all." More than six hundred years before, Xenophanes had said still better: "He sees as the whole, thinks as the whole, hears as the whole." At the present time, such a formula is not realised; but the unitarian solution, in which the whole universe should minister to the perceptions, the sensations, and the enjoyments of a single being, cannot, considering the infinitude of time to come, be regarded as an impossibility. France, in the time of Louis XIV and Louis XV, presented the example of a whole country contributing to the production of a brilliant and complete life, namely, that of the King, all social functions being organised with a view to his glory and pleasures. We may imagine a state of the world in which everything might likewise culminate in a single conscious centre, in which the universe might be reduced to a single existence, in which the conception of personal monotheism might become a truth. An all-knowing and all-powerful being may be the last term of god-developing evolution, whether we conceive him as enjoying (*jouissant*) by all (all also enjoying by him), according to the dream of Christian mysticism; whether we conceive him as an individuality attaining paramount power; or whether we conceive him as the resultant of a thousand million of beings, as the harmony, the sum-total of the universe.

Thus the universe might be consummated in a single organised being, in whose infinity would be summed up at once myriads of myriads of lives, those that are dead and those that are living. All animate nature would produce a central life, a grand hymn issuing from thousands of millions of voices, just as the animal springs from millions of organic cells, and the tree from millions of buds. A single consciousness would be the work of all, and all would participate in it; the universe would be an infinite polype, of which all the beings that have ever existed would be soldered together at their base, each living at once after its own life and the life of the whole.

Already we participate in the life of the universe (a life as yet very imperfect) through morality, science, and art. Religions are the epitomised and popular forms of this participation; in this their sacredness consists. But Nature aspires to a far closer and more intense communion, a communion which will attain its final term only when there shall arise a really perfect being. Such a being does not yet exist, since we have only three ways of verifying the existence of a being, namely, by seeing him, by hearing others speak of him, and by beholding his acts, and since by none of these three means is such a being as we are speaking of known; but we can conceive the possibility of a state in which, in the infinity of space, everything lives. At present, only a small quantity of matter is organised, and even that feebly organised; but we may conceive of an age in which all matter might be organised, in which thousands of suns united together might go to form a single being, feeling, enjoying, and imbibing, through its burning throat, a river of delights which might flow out of him in a stream of life. Such a living universe would present the two poles that every nervous structure presents, the pole, namely, which thinks, and the pole which enjoys. At present the universe thinks and enjoys through millions of individuals. Some day a gigantic mouth may taste with some relish the infinite; an ocean of intoxicating delight may flow into it; an inexhaustible discharge of life, conscious of neither rest nor fatigue, may gush forth into eternity. To coagulate this divine mass, the earth will, perhaps, have been taken and tempered like a clod, which we knead without thought of the ant or the worm that is concealed in it. What would you have? We do the very same thing. It is Nature's sole care, at every step, to gain a superior end at the expense of inferior individualities. Does a general, the chief of a State, take account of the poor people whose lives he sacrifices?

A single being summing up the fruition (*jouissance*) of the universe, an infinite number of individuals joyful in contributing to it, no contradiction is involved here, save to our superficial individualism. The world is but a series of human sacrifices; their sting might be removed by joy and by resignation. Alexander's companions lived on Alexander, and enjoyed Alexander. There are certain states of society in which the lower classes enjoy the pleasures of their nobles, take delight in their princes, call them "our princes," and make their glory their own. The animals that contribute to the maintenance of the man of genius, or of the good man, would feel they ought to be satisfied, if they knew what service they are rendering. Everything depends on the aim and object; and if some day vivisection on a large scale became necessary in order to discover the profound secrets of animate Nature, I can imagine creatures coming crowned with flowers to offer themselves up in the ecstasy of voluntary martyrdom. The useless slaughter of a fly is a censurable act; he who is sacrificed for ideal purposes has no right to complain, and his fate with regard to the infinite ($\tau\widehat{\omega}\ \theta\epsilon\widehat{\omega}$), is an enviable one. So many others die without leaving a trace in the construction of the tower of infinity! The sacrifice of one living being to the egoism of another is monstrous; but the sacrifice of a living creature to an end desired by Nature is justifiable. Strictly speaking, the man of purely selfish aims commits an act of cannibalism in eating flesh; only the man that works, to the best of his might, for the good and the true, has the right to do this. The sacrifice in that case is made to the ideal, and the victim has that which so many others have not, his small share in the work of eternity. In good old times, the immolation of an animal intended to be eaten was justly regarded as a religious action. Such slaughter committed under pressure of an absolute necessity should be disguised, it was thought, by garlands and some religious ceremony.

The majority have to think and live by proxy. The idea, which prevailed in the Middle Ages, of people praying for those who have no time to pray, is a very just one. The mass is devoted to labour; a few perform for them the high functions of life; this is humanity. The result of the obscure work of a thousand peasants, serfs of an abbey, was a Gothic chapel in the midst of a beautiful valley, shaded by tall poplars, to which pious people used to resort six or eight times a day to chant psalms to the Eternal. This constituted a rather noble way of doing worship, particularly when, among the ascetics, there were a St. Bernard, a Rupert de Tuy, and an abbot Jaochim. That valley, those rivers, those trees, those rocks would fain call upon God, but they were voiceless; the abbey gave them a tongue. Among the Greeks, a nobler race, this was done better by means of the flute and the sports of shepherds. Some day this will be done better still when a laboratory of chemistry or of physics shall supersede the abbey. But in our days the thousand rustics that were formerly serfs, being now emancipated, give themselves up, as is like, to a coarse merrymaking, without any ideal result whatever, on the lands of the aforesaid abbey. The tax imposed on these lands alone purifies them a little by making them contribute to a higher purpose.

There are some who live for all. Were this rule changed, nobody would live. The Egyptian, a subject of Chéphrem, who died building the pyramids, spent a better life than he that spends his useless days under his palm trees. Herein consists the dignity of the people; they desire no other; they will never be satisfied with egoism. Their wish is that, if they themselves do not reap enjoyment, there should be others who do. They are ready to die for the glory of a chief, that is to say, for something from which they themselves do not derive any direct advantage. I am speaking of the true people, the un-reflective mass given up to the instincts of race, whom reflection has not yet taught that the greatest folly that can be committed is to submit to be slain for anything whatever.

Thus, I sometimes conceive of God as the great inner festival of the universe, as the vast consciousness in which everything is reflected and echoed back. Each class of society forms, as it were, a system of wheels, an arm of the lever, in this vast machine. This is why each class has its own virtues. We are all functions of the universe; duty consists in each one of us acting his part well. The virtues of the plebeian ought not to be those of the noble; that which constitutes a perfect nobleman would be a blemish in a humble commoner. The virtues of each are determined by the requirements of Nature; the State in which there are no social classes is in the teeth of Providence. It signifies little that St. Vincent de Paul was not a great genius. Raphaël would have gained nothing by being well-ordered in his manners. The divine energy, which is in all, is brought forth by upright men, scholars, and artists. Each one has his part to play. The duty of Goethe was to be an egoist with reference to his work. The transcendent immorality of the artist is in its own way a supreme morality, if it helps towards the accomplishment of the particular divine mission with which each one is entrusted here below.

For myself I enjoy a taste of the whole universe by that kind of general sentiment which makes us feel sad in a sad town and merry in a merry one. I thus share the pleasures of the voluptuous, the debaucheries of the debauchee, the worldly-mindedness of the worldly, the sanctity of the virtuous man, the meditations of the scholar, and the austerity of the ascetic. By a sort of sweet sympathy I imagine myself as their consciousness. The discoveries of the scholar are my property; the triumphs of the ambitious are a festive season to me. I should feel grieved if the world were to suffer any want; for I have the consciousness of all that is in it. My only grief is that the present age is so debased that it no longer knows how to enjoy. I therefore take refuge in the past, in the sixteenth and seventeenth centuries, and in antiquity; all that has been of beautiful, of courteous, of true, and of noble, is like a paradise to me. With this idea I defy any misfortune to reach me; I carry with me the enchanting garden of my varied thoughts.

ANATOLE FRANCE

(ANATOLE JACQUES THIBAULT)

(1844–1924)

The Year 220 of the European Federation*

The son of a Parisian bookseller, Anatole France had great and versatile gifts as a journalist, playwright, novelist, and critic that won him election to the French Academy and a Nobel prize for literature. Though generally cynical about the perfectibility of human institutions, he was profoundly shaken by the repercussions of the Dreyfus Affair, and at the turn of the century began to write on political and social questions with a skeptical humanitarianism that has been compared to Voltaire's. *The White Stone* (1905) belongs to this period of his work, and reveals an attitude toward socialism that is sympathetic, if not entirely without ambivalence. The hero of the novel, recounting a dream in which he travels to the year 2270 on an airplane, describes his interview with citizens of the future.

*From Anatole France, *Sur la Pierre Blanche* (46th edition; Paris: C. Lévy, 1905), pp. 290–310; translated by the editors.

Anatole France, photograph, 1923. (From *Le Livre d'Or du Centenaire d'Anatole France, 1844–1944,* Paris: Calmann-Lévy [1949], by courtesy of M. Lucien Psichari.)

Hippolyte's Dream

I asked how it had been possible to construct a society composed entirely of workers.

Morin pointed out to me that there is among men a general propensity for work, and that it constitutes one of the fundamental characteristics of the race.

"In barbarian times," he said, "and right up to the end of the closed era, the aristocrats and the wealthy always showed a preference for manual labor. They hardly used their intellects, and then only under exceptional circumstances. Their tastes always inclined them to such activities as hunting and war, where the body plays a more important role than the mind. They rode, drove, fenced, and practiced pistol-shooting. Thus it may be said that they worked with their hands. Their labor was sterile or harmful, because prejudice forbade them to engage in any useful or beneficent work, and also because in their day useful work was most often performed under base and repellent conditions. It was not too difficult to impart a taste for work to everyone by restoring it to an honorable status. In barbarian times, men took pride in carrying a sword or a gun. Today, men are proud of wielding a spade or a hammer. There is in humanity a core that remains virtually unchanged."

When Morin told me that the very memory of currency had vanished, I asked him: "How do you carry on business without cash?"

He replied: "We exchange products by means of vouchers like that which you have received, comrade, and which correspond to the hours of work that we complete. The value of products is determined by the length of time required to produce them. Bread, meat, beer, clothes, an airplane represent x hours and x days of work. From each of these vouchers, the collectivity, or, as it was formerly termed, the state, deducts a number of minutes to be allocated to unproductive work, alimentary and metallurgical reserves, asylums and nursing homes, and so on."

"These minutes," Michel interposed, "are constantly on the increase. The Federal Committee decrees far too many great works, the burden of which thus falls on us. The reserve stocks are too extensive. The public warehouses are filled to overflowing with goods of all sorts. It is our minutes of work that lie buried there. Many abuses still exist."

"No doubt," Morin responded, "there is room for improvement. The wealth of Europe, which has accumulated through general and orderly labor, is immense."

I was curious as to whether these people had any other measure of work than time, and whether they considered the day's work of the digger or the plasterer equivalent to that of the chemist or the surgeon. I asked them candidly.

"What a silly question," exclaimed Perceval.

Nevertheless old Morin was kind enough to enlighten me. "All study, research, all work tending to make life better and more beautiful is encouraged in our workshops and laboratories. The collectivist state encourages advanced studies. To study is to produce, for nothing is produced without study. Study, like work, justifies one's existence. Those who devote themselves to long and arduous research are assured a peaceful and honorable existence. A sculptor can make the model of a figure in a fortnight, but he has taken five years to learn his art. And the state has paid him for his model during those five years. A chemist discovers in a few hours the special properties of a body. But he has spent months in isolating this body and years to fit himself for such an undertaking. During all that time he has lived at the expense of the state. A surgeon can excise a tumor in ten minutes, as a result of fifteen years of study and practice. Thus he has received vouchers from the state for fifteen years past. Every man who gives in a month, an hour, a few minutes the product of his whole life's work is simply repaying at one time to the collectivity what it has given him day by day."

"And this doesn't take into account," said Perceval, "that our great intellectuals, our surgeons, our lady doctors, our chemists, know very well how to profit from their work and their discoveries, how to add immeasurably to their pleasures. They manage to have allotted to themselves flying machines of 60 h.p., palaces, gardens, and vast parks. They are, for the most part, individuals keenly interested in getting hold of this world's goods, and they lead a more splendid and fulsome existence than the bourgeois of the closed era. The worst of it is that many of them are fools who should be hired for the flour-mills, like Hippolyte" [the narrator].

I bowed thanks for this compliment. Michel seconded Perceval, and bitterly complained that a complaisant state was fattening chemists at the expense of other workers.

I asked if speculation in vouchers did not lead to inflation or deflation.

"Speculation in vouchers," answered Morin, "is prohibited. As a matter of fact, it cannot be prevented altogether. There are among us, just as before, greedy and prodigal, industrious and idle, rich and poor, happy and wretched, contented and discontented men. But everybody can live, and that is already something."

I reflected for a moment; then I observed: "Monsieur Morin, as I listen to you, it seems to me that you have made equality and fraternity realities insofar as possible. But I fear that it is at the expense of liberty, which I have learned to cherish as the greatest good."

Morin shrugged, saying: "We have not established equality. We do not know what it means. We have assured a livelihood to everyone. We have made work honorable. After that, if the bricklayer thinks himself superior to the poet, and the poet to the bricklayer, it's their own affair. Every one of our workers imagines that his type of labor is the most important in the world. The advantages of this notion outweigh the disadvantages.

"Comrade Hippolyte, you seem to have read much in the books of the nineteenth century of the closed era, which are hardly opened nowadays. You speak their language, which to us has become a foreign tongue. It is hard for us to realize today that in former times friends of the people should have adopted as their motto: *Liberty, Equality, Fraternity.* Liberty cannot have a place in society, since it does not exist in nature. There is no free animal. It used to be said that a man who obeyed the laws was free. That was childish. Moreover, so strange a meaning was given to the word liberty in the last days of capitalistic anarchy that the word ended up as merely expressing a claim to privilege. The idea of equality is even less reasonable, and it is unfortunate in that it presupposes a false ideal. It is not our task to see that men are equal one to another. We must be concerned that each one gives his best and receives everything he needs. As to fraternity, we know all too well how brothers have acted toward brothers over the course of the centuries. We do not mean to say that men are bad. Nor do we say that they are good. They are what they are. But they live in peace when there is no longer any reason for them to fight one another. A single word epitomizes our social system: we say that we live in harmony. And it is certainly true that today all human forces act in concert."

"In the centuries," I said to him, "of what you call the closed era, people preferred to possess rather than to enjoy. I can imagine that, reversing the order of things, you prefer enjoyment to possession. But does it not distress you to have no property to leave to your children?"

"In capitalistic times," Morin replied heatedly, "how many were there who left inheritances? One in a thousand, one in ten thousand. Nor should we forget that many generations knew nothing of the right to bequeath. Be this as it may, the transmission of wealth through inheritance was perfectly conceivable when the family was in existence. But now . . ."

"What!" I cried, "you do not live in families?"

My astonishment, which I could not conceal, seemed funny to the lady comrade Chéron.

"We are quite aware," she said to me, "that there is marriage among the Kaffirs. But we European women do not bind ourselves with promises; or, if we make them, the law takes no cognizance of them. We do not believe that a human being's whole fate should hang on a word. There is, however, a relic of the customs of the closed era: when a woman gives herself, she swears fidelity on the horns of the moon. In reality, neither the man nor the woman makes any binding engagement. Yet it is not infrequent that their union lasts throughout their lives. Neither of them would want to be the object of a fidelity secured by an oath, instead of by physical or moral expediency. We owe nothing to anybody. Formerly a man convinced a woman that she belonged to him. We are less simple-minded. We believe that a human being belongs to himself alone. We give ourselves when we please and to whom we wish.

"Furthermore, we are not ashamed of yielding to desire. We are not hypocrites. Only 400 years ago men understood nothing of physiology, and their ignorance was the cause of gross illusions and cruel disappointments. Hippolyte, whatever the Kaffirs may say, society must be subordinate to nature, and not, as was too long the case, nature to society."

Perceval endorsed the words of her comrade, adding: "To show you how the sex question is handled in our society, I should tell you, Hippolyte, that in many factories the recruiting deputy does not even inquire about one's sex. The sex of an individual is of no interest to the collectivity."

"But the children?"

"What about the children?"

"Without any family, are they not neglected?"

"Where did you get such an idea? Maternal love is a very powerful instinct in woman. In the frightful society of the past, mothers braved poverty and shame in order to bring up their illegitimate offspring. Why should our women, who are exempt from shame and poverty, abandon their little ones? There are among us many good mates and many good mothers. But we also have a very large number—and constantly increasing—of women who get along without men."

At this point, Chéron made a rather strange remark. "We have notions about sexuality undreamed of in the barbaric simplicity of the closed era.

For a long time false conclusions were drawn from the fact that there are two sexes and only two: that a woman was absolutely female and a man absolutely male. The reality is far different. Some women are very much women, while others are hardly so at all. These variations, formerly concealed by clothing and way of life, and disguised by prejudice, are perfectly clear and open in our society. Indeed, they are accentuated and more marked with each successive generation. Ever since women have worked like men, and acted and thought like them, it is apparent that there are many who resemble men. Some day we may arrive at the point of creating neutrals and of producing female workers, as is said of the bees. It will be a great boon, for it will then become possible to increase the quantity of work without increasing the population to a degree disproportionate with the resources available for sustenance. We are equally apprehensive of a deficit or a surplus of births."

I thanked Perceval and Chéron for having been kind enough to instruct me on so interesting a subject; and I then asked whether education had been neglected in the collectivist society and whether theoretical science and the liberal arts still flourished.

This was old Morin's reply: "Education at all levels is highly developed. All the comrades know something; they do not know the same things, nor have they acquired any useless knowledge. Time is no longer wasted in the study of law and theology. Each person selects from the arts and sciences whatever suits him. We still have many ancient works, although the greater part of the books printed before the new era have vanished. Books are still printed, and in greater number than ever. And yet typography is on the point of disappearing. Phonography will replace it. Poets and novelists are already being published phonographically, while for plays a most ingenious combination of phonograph and camera has been devised to reproduce at the same time the words and gestures of the actors."

"You have poets and playwrights?"

"We have not only poets, but a special poetry of our own. We are the first to set boundaries to the realm of poetry. Previously, many ideas that could have been better expressed in prose appeared in verse. Narratives were recounted in rhyme. This was a survival of the days when legislative decrees and prescriptions for husbandry were set forth in verse. Today, poets sing only of delicate subjects that have no significance, and their grammar and language are as appropriate as their rhythms, their assonances, their alliteration. As for our theatre, it is almost exclusively lyric. A precise knowledge of reality and a life freed from violence have made us almost indifferent to drama and tragedy. The consolidation of classes and the equality of the sexes have deprived the old comedy of almost all its subject matter. But never before has music been so beautiful and so well loved. We especially admire the sonata and the symphony.

"Our society is favorable to the arts of design. Many prejudices that hinder the development of painting have disappeared. Our life is more pure and beautiful than bourgeois life, and we have a keen appreciation of form. Sculpture thrives even more than painting, ever since it has taken an intelligent part in adorning public buildings and private homes. Never has so much been done for the teaching of art. If you will but fly your airplane over one of our streets for a few minutes, you will be surprised at the number of schools and museums."

"And finally," I inquired, "are you happy?"

Morin shook his head. "It is not in human nature to enjoy perfect happiness. Happiness is not attainable without effort, and every effort brings in its train fatigue and suffering. We have made life endurable for everyone. That is something. Our descendants will do better. Our organization is not immutable. A mere fifty years ago it was different from what it is today. And subtle observers believe they can foresee great changes on the road ahead. That may be. But the progress of human civilization will henceforth be harmonious and peaceful."

"Do you not rather fear," I asked, "that the civilization with which you seem to be satisfied may be destroyed by an invasion of barbarians? There still remain in Asia and Africa, as you have told me, large black or yellow populations which have not entered into concord with you. They have armies, while you have not. If they should attack you . . ."

"Our defense is secure. Only the Americans and the Australians could engage in a struggle with us, for their state of knowledge is on a par with ours. But the ocean separates us and community of interest makes us sure of their friendship. As for the capitalistic Negroes, they are still in the stage of steel cannon, firearms, and all the old iron junk of the twentieth century. What could these ancient engines of war avail against a discharge of Y-rays? Our frontiers are protected by electricity. A zone of lightning encircles the Federation. A little bespectacled fellow sits somewhere before a keyboard. He is our one and only soldier. He has but to touch a key to pulverize an army of 500,000 men."

Morin stopped talking for a moment; then he continued, more deliberately: "Were our civilization threatened, it would not be by an outside enemy. It would be by the enemies within."

"There are such enemies, then?"

"There are the anarchists—many, fiery, and intelligent. Our chemists and professors of science and literature are almost all anarchists. They blame the regulation of labor and production for most of the evils that still beset society. They argue that humanity will be happy only in the state of spontaneous harmony born of the total destruction of civilization. They are dangerous. They would be still more so if we were to repress them. To do so, however, we have neither the means nor the desire. We do not possess any power of constraint or repression, and we find that good. In the ages of barbarism, men had great illusions regarding the effectiveness of penalties. Our fathers suppressed the whole judiciary. They had no further need of it. By abolishing private property, they ended at one blow theft and swindling. Since we carry electrical defenses, attempts against persons are no longer to be dreaded. Men have come to respect one another. Crimes of passion are still committed, but this kind of crime, when it goes unpunished, becomes more rare. Our entire judiciary body is composed of men of integrity who are elected and who pass judgment on violations and disputes, without recompense."

I rose and, thanking my companions for their kindness, requested of Morin the favor of asking him a last question: "You no longer have any religion?"

"On the contrary, we have a great many, including some rather new ones. To confine ourselves to France, we have the religions of Humanity, Positivism, Christianity, and Spiritualism. In some countries there remain Catholics, but they are few in number and divided into several sects, following the schisms that developed in the twentieth century when Church and State were separated. For a long time there has been no Pope."

"You are mistaken," said Michel, "There is still a Pope. Chance made me acquainted with him. He is Pius XXV, dyer, Via dell' Orso, Rome."

"What," I cried, "the Pope a dyer?"

"What is surprising about that? He has to have a trade like everyone."

"But his Church?"

"It is recognized by several thousand persons in Europe."

PIERRE TEILHARD DE CHARDIN
(1881–1955)

The Evolving Noosphere[*]

After a Jesuit education in France and a residence of some years on the Isle of Jersey, Teilhard de Chardin took the first of many journeys to other continents when he embarked for Cairo, to teach school and make initial explorations in the Fayum. Already a priest and a palaeontologist at the outbreak of World War I, he served as a regimental stretcher-bearer, refusing to accept a post as chaplain. A brief term on the faculty of the Institut Catholique in Paris was succeeded by long years in India and China, where he played an important role in the discovery of Peking man. In the meantime, Père Teilhard had been forbidden to teach because of his unorthodox views on original sin and human evolution. After 1946, he returned to France from China. He was enjoined by his religious superiors, however, from writing further on philosophical subjects, and, though elected to the most distinguished scientific bodies, was refused permission to publish his completed manuscripts. Much of his work was printed posthumously. In 1951, he came to the United States to work with research teams here, and died in New York. His conception of a collective human organism, the Noosphere, involves a transcendence of biological by psychosocial evolution. It is a utopian vision of new dimensions—a far cry from the "realistic" French utopias of the nineteenth century.

*From Pierre Teilhard de Chardin, *The Future of Man*, trans. Norman Denny (New York and London: Harper and Row and William Collins Sons, 1964), pp. 76–81, 113–23, 174–84, 300–3.

Teilhard de Chardin, S. J., photograph, 1952. (Wide World Photos.)

The Precise Point of Divergence . . . God or the World?

It seems to me clear above all else, setting aside the countless minor divergences, and ignoring the dull, inert mass of those who believe in nothing at all, that the spiritual conflict afflicting Mankind today arises out of the division of minds and hearts into the two profoundly separated categories of:

Those whose hopes are directed towards a spiritual state or an absolute finality situated beyond and outside this world;

Those who hope for the perfection of the tangible Universe within itself.

The first of these groups, by far the older, is pre-eminently represented in these days by the Christians, protagonists of a transcendent and personal God.

The second group, comprising those who for a variety of reasons have dedicated their lives to the service of a Universe which they conceive as eventually culminating in some form of impersonal and immanent Reality, is of very recent origin. Throughout human history this conflict between the 'servants of Heaven' and the 'servants of earth' has gone on; but only since the birth of the idea of Evolution (in some sort divinising the Universe) have the devotees of earth bestirred themselves and made of their worship a true form of religion, charged with limitless hope, striving and renunciation.

Are we to disdain the world and put it behind us, or live in it in order to master and perfect it? Mankind is rent asunder at this moment by these two concepts or rival mysticisms; and in consequence its vital power of adoration is disastrously weakened.

Such in my view is the nature of the crisis, more profound than any economic, political or social struggle, through which we are passing.

A Principle of Convergence. The Concept of Noogenesis

Any two forces, provided both are positive, must *a priori* be capable of growth by merging together. Faith in God and faith in the World: these two springs of energy, each the source of a magnificent spiritual impulse, must certainly be capable of effectively uniting in such a way as to produce a resulting upward movement. But in practical terms where are we to look for the principle and the generative medium which will bring about this most desirable evolutionary step?

I believe that the principle and the medium are to be found in the idea, duly 'realised', that there is in progress, within us and around us, a continual heightening of consciousness in the Universe.

For a century and a half the science of physics, preoccupied with analytical researches, was dominated by the idea of the dissipation of energy and the disintegration of matter. Being now called upon by biology to consider the effects of synthesis, it is beginning to perceive that, parallel with the phenomenon of corpuscular disintegration, the Universe historically displays a second process as generalised and fundamental as the first: I mean that of the gradual concentration of its physico-chemical elements in nuclei of increasing complexity, each succeeding stage of material concentration and differentiation being accompanied by a more advanced form of spontaneity and spiritual energy.

The outflowing flood of Entropy equalled and offset by the rising tide of a Noogenesis! . . .

The greater and more revolutionary an idea, the more does it encounter resistance at its inception. Despite the number and importance of the facts that it explains, the theory of Noogenesis is still far from having established itself as a stronghold in the scientific field. However, let us assume that, as all the observable evidence suggests, it will succeed before long in gaining in one form or another the place it deserves at the head of the structural laws of our Universe. Plainly the first result will be precisely to bring about the *rapprochement* and automatic convergence of the two opposed forms of worship into which, as I said, the religious impulse of Mankind is at present divided.

Once he has been brought to accept the reality of a Noogenesis, the believer in this World will find himself compelled to allow increasing room, in his vision of the future, for the values of personalisation and transcendency. Of Personalisation, because a Universe in process of psychic concentration is *identical* with a Universe that is acquiring a personality. And of transcendency because the ultimate stage of 'cosmic' personalisation, if it is to be supremely coherent and unifying, cannot be conceived otherwise than as emerging at the summit of the elements it super-personalises in uniting them to itself.

On the other hand, the believer in Heaven, accepting this same reality of a cosmic genesis of the Spirit, must perceive that the mystical evolution of which he dreams presupposes and consecrates all the tangible realities and all the arduous conditions of human progress. If it is to be super-spiritualised in God, must not Mankind first be born and grow in conformity with the entire system of what we call 'evolution'? Whence, for the Christian in particular, there follows a radical incorporation of terrestrial values in the most fundamental concepts of his Faith, those of Divine Omnipotence, withdrawal and charity. First, Divine Omnipotence: God creates and shapes us through the process of evolution: how can we suppose, or fear, that He will arbitrarily interfere with the very means whereby He fulfils His purpose? Then, withdrawal: God awaits us when the evolutionary process is complete: to rise above the World, therefore, does not mean to despise or reject it, but to pass through it and sublime it. Finally, charity: the love of God expresses and crowns the basic affinity which, from the beginnings of Time and Space, has drawn together and concentrated the spiritualisable elements of the Universe. To love God and our neighbour is therefore not merely an act of worship and compassion superimposed on our other individual preoccupations. For the Christian, if he be truly Christian, it is Life itself, Life in the integrity of its aspirations, its struggles and its conquests, that he must embrace in a spirit of togetherness and personalising unification with all things.

The sense of the earth opening and exploding upwards into God; and the sense of God taking root and finding nourishment downwards into Earth. A personal, transcendent God and an evolving Universe no longer forming two hostile centres of attraction, but entering into hierarchic conjunction to raise the human mass on a single tide. Such is the sublime transformation which we may with justice foresee, and which in fact is beginning to have its effect upon a growing number of minds, free-thinkers as well as believers: the idea of a spiritual evolution of the Universe. The very transformation we have been seeking!

A New Soul for a New World: Faith Renewed in the Progress of Mankind

From this standpoint it is at once apparent that, to unify the living forces of humanity, at present so painfully at odds, the direct and effective method is simply to sound the call-to-arms and form a solid block of all those, whether of the right or the left, who believe that the principal business of present-day Mankind is to achieve a breakthrough straight ahead by forcing its way over the threshold of some higher level of consciousness. Whether Christian or non-Christian, the people inspired by this particular conviction constitute a homogeneous category. Though they may be situated at the two extreme wings of Mankind on the march, they can advance unequivocally side by side because their attitudes, far from being mutually exclusive, are virtually an extension one of the other and ask only to be completed. What more do they need that they may know and love one another? The *union sacrée*, the Common Front of all those who believe that the World is still advancing: what is this but the active minority, the solid core around which the unanimity of tomorrow must harden?

Despite the wave of scepticism which seems to have swept away the hopes (too ingenuous, no doubt, and too materialistic) on which the nineteenth century lived, faith in the future is not dead in our hearts. Indeed, it is this faith, deepened and purified, which must save us. Not only does the idea of a possible raising of our consciousness to a state of super-consciousness show itself daily, in the light of scientific experience, to be better founded and psychologically more necessary for preserving in Man his will to act; but furthermore this idea, carried to its logical extreme, appears to be the only one capable of paving the way for the great event we look for—the manifestation of a unified impulse of worship in which will be joined and mutually exalted both a passionate desire to conquer the World and a passionate longing to be united with God: the vital act, specifically new, corresponding to a new age in the history of Earth.

I am convinced that finally it is upon the idea of progress, and faith in progress, that Mankind, today so divided, must rely and can reshape itself.

———◆———

The Present State of Mankind: The Phase of Planetisation

To open any book treating scientifically, philosophically or sociologically of the future of the Earth (whether by a Bergson or a Jeans) is to be struck at once by a presumption common to most of their authors, certain biologists excepted. Explicitly or by inference they talk as though Man today had reached a final and supreme state of humanity beyond which he cannot advance; or, in the language of this lecture, that, Matter having attained in *Homo sapiens* its maximum of centro-complexity on Earth, the process of super-molecularisation on the planet has for good and all come to a stop.

Nothing could be more depressing, but also, fortunately, more arbitrary and even scientifically false, than this doctrine of immobility. No proof exists that Man has come to the end of his potentialities, that he has reached his highest point. On the contrary, everything suggests that at the present time we are entering a peculiarly critical phase of super-humanisation. This is what I hope to persuade you of by drawing your attention to an altogether extra-ordinary and highly suggestive condition of the world around us, one which we all see and are subject to, but without paying any attention to it, or at least without understanding it: I mean the increasingly rapid growth in the human world of the forces of collectivisation.

The phenomenon calls for no detailed description. It takes the form of the all-encompassing ascent of the masses; the constant tightening of economic bonds; the spread of financial and intellectual associations; the totalisation of political regimes; the closer physical contact of individuals as well as of nations; the increasing impossibility of being or acting or thinking *alone*—in short, the rise, in every form, of the *Other* around us. We are all constantly aware of these tentacles of a social condition that is rapidly evolving to the point of becoming monstrous. You feel them as I do, and probably you also resent them. If I were to ask your views you would doubtless reply that, menaced by this unleashing of blind forces, there is nothing we can do but evade them to the best of our ability, or else submit, since we are the victims of a sort of natural catastrophe against which we are powerless and in which there is no meaning to be discerned.

But is it true that there is nothing to understand? Let us look more closely, once again by the light of our principle of complexity.

The first thing to give us pause, as we survey the progress of human collectivisation, is what I would call the inexorable nature of a phenomenon which arises directly and automatically out of the conjunction of two factors, both of a structural kind: first, the confined surface of the globe, and secondly, the incessant multiplication, within this restricted space, of human units endowed by ever-improving means of communication with a rapidly increasing scope for action; to which may be added the fact that their advanced psychic development makes them pre-eminently capable of influencing and inter-penetrating one another. Under the combined effect of these two natural pressures a sort of mass-hold of Mankind upon itself comes of necessity into operation.

But, the second noteworthy point, this phenomenon of holding, or cementing, turns out to be no sudden or unpredictable event. Looking at the picture as a whole we see that Life, from its lowest level, has never been able to effect its syntheses except through the progressively closer association of its elements, whether in the oceans or on land. Upon an imaginary earth of constantly increasing extent, living organisms, being only loosely associated, might well remain at the monocellular stage (if indeed they got so far); and certainly Man, if free to live in a scattered state, would never have reached even the neolithic stage of social development. The totalisation in progress in the modern world is in fact nothing but the natural climax and paroxysm of a process of grouping which is fundamental to the elaboration of organised matter. Matter does not vitalise or super-vitalise itself except by compression.

I do not think it is possible to reflect upon this twofold in-rooting, both structural and evolutionary, which characterises the social events affecting us, without being at first led to the surmise, and finally overwhelmed by the evidence, that the collectivisation of the human race, at present accelerated, is nothing other than a higher form adopted by the process of molecularisation on the surface of our planet. The first phase was the formation of proteins up to the stage of the cell. In the second phase individual cellular complexes were formed, up to and including Man. We are now at the beginning of a third phase, the formation of an organico-social super-complex, which, as may easily be demonstrated, *can only occur* in the case of reflective, personalised elements. First the vitalisation of matter, associated with the grouping of molecules; then the hominisation of Life, associated with a super-grouping of cells; and finally the planetisation of Mankind, associated with a *closed* grouping of people: Mankind, born on this planet and spread over its entire surface, coming gradually to form around its earthly matrix a single, major organic unity, enclosed upon itself; a single, hyper-complex, hyper-centrated, hyper-conscious arch-molecule, co-extensive with the heavenly body on which it was born. Is not this what is happening at the present time—the closing of this spherical, thinking circuit?

This idea of the planetary totalisation of human consciousness (with its unavoidable corollary, that wherever there are life-bearing planets in the Universe, they too will become encompassed, like the Earth, with some form of planetised spirit) may at first sight seem fantastic: but does it not exactly correspond to the facts, and does it not logically extend the cosmic curve of molecularisation? It may seem absurd, but in its very fantasy does it not heighten our vision of Life to the level of other and universally accepted fantasies, those of atomic physics and astronomy? However mad it may seem, the fact remains that great modern biologists, such as Julian Huxley and J. B. S. Haldane, are beginning to talk of Mankind, and to predict its future, as though they were dealing (all things being equal) with a brain of brains.

So why not?

Clearly this is a matter in which I cannot compel your assent. But I can assure you, of my own experience, that the acceptance of this organic and realistic view of the social phenomenon is both eminently satisfying to our reason and fortifying to our will.

Satisfying to the intelligence above all. For if it be true that at this moment Mankind is embarking upon what I have called its 'phase of planetisation', then everything is clarified, everything in our field of vision acquires a new sharpness of outline.

The tightening network of economic and psychic bonds in which we live and from which we suffer, the growing compulsion to act, to produce, to think collectively which so disquiets us—what do they become, seen in this way, except the first portents of the super-organism which, woven of the threads of individual men, is preparing (theory and fact are at one on this point) not to mechanise and submerge us, but to raise us, by way of increasing complexity, to a higher awareness of our own personality?

The increasing degree, intangible, and too little noted, in which present-day thought and activity are influenced by the passion for discovery; the progressive replacement of the workshop by the laboratory, of production by research, of the desire for well-being by the desire for *more*-being—what do these things betoken if not the growth in our souls of a great impulse towards super-evolution?

The profound cleavage in every kind of social group (families, countries, professions, creeds) which during the past century has become manifest in the form of two increasingly distinct and irreconcilable human types, those who believe in progress and those who do not—what does this portend except the separation and birth of a new stratum in the biosphere?

Finally, the present war; a war which for the first time in history is as widespread as the earth itself; a conflict in which human masses as great as continents clash together; a catastrophe in which we seem to be swept off our feet as individuals—what aspect can it wear to our awakened eyes except that of a crisis of birth, almost disproportionately small in relation to the vastness of what it is destined to bring forth?

Enlightenment, therefore, for our intelligence. And, let it be added, *sustenance and necessary reassurance for our power of will.* Through the centuries life has become an increasingly heavy burden for Man the Species, just as it does for Man the Individual as the years pass. The modern world, with its prodigious growth of complexity, weighs incomparably more heavily upon the shoulders of our generation than did the ancient world upon the shoulders of our forebears. Have you never felt that this added load needs to be compensated for by an added passion, a new sense of purpose? To my mind, this is what is 'providentially' arising to sustain our courage—the hope, the belief that some immense fulfilment lies ahead of us.

If Mankind were destined to achieve its apotheosis, if Evolution were to reach its highest point, in our small, separate lives, then indeed the enormous travail of terrestrial organisation into which we are born would be no more than a tragic irrelevance. We should all be dupes. We should do better in that case to stop, to call a halt, destroy the machines, close the laboratories, and seek whatever way of escape we can find in pure pleasure or pure nirvana.

But if on the contrary Man sees a new door opening above him, a new stage for his development; if each of us can believe that he is working so that the Universe may be raised, in him and through him, to a higher level—then a new spring of energy will well forth in the heart of Earth's workers. The whole great human organism, overcoming a momentary hesitation, will draw its breath and press on with strength renewed.

Indeed, the idea, the hope of the planetisation of life is very much more than a mere matter of biological speculation. It is more of a necessity for our age than the discovery, which we so ardently pursue, of new sources of energy. It is this idea which can and must bring us the spiritual fire without which all material fires, so laboriously lighted, will presently die down on the surface of the thinking earth: the fire inspiring us with the joy of action and the love of life.

All this, you may say to me, sounds splendid: but is there not another side to the picture? You tell us that this new phase of human evolution will bring about an extension and deepening of terrestrial consciousness. But do not the facts contradict your argument? What is actually happening in the world today? Can we really detect any heightening of human consciousness even in the most highly collectivised nations? Does it not appear, on the contrary, that social totalisation leads directly to spiritual retrogression and greater materialism?

My answer is that I do not think we are yet in a position to judge recent totalitarian experiments fairly: that is to say, to decide whether, all things considered, they have produced a greater degree of enslavement or a higher level of spiritual energy. It is too early to say. But I believe this can be said, that in so far as these first attempts may seem to be tending dangerously towards the sub-human state of the ant-hill or the termitary, it is not the principle of totalisation that is at fault but the clumsy and incomplete way in which it has been applied.

We have to take into account what is required by the law of complexity if Mankind is to achieve spiritual growth through collectivisation. The first essential is that the human units involved in the process shall draw closer together, not merely under the pressure of *external* forces, or solely by the performance of material acts, but directly, centre to centre, through *internal* attraction. Not through coercion, or enslavement to a common task, but through *unanimity* in a common spirit. The construction of molecules ensues through atomic affinity. Similarly, on a higher level, it is through sympathy, and this alone, that the human elements in a personalised universe may hope to rise to the level of a higher synthesis.

It is a matter of common experience that within restricted groups (the pair, the team) unity, far from diminishing the individual, enhances, enriches and liberates him in terms of himself. True union, the union of heart and spirit, does not enslave, nor does it neutralise the individuals which it brings together. It *super-personalises* them. Let us try to picture the phenomenon on a terrestrial scale. Imagine men awakening at last, under the influence of the ever-tightening planetary embrace, to a sense of universal solidarity based on their profound community, evolutionary in its nature and purpose. The nightmares of brutalisation and mechanisation which are conjured up to terrify us and prevent our advance are at once dispelled. It is not harshness or hatred but a new kind of love, not yet experienced by man, which we must learn to look for as it is borne to us on the rising tide of planetisation.

Reflecting, even briefly, on the state of affairs which might evoke this universal love in the human heart, a love so often vainly dreamed of, but which now leaves the fields of Utopia to reveal itself as both possible and necessary, we are brought to the following conclusion: that for men upon earth, all the earth, to learn to love one another, it is not enough that they should know themselves to be members of one and the same *thing*; in 'planetising' themselves they must acquire the consciousness, without losing themselves, of becoming one and the same *person*. For (and this is writ large in the Gospel) there is no total love that does not proceed from, and exist within, that which is personal.

And what does this mean except, finally, that the planetisation of Mankind, if it is to come properly into effect, presupposes, in addition to the enclosing Earth, and to the organisation and condensation of human thought, yet another factor? I mean the rise on our inward horizon of a cosmic spiritual centre, a supreme pole of consciousness, upon which all the separate consciousnesses of the world may converge and within which they may love one another: the *rise of a God*.

It is here that reason may discern, conforming to and in harmony with the law of complexity,[1] an acceptable way of envisaging 'the end of the world'.

The End of Planetary Life: Maturity and Withdrawal

The end of the world—for us, that is to say, the end of Earth. . . . Have you ever thought seriously, *in human terms*, about that sombre and certain eventuality?

Life at the beginning seemed modest in its requirements. A few hours in the sun were all it seemed to ask. But this was only a semblance, belied at the earliest stages of vitalisation by the tenacity with which the most humble cells reproduce themselves and multiply. This tenacity continues through all the enormous effusion of the animal kingdom, and bursts into the light of day with the appearance, in thinking Man, of the formidable power of pre-vision. It cannot but grow still more imperious with every forward stride of human consciousness. I have spoken of the impulse to act, without which there can be no action. But in practice it is not enough, if the impulse is to be sustained in face of the ever-growing onslaughts of the *taedium vitae*, for it to be offered nothing more than an immediate objective, even though this be as great as the planetisation of Mankind. We must strive for ever more greatness; but we cannot do so if we are faced by the prospect of an eventual decline, a

---

1. Which here culminates, we may note, in a sort of proof of the existence of God: 'proof by complexity'.

disaster at the end. With the germ of consciousness hatched upon its surface, the Earth, our perishable earth that contemplates the final, absolute zero, has brought into the Universe a demand, henceforth irrepressible, not only that all things shall not die, but that what is best in the world, that which has become most complex, most highly centrated, shall be saved. It is through human consciousness, genetically linked to a heavenly body whose days are ultimately numbered, that Evolution proclaims its challenge: either it must be irreversible, or it need not go on at all! Man the individual consoles himself for his passing with the thought of the offspring or the works which he leaves behind. But what will presently be left of Mankind?

Thus every attempt to situate Man and the Earth in the framework of the Universe comes inevitably upon the heavy problem of death, not of the individual but on the planetary scale—a death which, if we seriously contemplate it, must paralyse all the vital forces of the Earth.

In an attempt to dispel this shadow Jeans calculated that the Earth has many millions of years of habitability ahead of it, so that Man is still only on the threshold of his existence. He bade us warm our hearts, in this fresh dawn, with the *almost* limitless prospects of the glorious day that is only beginning. But a few pages previously he had talked of Mankind sadly growing old and disillusioned on a chilling globe, faced by inevitable extinction. Does not that first thought destroy the second?

Others seek to reassure us with the notion of an escape through space. We may perhaps move to Venus—perhaps even further afield. But apart from the fact that Venus is probably not habitable (is there water?) and that, if journeying between celestial bodies were practicable, it is hard to see why we ourselves have not already been invaded, this does no more than postpone the end.

We cannot resolve this contradiction, between the congenital mortality of the planets and the demand for irreversibility developed by planetised life on their surface, by covering it up or deferring it: we have finally to banish the spectre of Death from our horizon.

And this we are enabled to do by the idea (a corollary, as we have seen, of the mechanism of planetisation) that ahead of, or rather in the heart of, a universe prolonged along its axis of complexity, there exists a divine centre of convergence. That nothing may be prejudged, and in order to stress its synthesising and personalising function, let us call it the *point Omega*. Let us suppose that from this universal centre, this Omega point, there constantly emanate radiations hitherto only perceptible to those persons whom we call 'mystics'. Let us further imagine that, as the sensibility or response to mysticism of the human race increases with planetisation, the awareness of Omega becomes so widespread as to warm the earth psychically while physically it is growing cold. Is it not conceivable that Mankind, at the end of its totalisation, its folding-in upon itself, may reach a critical level of maturity where, leaving Earth and stars to lapse slowly back into the dwindling mass of primordial energy, it will detach itself from this planet and join the one true, irreversible essence of things, the Omega point? A phenomenon perhaps outwardly akin to death: but in reality a simple metamorphosis and arrival at the supreme synthesis. An escape from the planet, not in space or outwardly, but spiritually and inwardly, such as the hyper-centration of cosmic matter upon itself allows.

This hypothesis of a final maturing and ecstasy of Mankind, the logical conclusion of the theory of complexity, may seem even more far-fetched than the idea (of which it is the extension) of the planetisation of Life. Yet it holds its ground and grows stronger upon reflection. It is in harmony with the growing importance which leading thinkers of all denominations are beginning to attach to the phenomenon of mysticism. In any event, of all the theories which we may evolve concerning the end of the Earth, it is the only one which affords a coherent prospect wherein, in the remote future, the deepest and most powerful currents of human consciousness may converge and culminate: intelligence and action, learning and religion.

The Phases and Future of the Noosphere

We have found it possible to express the social totalisation which we are undergoing in terms of a clearly identifiable biological process: proceeding from this we may surely look into the future and predict the course of the trajectory we are describing. Once we have accepted that the formation of a collective human organism, a Noosphere, conforms to the general law of recurrence which leads to the heightening of Consciousness in the universe as a function of complexity, a vast prospect opens before us. To what regions and through what phases may we suppose that the extension of the rising curve of hominisation will carry us?

Immediately confronting us (indeed, already in progress) we have what may be called a 'phase of planetisation'.

It can truly be said, no doubt, that the human group succeeded long ago in covering the face of the earth, and that over a long period its state of zoological ubiquity has tended to be transformed into an organised aggregate; but it must be clear that the transformation is only now reaching its point of full maturity. Let us glance over the main stages of this long history of aggregation. First, in the depths of the past, we find a thin scattering of hunting groups spread here and there throughout the Ancient World. At a later stage, some fifteen thousand years ago, we see a second scattering, very much more dense and clearly defined: that of agricultural groups installed in fertile valleys—centres of social life where man, arrived at a state of stability, achieved the expansive powers which were to enable him to invade the New World. Then, only seven or eight thousand years ago, there came the first civilisations, each covering a large part of a continent. These were succeeded by the real empires. And so on . . . patches of humanity growing steadily larger, overlapping, often absorbing one another, thereafter to break apart and again reform in still larger patches. As we view this process, the spreading, thickening and irresistible coalescence, can we fail to perceive its eventual outcome? The last blank spaces have vanished from the map of mankind. There is contact everywhere, and how close it has become! Today, embedded in the economic and psychic network which I have described, two great human blocks alone remain confronting one another. Is it not inevitable that in one way or another these two will eventually coalesce? Preceded by a tremor, a wave of 'shared impulse' extending to the very depths of the social and ethnic masses in their need and claim to participate, without distinction of class or colour, in the onward march of human affairs, the final act is already visibly preparing. Although the form is not yet discernible, mankind tomorrow will awaken to a 'pan-organised' world.

But, and we must make no mistake about this, there will be an essential difference, a difference of order, between the unitary state towards which we are moving and everything we have hitherto known. The greatest empires in history have never covered more than fragments of the earth. What will be the specifically new manifestations which we have to look for in the transition to *totality*? Until now we have never seen mind manifest itself on this planet except in separated groups and in the static state. What sort of current will be generated, what unknown territory will be opened up, when the circuit is suddenly completed?

I believe that what is now being shaped in the bosom of planetised humanity is essentially a *rebounding* of evolution upon itself. We all know about the projectiles whose impetus is renewed by the firing of a series of staged rockets. Some such procedure, it seems to me, is what Life is preparing at this moment, to accomplish the supreme, ultimate stage. The first stage was the elaboration of lower organisms, up to and including Man, by the use and irrational combination of elementary sources of energy received or released by the planet. The second stage is the super-evolution of Man, individually and collectively, by the use of refined forms of energy scientifically harnessed and applied in the bosom of the Noosphere, thanks to the co-ordinated efforts of all men working reflectively and unanimously upon themselves. Who can say whither, coiled back upon our own organism, our combined knowledge of the atom, of hormones, of the cell and the laws of heredity will take us? Who can say what forces may be released, what radiations, what new arrangements never hitherto attempted by Nature, what formidable powers we may henceforth be able to use, for the first time in the history of the world? This is Life setting out upon a second adventure from the springboard it established when it created humankind.

But all this is no more than the outward face of the phenomenon. In becoming planetised humanity is acquiring new physical powers which will enable it to super-organise matter. And, even more important, is it not possible that by the direct converging of its members it will be able, as though by resonance, to release psychic powers whose existence is still unsuspected? I have already spoken of the recent emergence of certain new faculties in our minds, the sense of genetic duration and the sense of collectivity. Inevitably, as a natural consequence, this awakening must enhance in us, from all sides, a generalised sense of the organic, through which the entire complex of inter-human and inter-cosmic relations will become charged with an immediacy, an intimacy and a realism such as has long been dreamed of and apprehended by certain spirits particularly endowed with the 'sense of the universal', but which has never yet been *collectively applied*. And it is in the depths and by grace of this new inward sphere, the attribute of planetised Life, that an event seems possible which has hitherto been incapable of realisation: I mean the pervasion of the human mass by the power of sympathy. It may in part be passive sympathy, a communication of mind and spirit that will make the phenomenon of telepathy, still sporadic and haphazard, both general and normal. But above all it will be a state of active sympathy in which each separate human element, breaking out of its insulated state under the impulse of the tensions generated in the Noosphere, will emerge into a field of prodigious affinities, which we may already conjecture in theory. For if the power of attraction between simple atoms is so great, what may we not expect if similar bonds are contracted between human molecules? Humanity, as I have said, is building its composite brain beneath our eyes. May it not be that tomorrow, through the logical and biological deepening of the movement drawing it together, it will find its *heart*, without which the ultimate wholeness of its powers of unification can never be fully achieved? To put it in other words, must not the constructive developments now taking place within the Noosphere in the realm of sight and reason necessarily also penetrate to the sphere of feeling? The idea may seem fantastic when one looks at our present world, still dominated by the forces of hatred and repulsion. But is not this simply because we refuse to heed the admonitions of science, which is daily proving to us, in every field, that seemingly impossible changes become easy and even inevitable directly there is a change in the order of the dimensions?

To me two things, at least, seem certain. The first is that, following the state of collective organisation we have already achieved, the process of planetisation can only advance ever further in the direction of growing unanimity. And the second is that this growth of unanimity, being of its nature convergent, cannot continue indefinitely without reaching the natural limit of its course. Every cone has an apex. In the case of this human aggregation how shall we seek, not to imagine but to define the supreme point of coalescence? In terms of the strictly phenomenal viewpoint which I have adopted throughout this paper, it seems to me that the following may be said:

What at the very beginning made the first man, was, as we know, the heightening of the individual consciousness to the point where it acquired the power of Reflection. And the measure of human progress during the centuries which followed is, as I have sought to show, the increase of this reflective power through the interaction, or conjugated thought, of conscious minds working upon one another. Well, what will finally crown and limit collective humanity at the ultimate stage of its evolution, is and must be, by reason of continuity and homogeneity, the establishment of a sort of focal point at the heart of the reflective apparatus as a whole.

If we concede this the whole of human history appears as a progress between two critical points: from the lowest point of elementary consciousness to the ultimate, Noospherical point of Reflection. In biological terms, humanity will have completed itself and fully achieved its internal equilibrium only when it is psychically centred upon itself (which may yet take several million years).

In a final effort of thought let us remove ourselves to the ultimate summit where in the remote future, *but seen from the present*, the tide which bears us reaches its culmination. Is there anything further to be discerned beyond that last peak etched against the horizon?—Yes and no.

In the first place no, because at that mysterious pole crowning our ascent the compass that has guided us runs amok. It was by the law of 'consciousness and complexity' that we set our course: a consciousness becoming ever more centrated, emerging from the heart of an increasingly vast system of more numerous and better organised elements. But now we are faced by an entirely new situation: for the first time we have no multiple material under our hands. Unless, as seems infinitely improbable, we are destined by contact with other thinking planets, across the abysses of space and time, some day to become integrated within an organised complex composed of a number of Noospheres, humanity, having reached maturity, will remain alone, face to face with itself. And at the same time our law of recurrence, based on the play of interrelated syntheses, will have ceased to operate.

So in one sense it all seems to be over; as though, having reached its final point of Noospheric Reflexion, the cosmic impulse towards consciousness has become exhausted, condemned to sink back into the state of disintegration implacably imposed on it by the laws of stellar physics. But in another sense nothing will be ended: for at this point, and at the height of its powers, something else comes into operation, a primary attribute of Reflection concerning which we have hitherto said nothing—*the will to survive*. In reflecting upon itself the individual consciousness acquires the formidable property of foreseeing the future, that is to say, death. And at the same time it knows that it is psychologically impossible for it to continue to work in pursuance of the purposes of Life unless something, the best of the work, is preserved from total destruction. In this resides the whole problem of action. We have not yet taken sufficient account of the fact that this demand for the Absolute, not always easily discernible in the isolated human unit, is one of the impulses which grow and are intensified in the Noosphere. Applied to the individual the idea of total extinction may not at first sight appal us; but extended to humanity as a whole it revolts and sickens us. The fact is that the more Humanity becomes aware of its duration, its number and its potentialities— and also of the enormous burden it must bear in order to survive—the more does it realise that if all this labour is to end in nothing, then we have been cheated and can only rebel. In a planetised Humanity the *insistence upon irreversibility* becomes a specific requisite of action; and it can only grow and continue to grow as Life reveals itself as being ever more rich, an ever heavier load. So that, paradoxically, it is at that ultimate point of centration which renders it cosmically unique, that is to say apparently incapable of any further synthesis, that the Noosphere will have become charged to the fullest extent with psychic energies to impel it forward in yet another advance. . . .

And what can this mean except that, like those planetary orbits which seem to traverse our solar system without remaining within it, the curve of consciousness, pursuing its course of growing complexity, will break through the material framework of Time and Space to escape somewhere towards an ultra-centre of unification and wholeness, where there will finally be assembled, and in detail, everything that is irreplaceable and incommunicable in the world.

And it is here, an inevitable intrusion in terms of biology, and in its proper place in terms of science, that we come to the problem of God.

The Higher Freedom

Let us turn to cast an eye over the road that we have followed.

At the beginning we seemed to see around us nothing but a disconnected and disordered humanity: the crowd, the mass, in which, it may be, we saw only brutality and ugliness. I have tried, fortified by the most generally accepted and solid conclusions of science, to take the reader above this scene of turmoil; and as we have risen higher so has the prospect acquired a more ordered shape. Like the petals of a gigantic lotus at the end of the day, we have seen human petals of planetary dimensions slowly closing in upon themselves. And at the heart of this huge calyx, beneath the pressure of its infolding, a centre of power has been revealed where spiritual energy, gradually released by a vast totalitarian mechanism, then concentrated by heredity within a sort of super-brain, has little by little been transformed into a common vision growing ever more intense. In this spectacle of tranquillity and intensity, where the anomalies of detail, so disconcerting on our individual scale, vanish to give place to a vast, serene and irresistible movement from the heart, everything is contained and everything harmonised in accord with the rest of the universe. Life and consciousness are no longer chance anomalies in Nature; rather we find in biology a complement to the physics of matter. On the one hand, I repeat, the stuff of the world dispersing through the radiation of its elemental energy; and on the other hand the same stuff re-converging through the radiation of thought. The fantastic at either end: but surely the one is necessary to balance the other? Thus harmony is achieved in the ultimate perspective, and, furthermore, a programme for the future: for if this view is accepted we see a splendid goal before us, and a clear line of progress. Coherence and fecundity, the two criteria of truth.

Is this all illusion, or is it reality?

It is for the reader to decide. But to those who hesitate, or who refuse to commit themselves, I would say: 'Have you anything else, anything better to suggest that will account scientifically for the phenomenon of man considered as a whole, in the light of his past development and present progress?'

You may reply to me that this is all very well, but is there not something lacking, an essential element, in this system which I claim to be so coherent? Within that grandiose machine-in-motion which I visualise, what becomes of that pearl beyond price, our personal being? What remains of our freedom of choice and action?

But do you not see that from the standpoint I have adopted it appears everywhere—and is everywhere heightened?

I know very well that by a kind of innate obsession we cannot rid ourselves of the idea that we become most masters of ourselves by being as isolated as possible. But is not this the reverse of the truth? We must not forget that in each of us, by our very nature, everything is in an elemental state, including our freedom of action. We can only achieve a wider degree of freedom by joining and associating with others in an appropriate way. This is, to be sure, a dangerous operation, since, whether it be a case of disorderly intermingling, or of some simple form of co-ordination, like the meshing of gear-wheels, our activities tend to cancel one another out or to become mechanical—we find this only too often in practice. Yet it is also salutary, since the approach of spirit to spirit in a common vision or a shared passion undoubtedly enriches all; in the case of a team, for example, or of two lovers. Achieved with sympathy, union does not restrict but exalts the possibilities of our being. We see this everywhere and every day on a limited scale. Why should it not be worth correspondingly more on a vast and all-embracing scale, if the law applies to the very structure of things? It is simply a question of tension within the field that polarises and attracts. In the case of a blind aggregation, some form of unification brought about by purely mechanical means, the principle of large numbers comes into play. That is true: but where it is a matter of unanimity realised from *within* the effect is to personalise our activities, and, I will add, to make them unerring. A single freedom, taken in isolation, is weak and uncertain and may easily lose itself in mere groping. But a totality of freedom, freely operating, will always end by finding its road. And this incidentally is why throughout this paper, without seeking to minimise the uncertainties inherent in Man's freedom of choice in relation to the world, I have been able implicitly to maintain that we are moving both freely and ineluctably in the direction of concentration by way of planetisation. One might put it that determinism appears at either end of the process of cosmic evolution, but in antithetically opposed forms: at the lower end it is forced along the line of the most probable *for lack of freedom*; at the upper end it is an ascent into the improbable through *the triumph of freedom*.

We may be reassured. The vast industrial and social system by which we are enveloped does not threaten to crush us, neither does it seek to rob us of our soul. The energy emanating from it is free not only in the sense that it represents forces that can be used: it is moreover free because, in the Whole no less than in the least of its elements, it arises out of a state that grows ever more spiritualised. A thinker such as Cournot might still be able to suppose that the socialised group degrades itself biologically in terms of the individuals which comprise it. Only by reaching to the heart of the Noosphere (we see it more clearly today) can we hope, and indeed be sure, of finding, all of us together and each of us separately, the fullness of our humanity.

The End of the Species

... Man now sees that the seeds of his ultimate dissolution are at the heart of his being. The *End of the Species* is in the marrow of our bones!

Is it not this presentiment of a blank wall ahead, underlying all other tensions and specific fears, which paradoxically (at the very moment when every barrier seems to be giving way before our power of understanding and mastering the world) is darkening and hardening the minds of our generation? As psychiatry teaches us, we shall gain nothing by shutting our eyes to this shadow of collective death that has appeared on our horizon. On the contrary, we must open them wider.

But how are we to exorcise the shadow?

It may be said that timidly, even furtively (it is remarkable how coy we are in referring to the matter) two methods are used by writers and teachers to reassure themselves and others in face of the ever more obsessive certainty of the eventual ending of the human species: the first is to invoke the infinity of Time and the second is to seek shelter in the depths of Space.

The Time argument is as follows. By the latest estimates of palaeontology the probable life of a phylum of average dimensions is to be reckoned in tens of millions of years. But if this is true of 'ordinary' species, what duration may we not look for in the case of Man, that favoured race which, by its intelligence, has succeeded in removing all danger of serious competition and even in attacking the causes of senescence at the root.

Then the Space argument. Even if we suppose that, by prolonging its existence on a scale of planetary longevity, the human species will eventually find itself with a chemically exhausted Earth beneath its feet, is not Man even now in process of developing astronautical means which will enable him to go elsewhere and continue his destiny in some other corner of the firmament?

That is what they say, and for all I know there may be people for whom this sort of reasoning does really dispel the clouds that veil the future. I can only say that for my part I find such consolations intolerable, not only because they do nothing but palliate and postpone our fears, which is bad enough, but even more because they seem to me scientifically false.

In order that the end of Mankind may be deferred *sine die* we are asked to believe in a species that will drag on and spread itself indefinitely; which means, in effect, that it would run down more and more. But is not this the precise opposite of what is happening here and now in the human world?

I have been insisting for a long time on the importance and significance of the technico-mental process which, particularly during the past hundred years, has been irresistibly causing Mankind to draw closer together and unite upon itself. From routine or prejudice the majority of anthropologists still refuse to see in this movement of totalisation anything more than a superficial and temporary side-effect of the organic forces of biogenesis. Any parallel that may be drawn between socialisation and speciation, they maintain, is purely metaphorical. To which I would reply that, if this is so, to what undisclosed form of energy shall we scientifically attribute the irreversible and conjugated growth of Arrangement and Consciousness which historically characterises (as it does everywhere else, in indisputably 'biological' fields) the establishment of Mankind on Earth?

We have only to go a little further, I am convinced, and our minds, awakened at last to the existence of an added dimension, will grasp the profound identity existing between the forces of civilisation and those of evolution. Man will then assume his true shape in the eyes of the naturalists—

that of a species which, having entered the realm of Thought, henceforth folds back its branches upon itself instead of spreading them. Man, *a species which converges*, instead of diverging like every other species on earth: so that we are bound to envisage its ending in terms of some paroxysmal state of maturation which, by its scientific probability alone, must illumine for us all the darkest menaces of the future.

For if by its structure Mankind does not dissipate itself but concentrates upon itself; in other words, if, alone among all the living forms known to us, our zoological phylum is laboriously moving towards a *critical point of speciation*, then are not all hopes permitted to us in the matter of survival and irreversibility?

The end of a 'thinking species': not disintegration and death, but a new break-through and a re-birth, this time outside Time and Space, through the very excess of unification and co-reflexion.

It goes without saying that this idea of a salvation of the Species sought, not in the direction of any temporo-spatial consolidation or expansion but by way of spiritual escape through the excess of consciousness, is not yet seriously considered by the biologists. At first sight it appears fantastic. Yet if one thinks about it long and carefully, it is remarkable how it sustains examination, grows stronger and, for two particular reasons among others, takes root in the mind.

For one thing, as I have said, it corresponds more closely than any other extrapolation to the marked (even challenging) urgency of our own time in the broad progress of the Phenomenon of Man. But in addition it seems to be more capable than any other vision of the future of stimulating and steadying our power of action by counteracting the prevailing pessimism.

Finally, there is a fact which we must face.

In the present age, what does most discredit to faith in progress (apart from our reticence and helplessness as we contemplate the 'end of the Race') is the unhappy tendency still prevailing among its adepts to distort everything that is most valid and noble in our newly aroused expectation of an 'ultra-human' by reducing it to some form of threadbare millennium. The believers in progress think in terms of a Golden Age, a period of euphoria and abundance; and this, they give us to understand, is all that Evolution has in store for us. It is right that our hearts should fail us at the thought of so 'bourgeois' a paradise.

We need to remind ourselves yet again, so as to offset this truly pagan materialism and naturalism, that although the laws of biogenesis by their nature presuppose, and in fact bring about, an improvement in human living conditions, it is not *well-being* but a hunger for *more-being* which, of psychological necessity, can alone preserve the thinking earth from the *taedium vitae*. And this makes fully plain the importance of what I have already suggested, that it is upon its point (or superstructure) of spiritual concentration, and not on its basis (or infra-structure) of material arrangement, that the equilibrium of Mankind biologically depends.

For if, pursuing this thought, we accept the existence of a critical point of speciation at the conclusion of all technologies and civilisations, it means (with Tension maintaining its ascendancy over Rest to the end of biogenesis) that an *outlet* appears at the peak of Time, not only for our hope of escape but for our expectation of revelation.

And this is what can best allay the conflict between light and darkness, exaltation and despair, in which, following the rebirth in us of the Sense of Species, we are now absorbed.